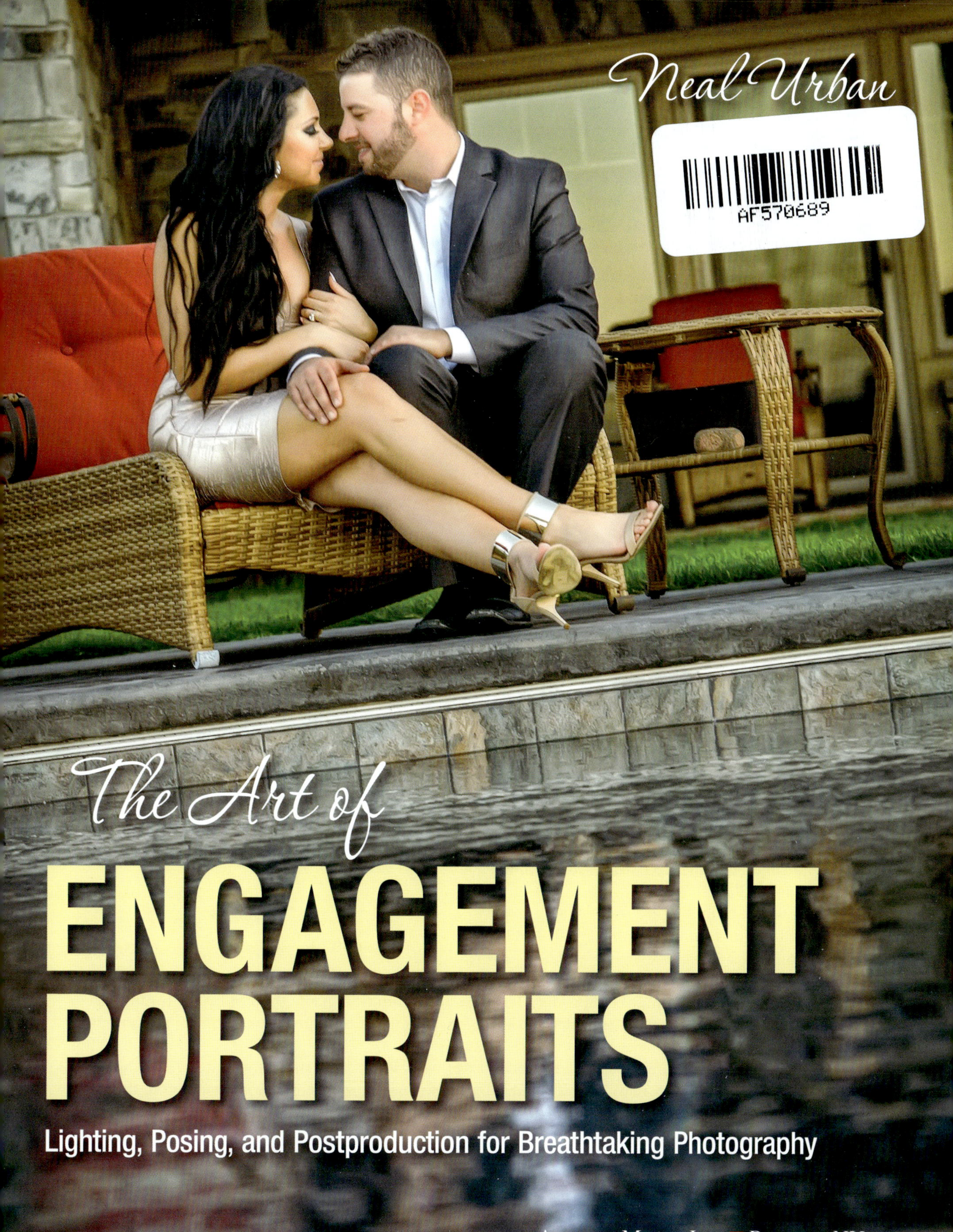

Neal Urban

The Art of ENGAGEMENT PORTRAITS

Lighting, Posing, and Postproduction for Breathtaking Photography

Amherst Media, Inc. ■ Buffalo, NY

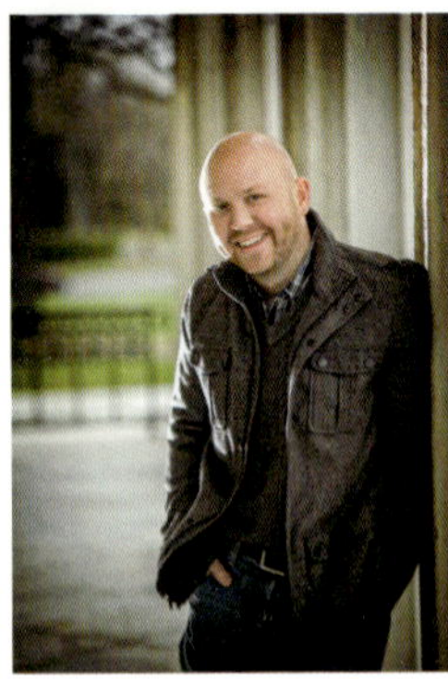

About the Author

Neal Urban is a wedding photographer from Buffalo, NY, whose work for discerning clients takes him to exotic locations coast to coast. Neal has earned numerous Accolades of Excellence Awards in WPPI's annual print competition (Wedding & Portrait Photographers International). In 2011, he was the winner of *Photo District News'* Top Knots People's Choice Award. Neal was also recently a featured photographer in the Chinese edition of *Cosmopolitan Brides* as well as in *Rangefinder* magazine, which called him "one of the most sought after wedding photographers in the industry." He is the author of *Dream Weddings: Create Fresh and Stylish Photography* (Amherst Media, 2014.)

Published by:
Amherst Media, Inc.
P.O. Box 586
Buffalo, N.Y. 14226
Fax: 716-874-4508
www.AmherstMedia.com

Publisher: Craig Alesse
Senior Editor/Production Manager: Michelle Perkins
Editors: Barbara A. Lynch-Johnt, Beth Alesse, Harvey Goldstein
Associate Publisher: Kate Neaverth
Editorial Assistance from: Sally Jarzab, John S. Loder, Carey A. Miller
Business Manager: Adam Richards
Warehouse and Fulfillment Manager: Roger Singo

ISBN-13: 978-1-60895-747-7
Library of Congress Control Number: 2014933304
10 9 8 7 6 5 4 3 2 1

Contents

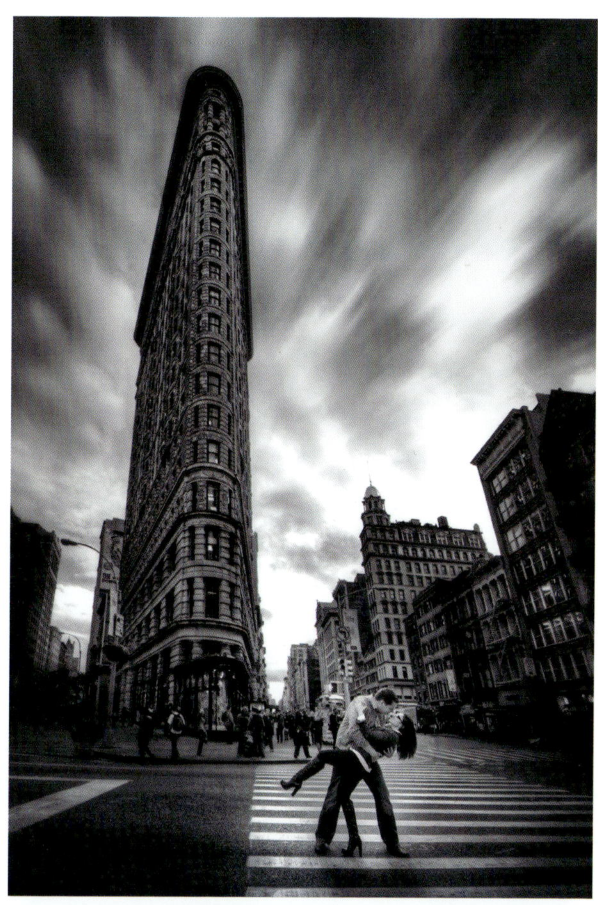

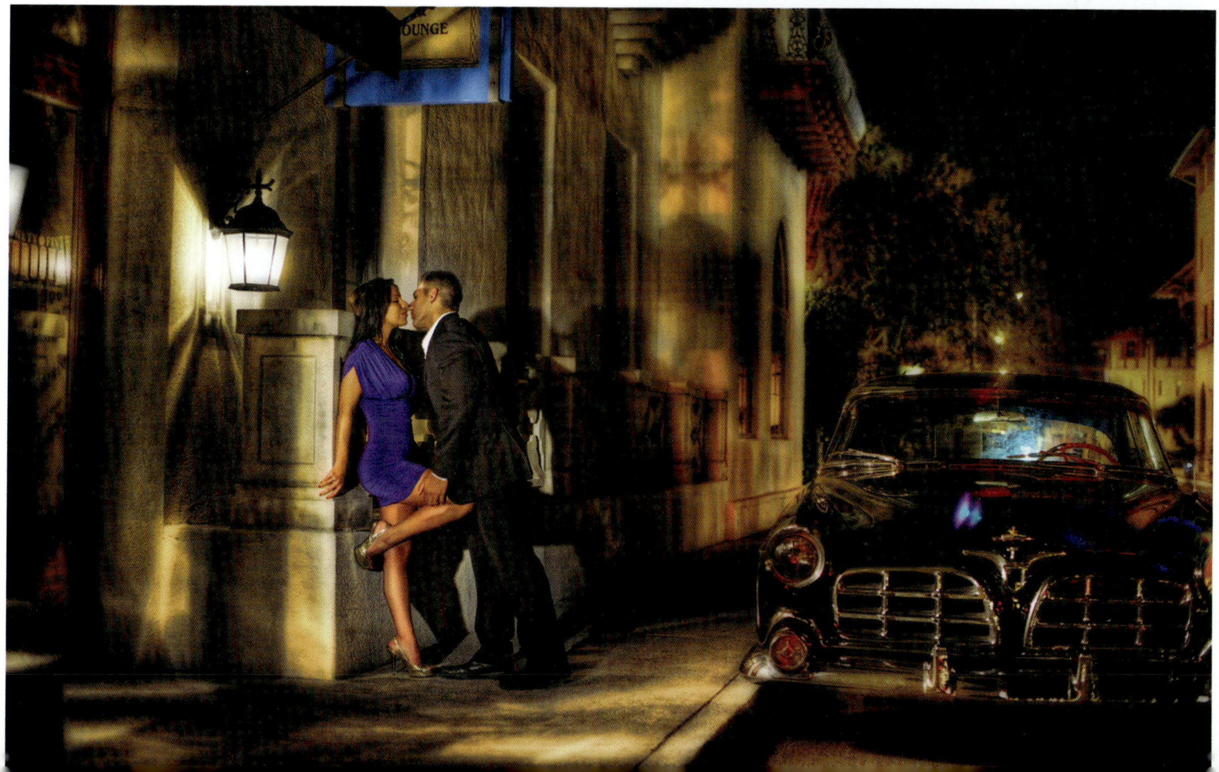

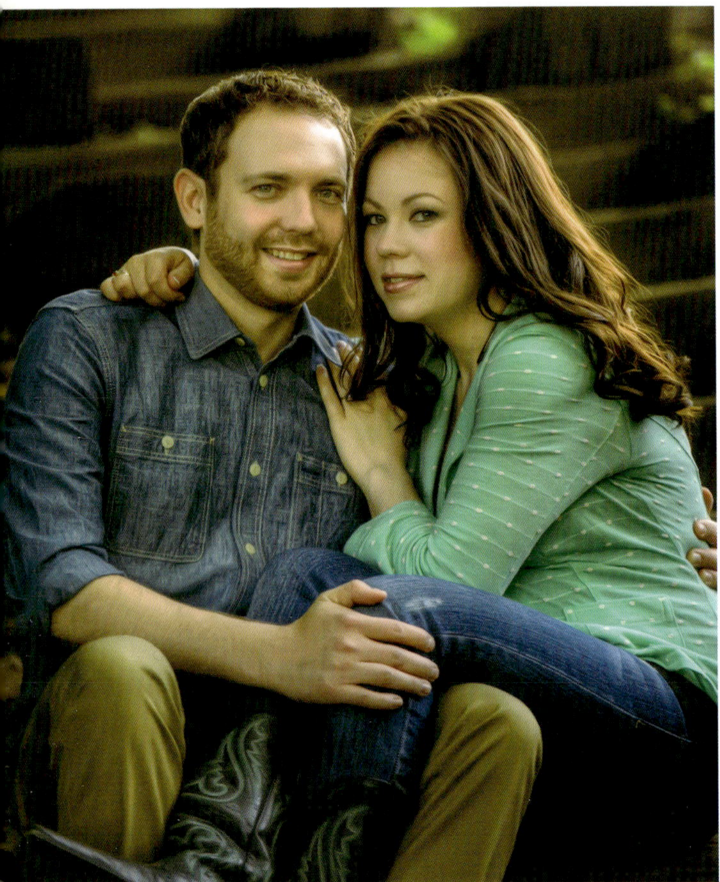

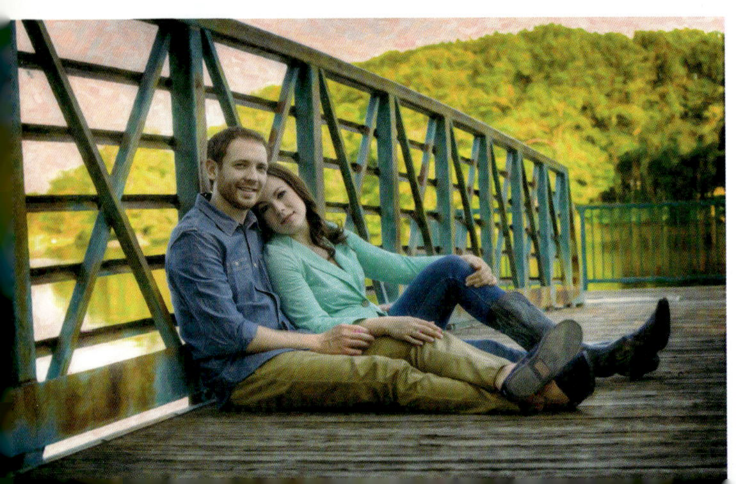

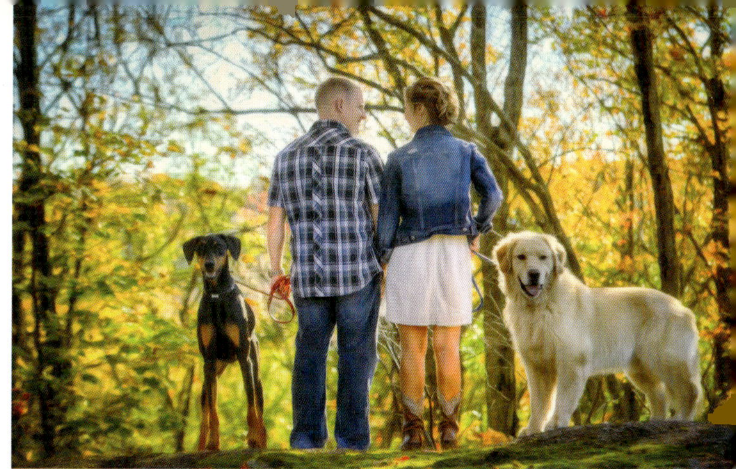

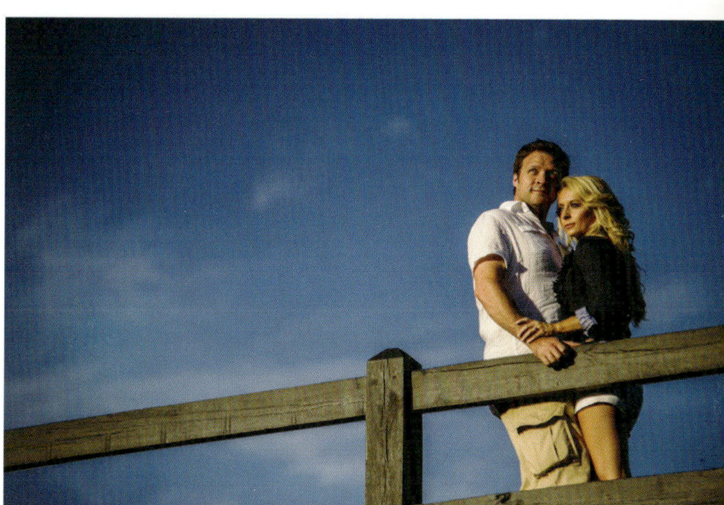

1 Why Do an Engagement Session?

As we do at our weddings, my wife Danielle and I shoot engagement sessions together, giving us a chance to get to know the couple—and a chance for them to get to know *us*. We find that the engagement session is an important first step in the overall wedding photography process. A great engagement session sets the stage for everything that is to come.

Benefits to the Couple

Most couples don't like being in front of the camera. Time after time, we hear couples say that they're "not very photogenic" or "never take good pictures." It's simply not true—and showing them that we can make them look great in their engagement images gives even the most nervous bride or groom a sense of ease in front of the camera on their wedding day. (It's especially helpful for the guys, very few of whom are naturally comfortable in front of the camera.)

Having worked with us, they also know what to expect—how we work, how we give directions, how we set up our lighting. They've had a chance to get used to our rhythms and won't be surprised when I start making goofy jokes to loosen them up or be put off if I hop into the frame to demonstrate how I want the bride to pose.

Engagement Session Packages

Engagement sessions are part of many of our packages, but we also offer packages without them. Some clients choose these for financial reasons. They're also a good option for out-of-town clients who hire us to travel in for just their wedding but opt to do an engagement session with a photographer in their own area. Likewise, couples in *our* area who will be traveling out of the region for their weddings sometimes book us for an engagement session here—especially if they really want to work with us and we're already committed for their wedding date.

Benefits to the Family and Friends

A great engagement session doesn't just boost the couple's confidence, though—it also lets the

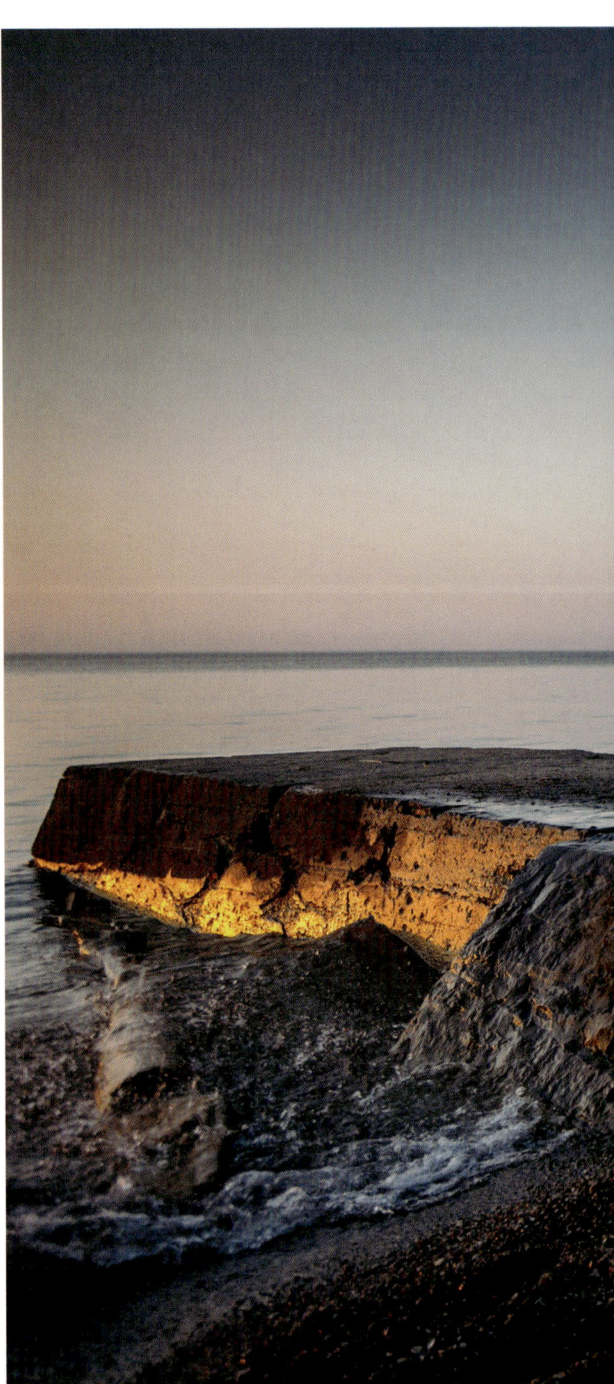

family know that the photographer they hired to document this special event is going to do a great job. Seeing those results helps everyone feel a little more laid back on the wedding day.

For the bridal party, seeing the couple's engagement shots (usually on Facebook or via other social media sites) gives them a taste of the style of photos they'll be in. It gets them even more excited for the big day. As soon as we share the tagged couple's photos on Facebook, friend requests always start rolling in from the whole wedding party. (And having more people following and liking our Facebook posts is definitely a good thing!)

The engagement session is an important first step in the overall wedding photography process.

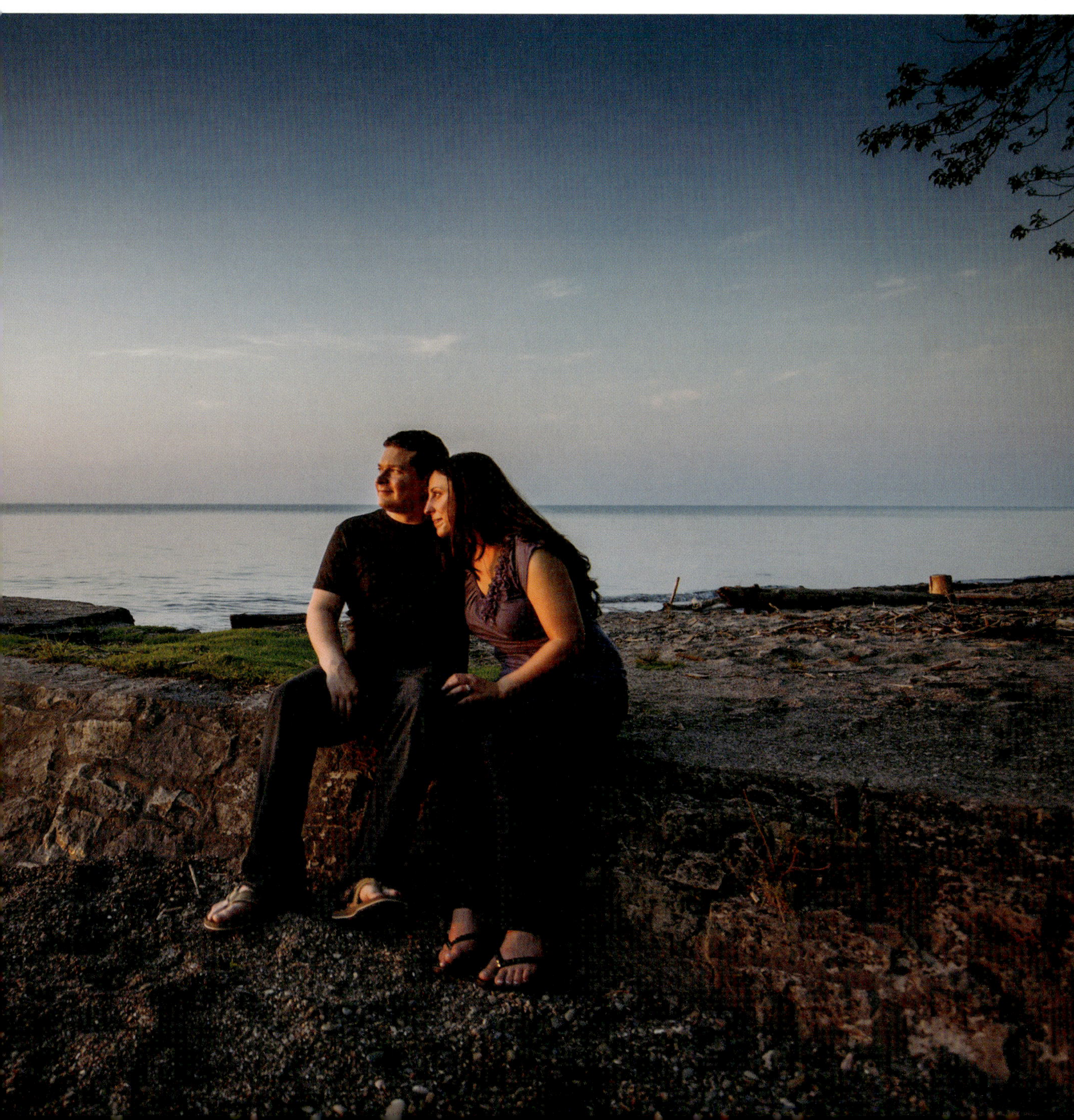

2 Scheduling the Session

Month and Day

I like to photograph our clients at a time of year that is visually different from the time of year when they're getting married (more on this in section 25). Since weekends are reserved for wedding bookings, we schedule our engagement sessions for weeknights, Monday through Thursday. (We reserve Fridays to prep for weekend events—and to shoot Friday weddings, which are increasingly popular.) If necessary, we will consider booking a Sunday engagement session—but that's an accommodation we primarily make for out-of-town clients who have more limited windows of opportunity.

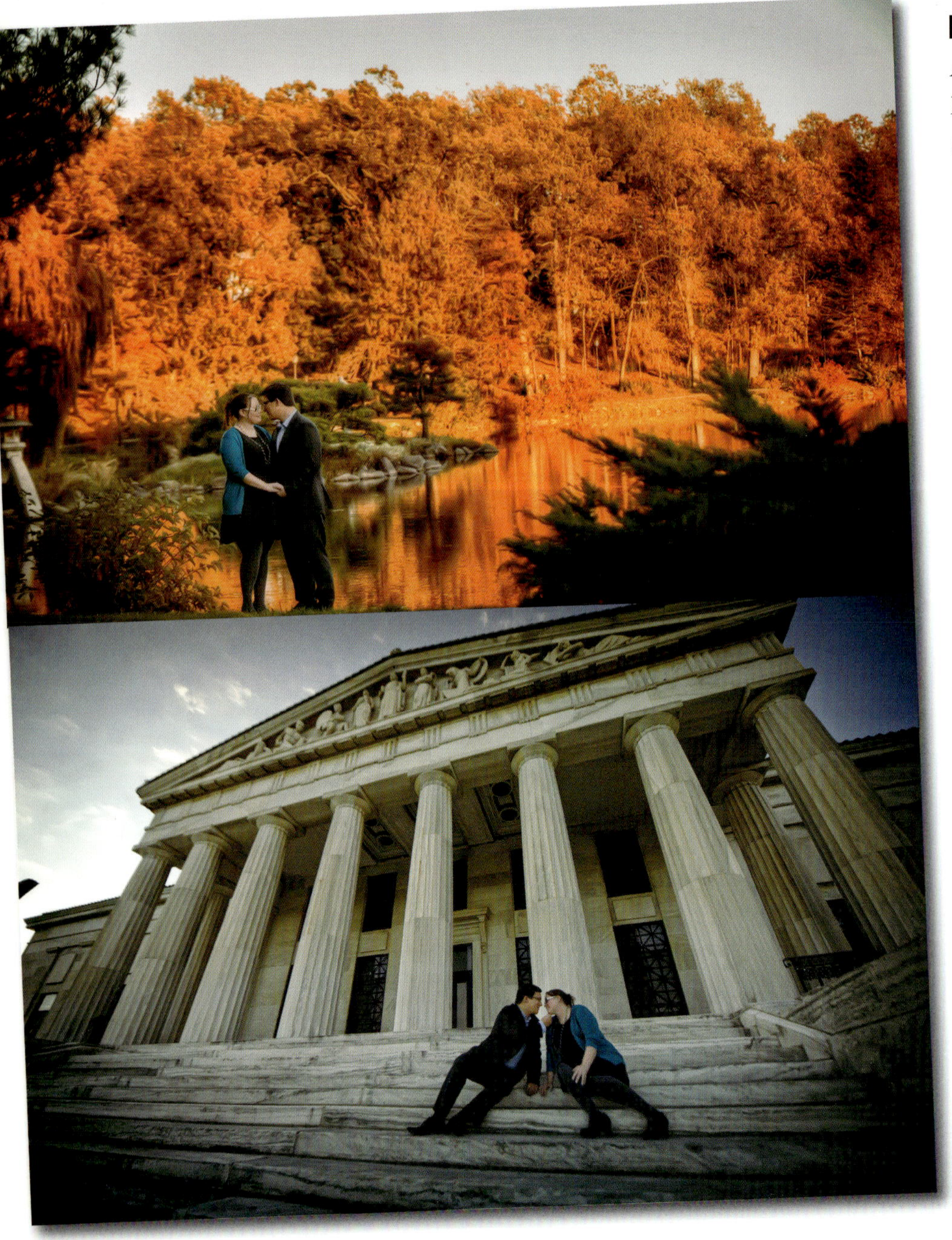

Booking

A lot of couples like the look of fall engagement sessions. However, that's also one of our busiest times of year for wedding photography, so we ask couples to book their engagement sessions at least six weeks in advance so we can guarantee them a date. Since we shoot on weekdays, this also gives them leeway to make plans to leave work early—which is especially important at times of year when the sun sets earlier or if the bride-to-be wants time to have her hair and makeup professionally styled.

Autumn engagement sessions are very popular. These two shots, created using adjacent areas in a city park, let us give the couple two very different looks.

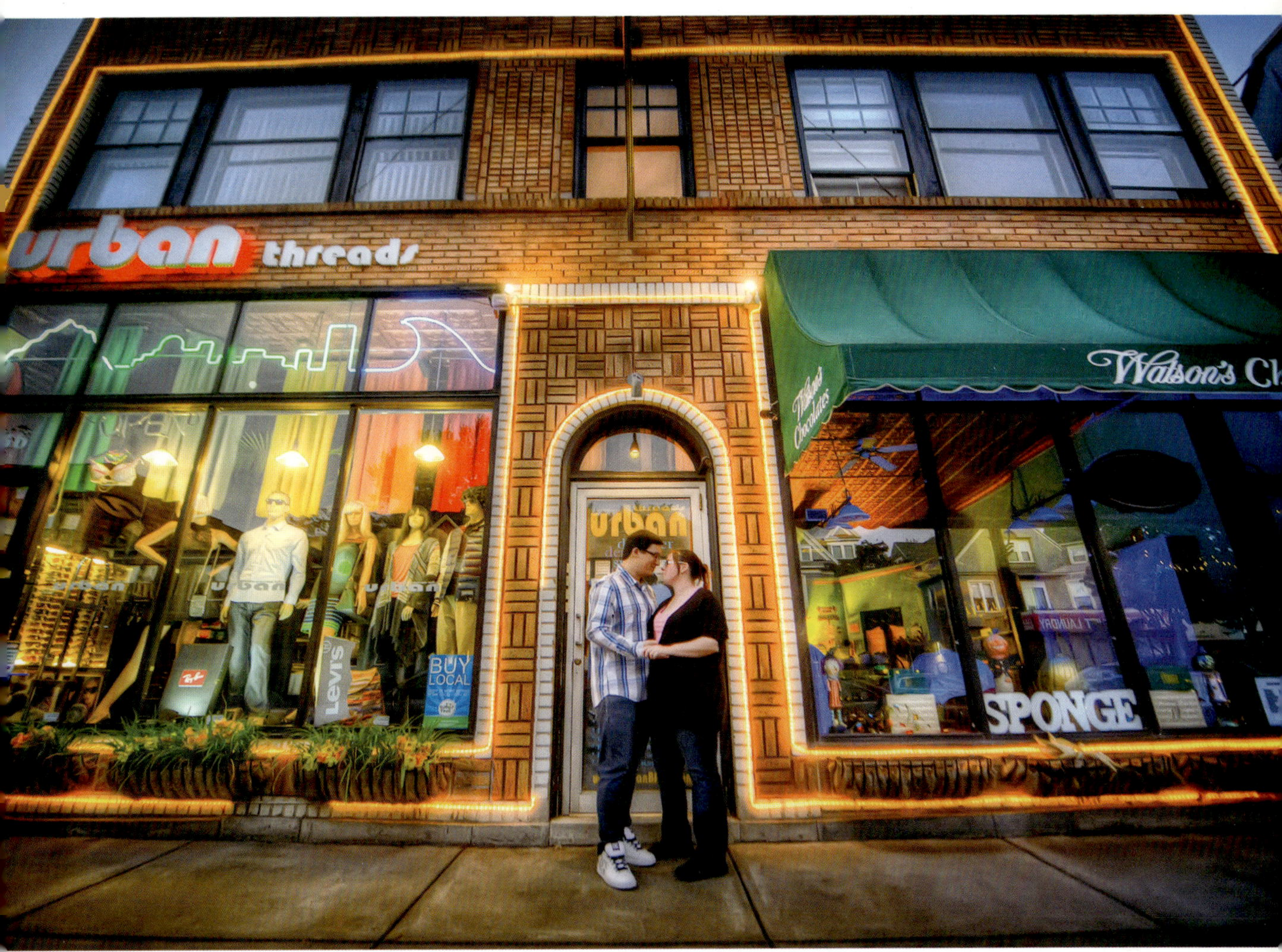

▲ A third look was easily achieved for the same couple by driving to a nearby shopping area.

Danielle handles our scheduling, so when clients call she is ready with a few open dates to consider. In addition to our own schedules, we have to take into account any special locations the client has chosen for their images. If there are specific times or dates required by those venues, we will build the schedule for the session based on those specifications. (More on location selection and working with venues in section 4.)

Time Frame

We like to start our sessions a little before sunset so we can get a few late-afternoon shots in and get the couple loosened up; that way we're all ready to go when the beautiful Golden Hour light makes its appearance (more on this in sections 33 and 34). We tell our couples to allow from ninety minutes up to about two hours for the session. We also suggest that they not make specific dinner reservations (or other time-sensitive plans) immediately after the session. If we're getting great stuff or there's an amazing sunset, we don't want to cut things short!

3 Clothing Selection

Two Styles

We ask our clients to prepare two outfits for the session. One should be a nice but casual outfit—not "sweatpants casual," but comfortable and relaxed. Lots of our couples opt for jeans or even jerseys from their favorite teams for this look.

The second outfit should be something dressy but not formal—the kind of outfit they'd wear for a date night at a nice restaurant. For the ladies, this usually means a dress and heels; for the guys it could be a suit, or trousers and a button-down shirt with a tie. It all depends on them and their personal style.

Themes

We like to ask clients if they have planned a theme for their wedding. If so, that's something we can carry through into the engagement photography. In this case, the couple's theme was *Beauty and the Beast*, so they selected outfits in those characters' respective signature colors—and even brought along a few props. The theme also inspired some of our location selections.

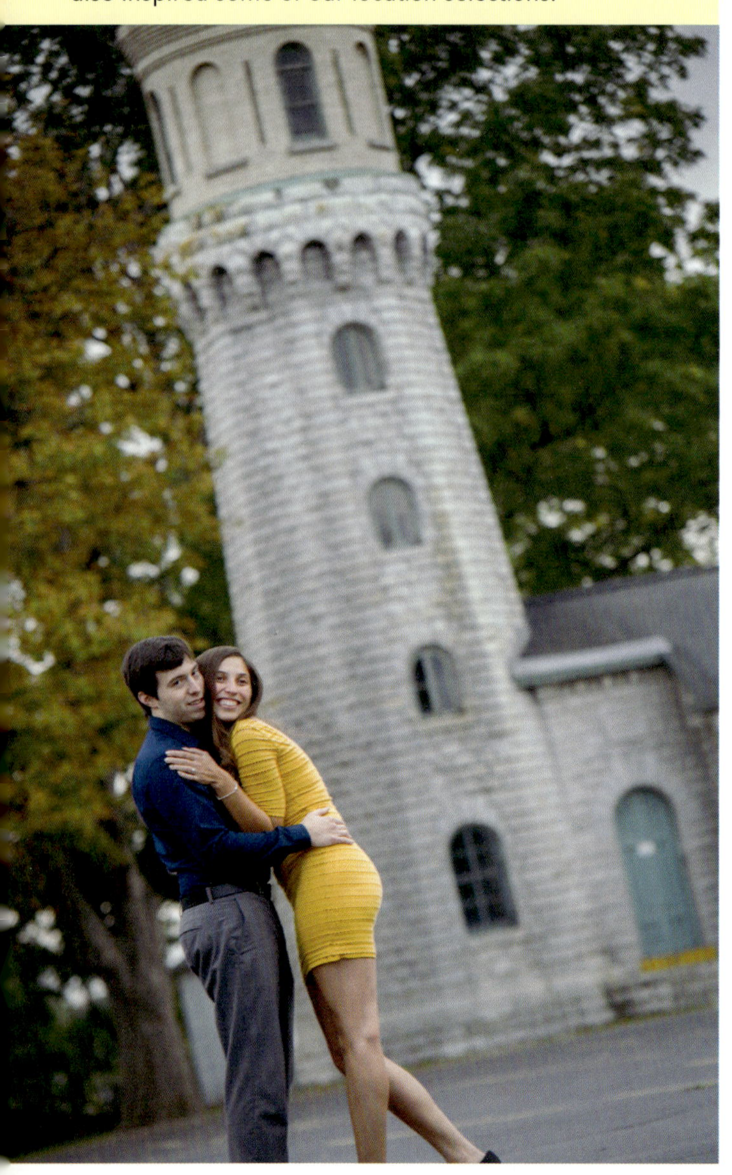

What to Choose (and What to Avoid)

In the past, we asked clients to avoid black or white clothing and to select more earth-tone colors. Lately, we've been trying to go for more bold colors in our engagement sessions.

We ask them to avoid any crazy patterns or logos. Those will only date the photograph and draw more attention to the outfit than the person. Naturally, the clothing for outdoor sessions should also make sense for the time of year and the selected locations.

Clothing Changes

We'll tell the couple what outfit to arrive in based on the order of the locations we'll be shooting. The time required for outfit changes can be an issue—we *have* missed opportunities. When that happens, though, we just add in some speedlights and deal with it! (We'll look at how we work the clothing changes a bit more in section 35.)

Lots of our couples opt for jeans or even jerseys from their favorite teams for this look.

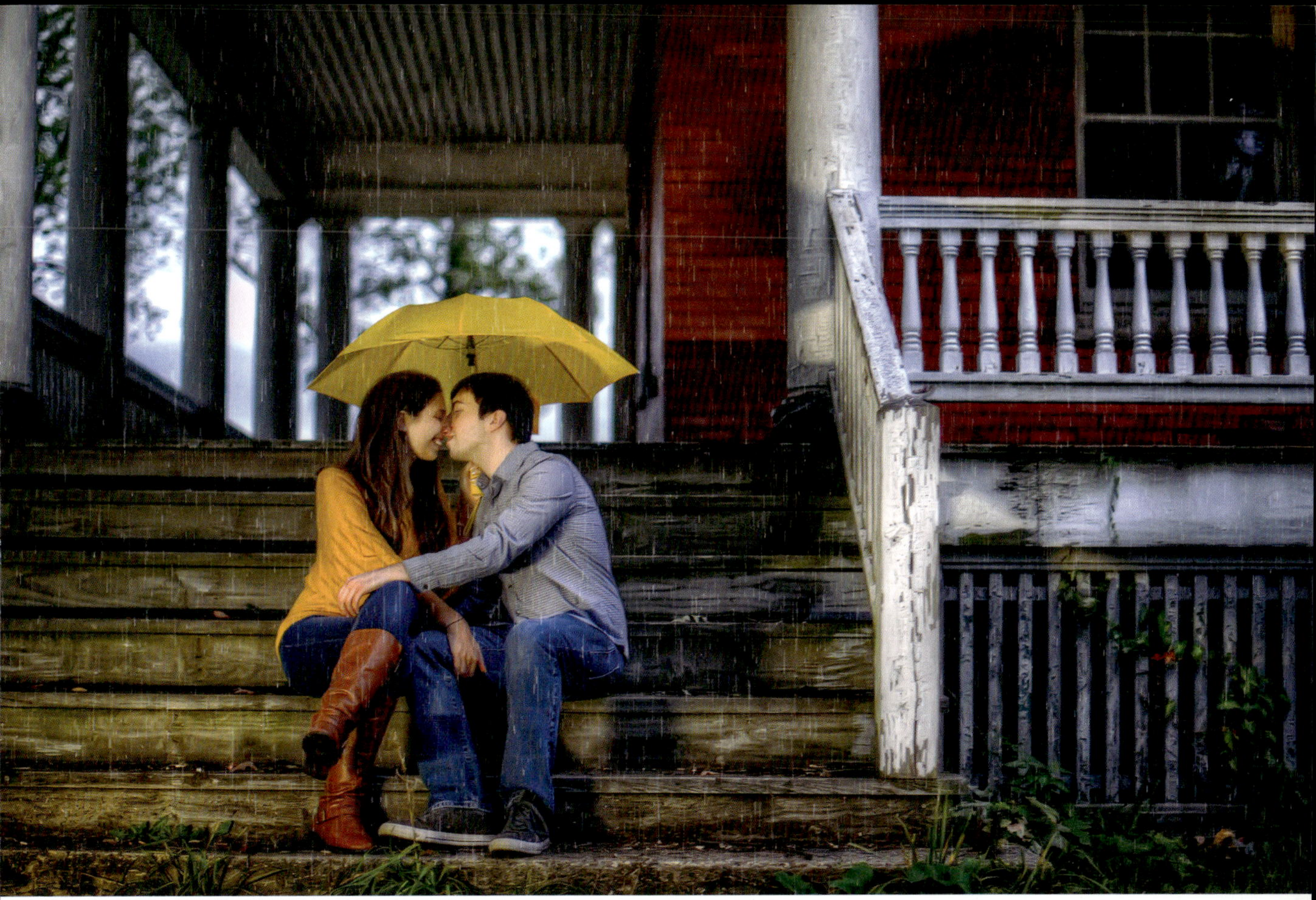

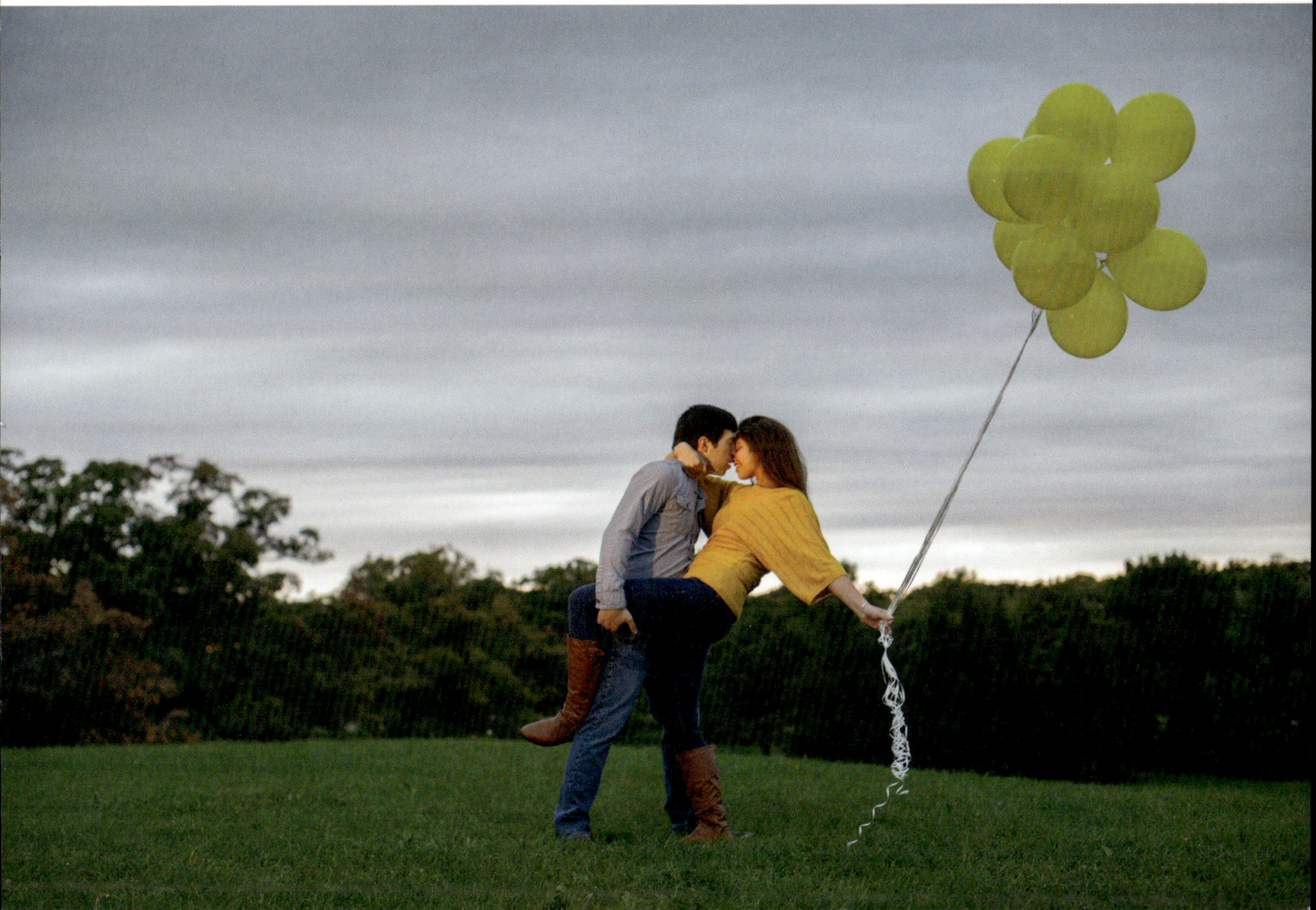

4 Selecting Locations

A Meaningful Choice

During our first meeting with the couple (or over the phone, if a face-to-face meeting isn't possible), we ask them about locations they might like to use for their engagement session.

Specifically, we want to know if there's anywhere that is really personal to them—perhaps the place they met, the place they went on their first date, or where they got engaged. Any of those places might make a good location for their session. That's especially true if these are places we wouldn't be able to visit on the couple's wedding day.

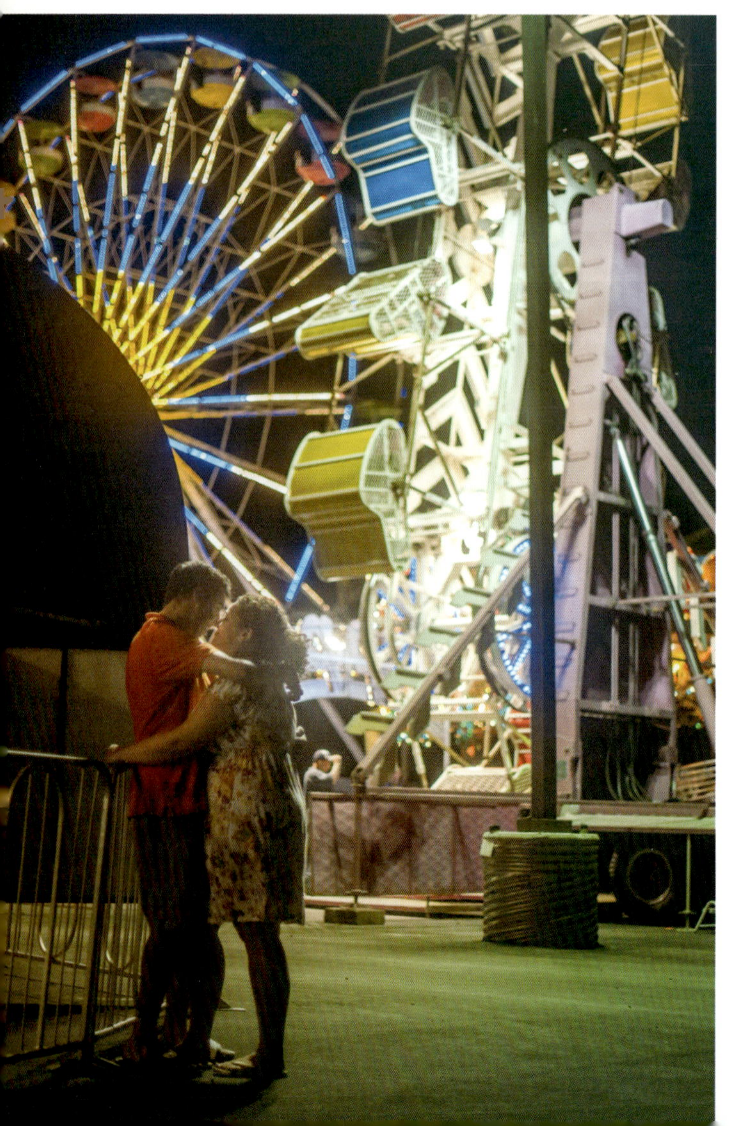

Their Shared Interests

What does the couple like to do for fun? Do they love walking in the park? Fishing on a lake? Going to the movies? Cooking together? Attending sporting events? Or maybe sampling some good wines? Shared interests can suggest locations that would suit their personalities and make the images more meaningful to them. One of our couples (see section 12) had a family cottage and loved spending time there; it was a meaningful location to them and reflected a shared interest.

A List of Suggestions

If couples don't have their own ideas about locations for their engagement images, we have a long list of local sites that work well—and we can usually guide them to a good choice. If, for example, a couple says their wedding has a vintage theme, there's a nearby farm with beautiful settings for that kind of look. If they want to bring their dogs along for the shoot (more on this in section 31), we know which locations accommodate pets—and which prohibit them.

If the couple selects a privately owned location where permission will be needed (such as a restaurant or theater), we have them contact the venue directly to make the arrangements

Popular Locations

In every region, there are popular locations for wedding images. In addition to being congested with photographers and wedding parties on the weekends, these locations have become so "expected" that they don't make the couple's images look special. When couples request one of these locations for their wedding day images, we suggest going there for engagement images instead. This lets us go mid-week (so there's less traffic) and in the evening (so the images will look different). We also try to shoot from unexpected angles and in different parts of the scene. More on this in section 22.

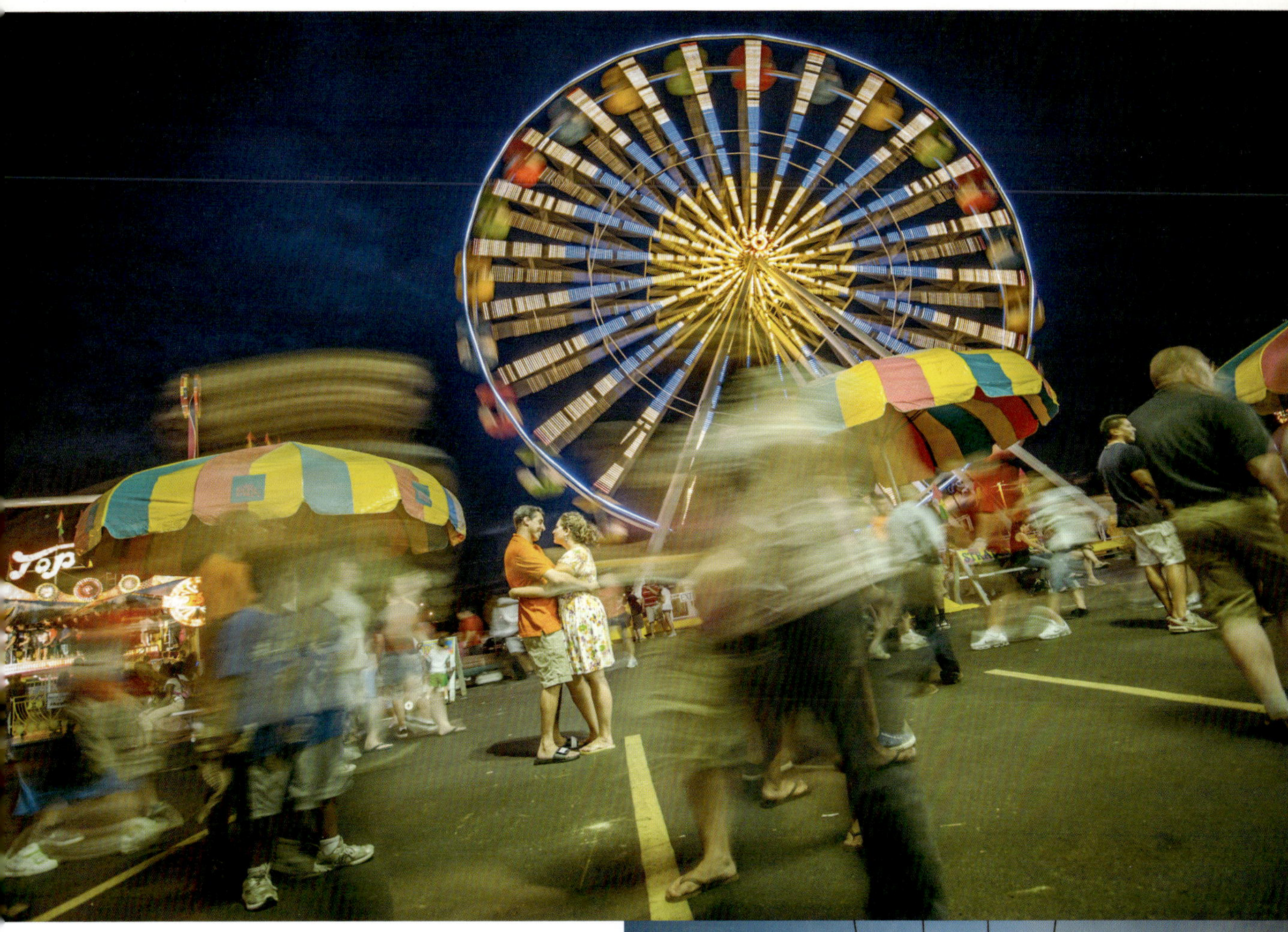

and cover any fees that might be required by the venue. For public parks, or anywhere a permit is required, we make the needed arrangements.

Check Social Media

A good way to learn about your couple is through social media. If you're Facebook friends with them, check out their posts and photos. With one couple (*this page and facing page*), we settled on a location only after visiting the bride-to-be's Facebook page and discovering that she and her fiancé went to a lot of fairs and carnivals—a friend even commented that they were the people to ask if you wanted to know about any local fairs coming up that weekend! One of the largest county fairs in the country happens to be in our area, and it was going on when we wanted to take their images, so it was a natural choice.

The Gear

For an engagement session, we pack pretty much everything we'd pack for a wedding—although not as many batteries, since we'll only be shooting for a couple hours. This includes:

- two cameras
- three speedlights
- Ice Light
- bounce board
- small softbox
- snoot
- umbrella (white or clear—in case of rain)
- stain stick
- Tylenol and water
- first-aid kit
- hair clips
- facial tissues
- insect repellent
- lint roller
- for shoots with pets, dog treats and a squeaky toy

My camera is equipped with two memory card slots, and each has a 32G card. I shoot RAW and the files write to both cards so I have an immediate backup of all the images.

Watch the Weather

The morning of the session, we check the weather. If anything looks like it will be a problem, we keep checking. However, we won't cancel right away if it's raining in the morning. Our sessions don't start until about 4:00PM and rescheduling can be difficult for everyone, especially during peak season. If things really aren't looking good, we'll give the clients a call around noon. This gives them time to cancel their hair or makeup appointment if necessary.

The Location

Many locations in our area are familiar to us from previous sessions—but if we'll be shooting at a new location that's not too far away, we like to visit before the session and check it out.

When packing up for the session, we make sure we also have the address for the site, along with the phone number and the name of the contact person at the venue. Especially if it's a new location for us, we'll make a point of asking for that contact person when we arrive and introducing ourselves to them. This simple gesture of respect is a good way to ensure we'll be welcomed on future visits.

If the location where we'll be shooting requires a permit or business insurance, we also make sure we have that information. In fact, we each keep a copy of our insurance certificate on our iPhones—and there's a paper copy in the camera bag just in case.

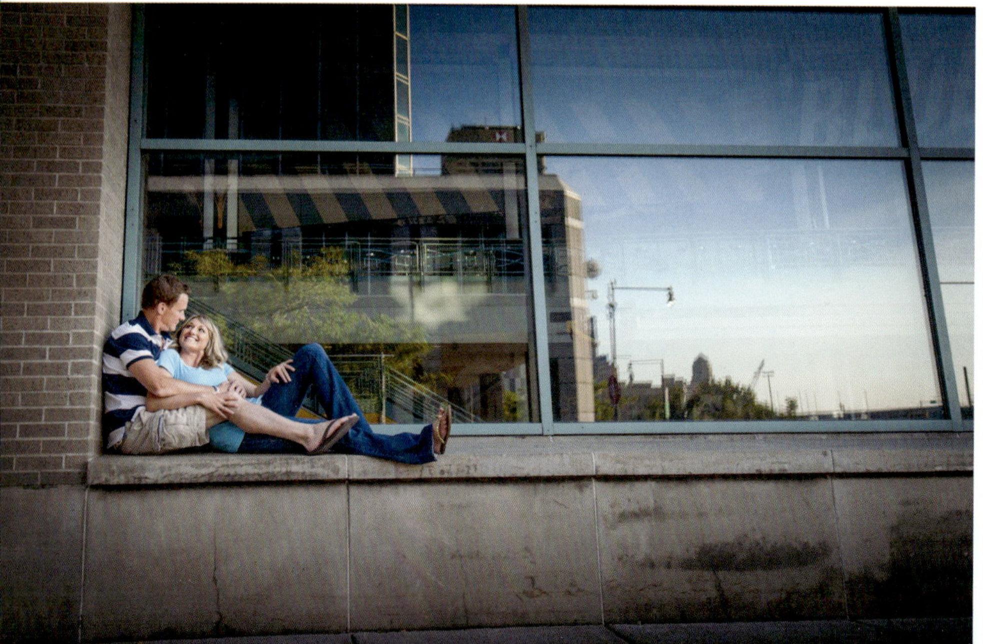

This simple gesture of respect is a good way to ensure we'll be welcomed on future visits.

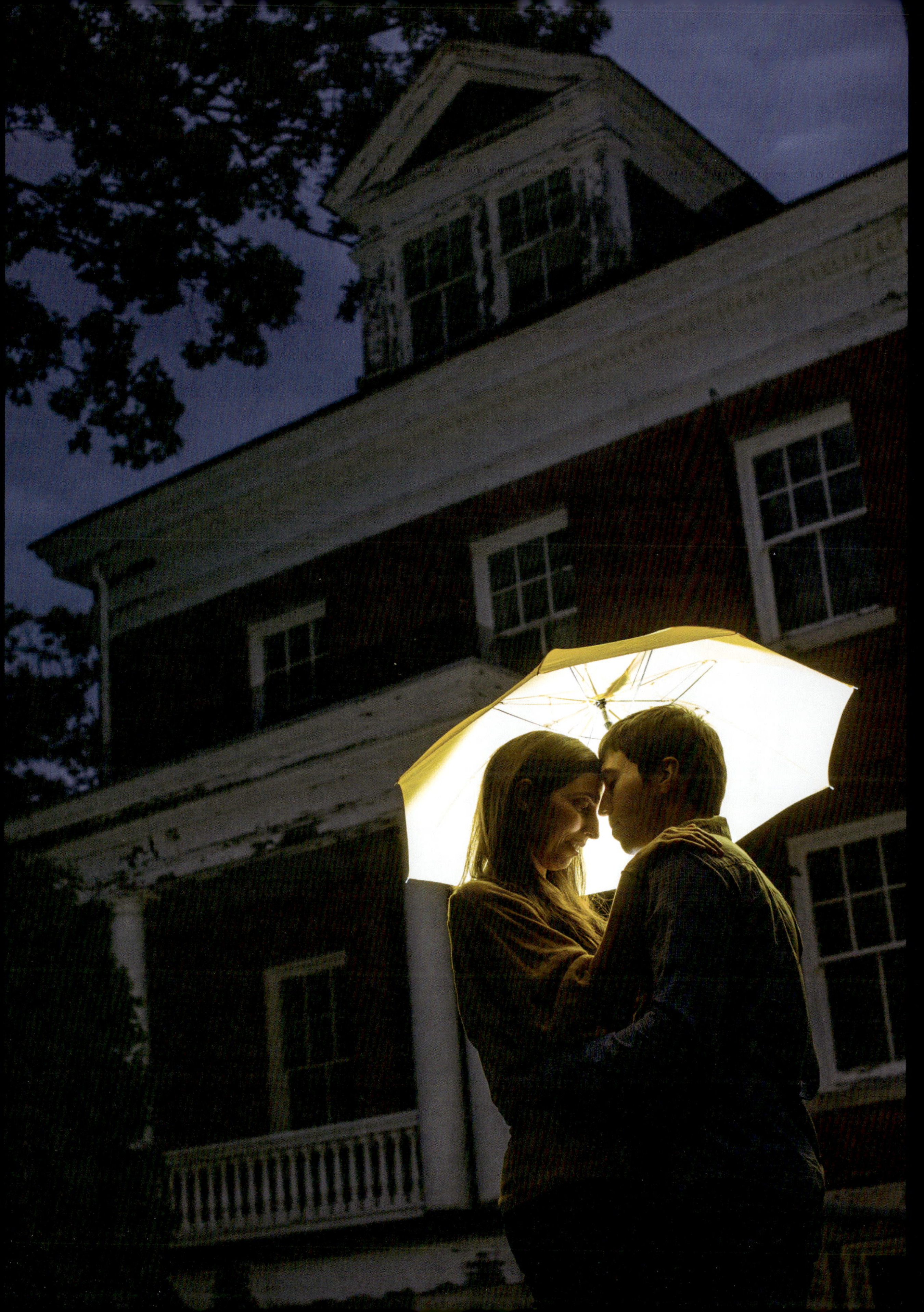

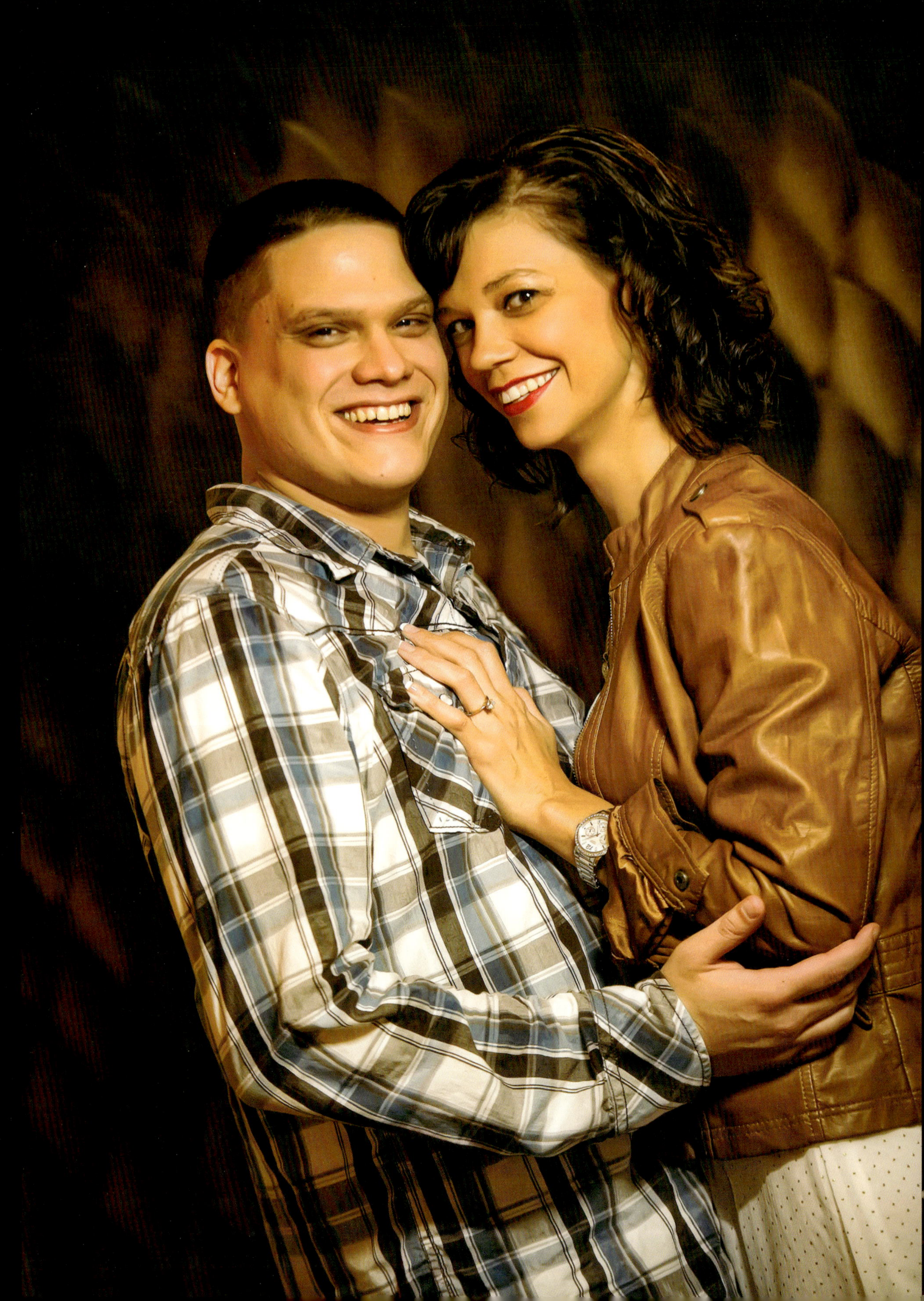

Preparation

Part of the reason ample preparation is important is that things don't always go as planned. Cameras malfunction (trust me!), clients arrive late, rain storms roll in at the last minute, and locations sometimes aren't as great-looking as they were described (or, often, as the venue's web site showed).

As a professional, you have to know how to roll with the punches and produce great images even when things aren't going your way. A location doesn't have to be fancy or really beautiful to create something good. And remember: that's *your* responsibility, not your client's problem.

Keep Moving and Shooting

If the location presents a challenge, do a few shots at the planned site (especially if it's one that's meaningful to your clients) and play with the lighting. Then, keep moving.

Keep your mind open as you check the less obvious options and think about using a small part of the background rather than the entire scene. For the image on the facing page, we were shooting in a museum where many of the backgrounds were very complex. As we walked around, I saw a huge fish mural—and the scales created a nice backdrop for a close portrait of the couple.

This is also the time to go to all your "safe" shots—images that you know can work anywhere. Look for tall grass or trees (more on this in sections 19 and 20). Pose them on the ground and shoot from a high angle to use the foliage as the background. Think about adding light on the couple to make the background exposure drop down for a more subdued view.

If all else fails, hop in your cars and have them follow you; pull over if you see a great scene or some perfect light. If it's later in the day, cross your fingers and hope for a great sunset—sometimes you do get lucky!

A Textured Wall Almost Always Works

Next Two Pages ➤

If you're struggling to find a good background at your location, scout around for a textured wall. This will make a good background for just about any couple in any clothing style. It's a go-to look to have in your arsenal—and a clean, classic style to try even when the location *does* offer other good alternatives.

◀ Part of a fish mural provided a nice background for this close portrait.

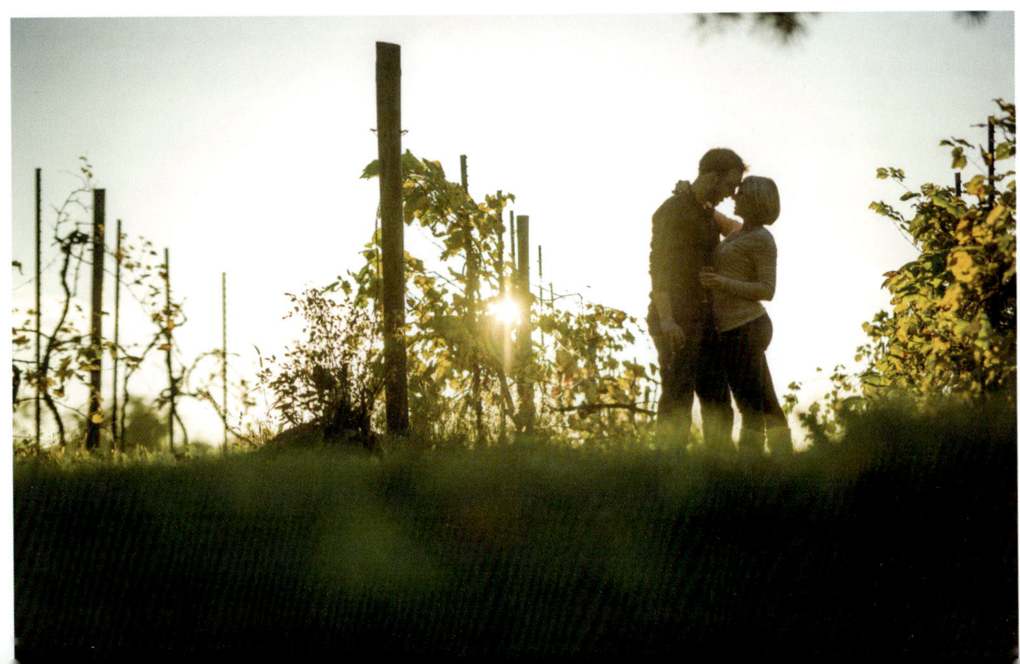

➤ Beautiful backgrounds aren't always at eye-level. Getting down low let me create a totally different look with the couple almost in silhouette.

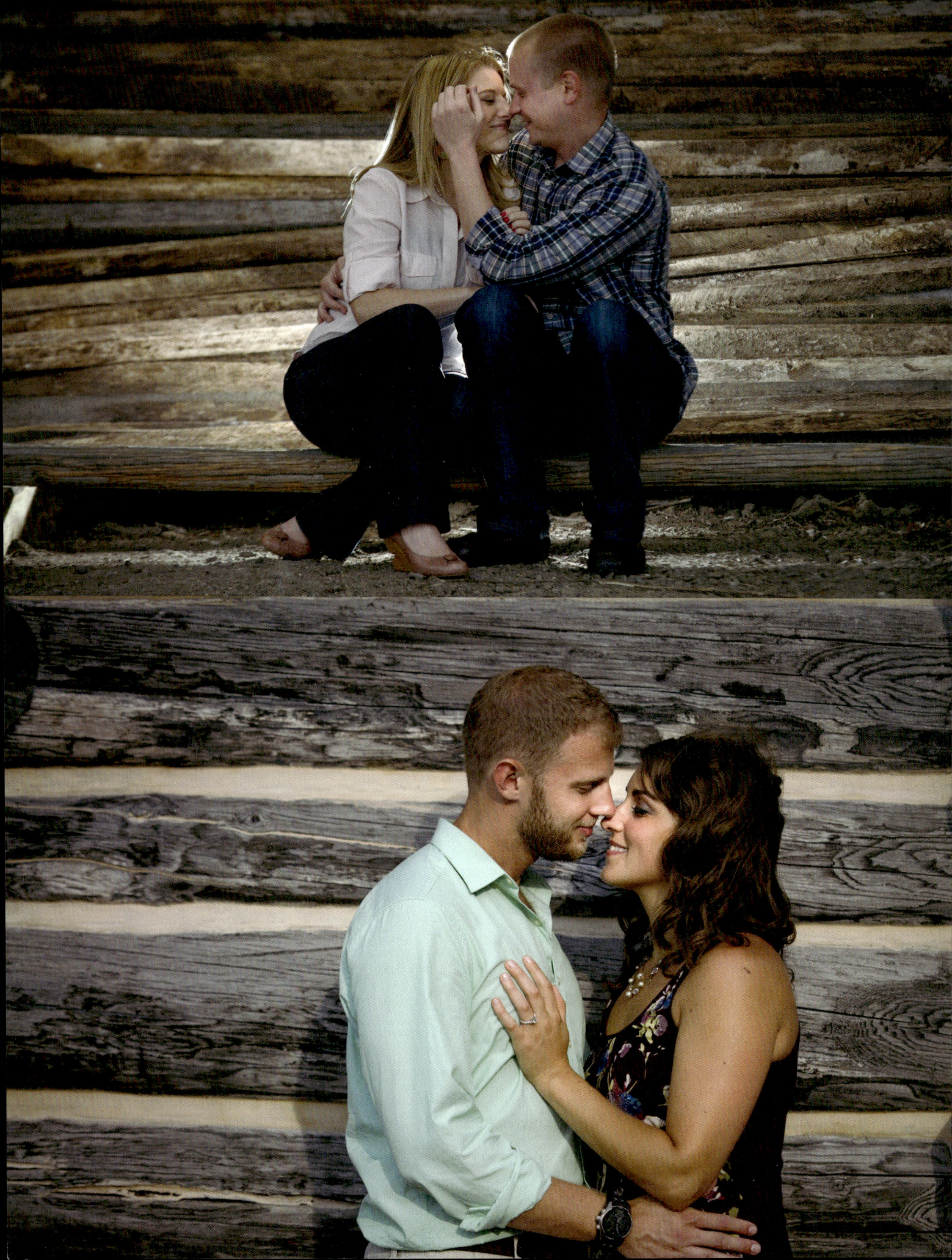

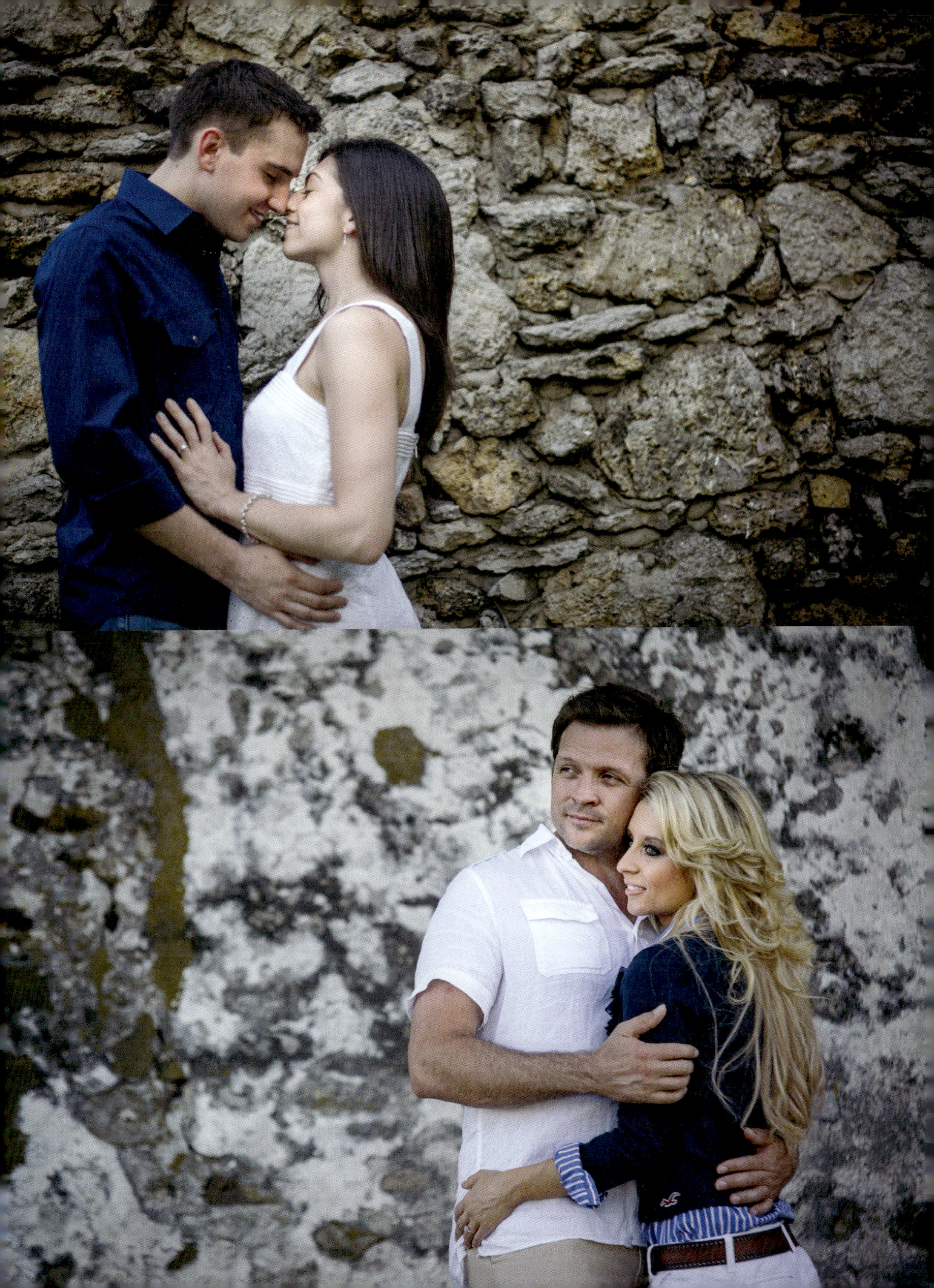

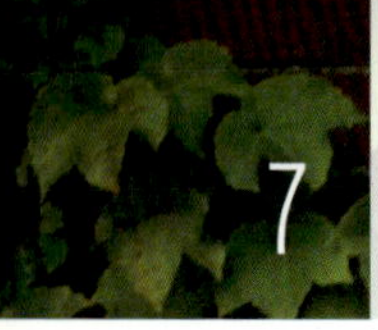

7 Kicking Off the Session

Arrival at the Location

We have the couple meet us at the first location, dressed in the outfits (casual or dressy) we've selected to suit that part of the session.

In our conversation before the session, we make sure to ask what kind of car they'll be driving—and we let them know how to identify our vehicle. Since this is often our first face-to-face meeting, it's important to be able to find each other easily.

We also remind them to arrive on time. We set the arrival time for about thirty minutes before we actually want to start shooting. This gives us a little wiggle room. It also allows some time for the inevitable small talk when we all arrive, so we (and they) don't feel hurried.

As we walk from the cars to the first shooting area we have in mind, I walk ahead while Danielle trails behind and watches how the couple interacts. If they naturally hold hands or kiss or touch each other, that's a good sign. We know they're comfortable with public displays of affection. If they're a little more reserved (or, as is the case with many couples who have been together a long time, less physically demonstrative) we know to give them a little extra coaching and encouragement as we start the session.

Telling Them What to Expect

If we haven't met the couple face-to-face yet, this is also the time when we'll give them a little rundown of what to expect during the session. We

▼ Give them a moment alone, not knowing where you are—and then see what happens.

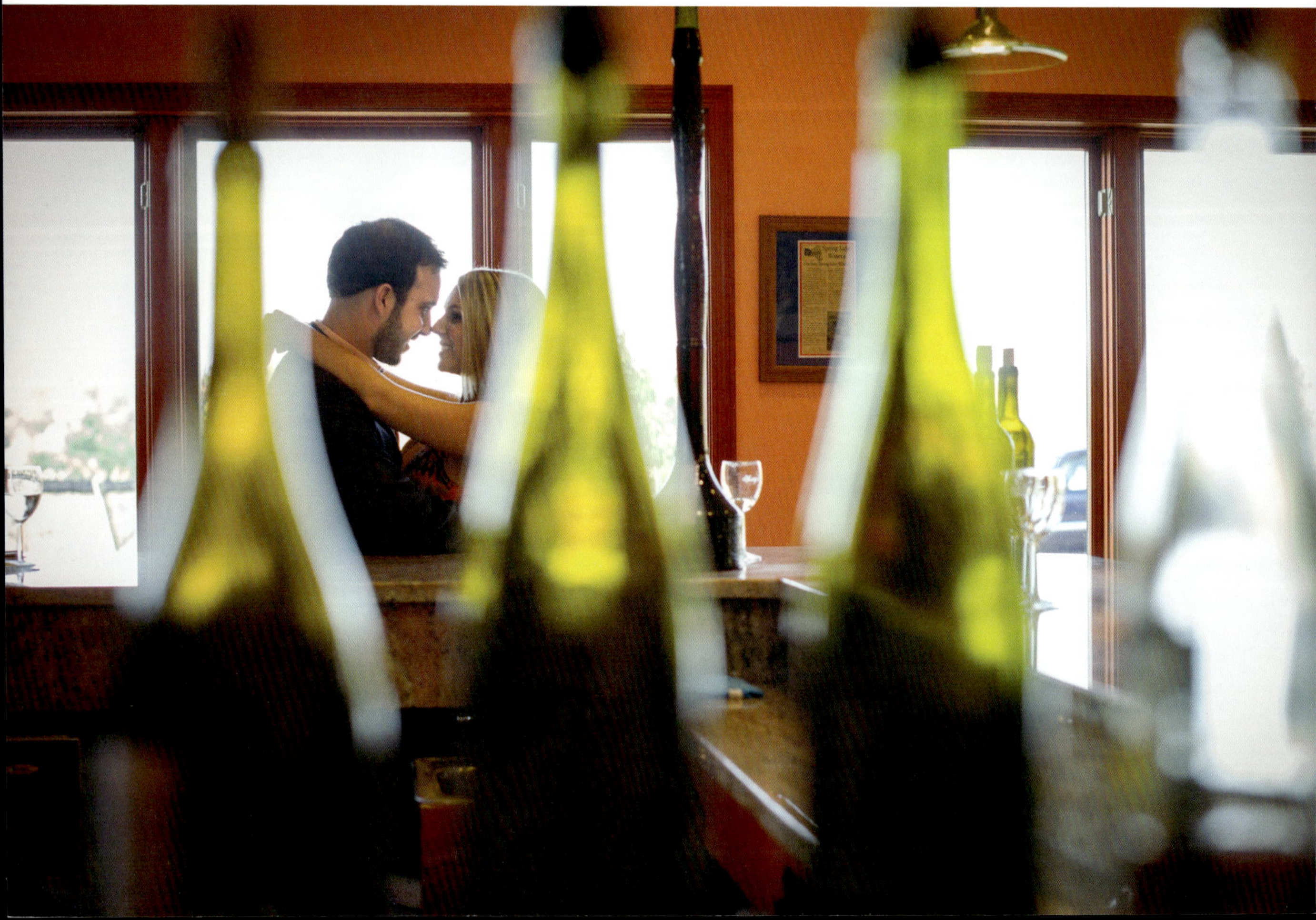

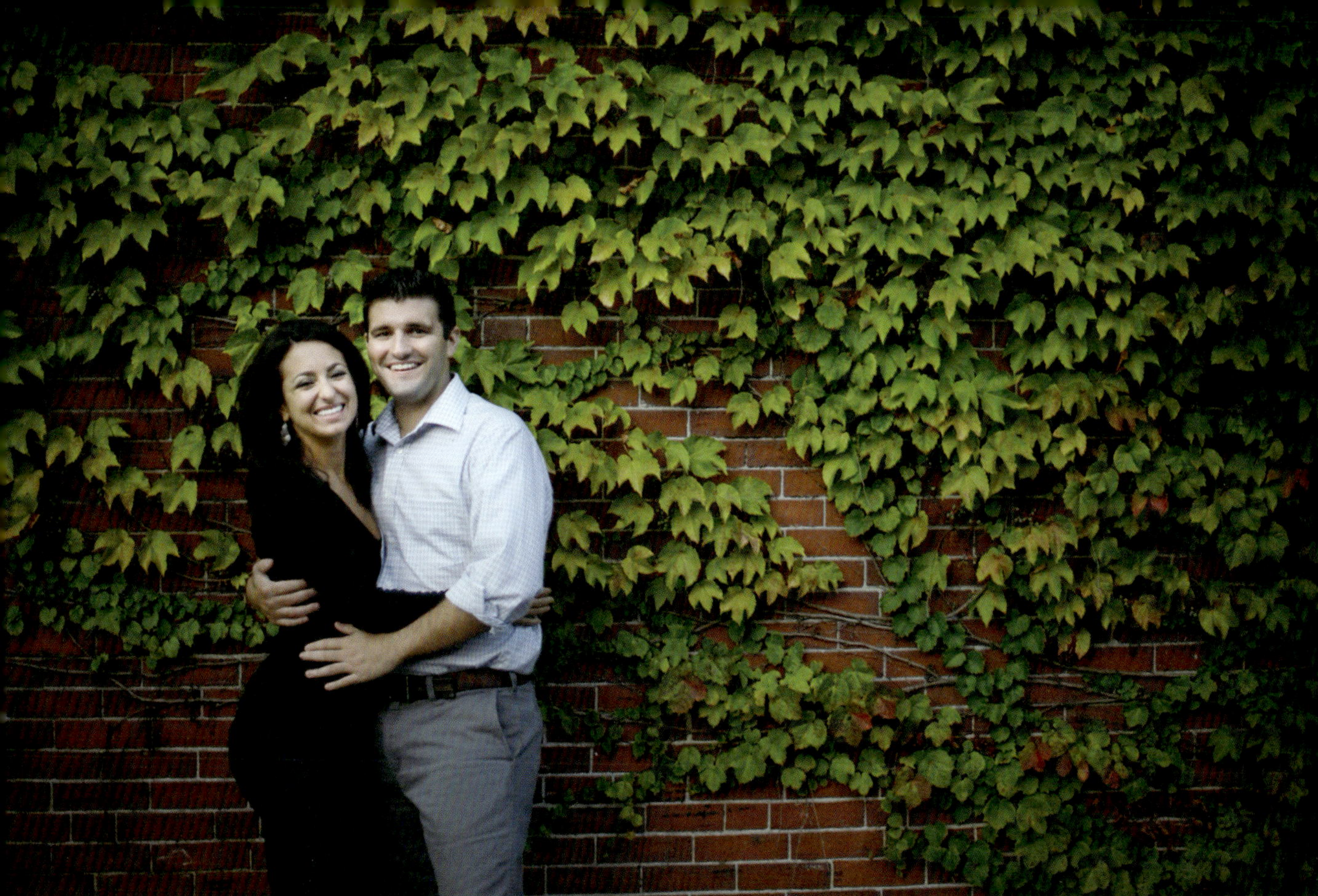

Keeping up a silly banter with the couple helps produce genuine smiles.

ask them to relax and be themselves as much as possible. We want them to be playful and physically expressive. We request the bride-to-be try to keep her ring visible as they pose.

We tell them to let us know if something we're asking them to do feels uncomfortable or just "not them." If that happens, we want to know so we can stop doing that and try something that suits them better.

Start Shooting

As we get started shooting, I tell them that we're just going to walk around a little bit—but we'll stop a lot when I see a setting or light I like. Sometimes, we'll work quickly; other times, we'll spend a little more time at a location so I can play with the lighting or just work on getting everything perfect. This helps introduce them to the rhythm of shooting—putting us better in sync when it comes to shooting their wedding day.

Humor and Positive Reinforcement

No matter how the first frame I shoot comes out, whether it's really good or really bad, I look at it and proclaim, "Looks great. That's a wrap!" The couple inevitably laughs—it loosens them up and is a subtle way to communicate how easy and unintimidating the whole session will be.

As we get going, I show them a few good shots on the back of the camera. Seeing for themselves how great they look is a real confidence booster. It helps them be more demonstrative and genuine with each other, which always makes for better expressions and poses.

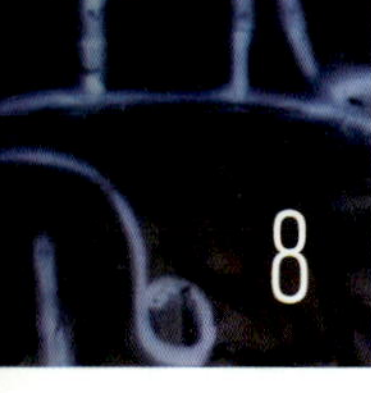

8 Gritty Scenes

Graffiti

Graffiti makes a cool backdrop; whether it's colorful and vibrant or a bit more subdued (as here), it adds texture and interest to the background and helps your images stand out.

However, there is some street art that shouldn't be used. Take a careful look (or take a couple practice shots) and study the art before you put the couple in front of the image. Sometimes, the graffiti can be too busy, so you'll have to make sure that your subjects don't get lost in the image. At one wedding I shot, I didn't really study the art beforehand and only noticed the profane words and images in the background when I got home from the shoot. I had to do a lot of work to remove the problem areas with Photoshop's Clone tool. It was a real headache.

This look isn't for everyone, but for some couples it's a nice fit. I offer sessions like these by request to couples for whom it makes sense as part of the session.

Interaction

Before the shoot, I always advise the couple to be physical with each other during the session—and, no, that doesn't mean beating each other up. What I want is to see a lot of contact between them. I want them to act as if they can't keep their hands off each other. I want them to grab each other and throw each other around if the spirit moves them.

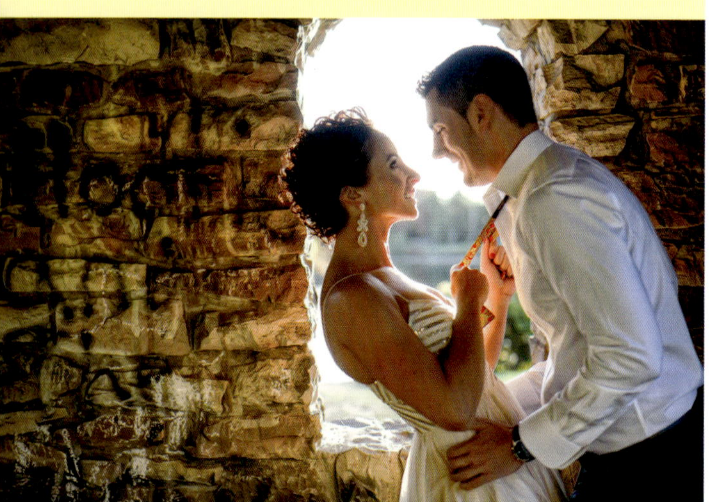

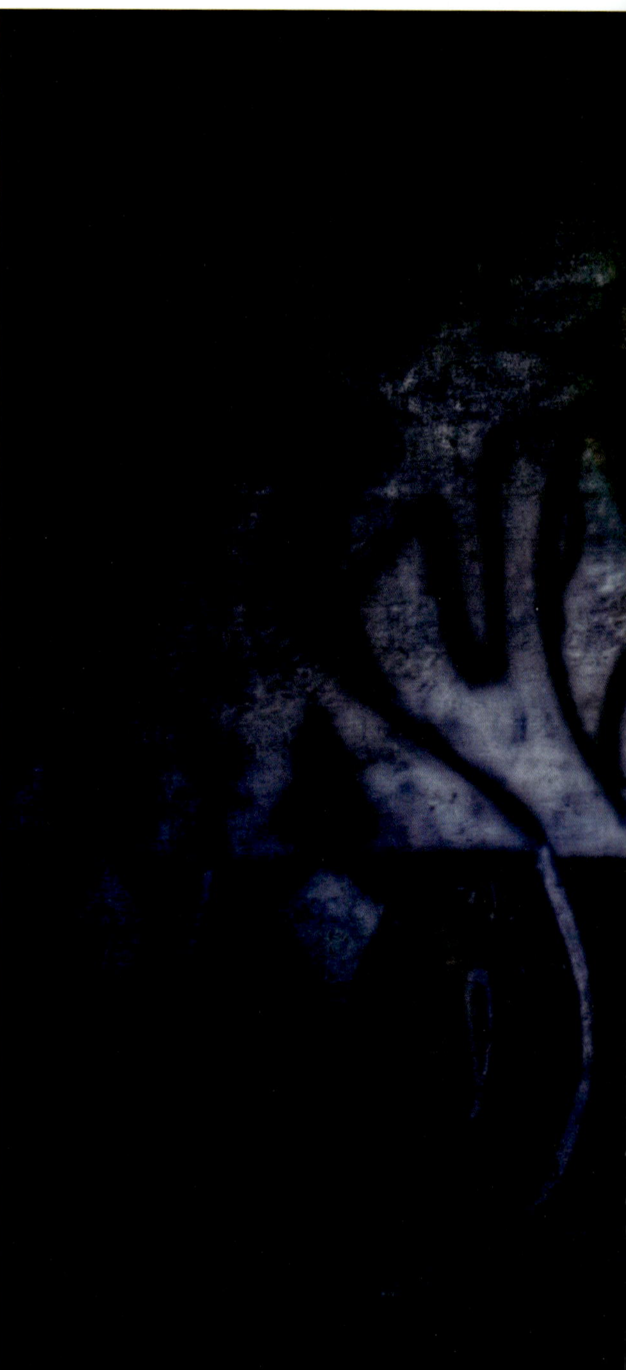

Location and Lighting

For this engagement session, we were working in a structure that had walls and window openings, but no roof. In the image below, you can see that this allowed the sun to peek over the wall and light the couple with a warm glow. The wall behind them was also lit by natural light only, but it was in the shade and was rendered in darker, cooler tones.

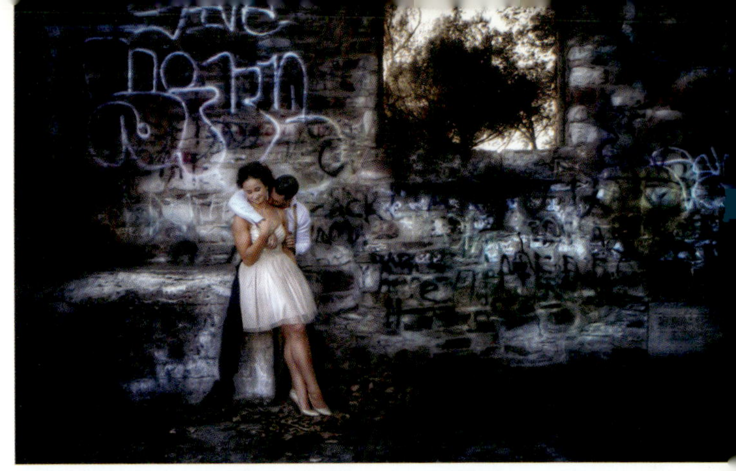

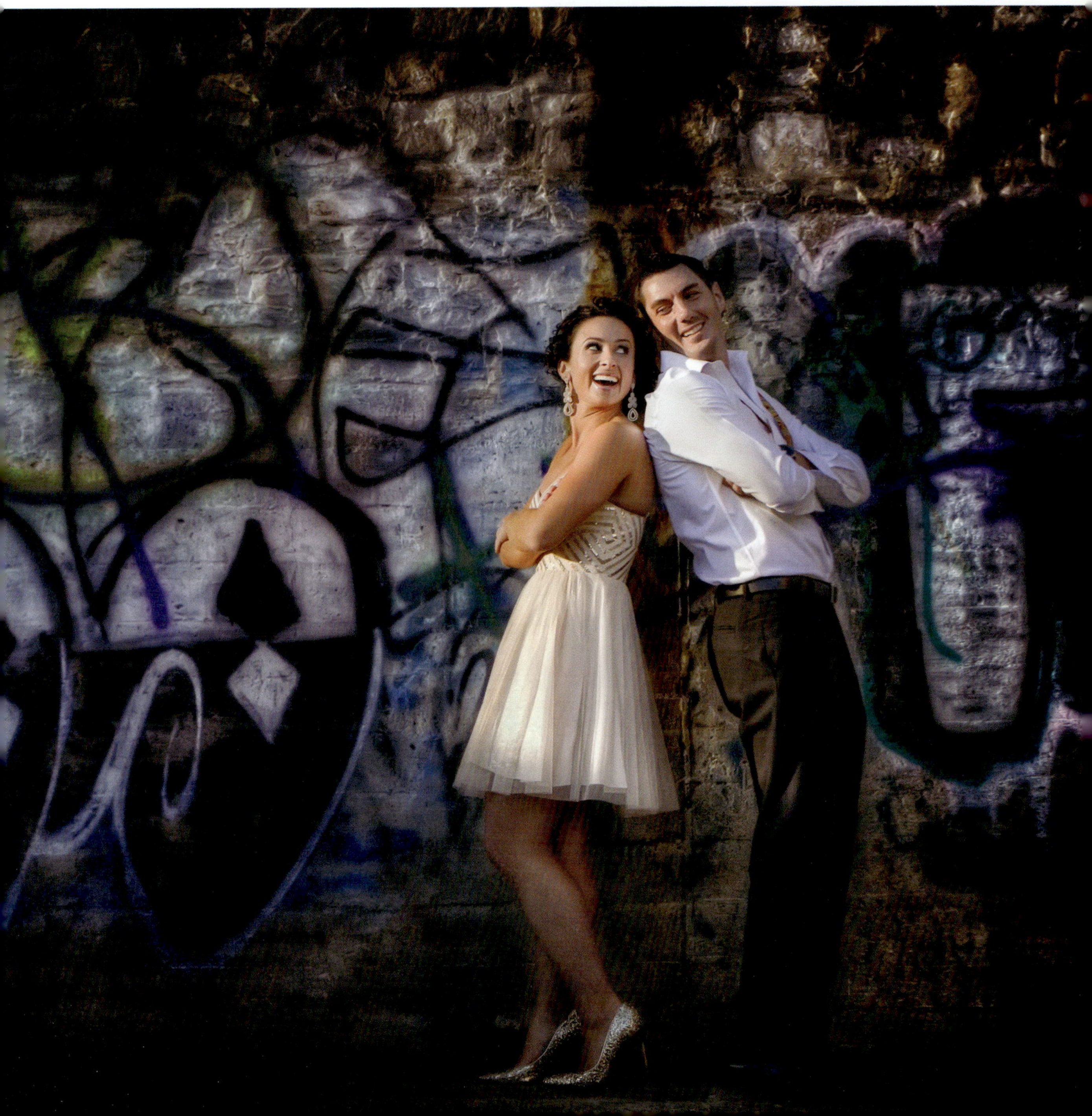

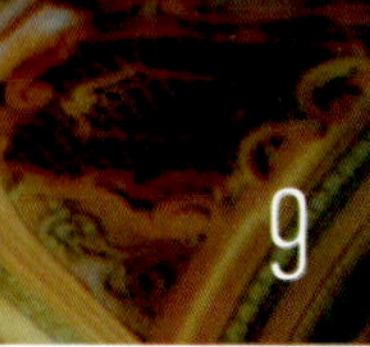

9 Architectural Scenes: Leading Lines

Architectural backgrounds, whether indoors or out, tend to include lines. With smart subject placement, you can use these lines to show the space without losing the couple in the scene.

At the Theater

Our first example (*top, left*) was shot in a historic downtown theater we booked in case rain cut short our night photography session on the street outside. The couple was posed in a hallway with lines all around that direct your eye to them. I photographed from a balcony to get this perspective. To add to the effect, I placed an SB900 flash (with round diffuser cap) on the floor in front of them. This created a pool of light around the couple, who are accented with rim light. The couple's shadows create another set of leading lines that draw your eye toward them. I shot in TTL to balance the flash with the existing light, then toned down the highlights in Lightroom. I also cloned out the flash itself.

Public Art

This geometrical sculpture (*bottom, left*) sits in a public courtyard. I was attracted to the symmetry it presented as a background element. If you look closely at how the couple is posed, you'll see that their positions coordinate with this symmetrical approach. Each has their outside arm raised to connect with the sculpture. The woman's second hand was lifted to the man's cheek, and his other arm wrapped around her waist to rest on her hip.

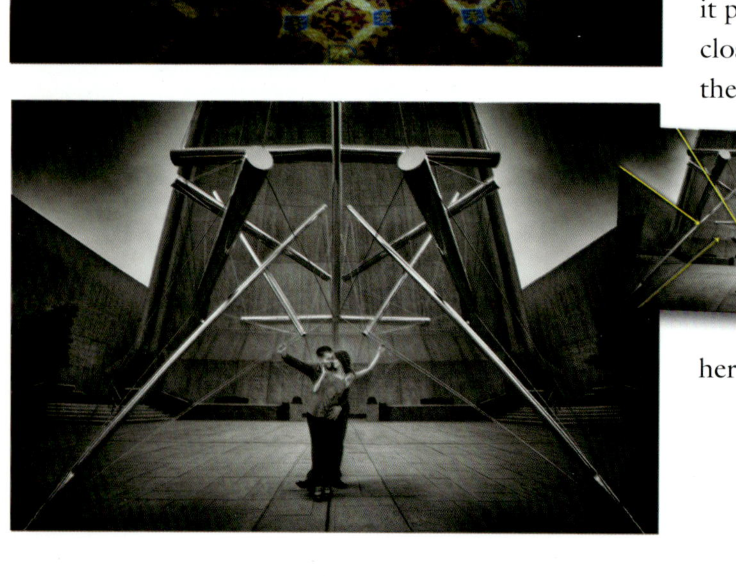

There was one little problem, though: the building on the right-hand side of the scene didn't work. To make that part of the scene fall into line, I duplicated the left half of the image and flipped into onto the right half of the frame (masking out the couple). To make the mirroring a little less obvious, I got rid of a couple branches in the background. The end result is a image where all the leading lines point toward the couple.

Once we had the timing down, I had them head out into the crosswalk. For the first couple of shots, I photographed them as they walked—but I really though the setting called for a more eye-catching pose, so I asked them for a dip. To pump up the drama in postproduction, I added a little motion blur to the already cloudy sky.

Again, note how the leading lines throughout the scene draw your eyes right to the couple in the crosswalk.

A New York City Icon

This shot (*right*) was the last of the session—in fact, we only had a couple minutes to execute it before the couple had to catch their plane for home. Fortunately, we'd scouted the area around New York City's Flatiron building the day before at the time we planned to shoot (rush hour—about 5:00 or 5:30PM).

I knew the shot I wanted, so we timed out the traffic and determined the best moment to go into the middle of the street. I wanted to make it look like they had the city to themselves, which meant finding a moment when cars weren't moving and people weren't crossing the street.

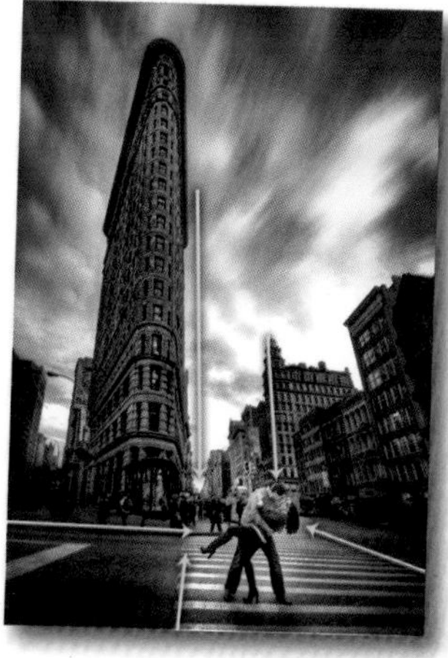

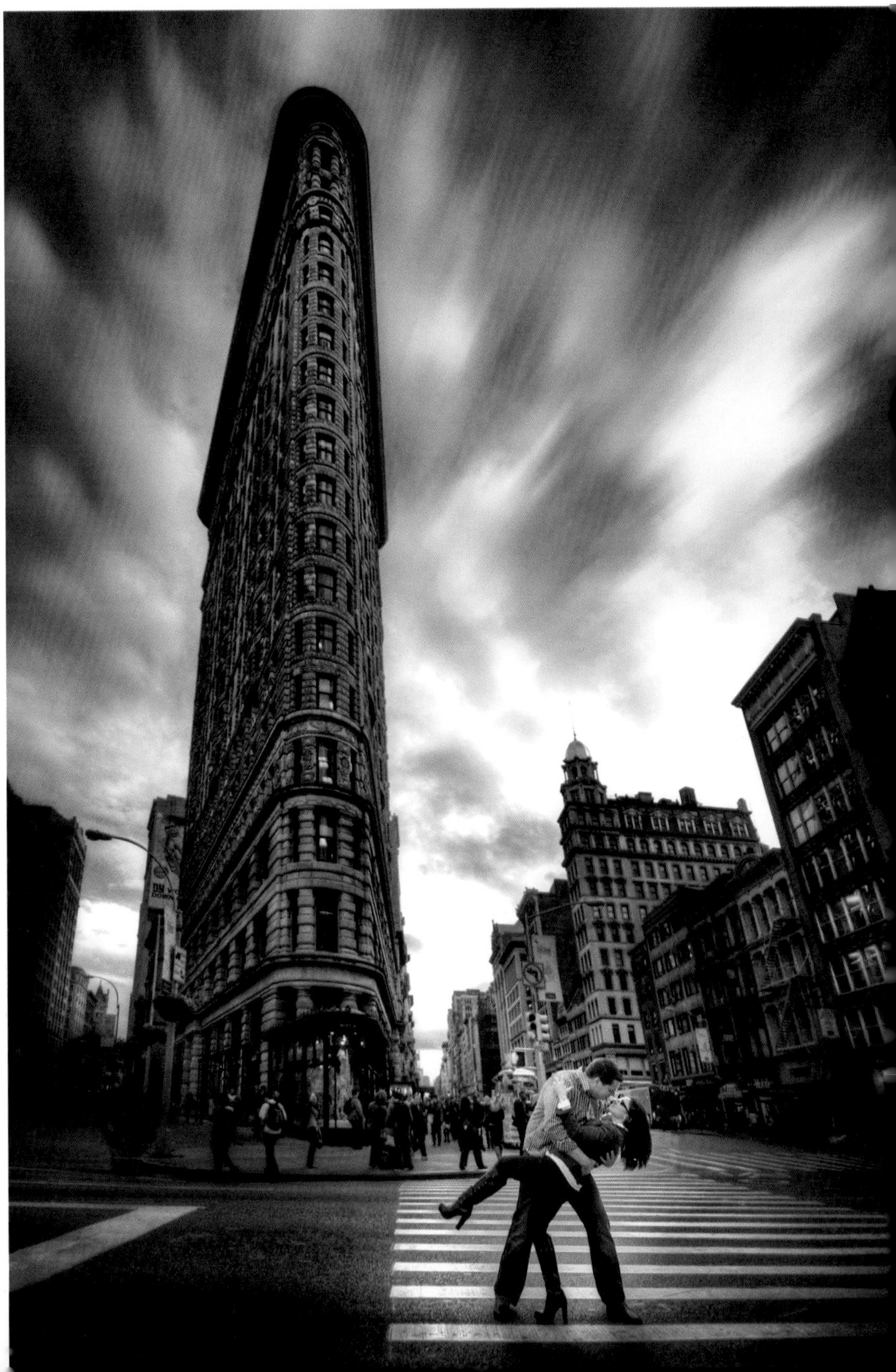

10 Architectural Scenes: Framing

Another way to make your couple stand out amidst a complex architectural scene is through the use of framing.

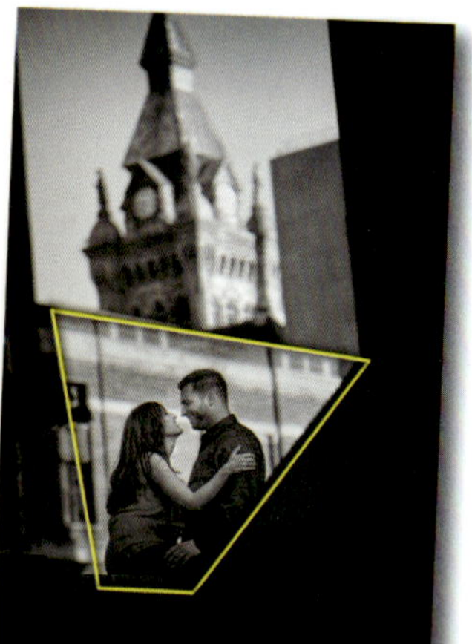

Light and Shade

I was drawn to the scene below because I liked how the setting sun was hitting the buildings in the background. I posed the couple at the foot of a shaded building in the foreground. The dark lines of that building, along with the roof line of the lower building in the background, framed the couple. I positioned them for good lighting on their faces, then added a little fill.

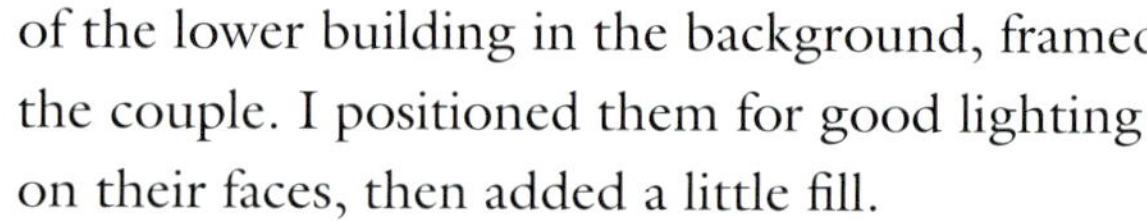

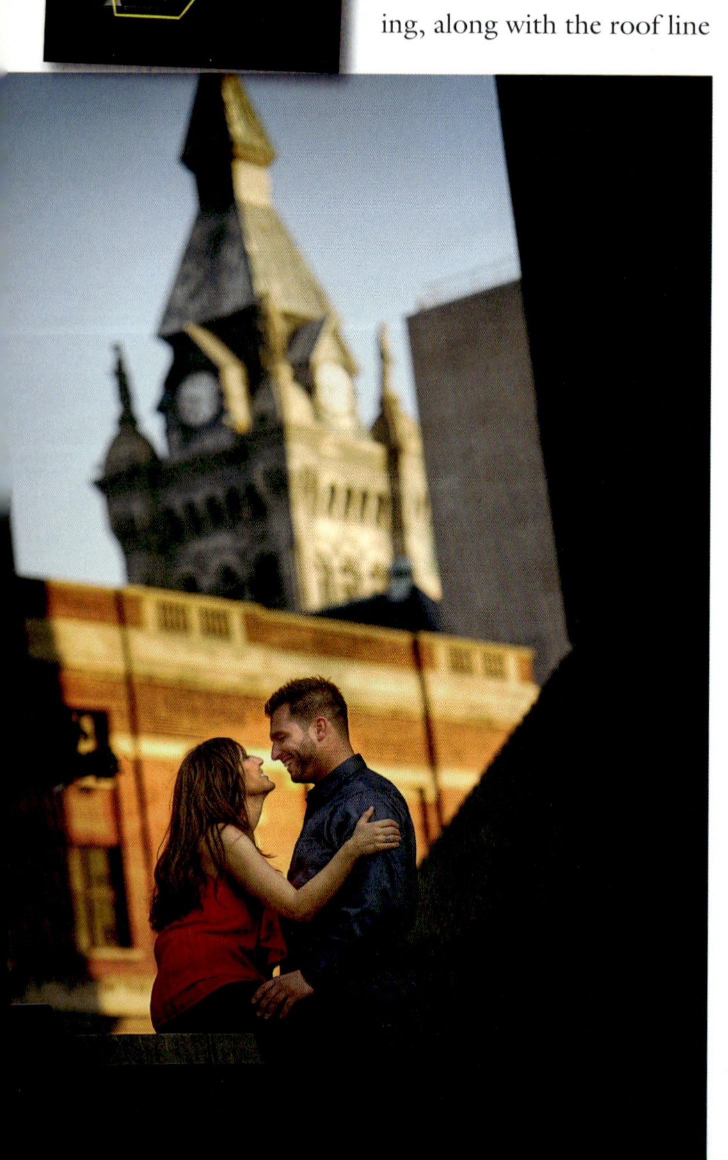

In the Circle

Buffalo's art-deco city hall (*below*) is a popular place for photos. I'm always trying to give my

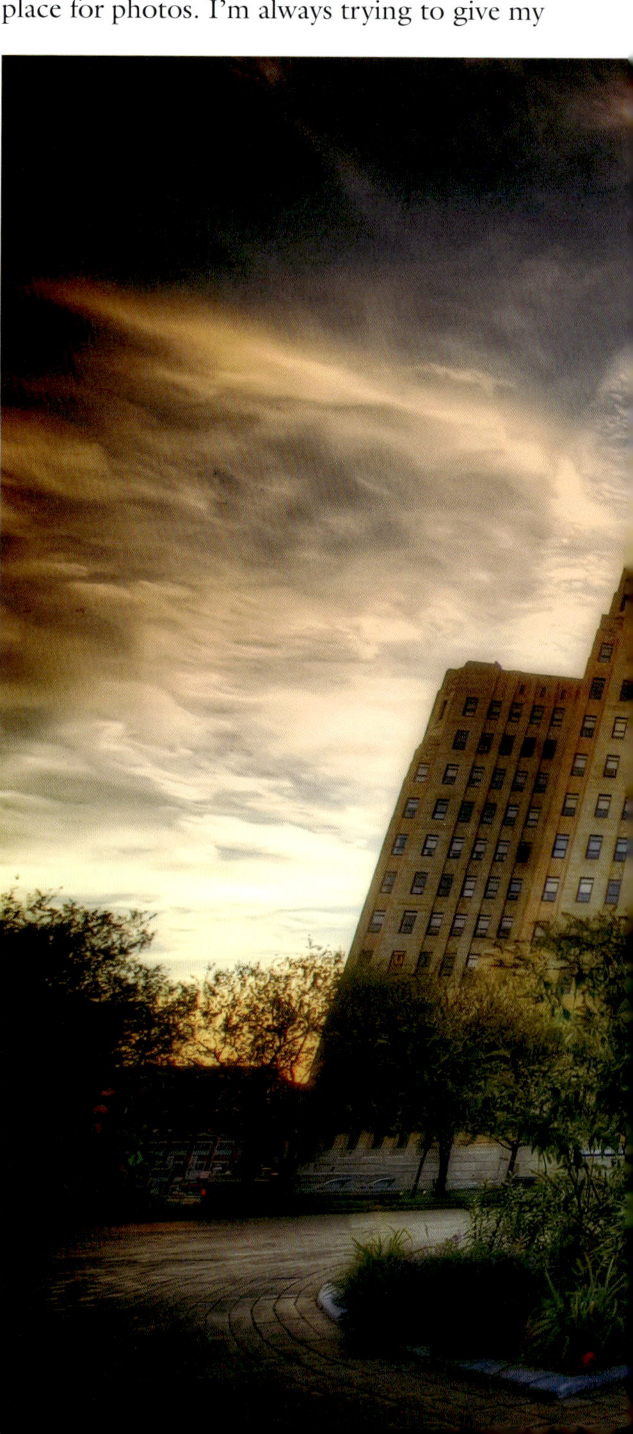

couples a different look, so instead of shooting on the steps of the building, we went across the street and shot in a large public circle with the iconic building in the background. Shooting at sunset, I framed the couple with the lines of the bench. In postproduction, I also dodged the area to put them in the lightest part of the frame. Once the sun dropped, we headed to a local bowling alley; images from that session are in section 16.

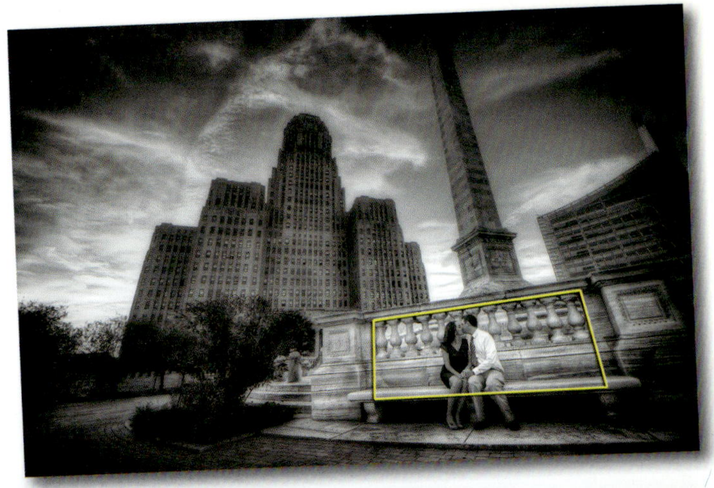

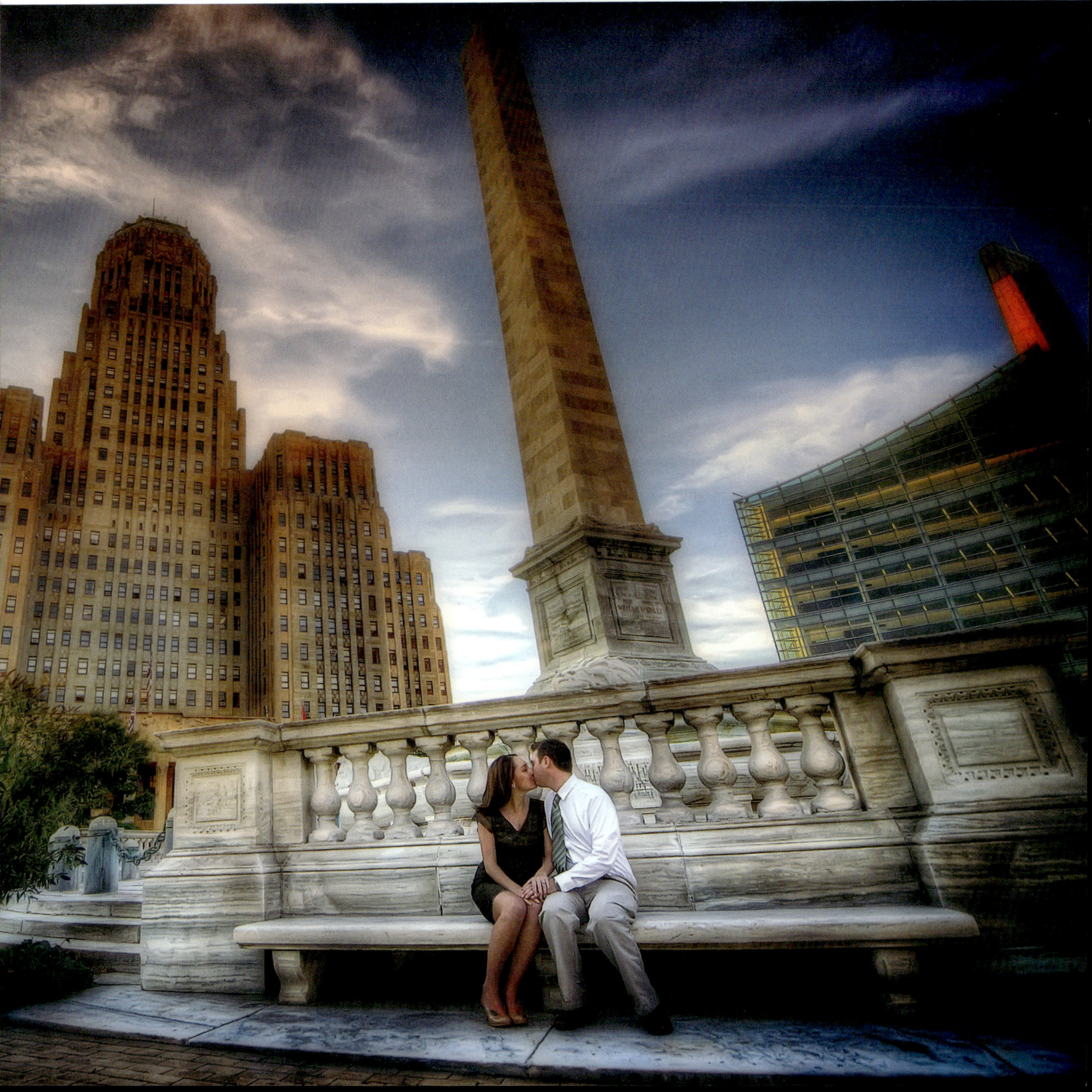

11 Beach Scenes

While we were shooting at an art center, I climbed to the top of a tower on the grounds to scout for nearby locations. I saw there was a break in the clouds, so I knew the sun was going to peek out for a great sunset (when it comes to sunset, lots of clouds means great color). We raced to the beach, on the shore of Lake Erie, to capture it. Even though the weather wasn't great, it was cold and windy, the sunset gave the images a warm glow.

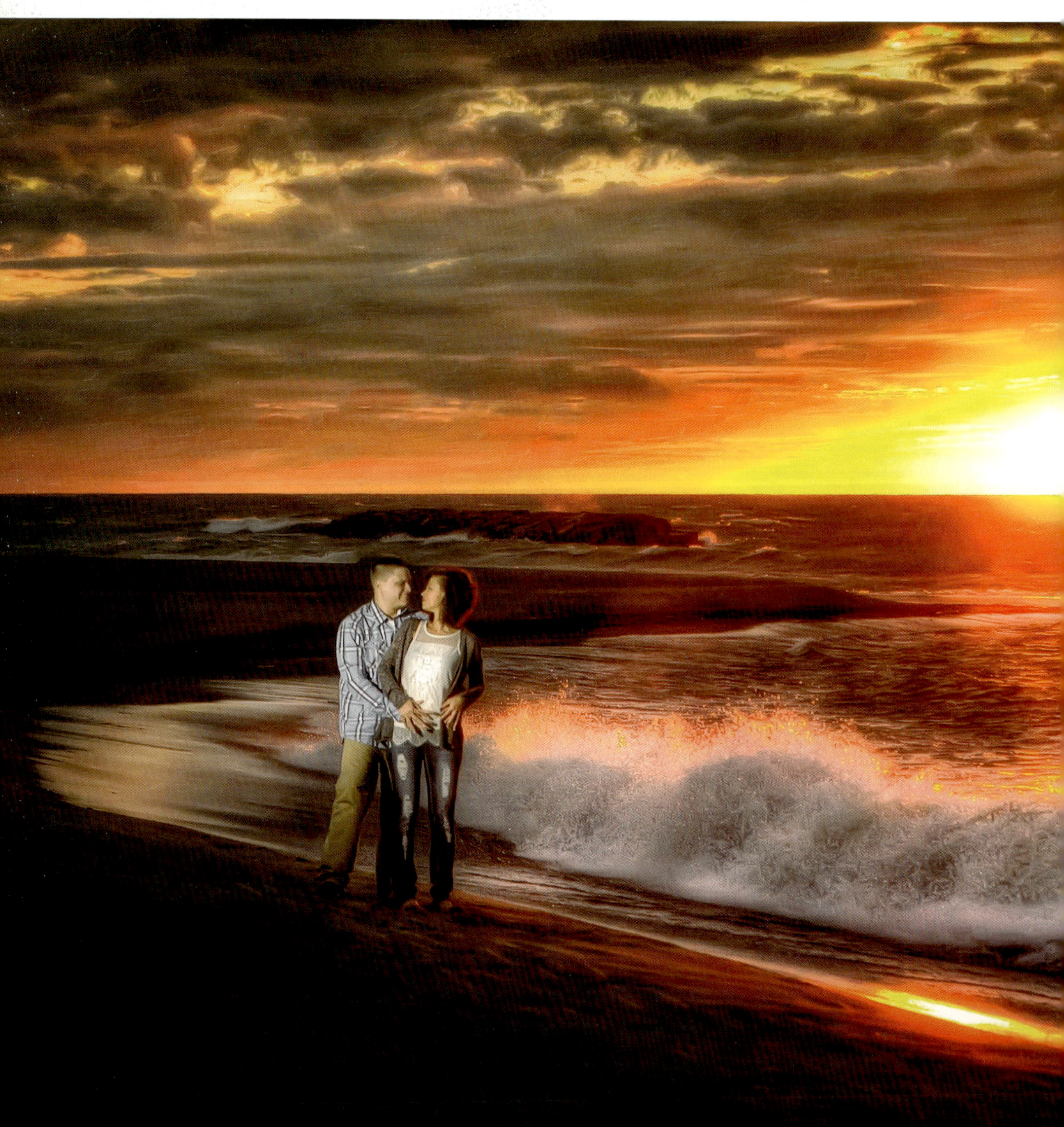

Adding Flash

I backlit the couple with the sun, then had Danielle stand to camera left with an SB900 to light them from the front. This light also brought out some of the detail on the front edge of the wave behind them (the sunlight from behind created the highlight in its crest).These images are pretty much straight out of the camera—I just boosted the vibrance a bit and added a vignette.

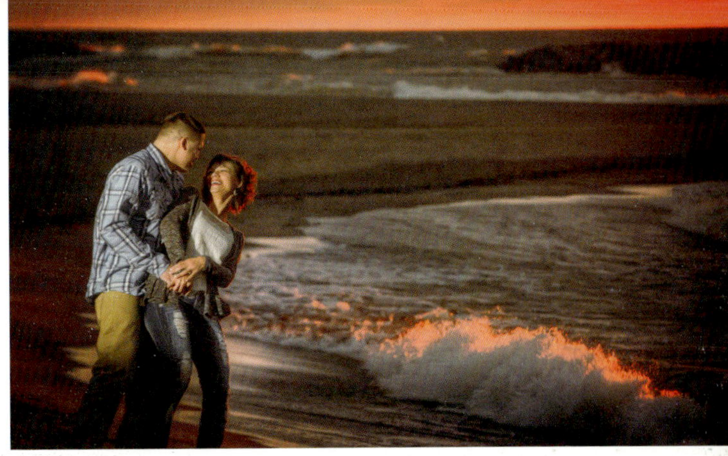

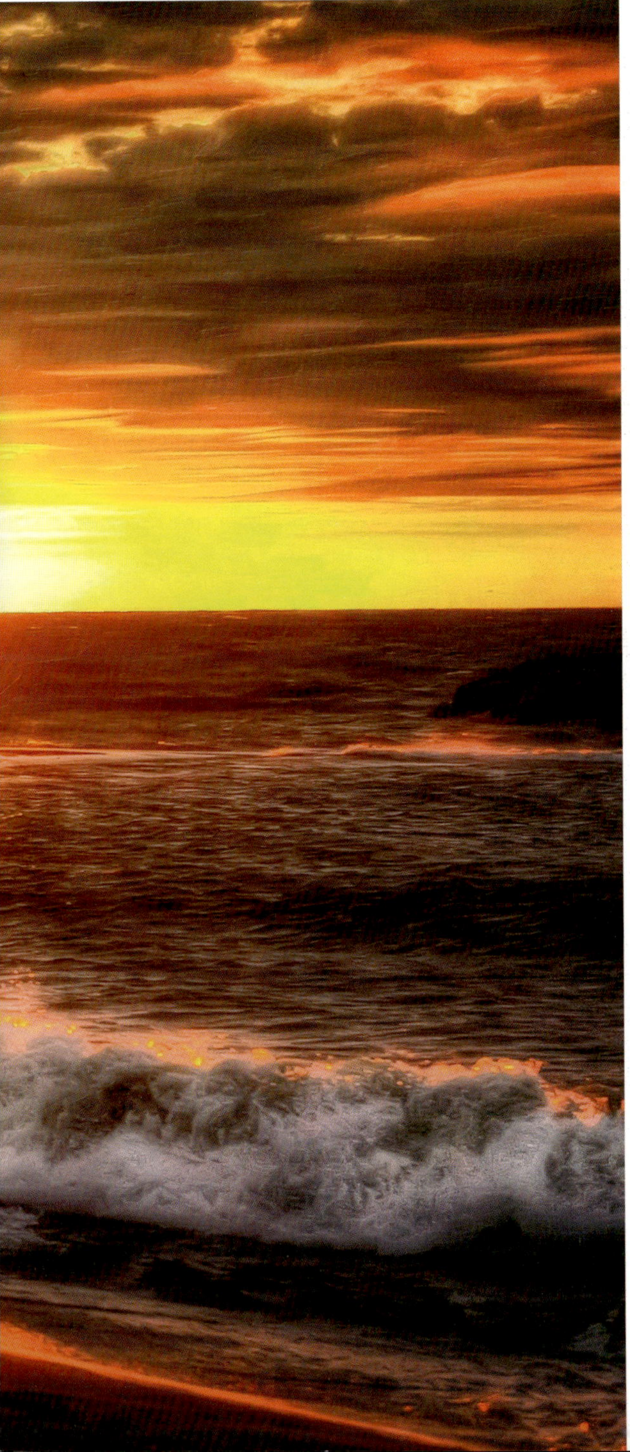

Natural Light Only

For some different looks, I also photographed the couple using the natural light only.

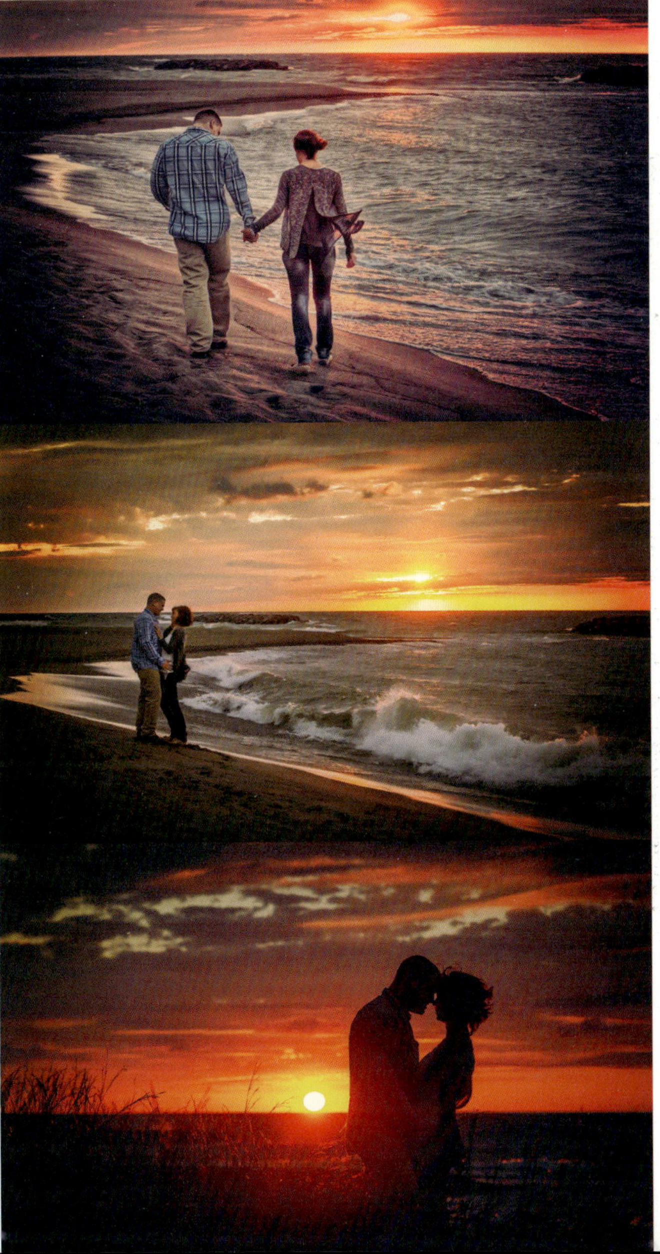

12 Rustic or Vintage Scenes

The rustic or vintage look is quite popular, so when couples tell us that's their style (or wedding theme), we have a few go-to locations we like to use for their engagement portraits. In this case, the couple had their own location in mind: a family cottage built by the grandfather of the bride-to-be. That made the setting not only appropriate to their style and event but also personally meaningful.

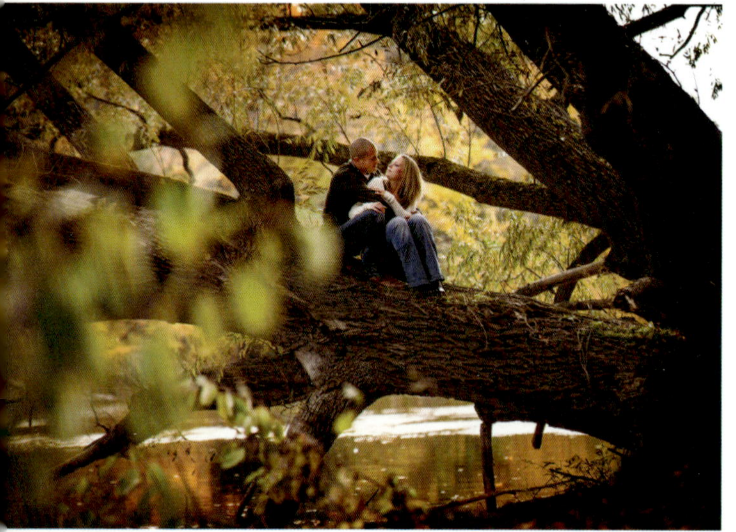

An October Session

For warm colors in the foliage, we shot in October, starting our session in the late afternoon—around 6PM. After photographing them with the fishing cottage (*below*), I wanted to create some images that showed this couple's more adventurous side. For the image to the left, I had them pose up on a sturdy tree branch near the water. They also took the canoe out for a paddle (*facing page*). For a different perspective, I positioned myself up in a tree (not super high) and had them row over to me for the shot.

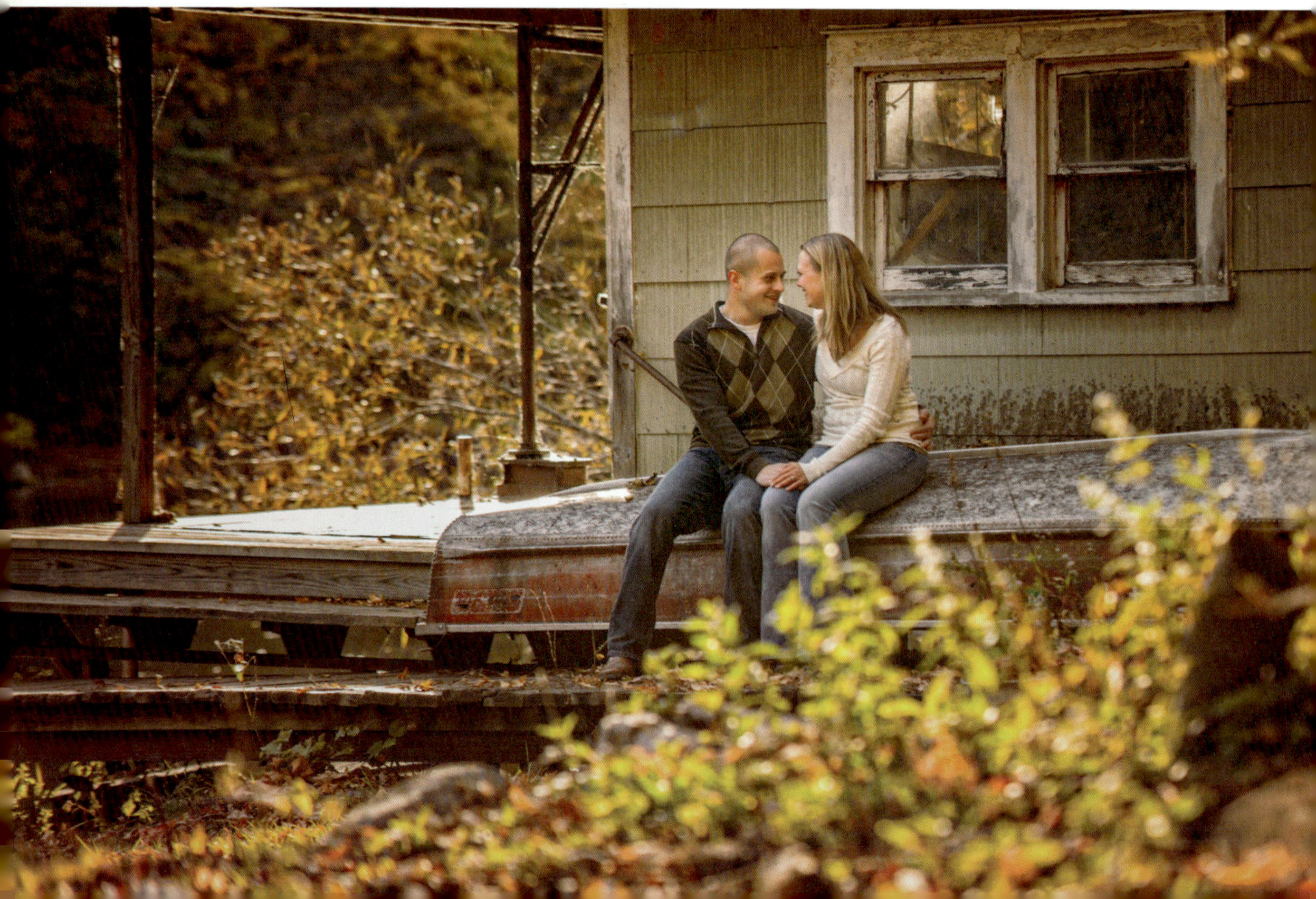

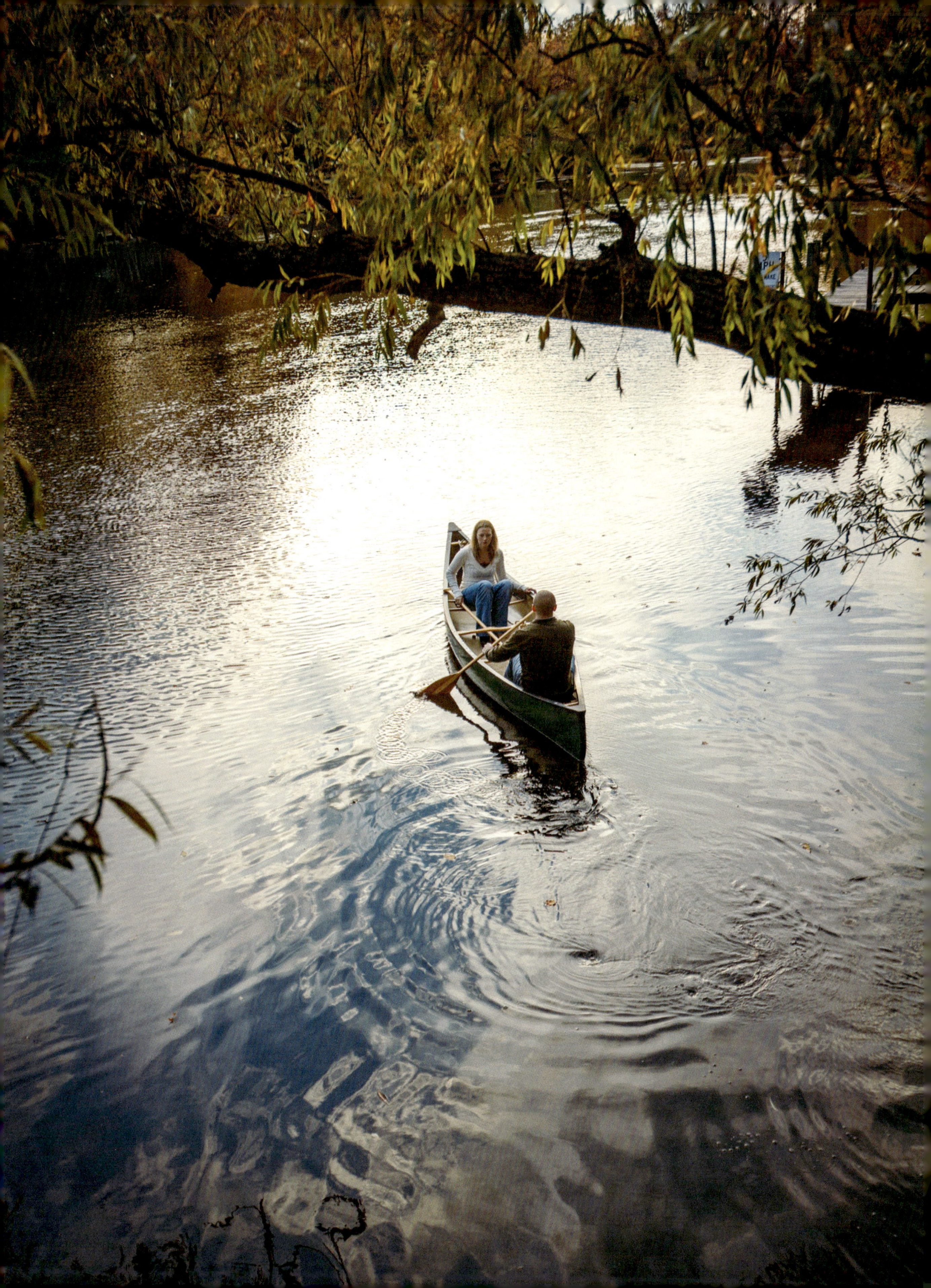

13 Winery

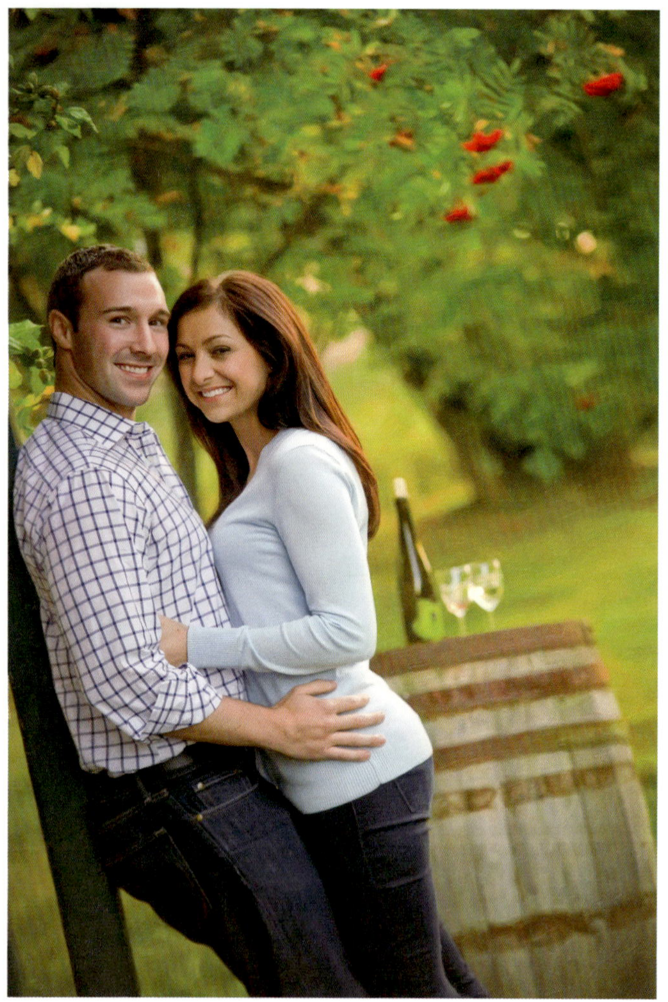

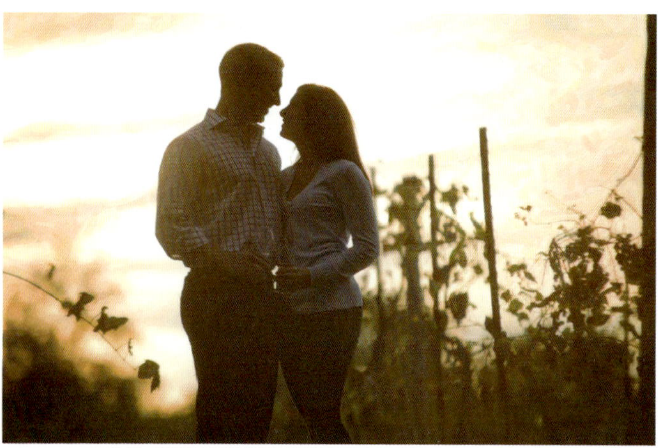

Many couples choose wineries as their wedding location, but we also like them for engagement shoots. At most wineries, you'll find a lot to work with—barrels, vines, wine glasses and bottles, etc. These images were created at Spring Lake Winery in Lockport, NY.

Next to the Barn

The image to the left (*top*) was created next to a barn, under an overhang. I had the man lean up against a post then brought his bride-to-be in for a casual pose that makes them both look great. An image like this is perfect for the couple's "save the date" card. Because it's not intensely romantic, an image like this also makes a perfect gift for their parents—and it *is* important to have images that will please everyone. The sunlight from behind them adds to the natural look of the shot.

Because it's not intensely romantic, an image like this also makes a perfect gift for their parents . . .

Almost a Silhouette

For our next look with this couple, we moved into the vines for an image that gives viewers a better sense of the location. With the sun dropping, I posed the couple amidst the vines and put their faces in profile. I wanted to keep the look of the location, so I didn't let this drop to a pure silhouette; we still see some of the shadow detail throughout the frame. Dropping the shadows in Lightroom gave the image more of the vintage feel I was after.

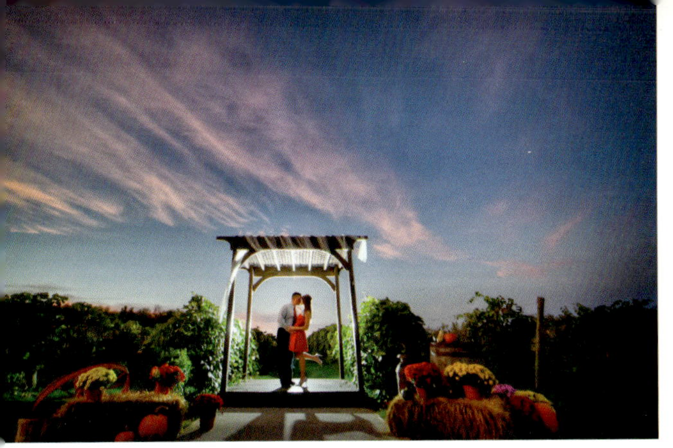

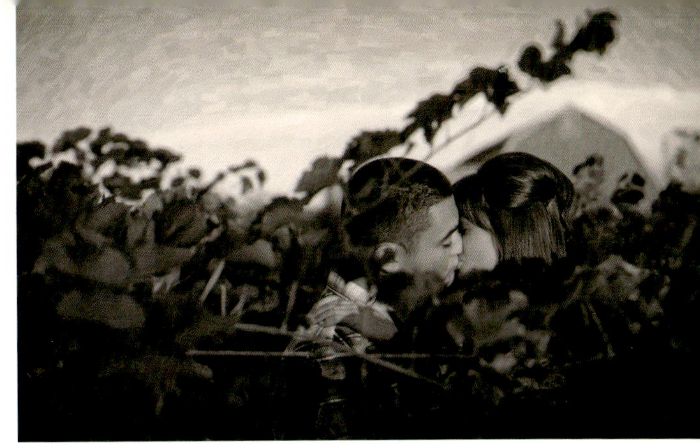

The Gazebo

The gazebo (*top left*) is where people usually get married; it was a perfect spot to frame the couple. I placed an SB900 flash behind them, pointing it up to light the area around them. It also bounced back down onto the front of the couple from the ceiling above—sort of like shooting into an umbrella.

Through the Leaves

Using foliage in the foreground can give your images a "stolen moment" look (*top right*). Here, I shot the couple from the other side of the row of vines. The sun was peeking through a break in the row of trees behind the camera and created a spotlight effect on them.

Adding Props

To tell a little story, as if the couple just wandered off for some alone time, I posed them in the vines with her holding a wine glass and him carrying a wine bottle (*below*). The sun was setting to camera left for great light on their faces. The lines and shadows all lead your eyes to the centered couple.

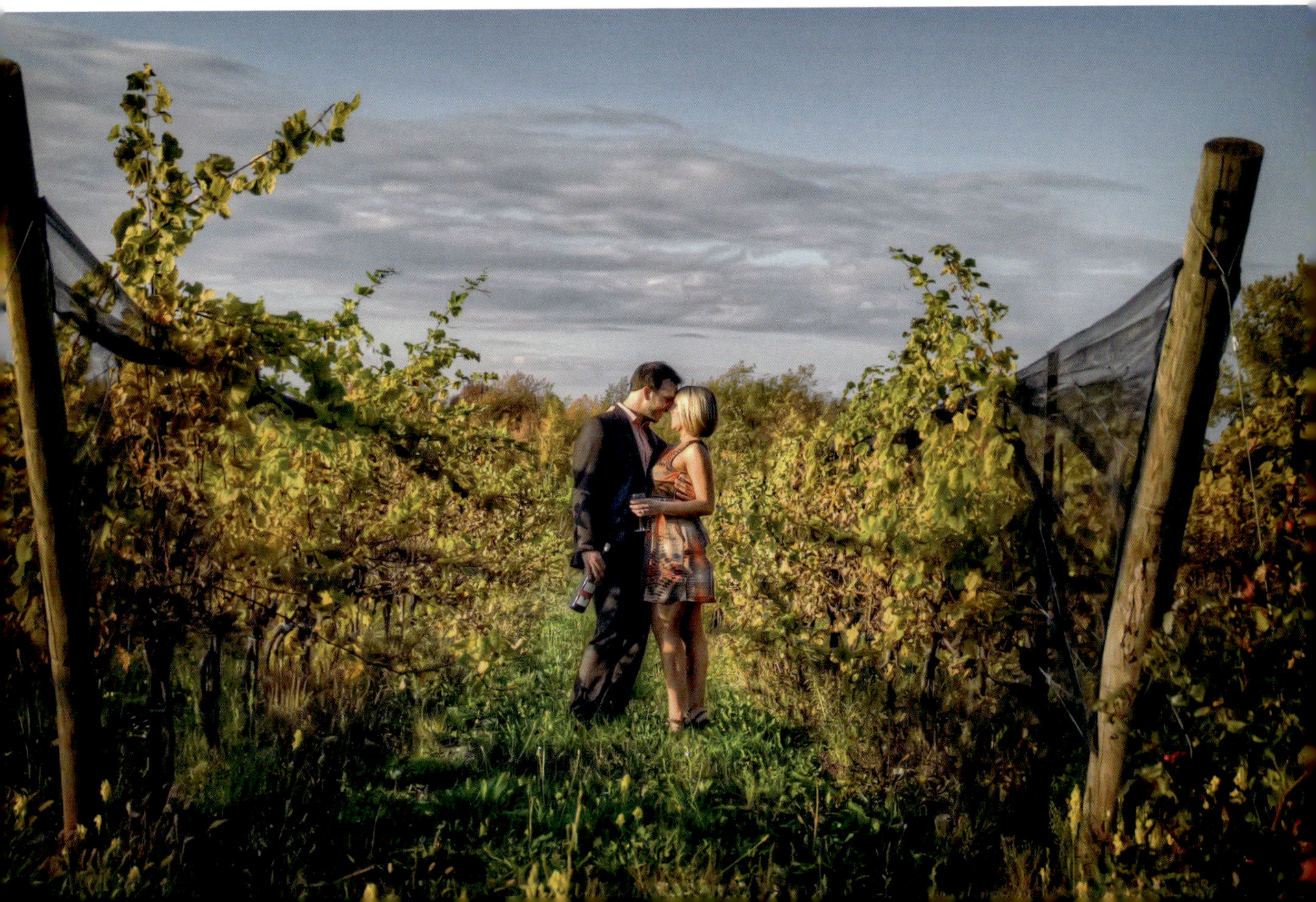

14 The Couple at Home, Part 1

Couples are at ease in their own environment, which makes their home a great option for shooting. Home shoots are also nice because you can have music playing, enjoy some snacks and wine—it just makes the session feel personal. From a logistical standpoint, access to bathrooms and private changing areas are another plus.

Evening Image

For a near-sunset image (*below*), we pulled the patio furniture over near the infinity pool. As the sun ducked behind a cloud, I shot this from across the pool. I positioned my camera at water level to get a nice reflection.

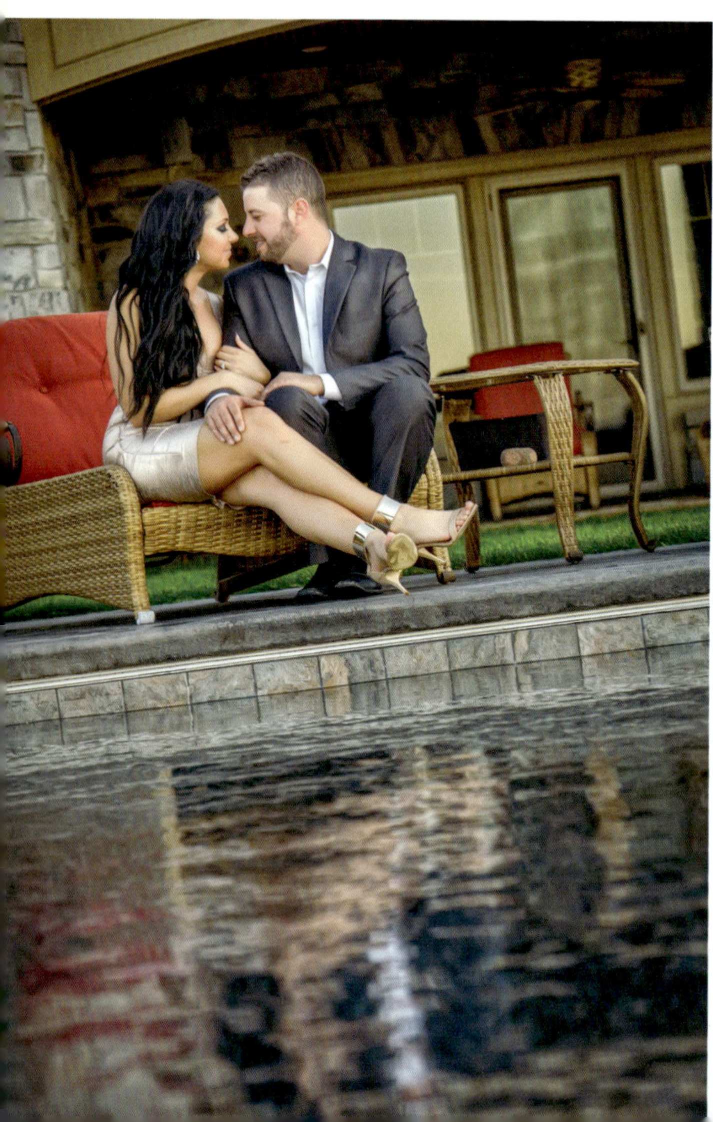

Night Image

Later in the day, at the same location, we pulled in plants to frame the couple standing at the edge of the pool (*below*). I placed one SB900 flash behind them, pointing it up at their faces. This lit up the plants and created rim light on the couple.

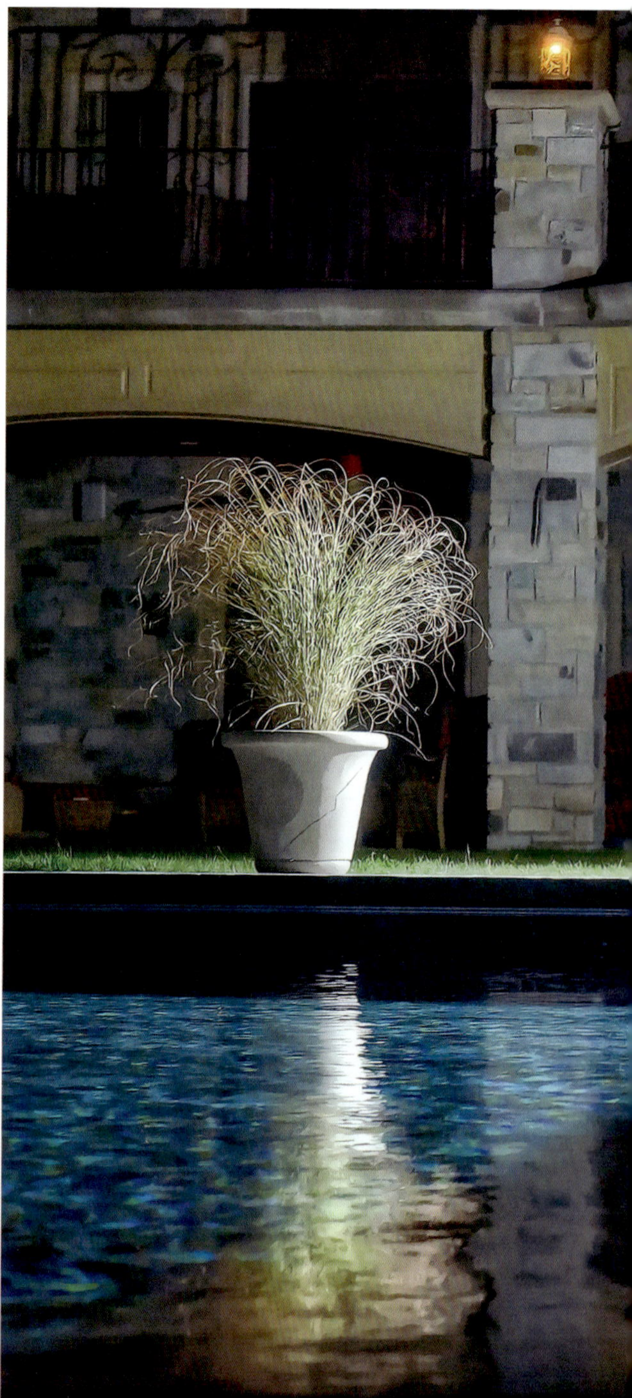

Be True to Who They Are

Engagement portraits are best when they are true to who the couple really is together—and when they let each person's personality come out. This couple likes to stay home and cook, so we did their shoot in their newly remodeled kitchen. I planned to have her looking at the camera, but she didn't think we were shooting and grabbed a sip of wine—and it looked perfect. The pose captured their personalities; he's a serious kind of guy, while she's a bit more free-spirited.

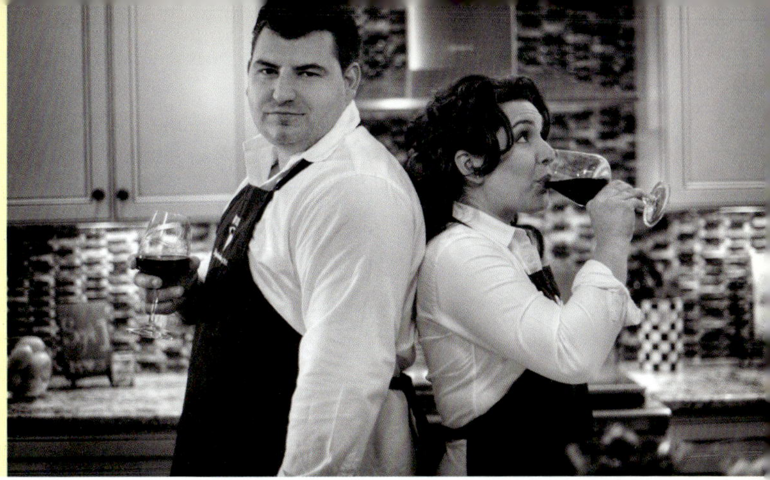

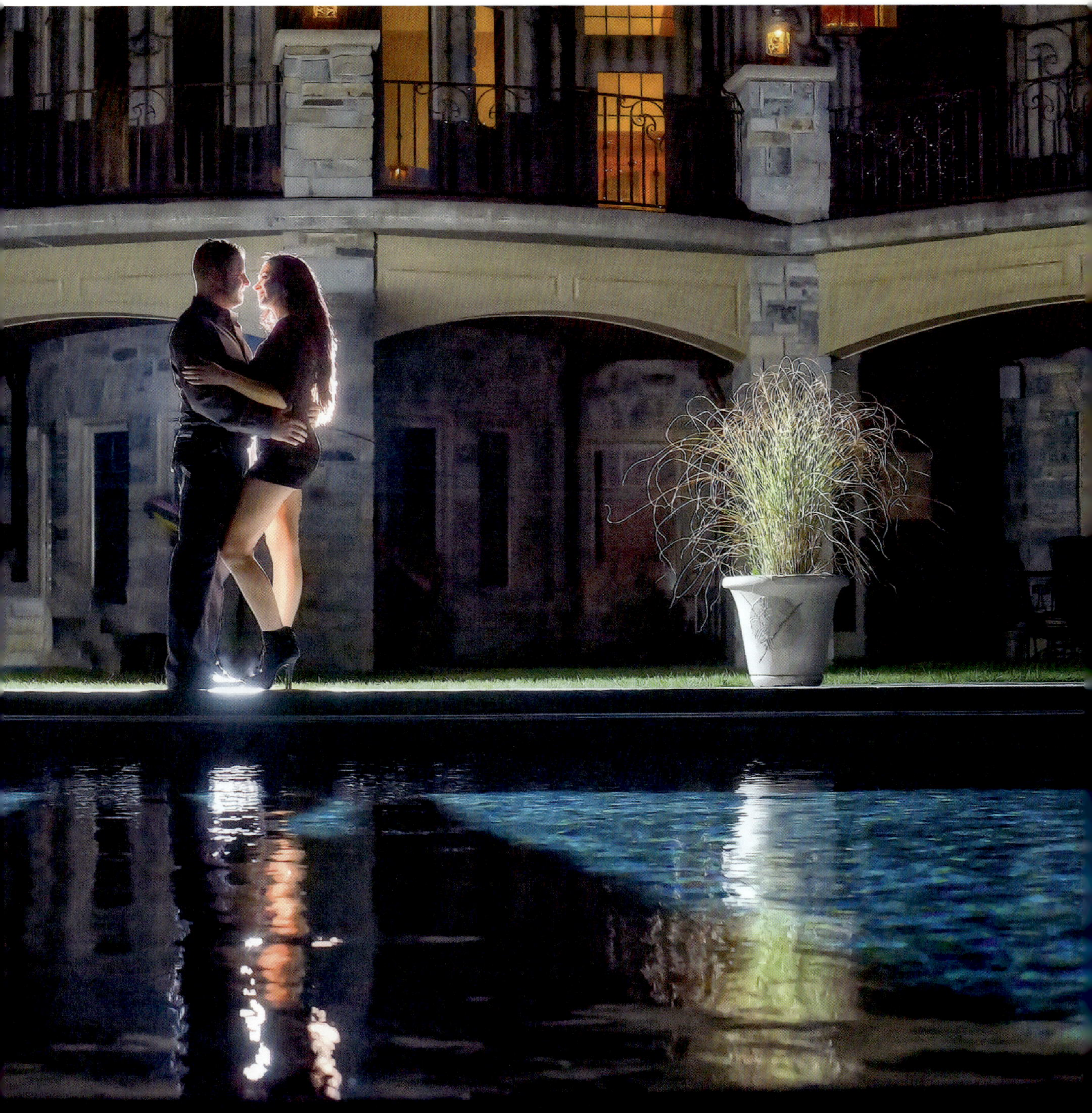

The Couple at Home, Part 2

Seated Posing

For images where the couple will be seated, I have them start by sitting down naturally. Then, I give them some guidance to help them refine the pose. If need be, I'll sit next to them on the couch and demonstrate exactly what I want. I also give plenty of verbal feedback.

A High-Key Look

The image below was shot with natural light. I wanted a high-key look, so I let the windows behind them blow out. Then I brought them down just a bit in Lightroom.

Especially for images where the couple is dressed up, I encourage the girl to engage the guy—it helps him relax and have fun with the session. Here, she's pulling him in close and has her hand on his chest. His hand on her knee also draws her closer for a more romantic feel.

A Magical Setting

Especially with couples who have been together a long time, it's important to keep reminding them to make physical contact. Encourage them to tease each other and to engage both in their body language and expressions. Their connection is what will bring the image to life.

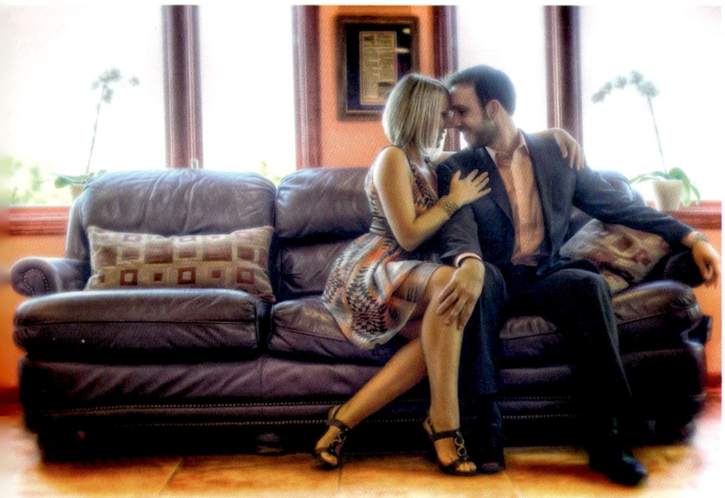

For the image below, the sun was setting behind the couple. I placed an SB900 flash (at a low setting) right behind them on the couch then added an Ice Light to camera right for fill. The room lights were also left on. I'd reminded her to keep her ring visible, so she used her left hand to draw him in for a kiss.

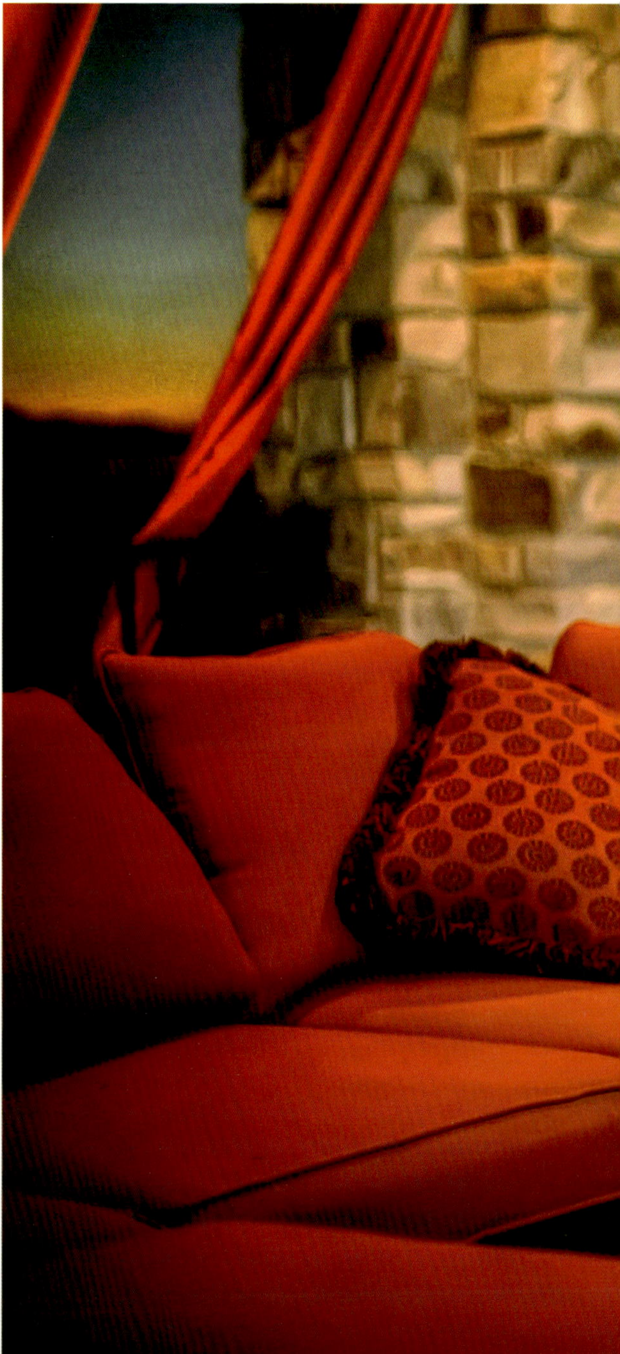

The Dog Whisperer

April and John had made some fancy renovations to their home, so they decided to do their engagement shoot there—in the place where, after a hard day's work, they come to enjoy each other's company, cook, and spend time with their dog. I posed April and John on a chair and asked them to get comfortable. The dog was sitting on the other chair and mostly kept his eyes locked in on me. When I asked April and John to kiss, however, the dog shot them a glance. It was perfect. (More on couples and their pets in section 31.)

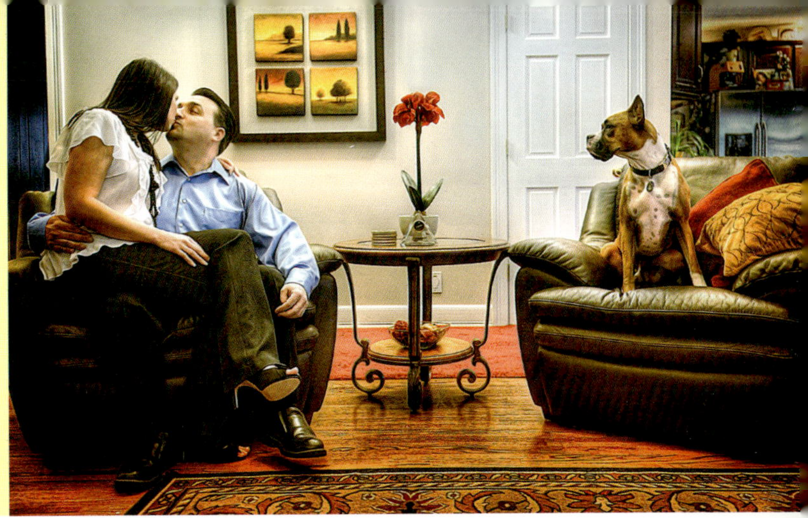

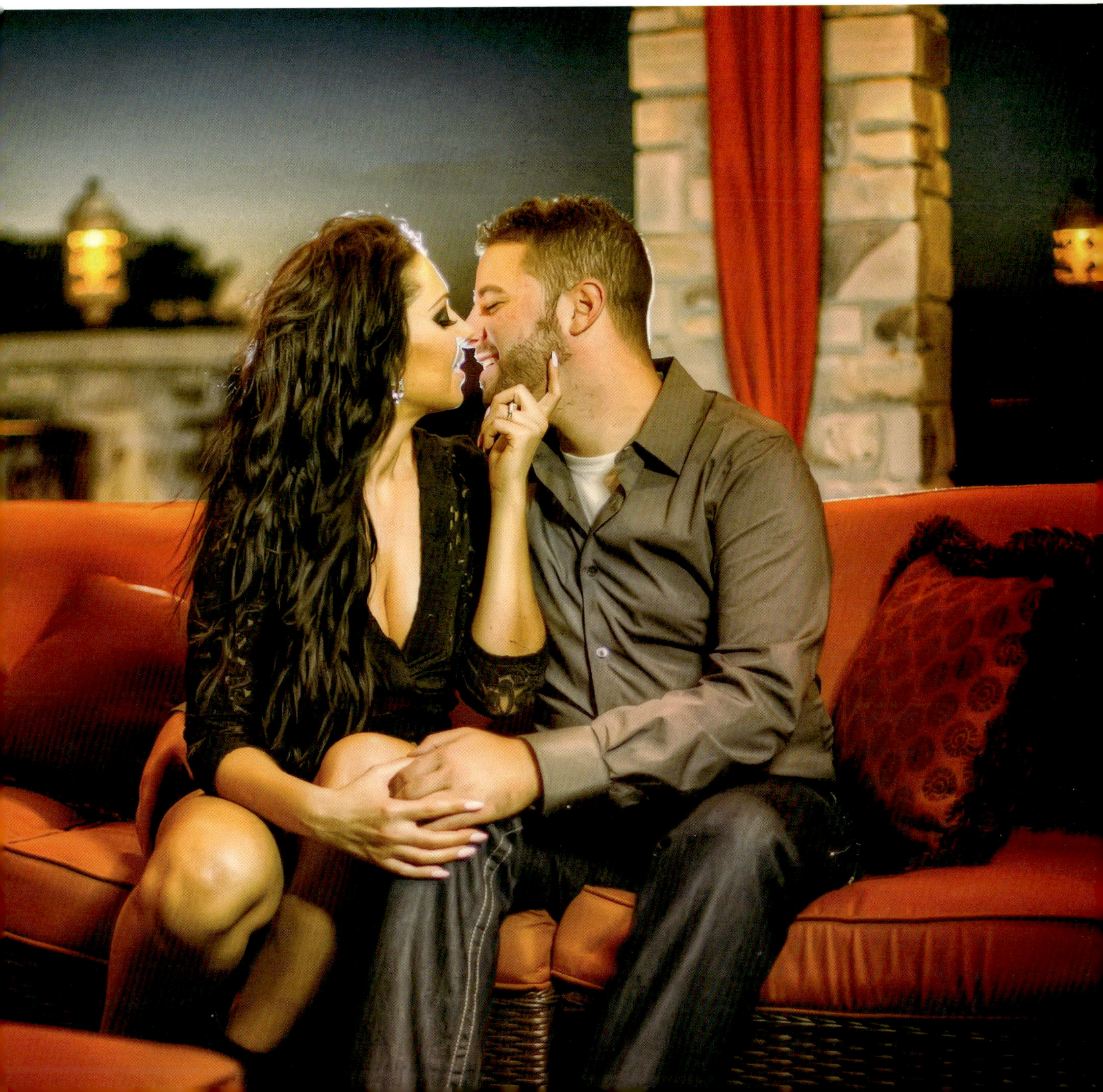

Special Places: Bars

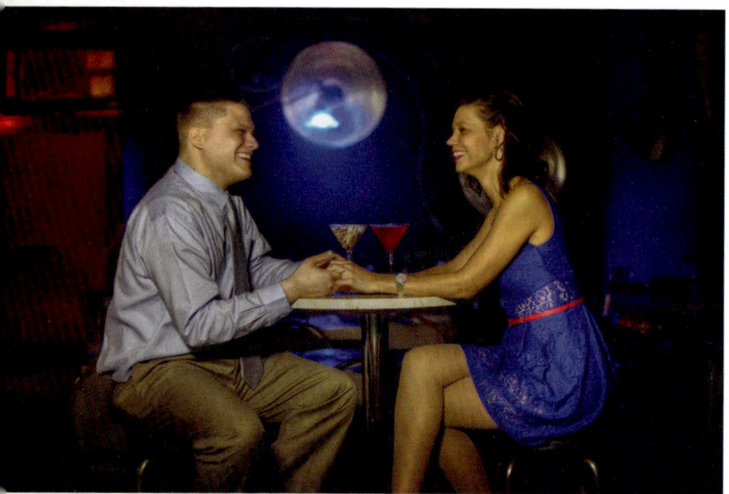

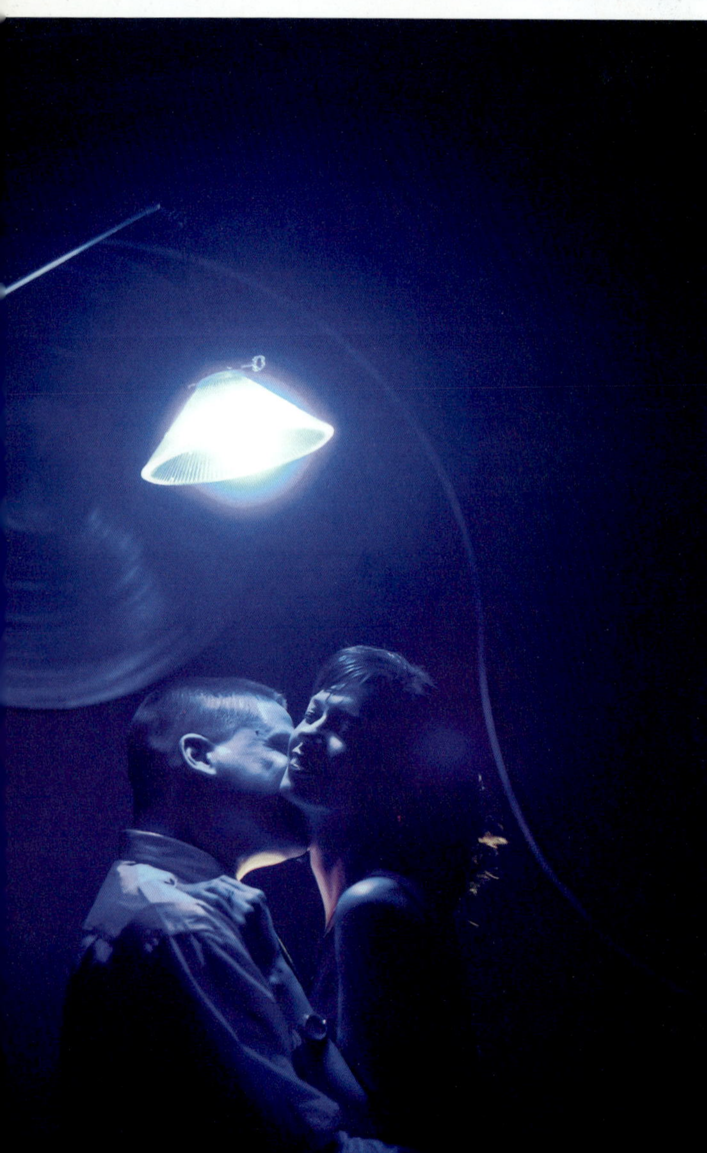

At the Bar

The images to the left were taken at a bar where the couple went on their first date. These were created at the end of the day, so we could all enjoy a drink together and end our session somewhere personal to them. Whenever you anticipate shooting at a public venue like this, it's a good practice to call ahead and ensure the venue isn't too crowded.

For the top image, I shot using the room lights plus an Ice Light above them to camera left for fill. What you can't see is the pool table that was between us. I shot over the table and used the light above it to illuminate them.

In the background of that shot (reflected in a mirror) you can see the blue lamp that was used as the main light for the bottom image. For this image, I had them dance under the light. The man held an SB900 (set low) in his far hand for a little accent lighting that separates them from the background.

At the Bowling Alley

The images on the facing page were taken at the site of another couple's first date—a local bowling alley and bar. When I asked the guy what he liked to do at the facility, he said he mostly played video games. So, for one image I had him do just that. I posed her to show her reflection in the foreground screen (*facing page, top*).

For an nice shot at the vintage bar (*facing page, bottom*), I switched to a 14mm lens. To camera left, Danielle held an Ice Light that helped keep the couple in balance with the neon and red room lights in the background. Their gaze and pose show the connection they share.

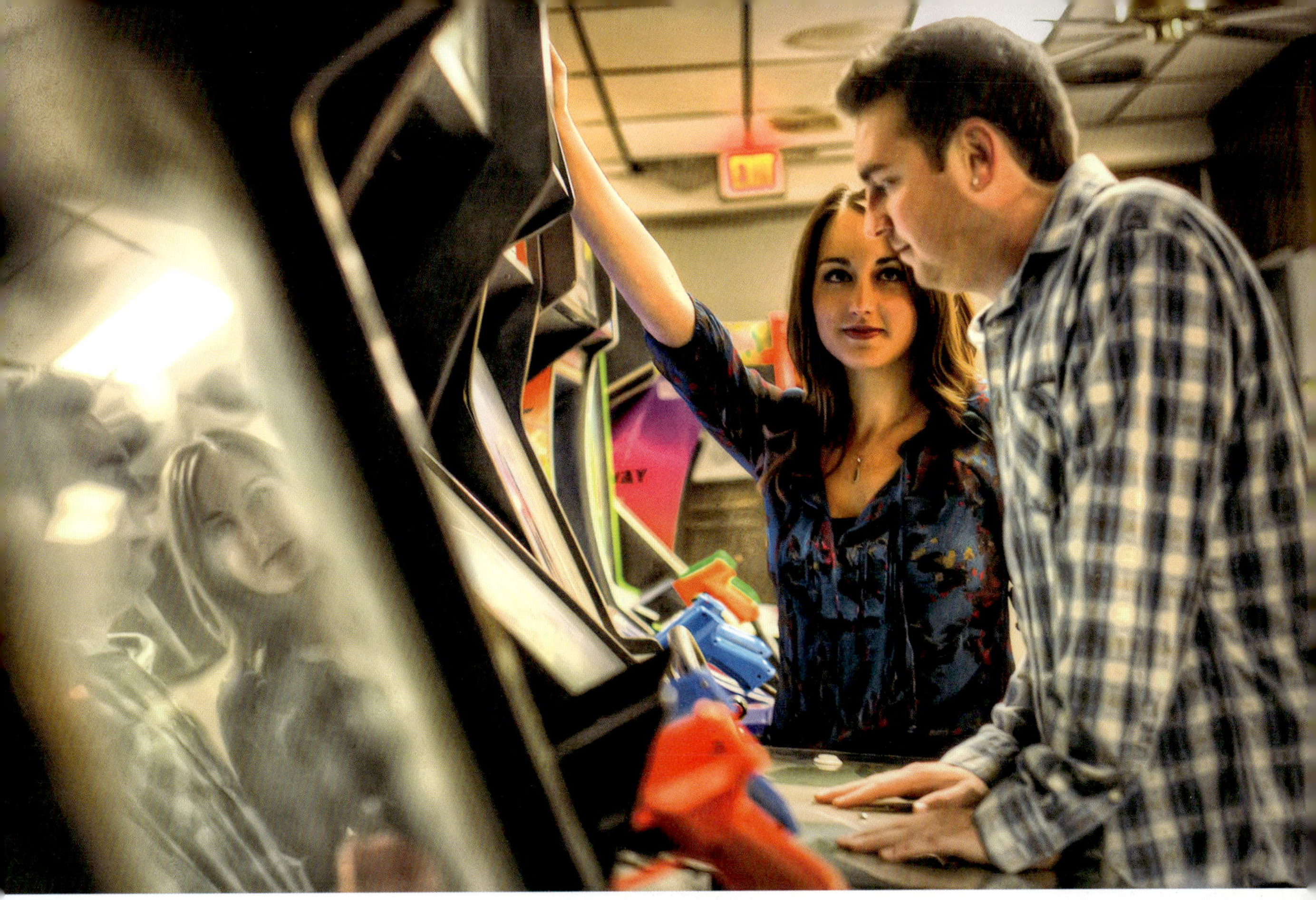

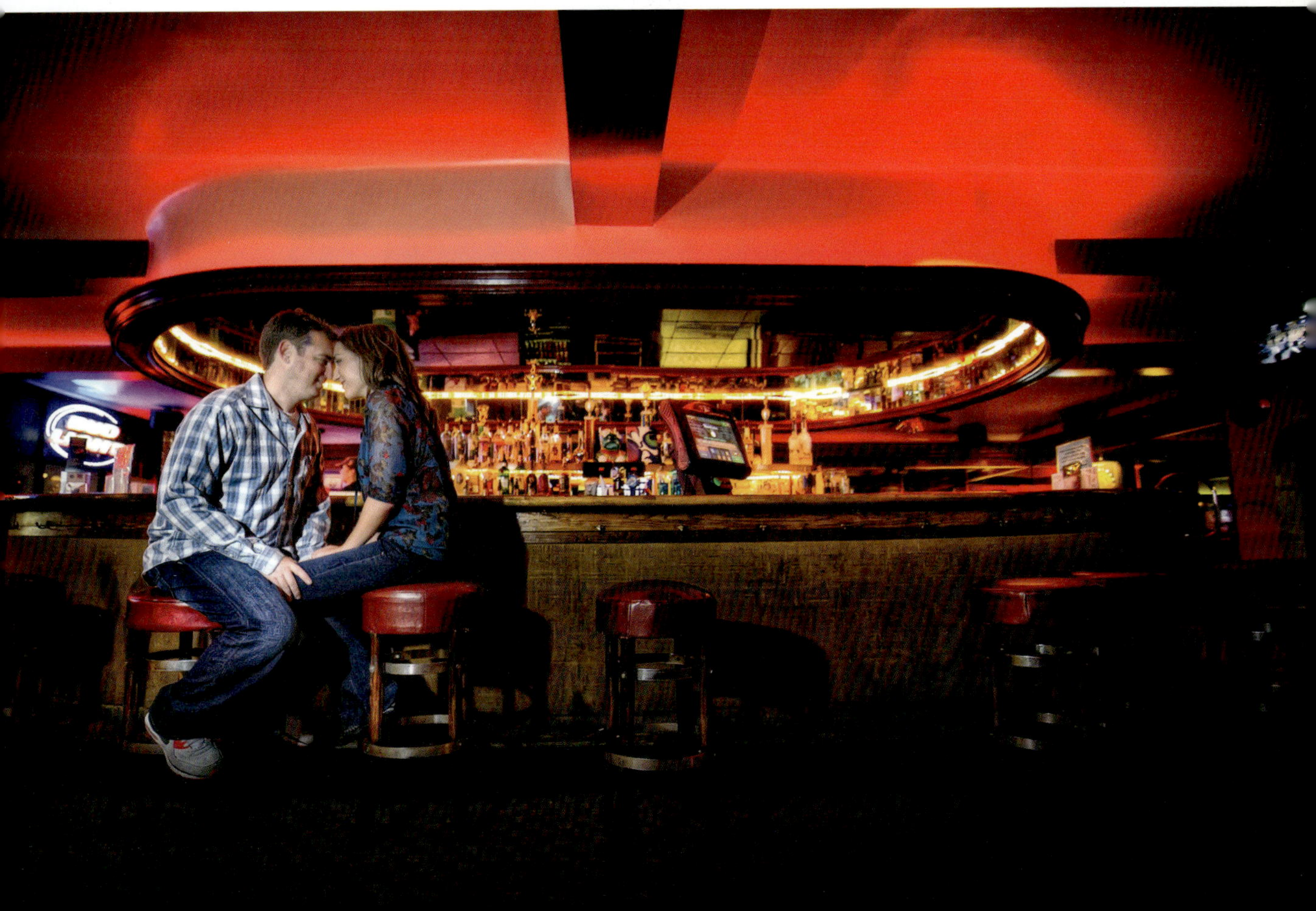

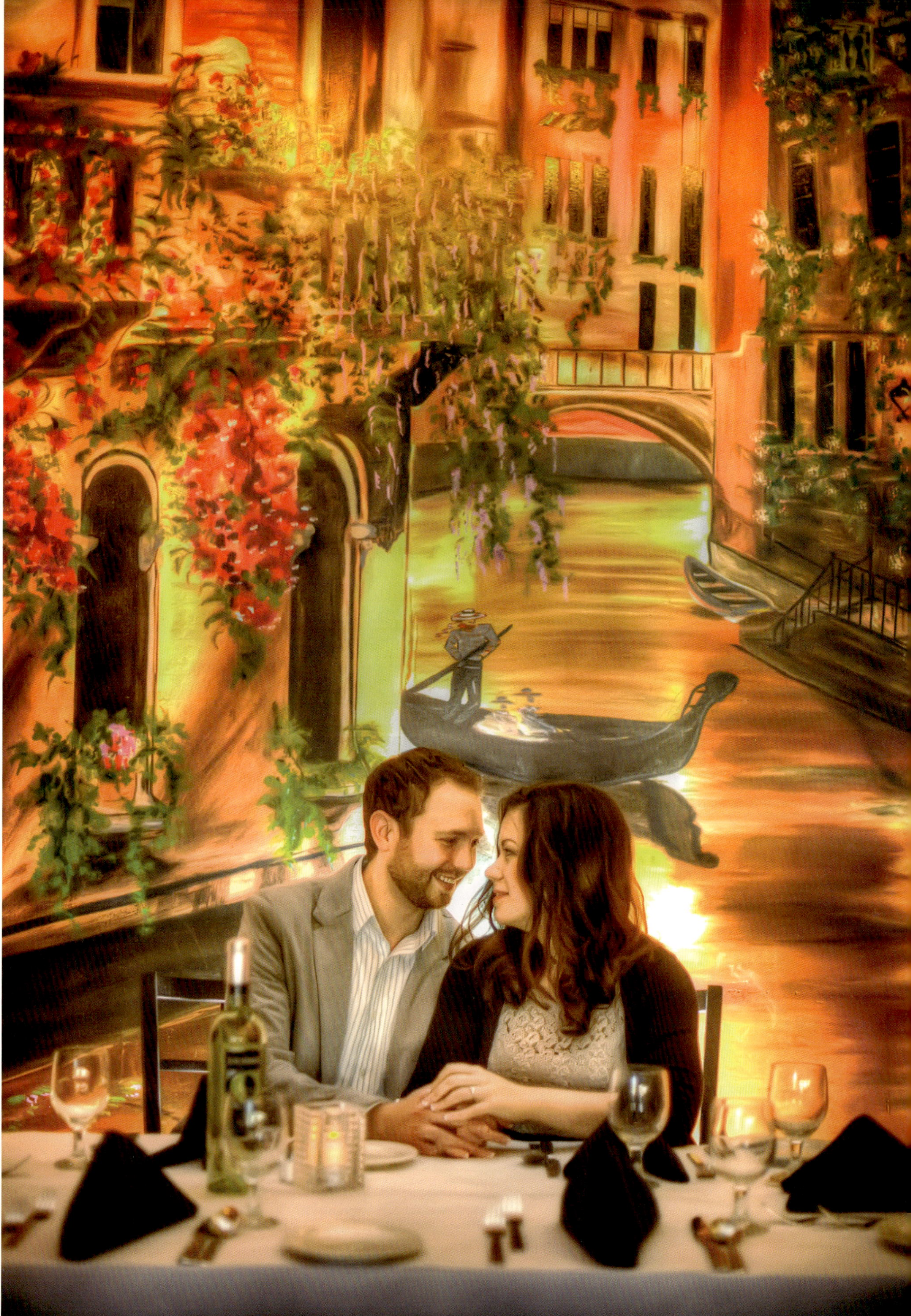

When we ask couples for special places that might be good for their engagement portraits, restaurants are commonly on the list. Special meals at a favorite eatery are highlights in many couples' romances.

A Relaxed Start

Here, we revisited the restaurant that was the site of this couple's first date—but they also go back there all the time, so it's a place they know and love. This was where we began our session to kick things off on a very personal note that also felt natural to them.

To get us started in an easy, relaxed way, I had them sit at a table (*facing page*). This is a good first pose to help people relax because it's something we do every day and there are plenty of things around them to interact with (tables, chairs, glasses, etc.).

To separate them from the detailed mural in the background, I added an SB900 behind them. In front of them and slightly to camera left, Danielle held an Ice Light in position.

A Private Moment

Next, we moved to the bar, where I asked them just to talk, touch, and enjoy the moment—whatever they would do if we were not there. The bride-to-be happens to be a photographer, and I knew it would be hard for her to avoid watching what we were doing, so Danielle went to another room and I ducked around the corner behind a plant to make them feel more alone. Using the available light, I sniped this shot (*below*) as they relaxed together. A little dodging and burning in postproduction completed the look and made them look like they were all alone in the world, lost in the moment.

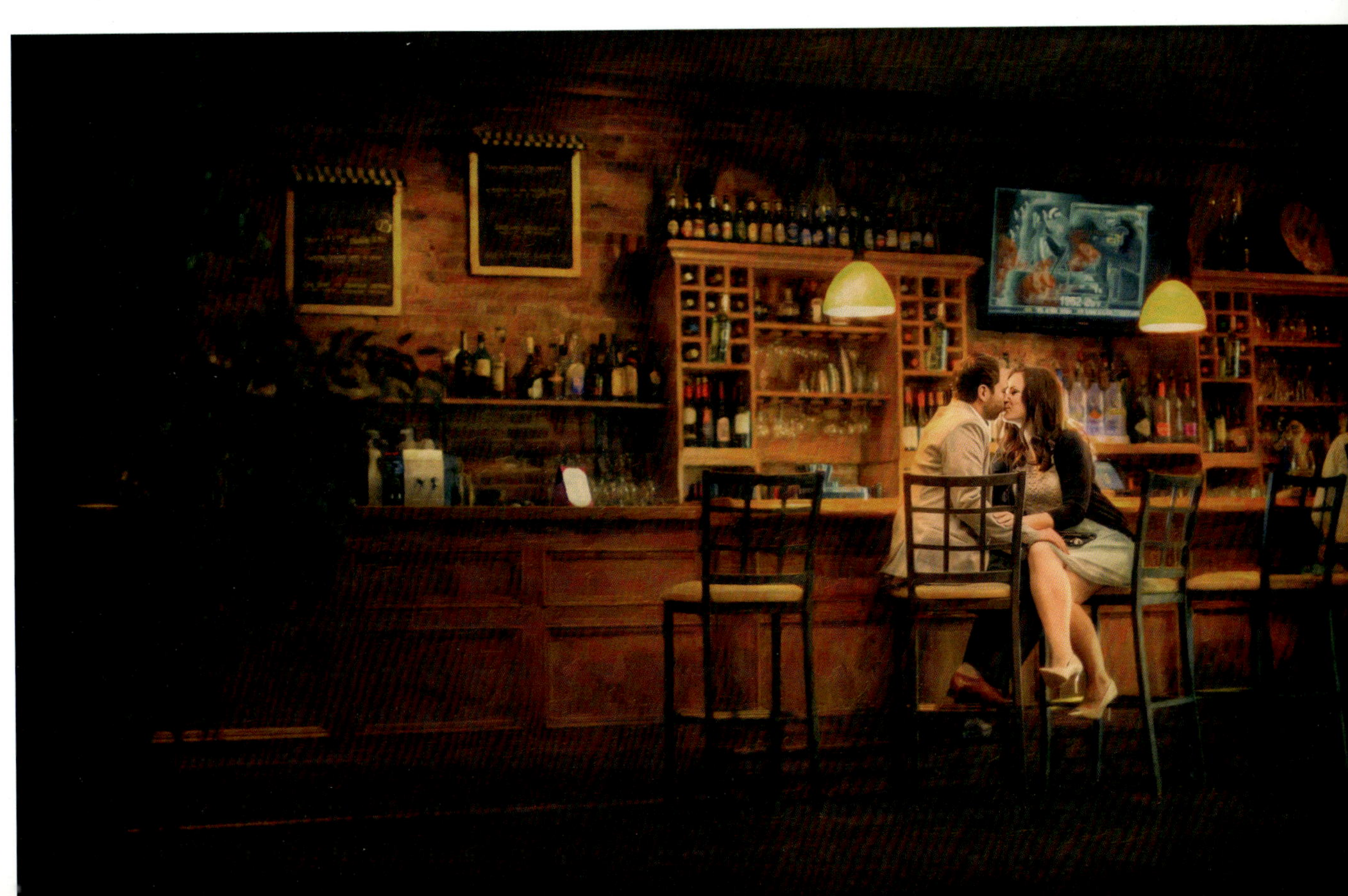

Special Places: Parks

A Real Proposal

The image below started out as a "couple shoot," but he warned me that he'd be bringing the ring. Our session was at a park where the couple enjoyed fishing and spending time together.

When I had them walk over toward this wall, he gave me the heads up that it was time. Just then, two kids appeared atop the wall. I was worried that the image was going to be ruined—but as he dropped to one knee, the kids sat down and watched quietly while he declared his love to the surprised bride-to-be! It ended up being a perfect moment. I simply captured it with natural light and a long lens.

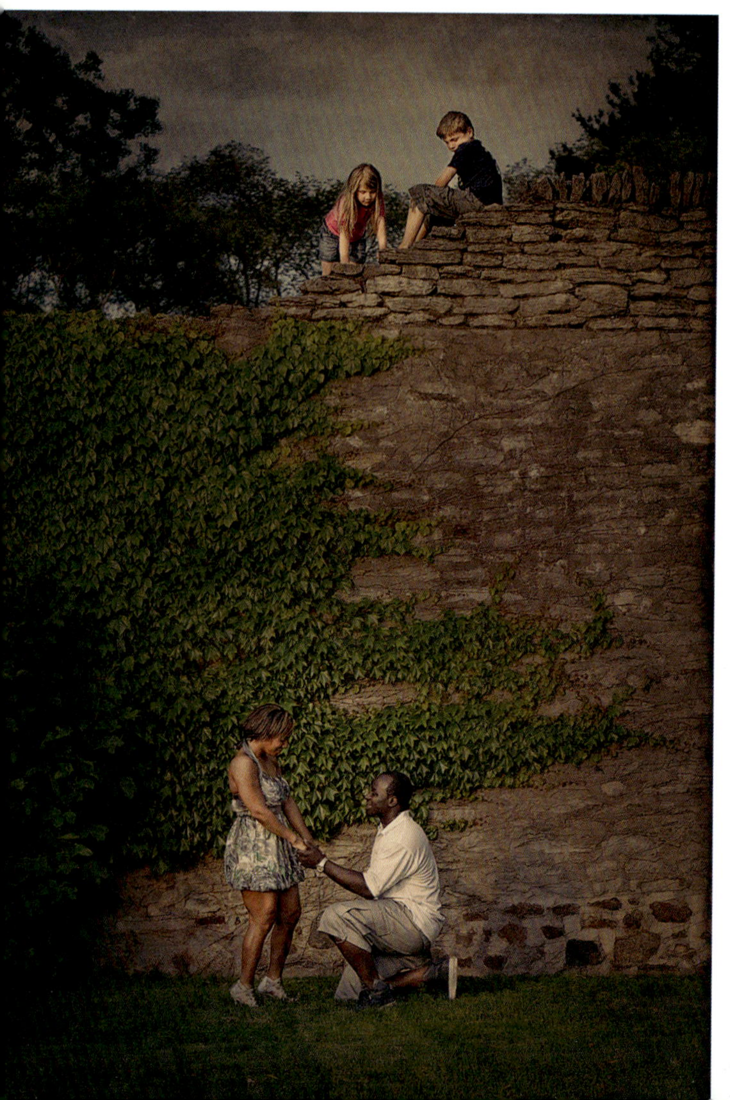

By the Water

The couple in the image below also felt a strong personal connection to the park where we decided to shoot some of their images. They had just moved to the city and were having a *Great Gatsby* theme at their wedding, so we wanted to do engagement shots that had a totally different feel. Shots with a village, rural, or natural themes provided a nice point of contrast.

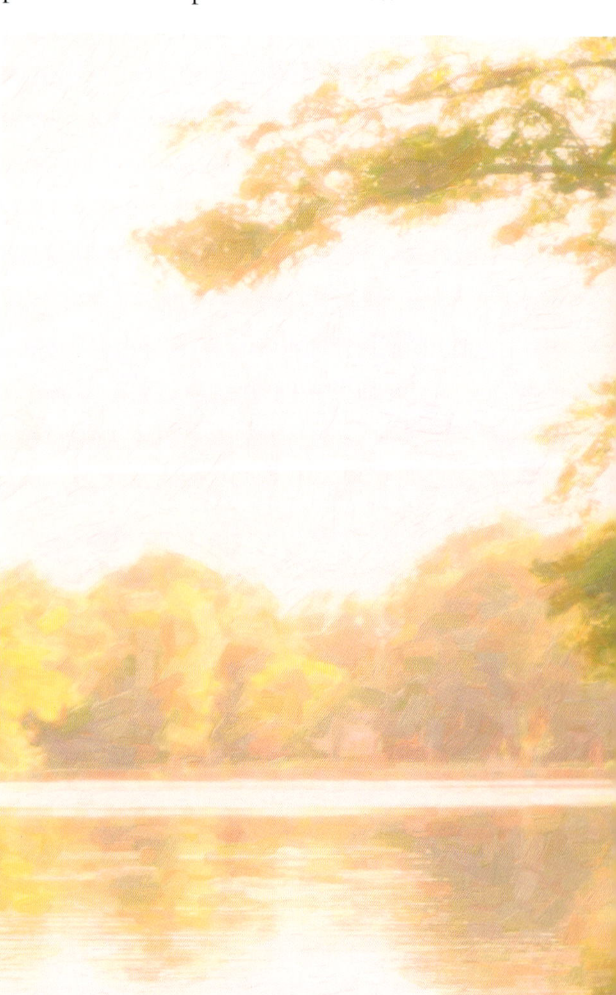

We created this image just before sunset while the sky was still bright. After testing its stability to ensure we wouldn't have a disaster, I posed the couple out on the rustic boat dock. Then, I followed along the shore to find a spot where I had a nice reflection of them showing in the water.

To add the sunburst effect in Photoshop, I duplicated the background layer and went to Image > Adjustments > Threshold. I moved the slider to the right until I saw the white poking through the tree and hit OK. After blacking out any other white objects, I set the layer blending mode to Screen and went to Filter > Blur > Radial Blur. I chose Zoom and 100 percent, then clicked and dragged the blur center over the sun.

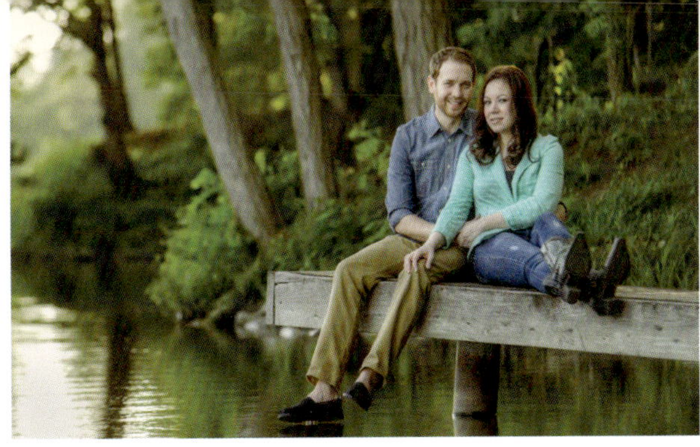

▲ I also shot a closer view. Couples usually purchase images like the one below—but moms love images like the one above.

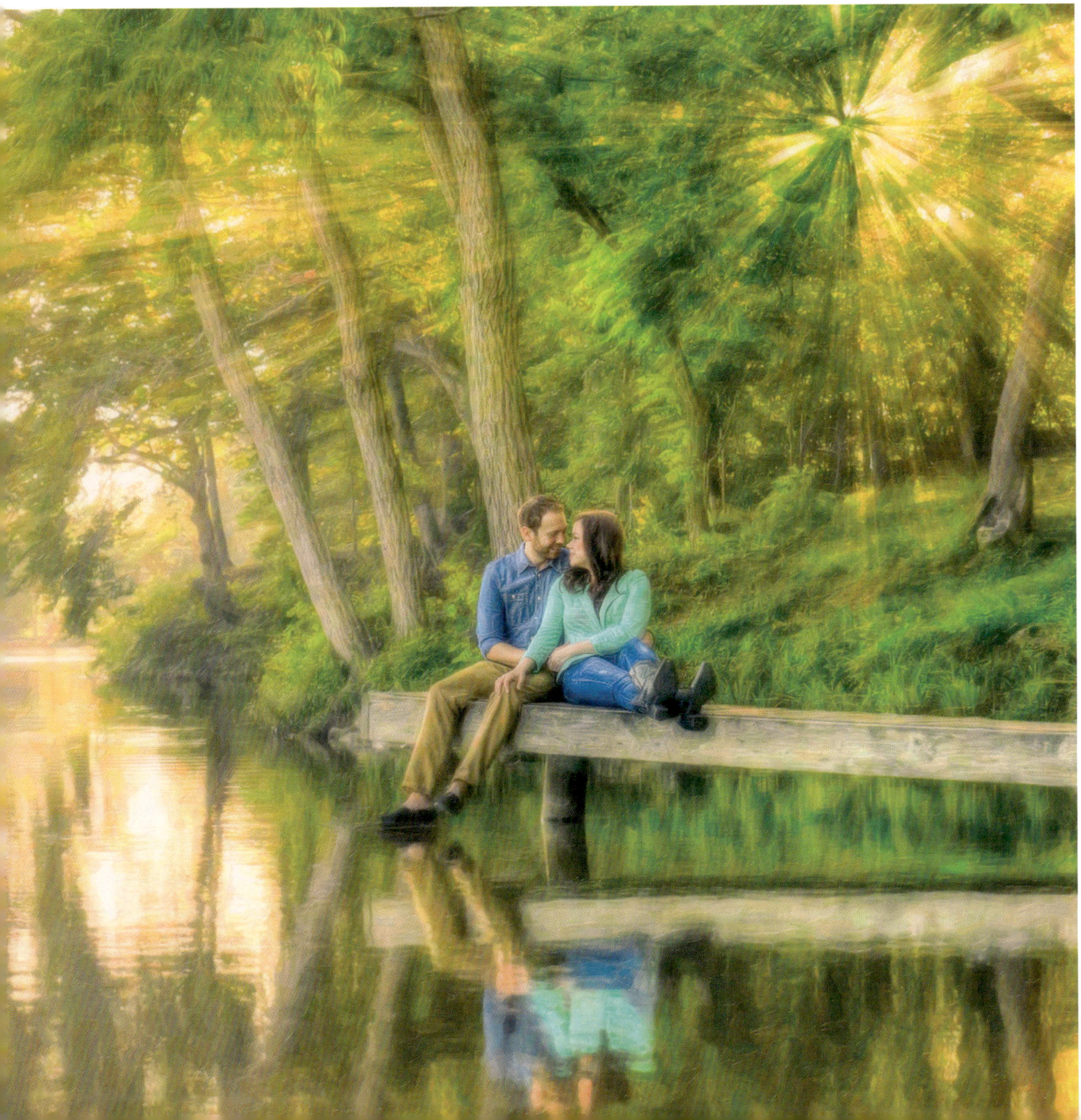

19 Two Looks in the Tall Grass

The sun was almost done and we'd completed our beach poses when I saw some tall grass and decided to hide the couple in it (*below*). I added an SB900 flash behind them and an Ice Light from camera left. For another look—the sunset colors were totally different—I flipped myself around and had them stand (*below*). He held the SB900 in his hand and we picked up the last of the light from the setting sun on their faces.

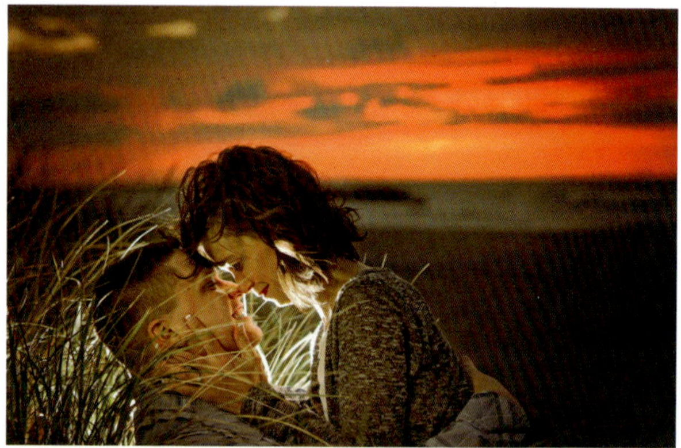

Amazing Location Not Required

Even if you don't have an amazing location, you can hide people in the tall grass. Here, we were next to a parking lot, but there was tall grass popping up from the landscaping. I photographed them through it to make it look like a field. There was a building just out of frame to the right.

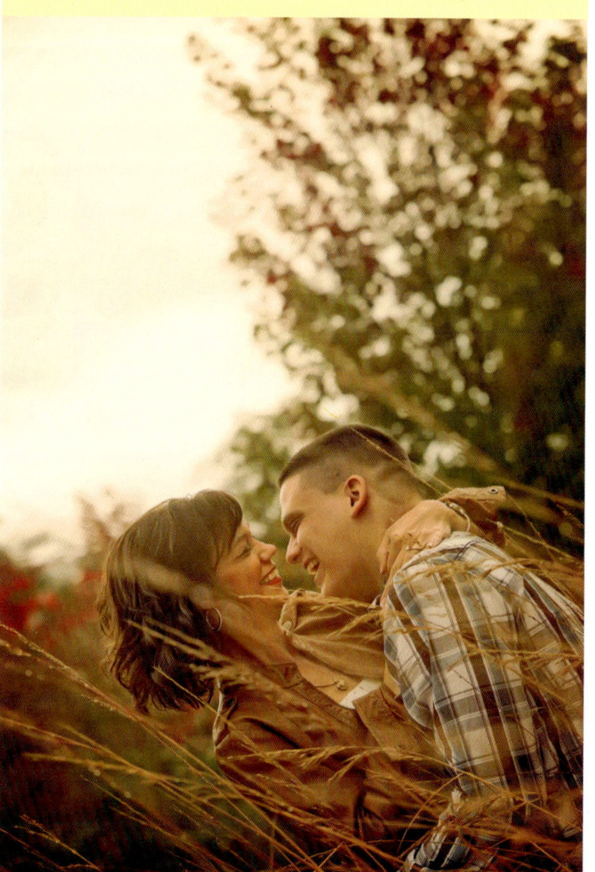

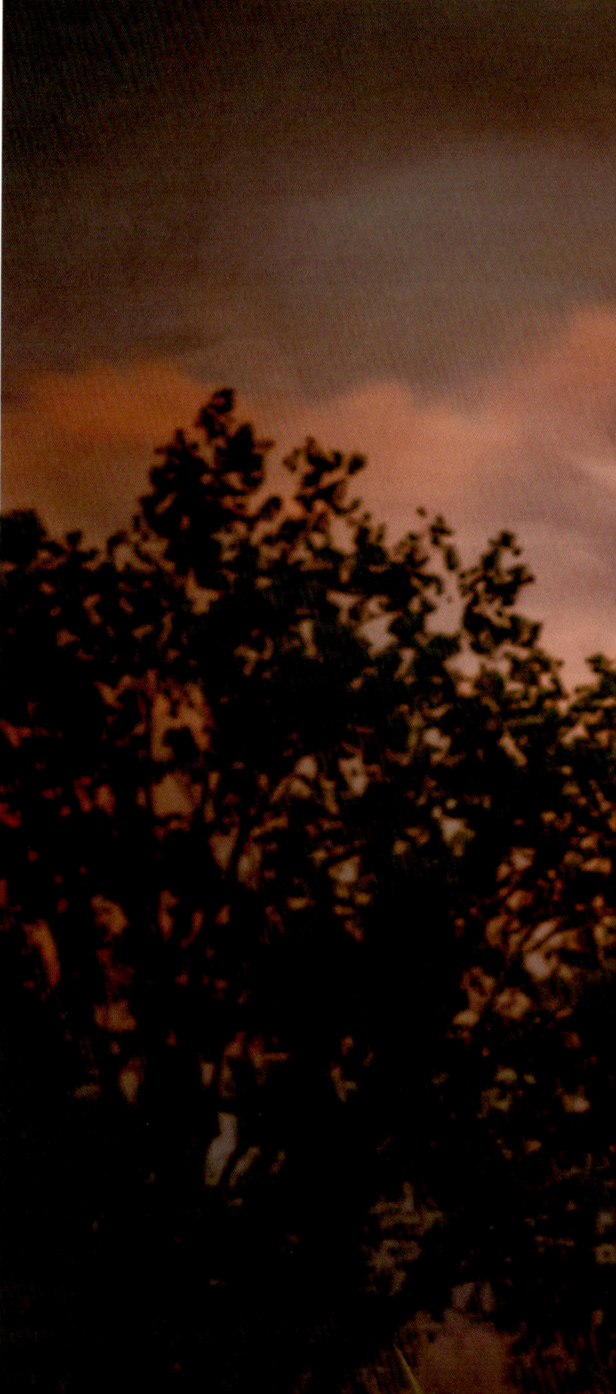

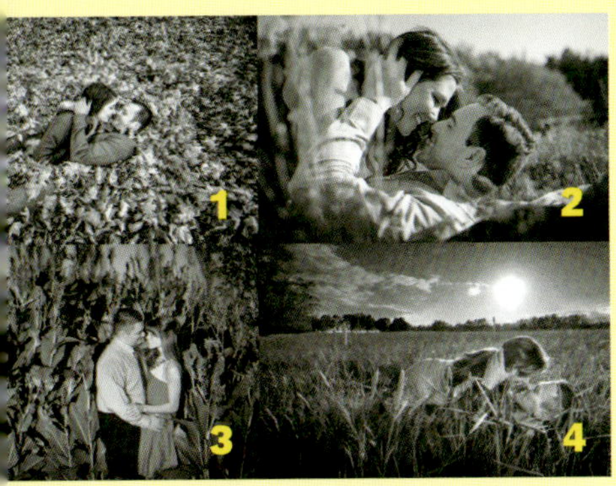

Use the Scene More Completely | *Next Two Pages* ➤

Immerse your subjects in whatever the scene has to offer—literally. Position them in the tall grass, amidst the flowers, or atop a pile of leaves. The images on the next two pages show what I mean. **Image 1:** Playing in the leaves helped the couple connect and showed the autumn scene. **Image 2:** Lying down in the grass, with foliage and flowers in the foreground, made this simple location look great. **Image 3:** Backed up to a wall of flowers and foliage, the couple faced the sunset for that nice orange glow. **Image 4:** The terrain was quite flat. Getting the couple down into the grass let me fill the background. I added an SB900 at full power slightly to camera right to overpower the backlighting from the sun.

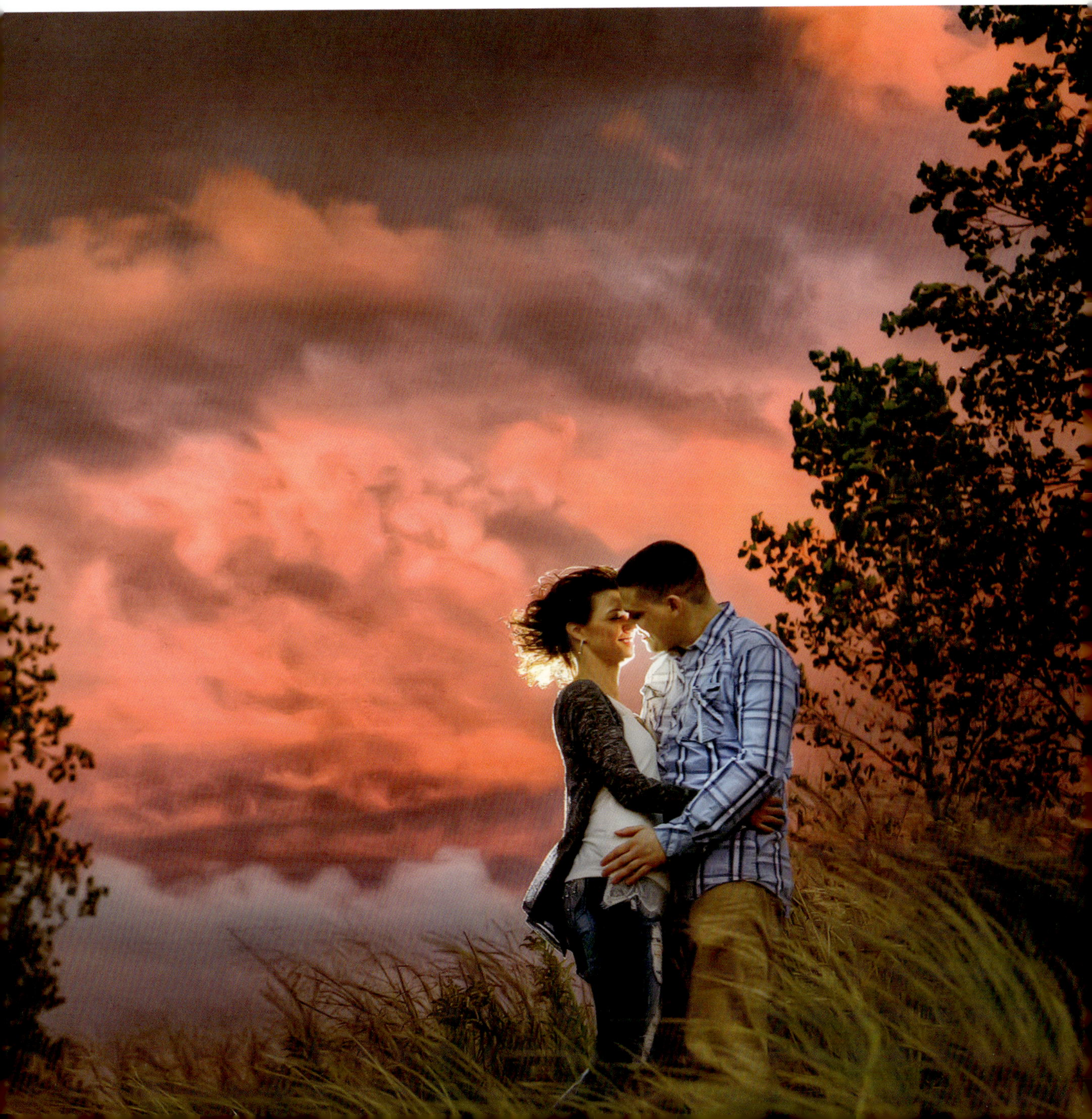

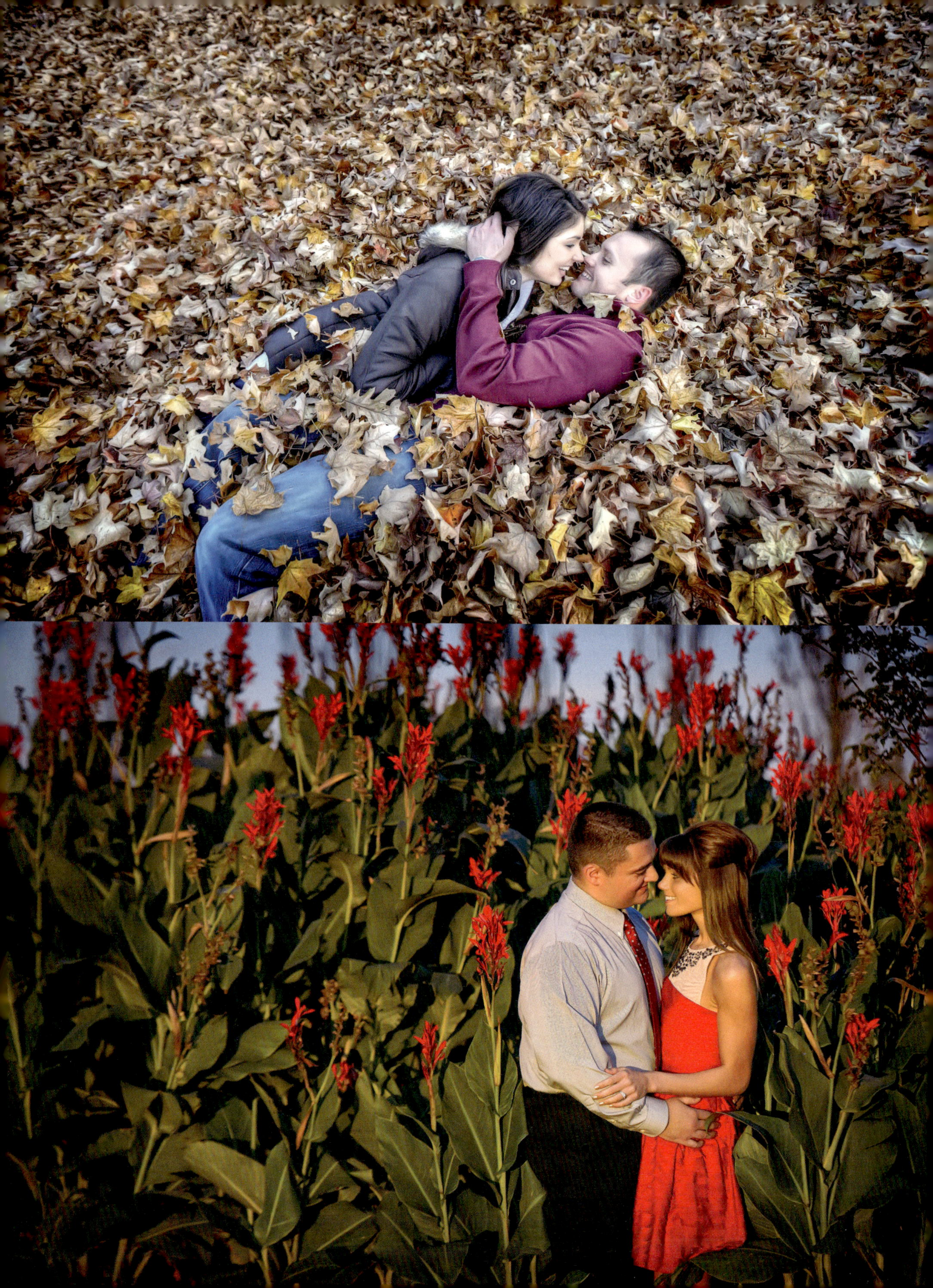

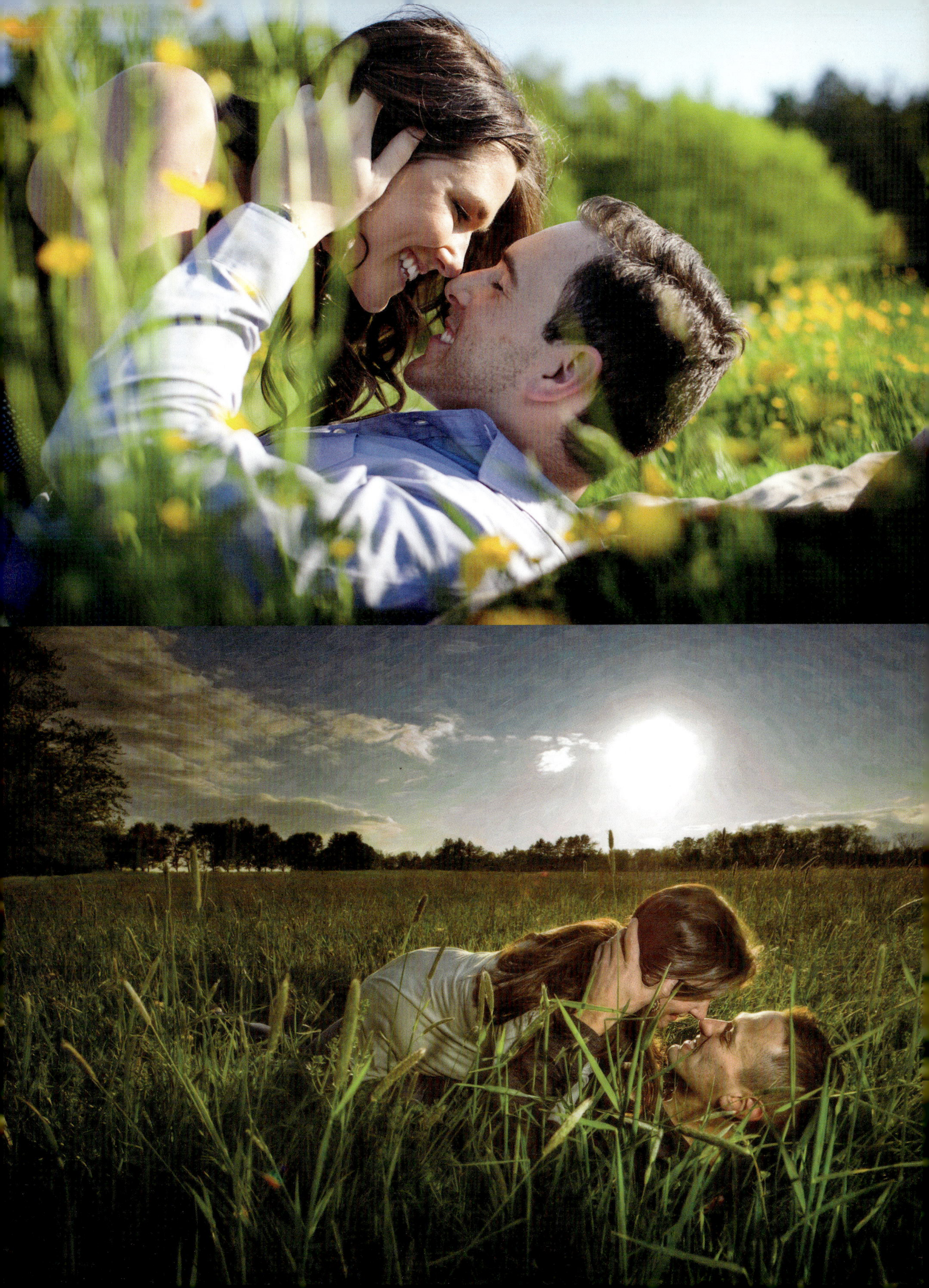

20 Amidst the Trees

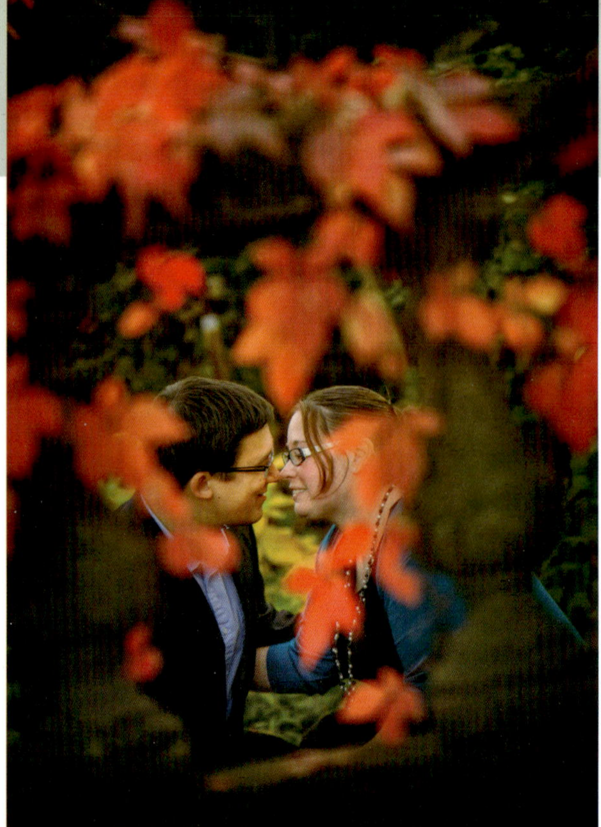

Get Things Started

A shot like this is a good way to get things clicking at the session. Because you're shooting from a distance and giving them some privacy, the shot is easy and unintimidating for them. It also gives you something interesting to show them on the camera right off the bat. Most people are not used to seeing this kind of foreground blur—so even though the shot is actually easy to execute, it looks pretty impressive.

Make the Most of the Scene

Just as we used tall grasses in section 19, this is another way to make something artistic—even if all you have to work with is a tree.

Lighting

With one exception, these images were created with available light only. For the photo below, I added a Lowel light (zoomed in to work as a spotlight) just to punch through the opening in the leaves and illuminate the couple.

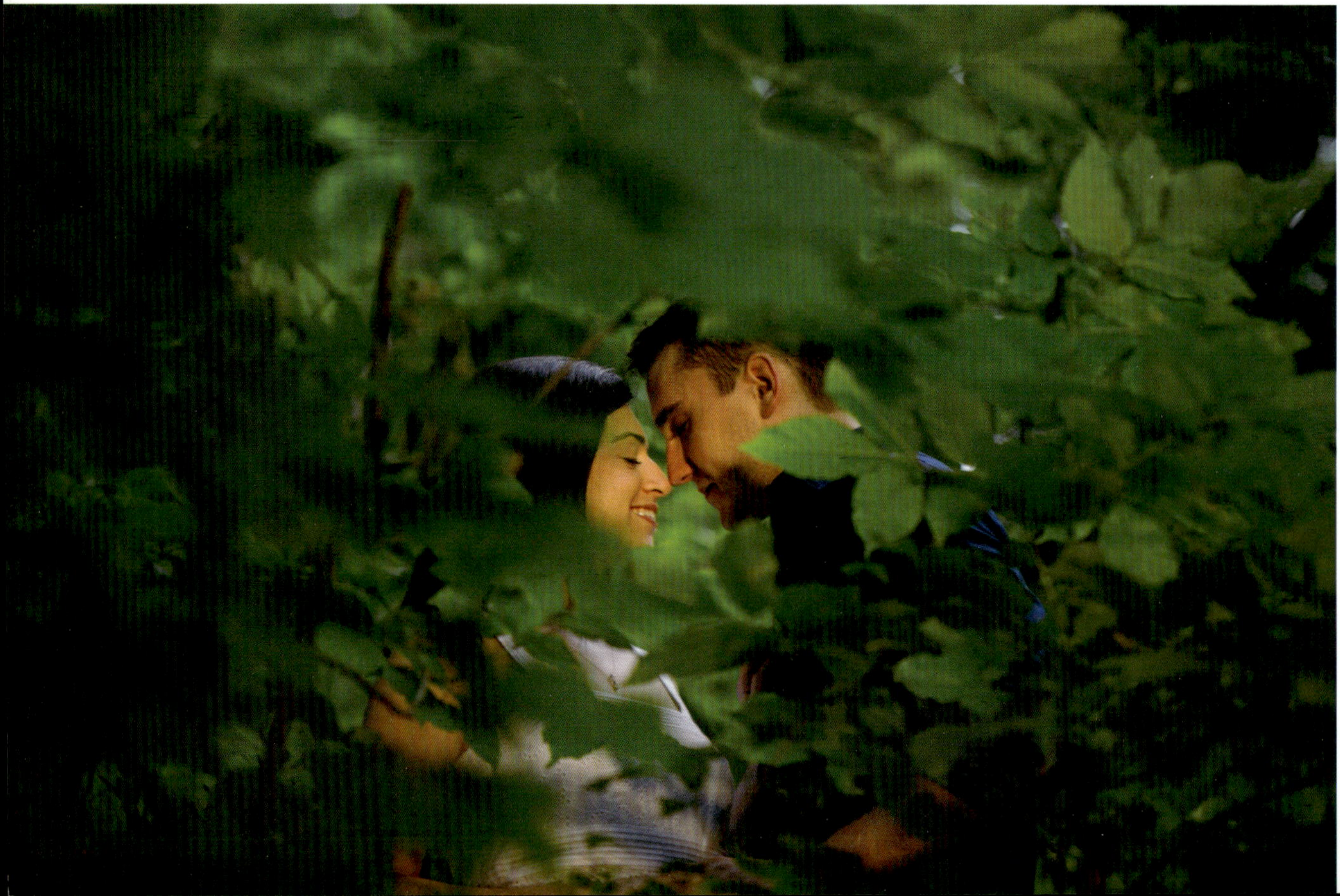

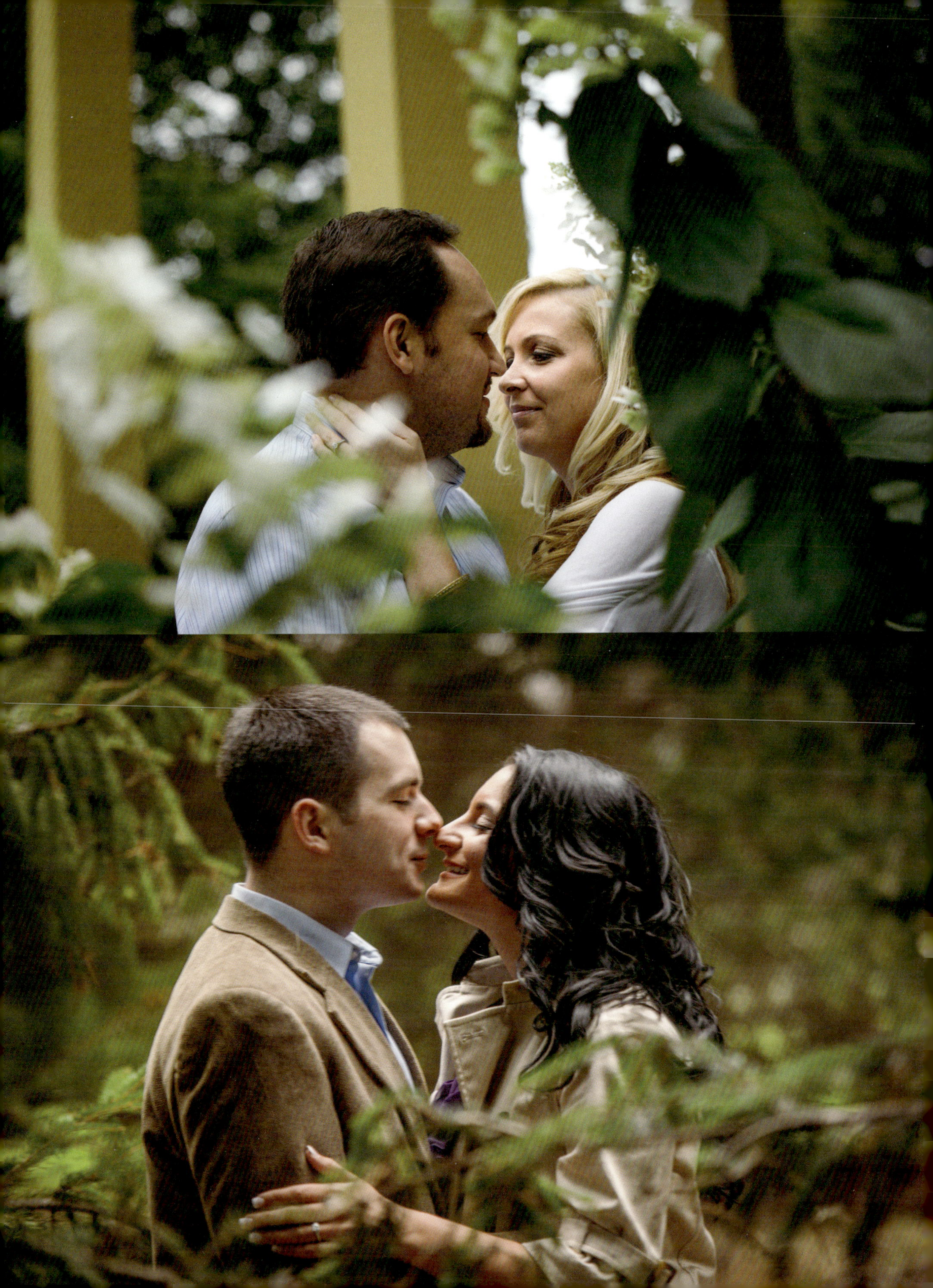

21 Many Looks, One Location

Creating a nice variety of looks for your couple doesn't mean you have to spend a lot of time traveling from location to location. Learning to identify and use of all the potential backgrounds in a given area will expedite your sessions and avoid breaking up the rhythm of the shoot with too many travel breaks.

The Family Ranch

These images were all created on the bride's family ranch—and with natural light only. She had described the property to me over the phone, but I really had no idea what I was going into. In the end, what we created was a series of images that tells a story of the whole property.

In the Woods and Field

We began the session in the woods. In fact, the image directly below *(1)* is the very first frame I shot. Deep in the woods, I looked for nice lighting opportunities—like a shaft of light on some trees *(2)*. Here, I exposed for the highlights and let the rest of the frame go dark as a natural vignette around them.

As we walked out of the forest, I photographed the couple backlit on the path and framed by the foliage *(3)*. In the distance, you can see a field beyond the couple on the path. That's where I had them lie down amidst the yellow flowers to create our next look *(4)*. Late afternoon sun made the image glow.

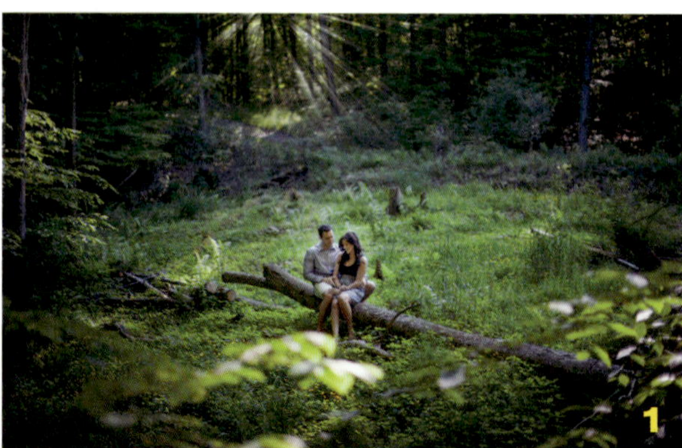
1

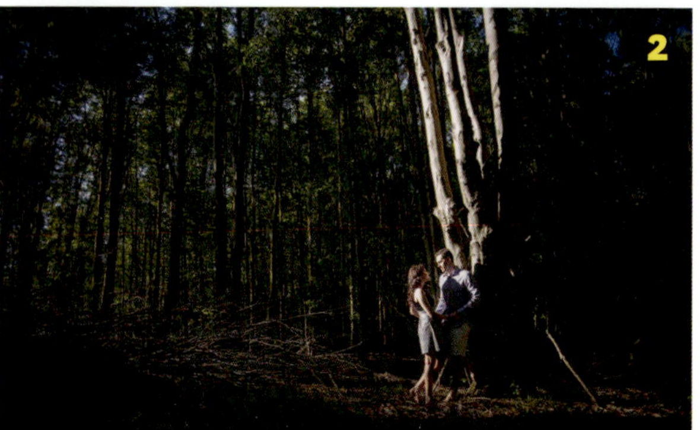
2

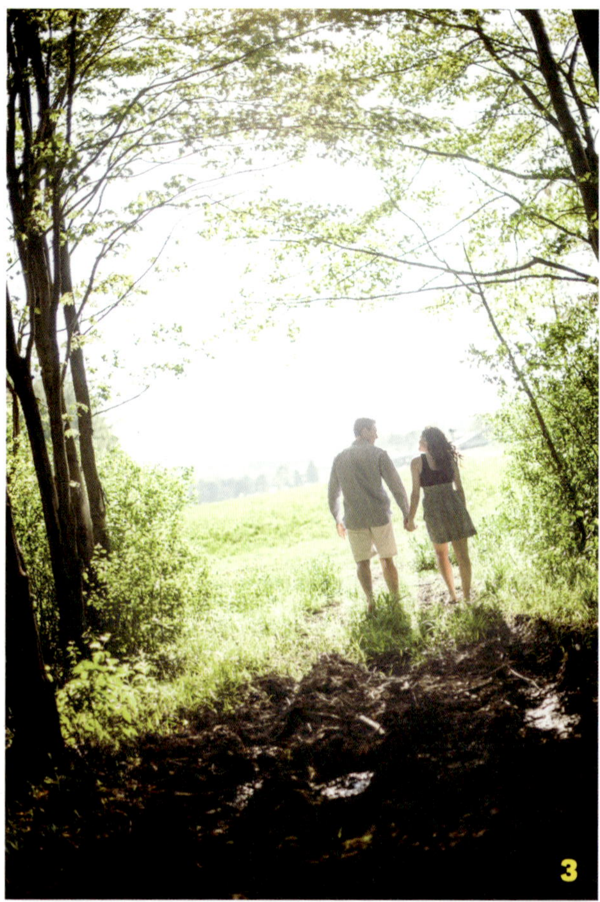
3

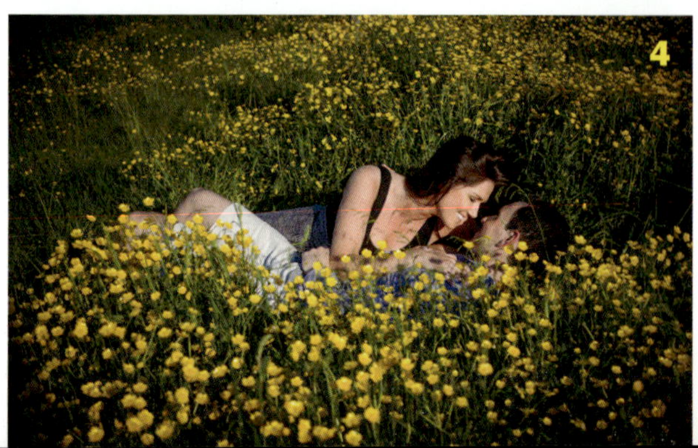
4

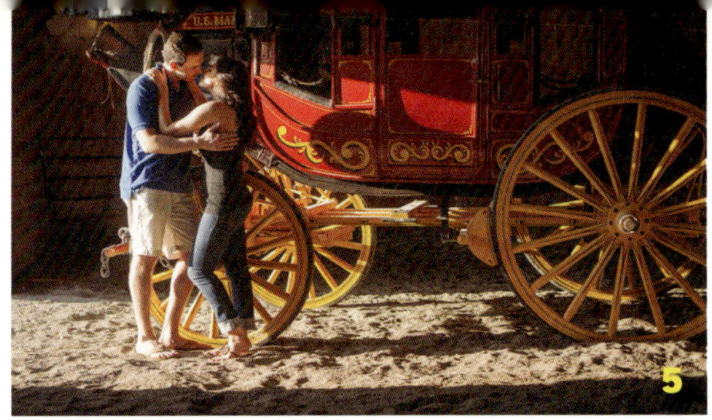
5

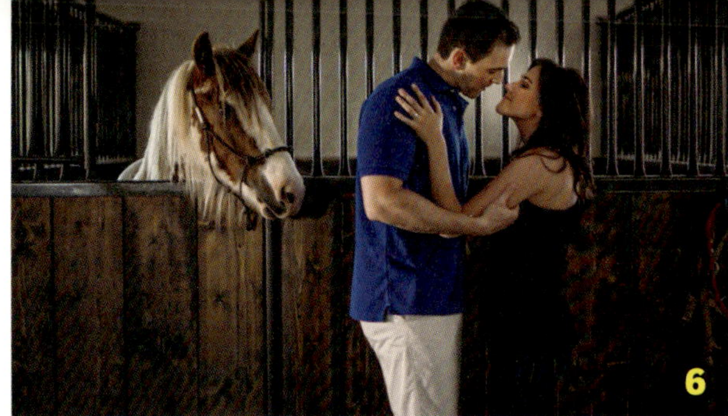
6

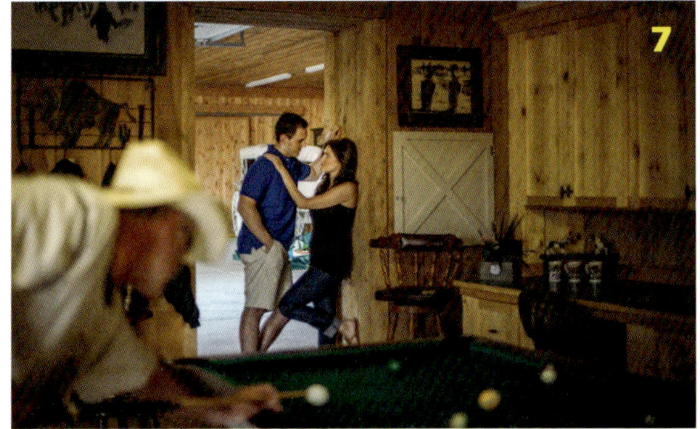
7

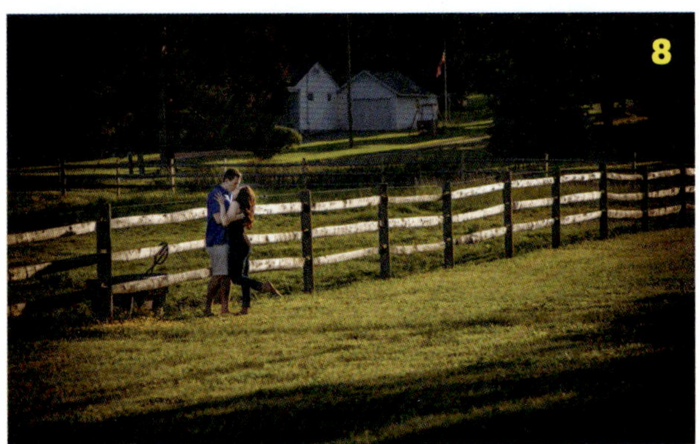
8

The Barn and Tavern

We moved into the barn for our next images *(5, 6)*, using window and door light to capture images of the couple with a carriage and one of the resident Clydesdale horses. Moving into the tavern area, I asked her dad to shoot some pool while I photographed them in the background *(7)*. He'd been very involved with the shoot, helping us get around the property on four-wheelers, so I wanted to include him in some way.

A Final Look

For one last look, with rim light from the setting sun, we moved back outside for a wide view of the property with the couple in the foreground *(8)*, then a closer view of the two embracing *(9)*.

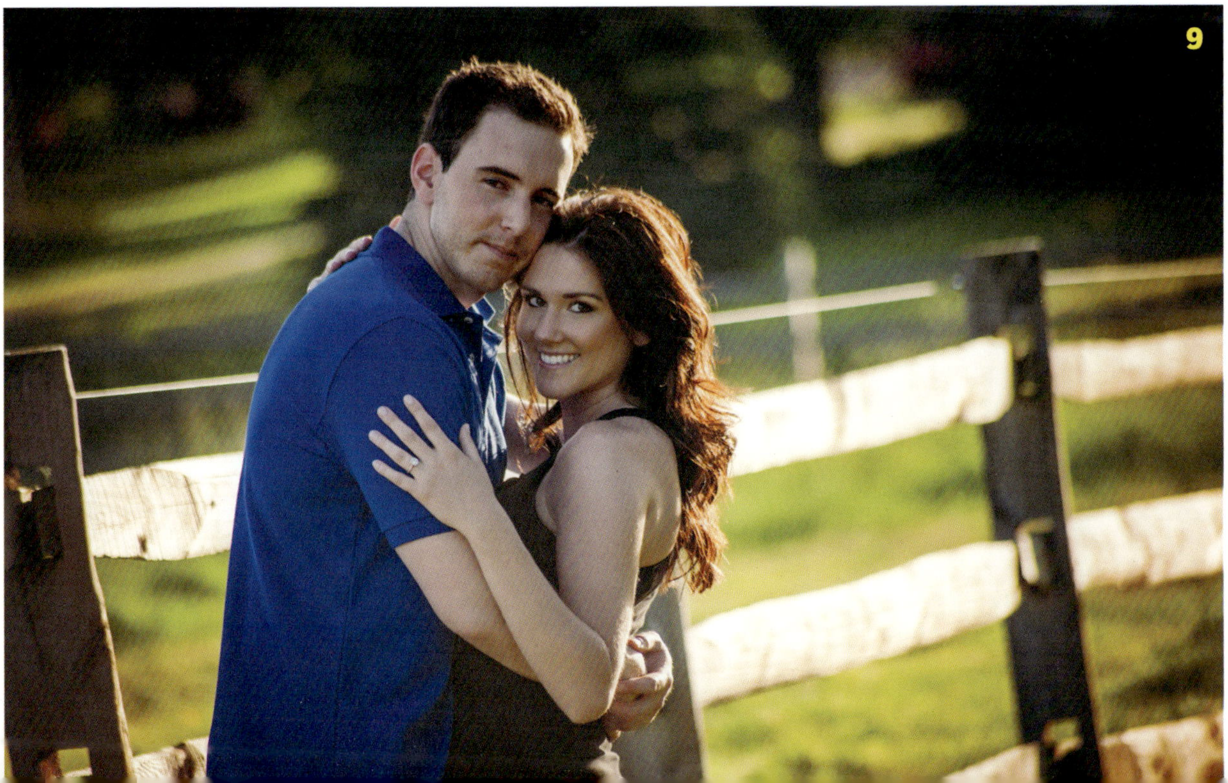

9

22 Beyond the Expected

I like to have everybody's images look different from their friends' images—and part of how I do that is by choosing different locations for their sessions. However, in every city or region, there are places that couples *want* to go for their photography. In our area, the back steps of the Albright Knox Art Gallery is one of those places.

Make the Familiar Look Special

In section 41, you can see a broader view of this same location—and a pose that would be typical for daytime wedding portraits in this spot. To make it look different, I take couples there in the evening. This changes the whole look of the space—and all the wedding parties that typically crowd the steps in the afternoon are off at their receptions by this hour, so we have the spot to ourselves.

To further change the look of the images, I add light, use different poses, and work in different parts of the general location. Simply shooting from different camera angles and heights lets me make use of less commonly seen parts of the background and design more artistic compositions.

In this way, the couple can shoot at an "expected" location but have images that are wholly their own.

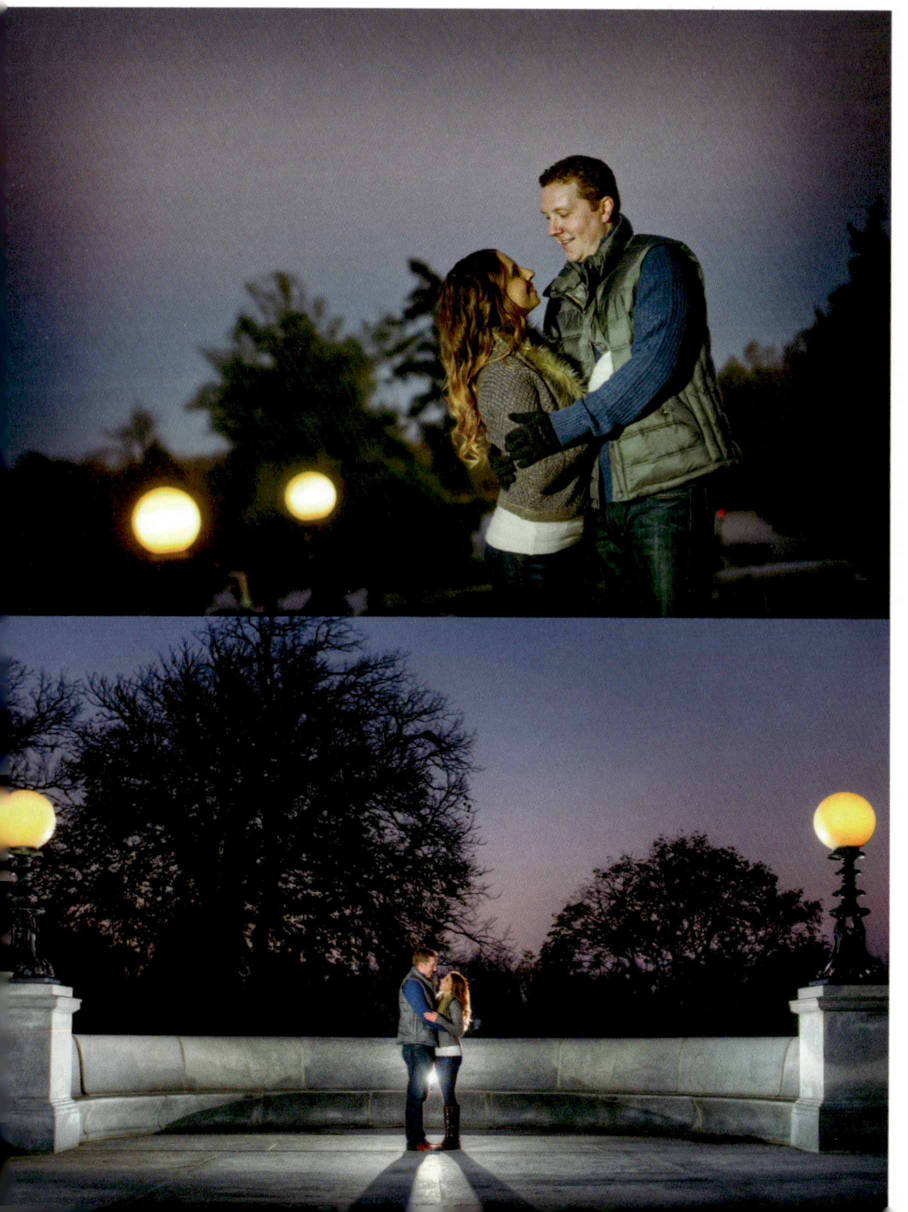

Lighting

For most of these images, I used the Ice Light as the main light on the couple. The exception is for the bottom image on this page, where the main light was an SB900 (because the needed working distance required more power).

For the bottom image on this page and the shots on the facing page, an SB900 behind the couple added backlighting and illuminated the otherwise very dark scene.

◀ ▶ Adding light on the scene and subjects transformed the expected scene into something more special.

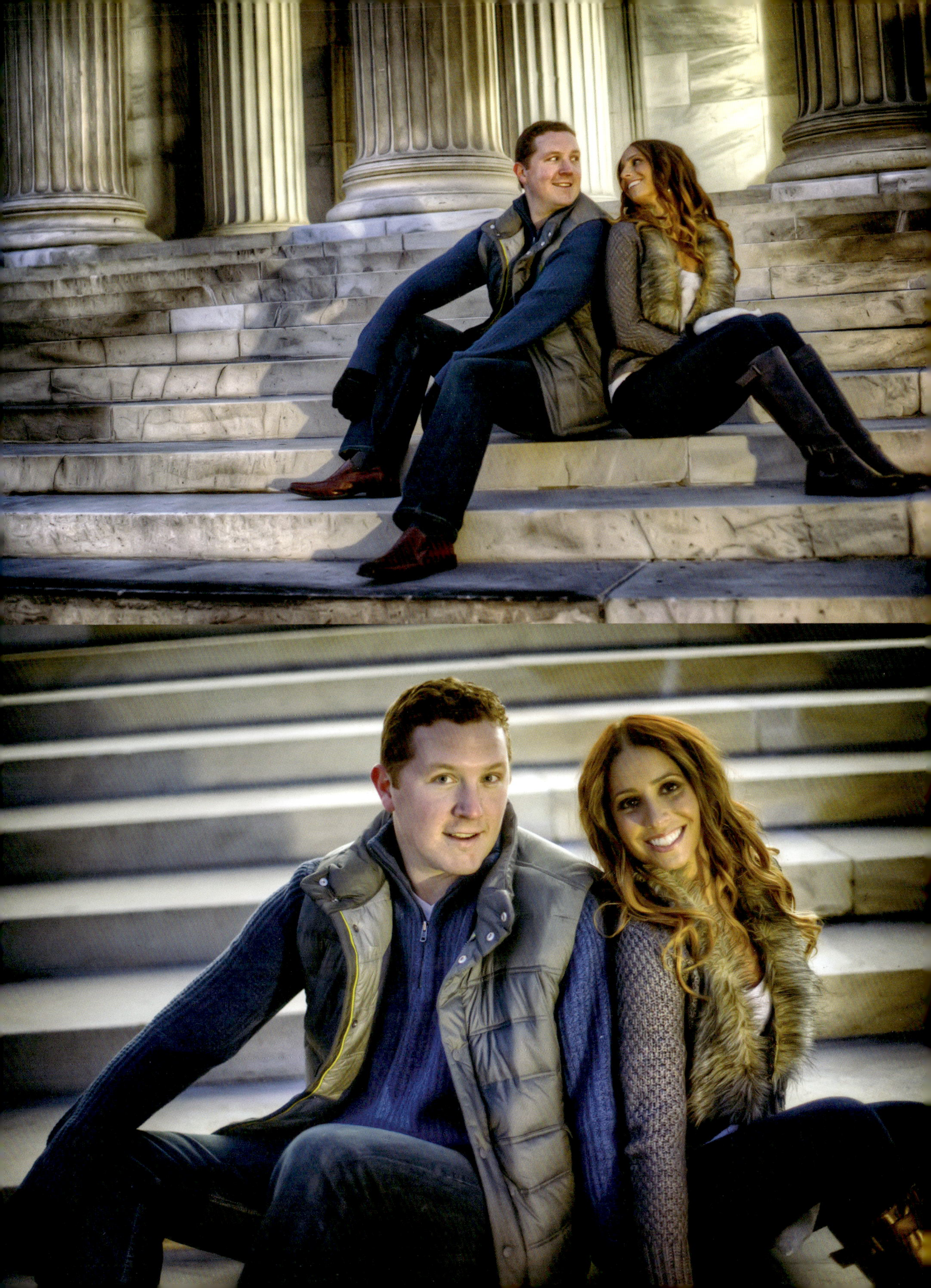

Make It Your Own

When couples come to us with a specific theme in mind for their engagement session, we're happy to go with their concept. However, we always want to do it in an original way. As a professional photographer, you don't want simply to be duplicating images your clients have pulled off Pinterest. Make something that is *your* own—and give your clients images that are uniquely *their* own.

Flipping the Camera Position

After posing the couple for the image below, I rotated around them. With the setting sun now at their backs, I was able to capture a nice range of silhouettes, adding another look to the collection.

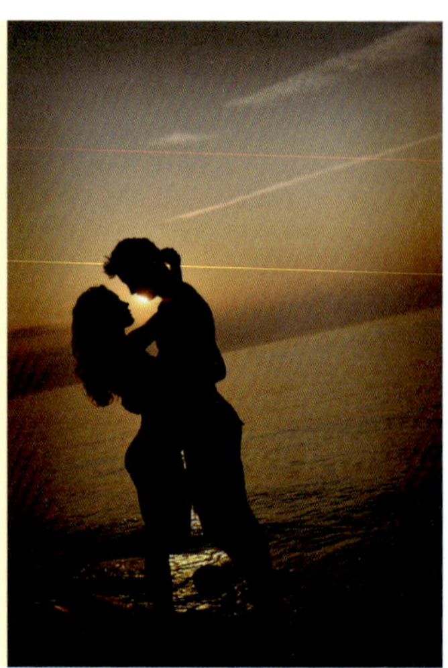

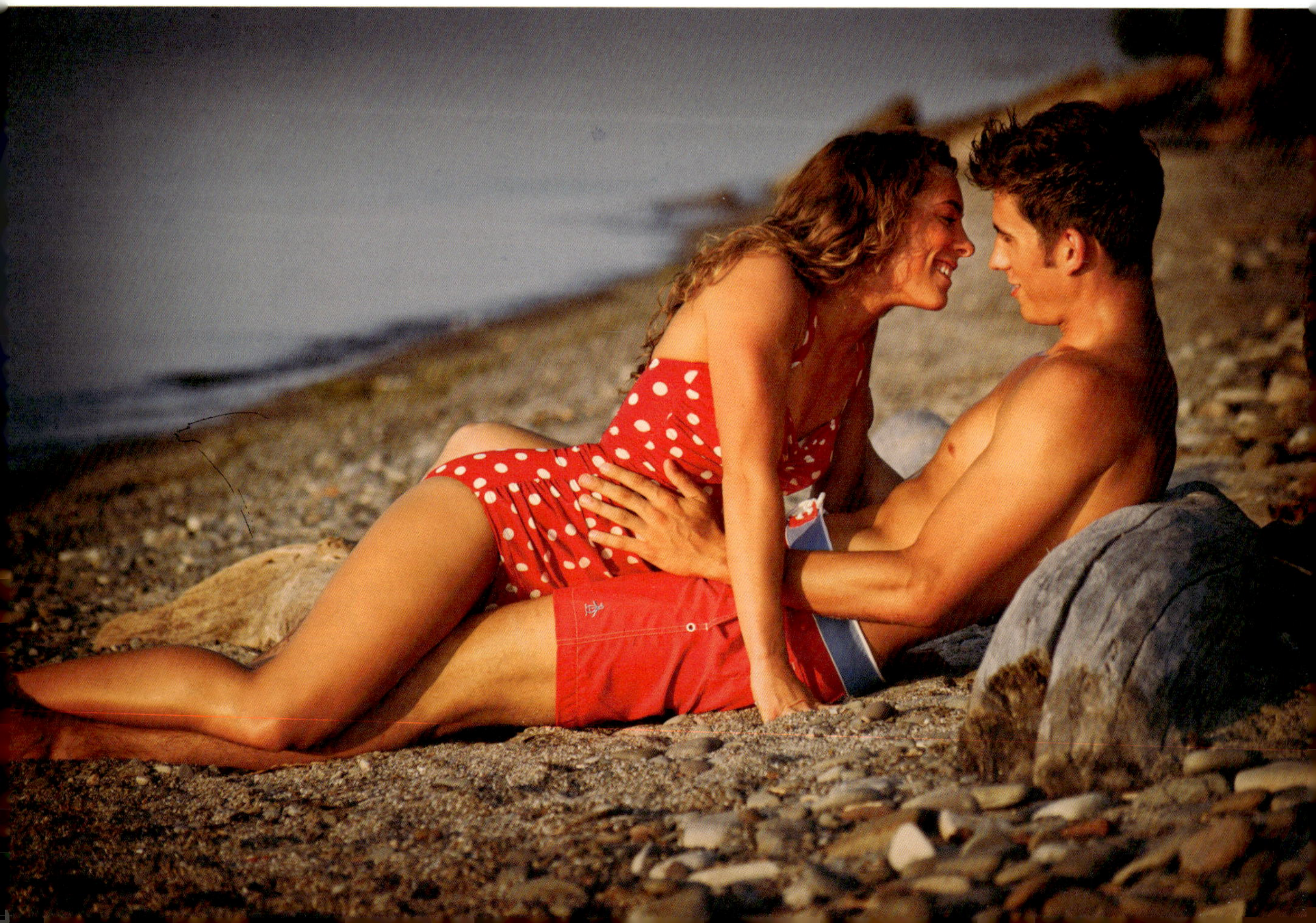

The Notebook

This couple suggested using the epic romantic movie *The Notebook* as the theme for their engagement session. I knew there were key scenes in the film that took place at a beach, so that's where we decided to begin our session. We went to the south shore of Lake Ontario. The couple brought along vintage-style swimwear to help set the mood. The image below was shot at sunset. Once we found the right location, I positioned them relative to the light for a flattering look.

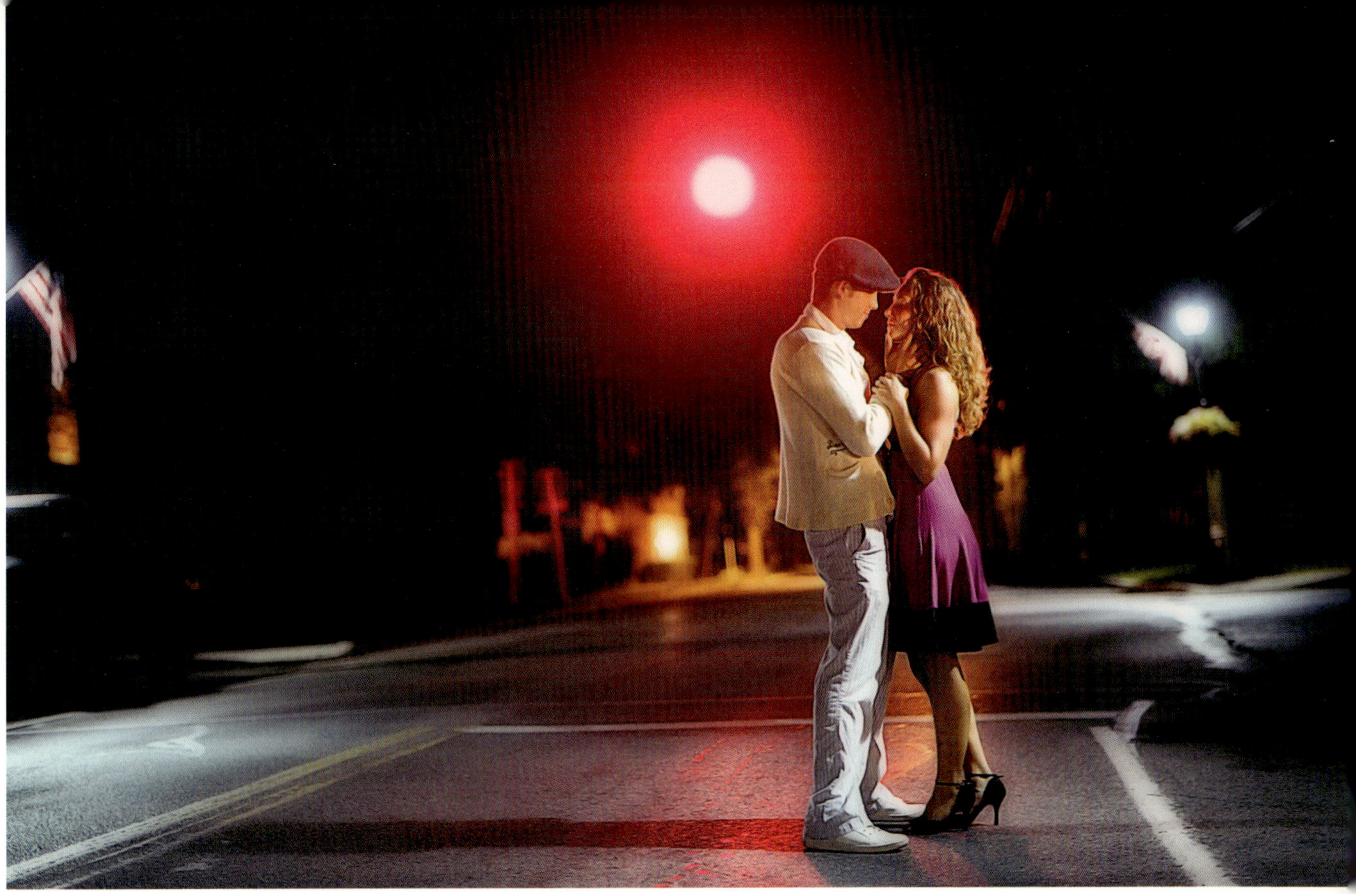

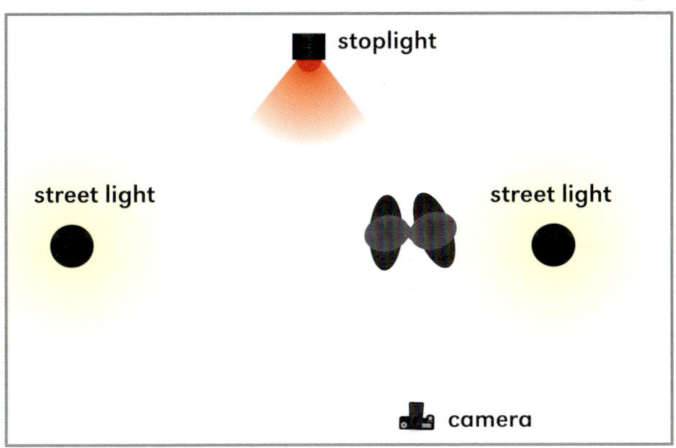

Street Scene

After the sun had set and we concluded our shooting at the beach, we decided to check out a nearby village. There's another key scene in *The Notebook* that takes place on an empty street at night, so this seemed like a logical choice. Not anticipating this second scene, however, I hadn't packed a lot of lighting gear. Happily, the village lights were ample for the scene I envisioned. I positioned the couple under a street light to camera right, which served as the main light. The town's one blinking red light in the background added rim light on both subjects. A more distant streetlight at camera left added a little kick of light on the groom's back. Aside from a bit of sharpening, no postproduction was needed.

One Light, Two Looks

In the background of the image above, you can see a lamp post with a flag. That's the same light I used here. The couple was just moved closer to a building for an entirely different look.

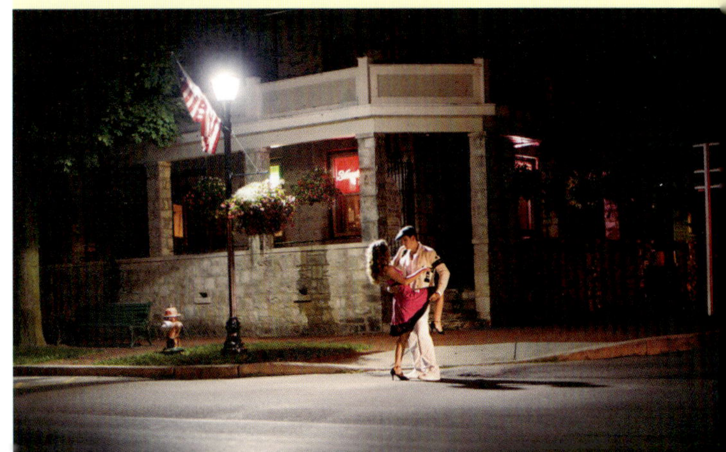

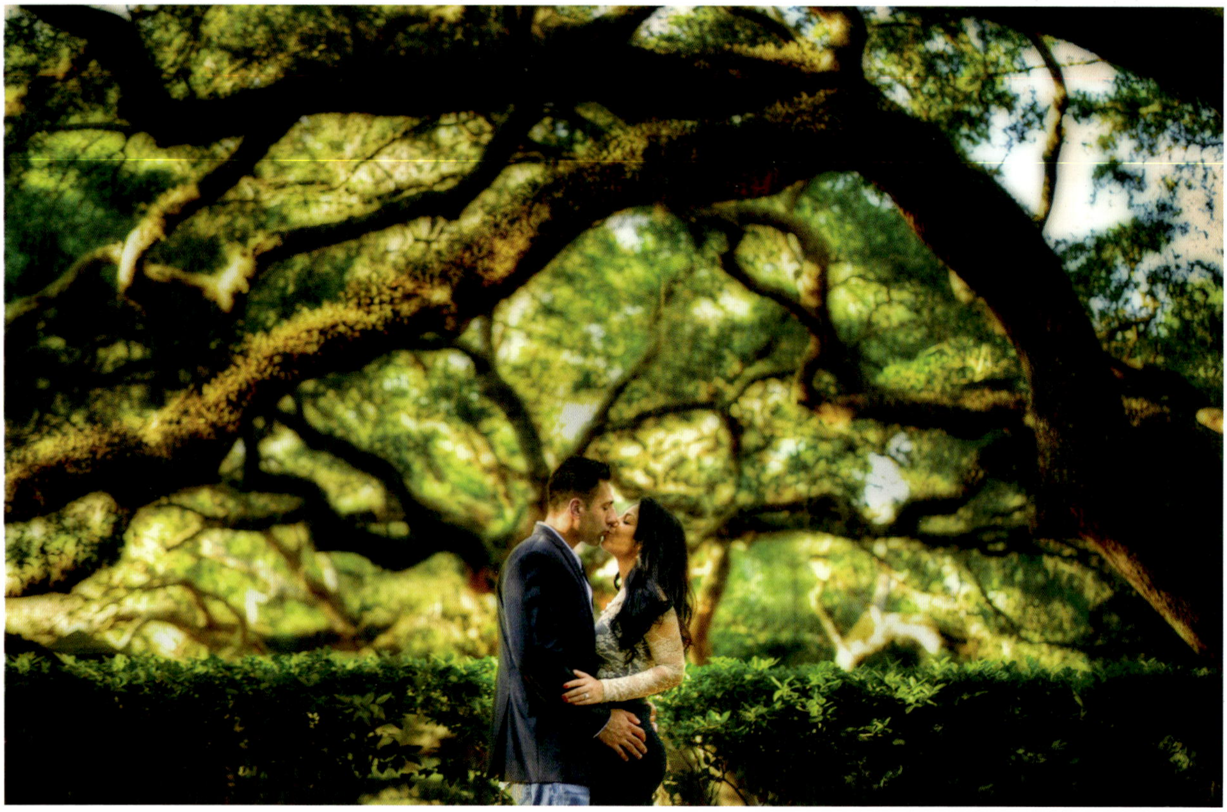

Unexpected Backgrounds

This couple decided to hold their wedding in their hometown of Buffalo, NY. But since they now live in Florida, I suggested doing their engagement session there to give the images a totally different look. We settled on a shoot at the historic St. Augustine lighthouse—but when I saw the beautifully arched oak trees (*above*), I knew that we had a perfect background. With the sun dropping to camera left, I positioned them under the arch of a branch for beautiful framing.

In Photomatix, I dodged the background a bit so the couple didn't get lost in all the texture. I also burned down the bark areas to reduce the detail. Finally, adjusting the vibrance brought up the greens and yellows without impacting the couple's skin tones.

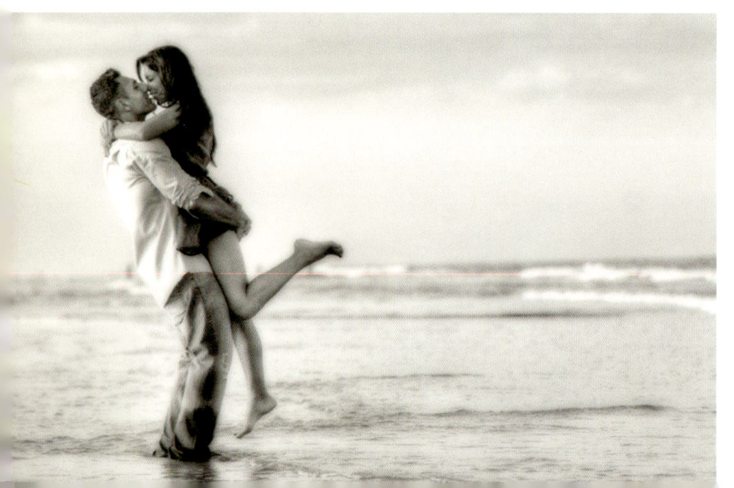

Black & White at the Beach

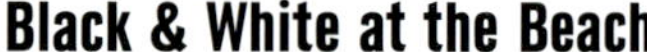

After shooting around the lighthouse, we headed to the beach for portraits with a more romantic feel (*left*). With the sun low to camera left, the couple played in the surf. To get them to interact

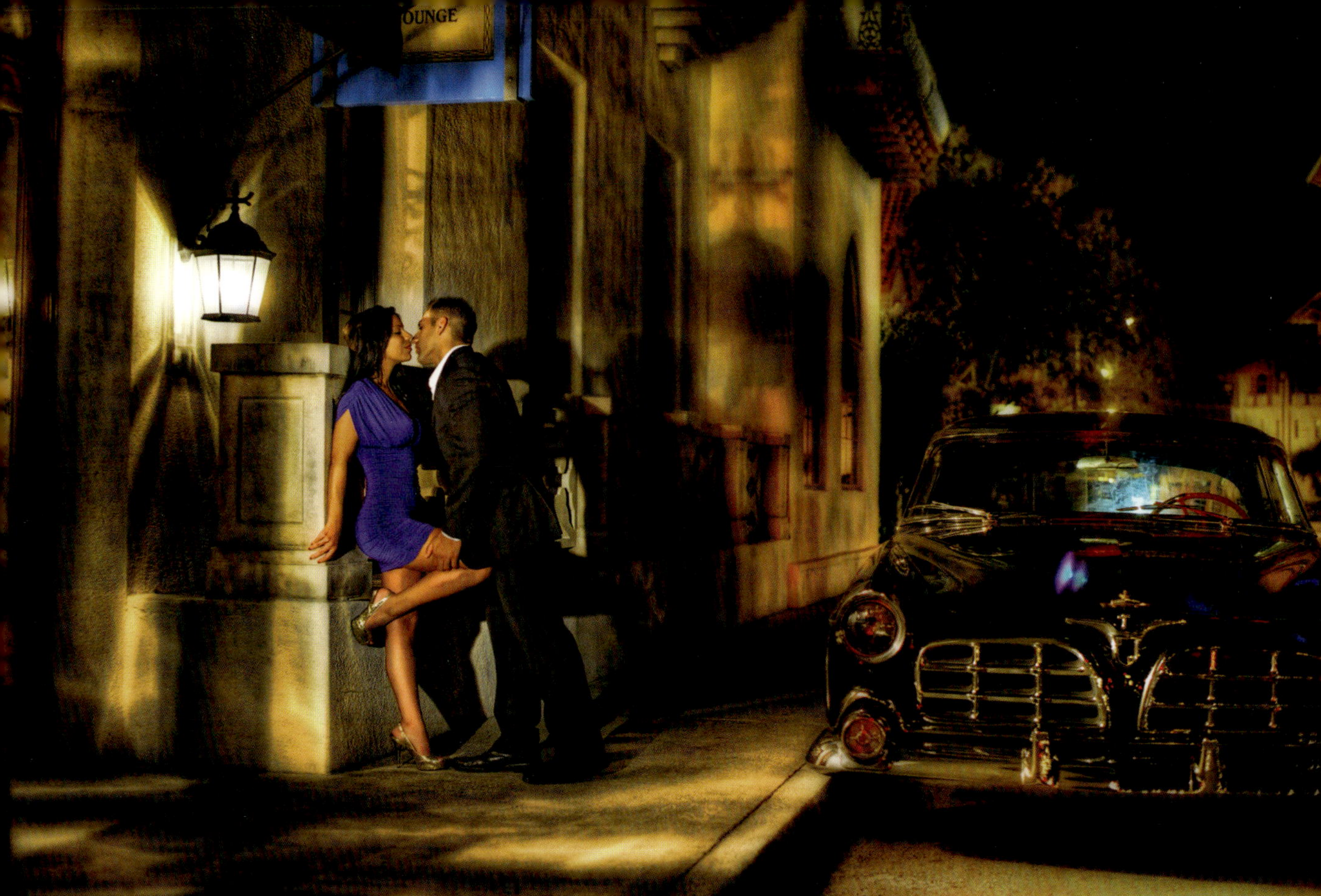

naturally, I asked her to jump into his arms and kick her feet. They were having fun with it, so we did this a few times until I had just the look I wanted.

Since most of the other images from this tropical session featured very vibrant colors, I decided to present the beach images in black & white, adding some variety to the overall package.

City Style

After our sunset images at the beach, we traveled into town to take advantage of the Spanish-style architecture. As we walked along the streets, we happened upon a classic car parked in front of a restaurant (*above*). It was too good to pass up!

I envisioned the pose I wanted to use, then quickly demonstrated it to them. Giving the couple a brief, funny demonstration is the simplest way to handle the posing—and it definitely helps to loosen them up. Once she was in position against the wall, I had him put his arm around her waist and draw her closer.

The light on the scene came from the wall lamp and the streetlights in the area, plus a Lowel tungsten light held to camera left.

I used Photomatix to bring down the wall lamp as well as to enhance the street detail and the reflections on the car. I masked out the skin tones to keep them natural.

Lightroom or Photomatix?

Lightroom has come a long way, and today I use Photomatix much less often than I did when this image was shot. However, for a scene that needs the kind of tonal enhancements this one did, I would still probably opt for Photomatix.

25 Opposite Seasons

To give the couple the most diversity in their images, we like to shoot the engagement session during a different season than their wedding. This couple was planning a December 7 wedding, so we wanted to shoot them in the heart of summer when everything was really green. This let us ensure that the engagement session scenes would contrast with the early winter wedding scenes (when there could be snow, or there could still be late-autumn leaves on the trees). I wanted nothing but *green* in these images.

We shot at historic Knox Farm State Park in East Aurora, NY. I chose to work with the couple close to sunset (about thirty minutes before) so that the low sun would provide some nice directional light on the bride- and groom-to-be. Trees blocked the overhead light on this bright but overcast day. The result was a nice tunnel effect, especially in the shot below.

All that was needed was a little dodging and burning in postproduction to complete the look.

A Winter Wedding

Images from the couple's winter wedding (*below*) contrast beautifully with the images from their engagement session (*right and facing page*).

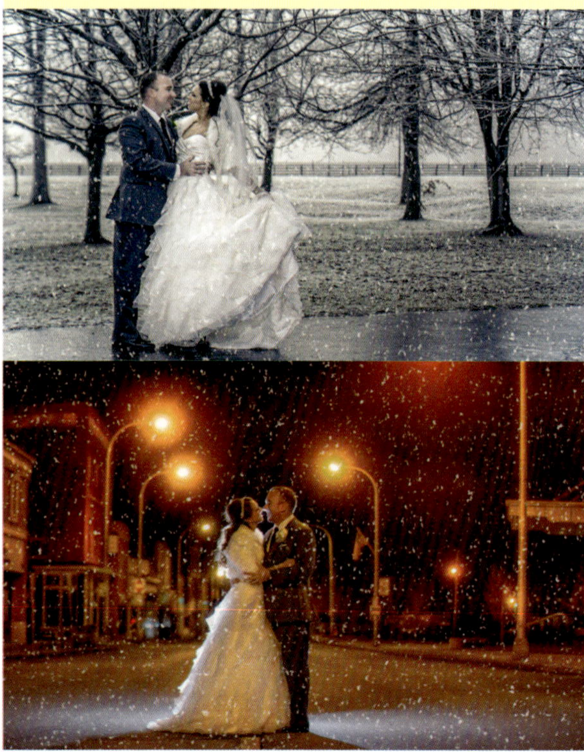

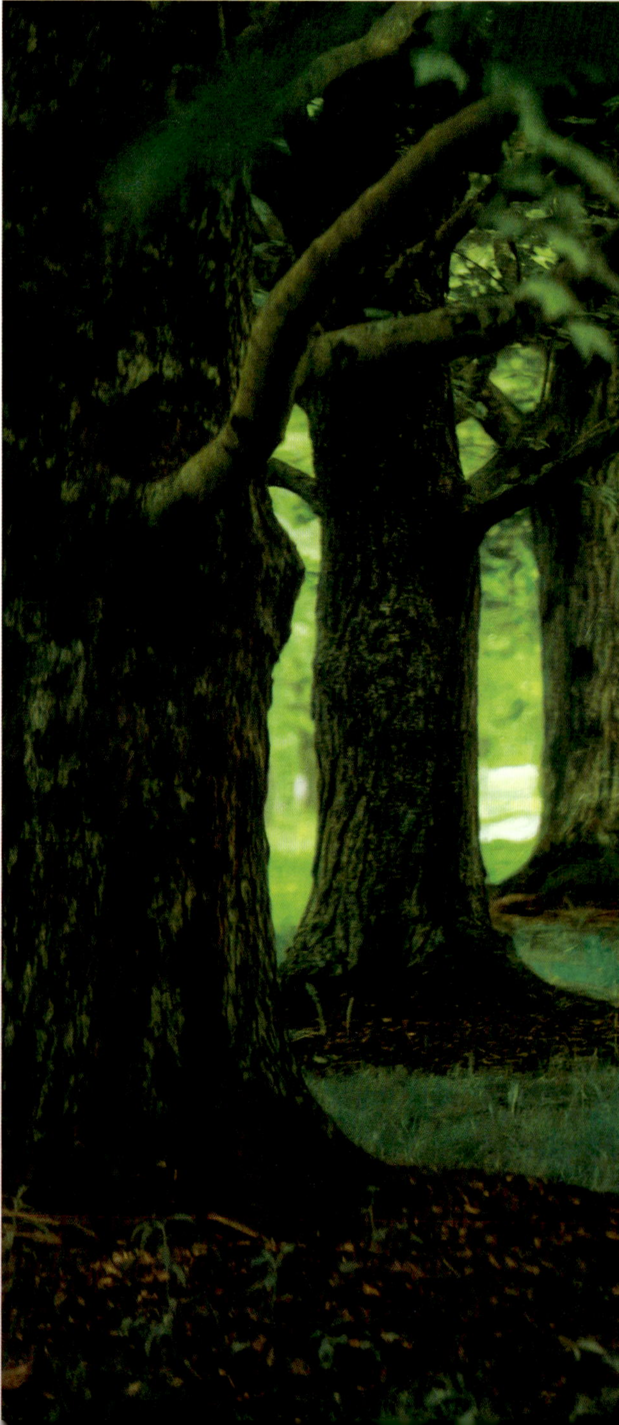

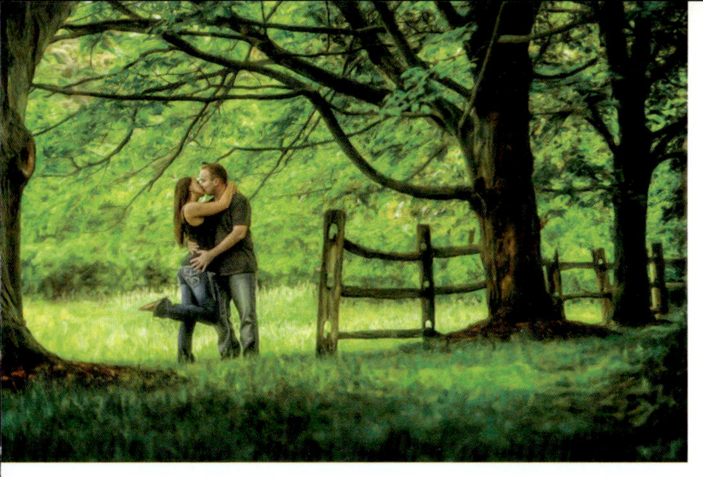

This couple was planning a December 7 wedding, so we wanted to shoot them in the heart of summer when everything was really green.

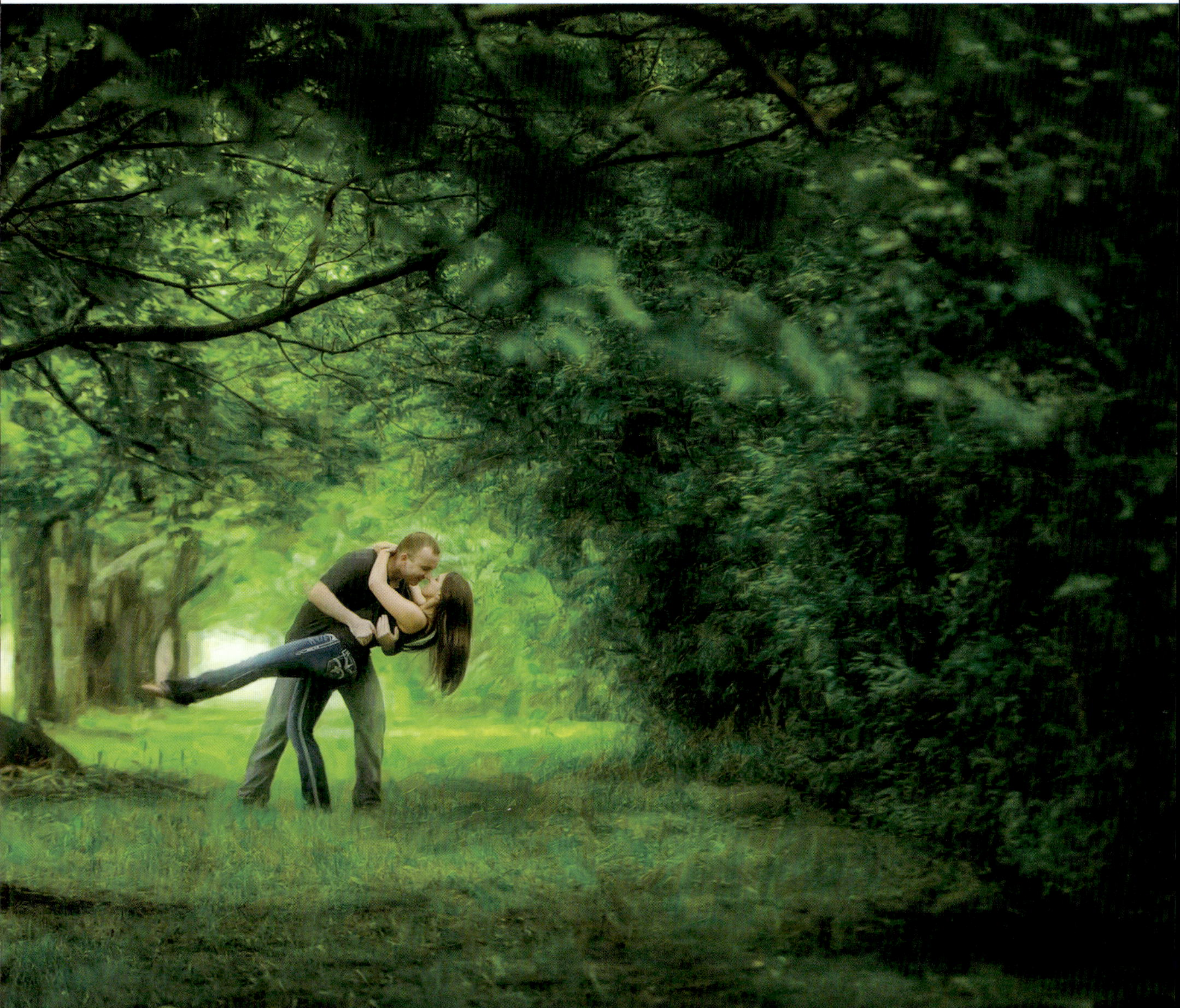

Spring/Summer Sessions

For couples planning fall or winter weddings, spring or summer engagement sessions provide the seasonal contrast we like to present. As seen in section 25, it's a chance to capture the green leaves and blue skies of summer—and even some summer activities.

Fourth of July

Nothing says "all-American summer" like flowers and Fourth of July decorations in a quaint village setting. That's what we wanted to capture in the image below. For fill light on the couple, Danielle held a reflector just out of view in the doorway to camera left. The lamp post, the red/green/blue colors—it all comes together for a perfect look (*bottom left*).

With the same couple, we also created images at a park to show the green of midsummer (*bottom right*). Here, the foliage was so dense that the sunlight was barely peeking through, so we had to add light on the couple. Danielle stood to camera left with an SB900 flash in a softbox for light that looks like a sunbeam cutting through and sweeping across the couple.

At the Shore

Summer is a time when people flock to the water, so that's the setting we chose for the next couple (*facing page*). We also took advantage of the nice weather to capture them isolated against another hallmark of summer: vibrant blue skies. For these images, we were working a little earlier than we tend to shoot—so the sun was a bit high in the sky. I made it work just by controlling the angle of their faces toward it. (For some other images from this session, see section 33.)

Our next stop was a nearby marina. For this setting, the couple changed into their dressier outfits. Boats have a very summery look; while we didn't have plans to shoot on a boat, I knew

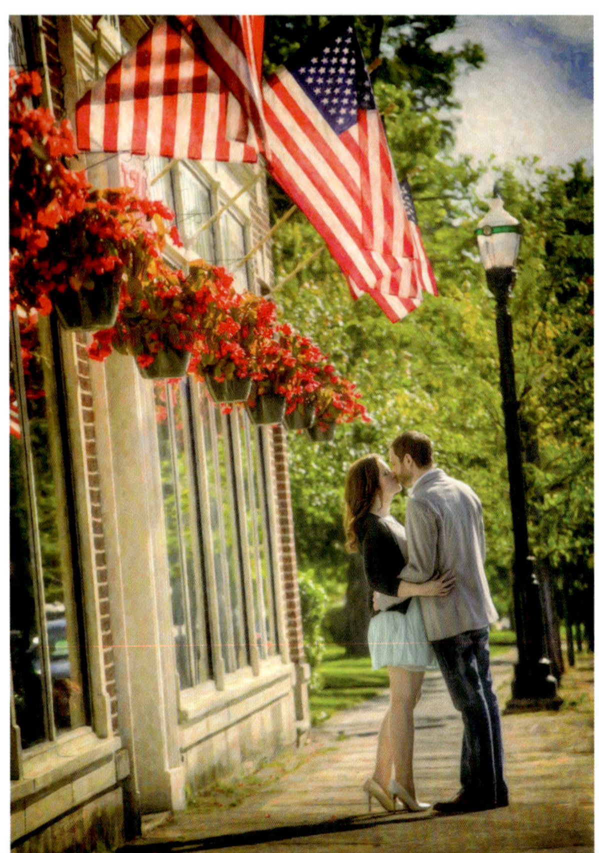

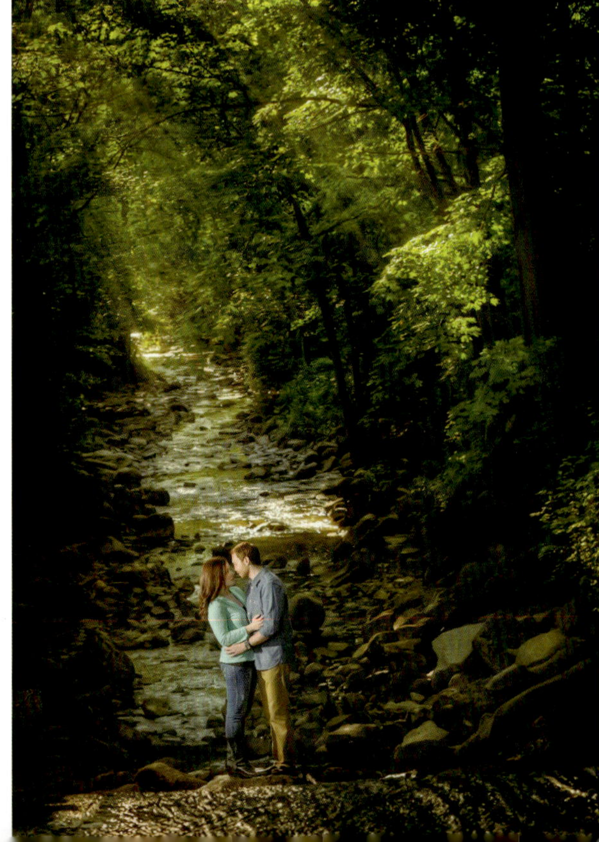

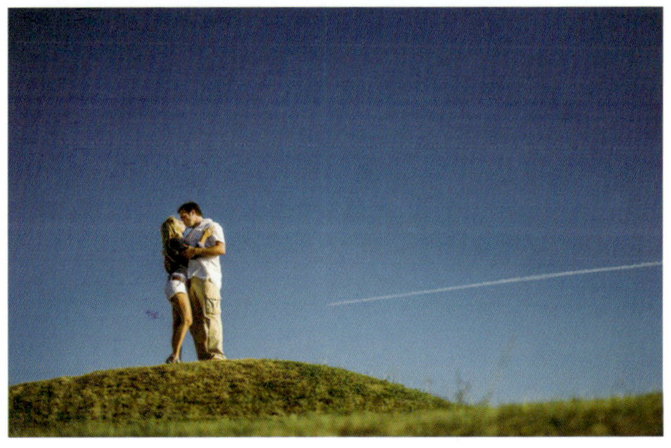

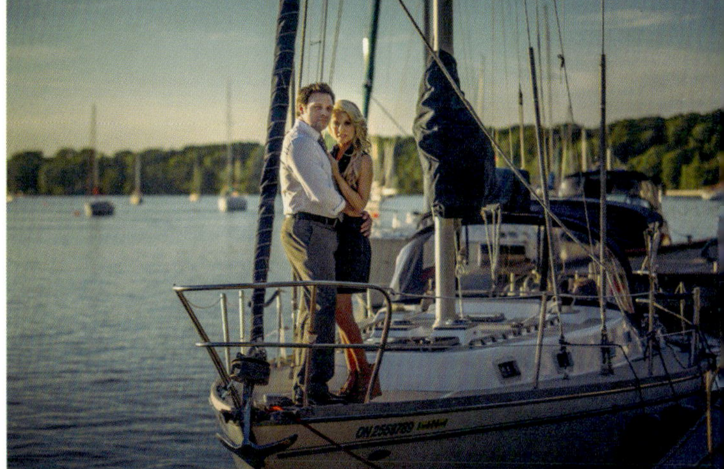

the scene would look nice. As luck would have it, though, we happened upon some people hanging out on their boat. When we explained what we were doing, they happily gave us permission to come on board and create some images with the couple. You have to take advantage of the locations and props you find! And when you say you're doing a shoot for a wedding, people are almost always willing—and often provide you with unplanned opportunities.

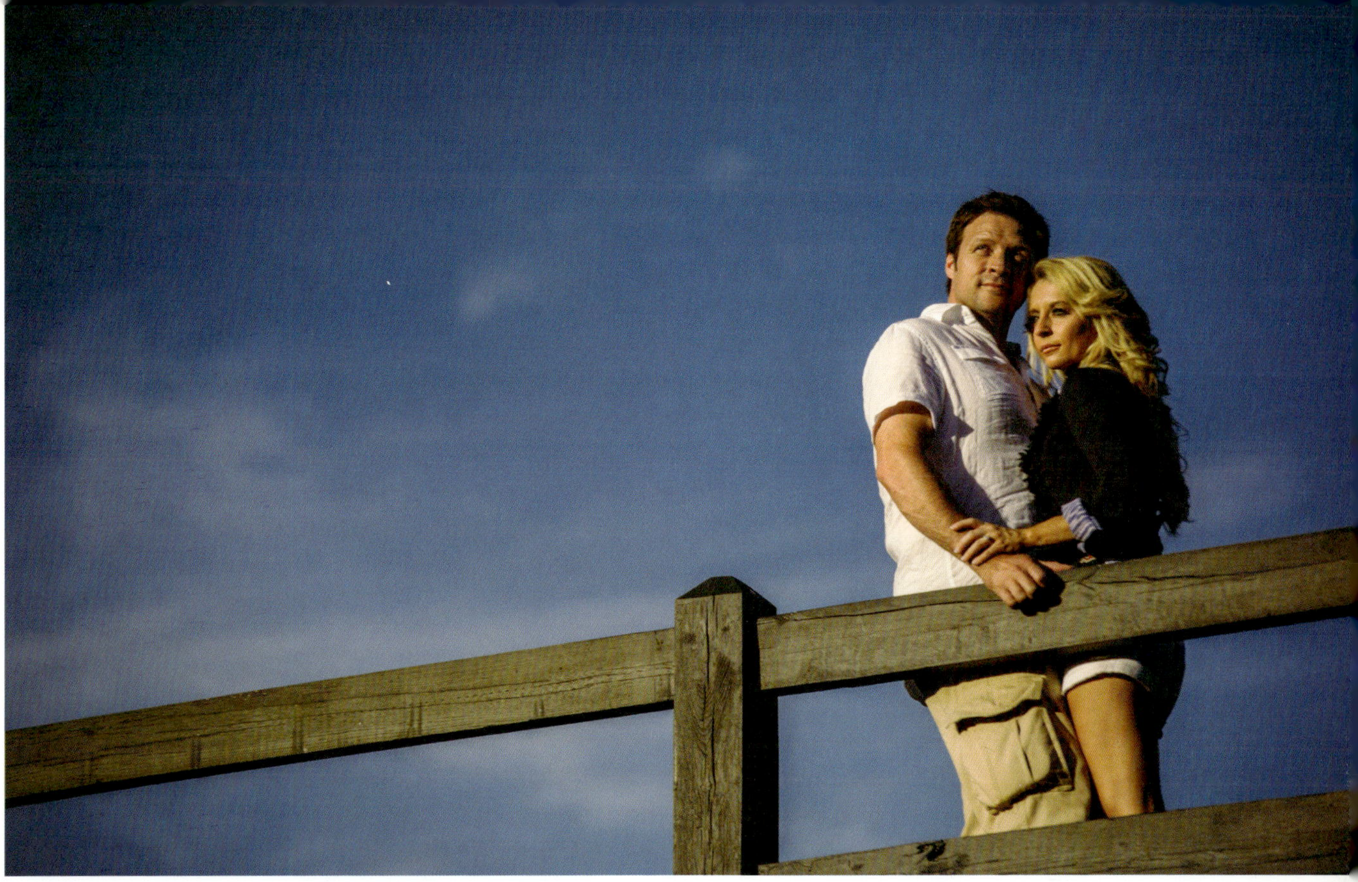

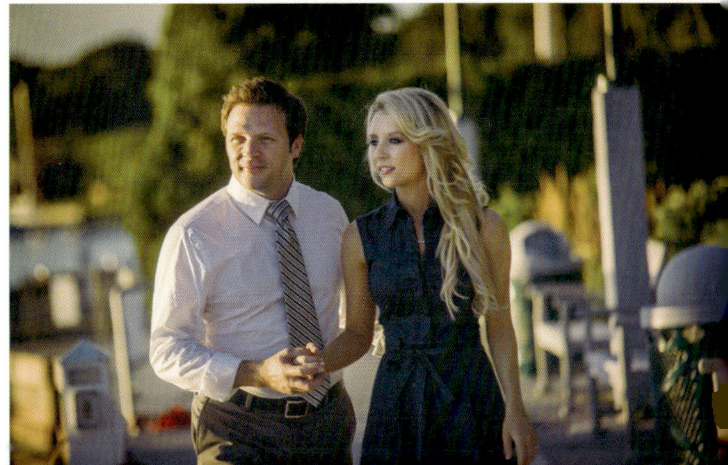

27 Autumn Sessions

In our area, autumn is the most popular season for engagement photography. Not only does it offer a nice scenic contrast for couples having summer weddings, but a lot of locations are just prettier at this time of year. An additional advantage is that the temperatures are cooler, so people (especially the guys) feel a lot more comfortable being dressed up.

Location Selection

If you're planning an autumn session, it only makes sense to take advantage of the colors—so

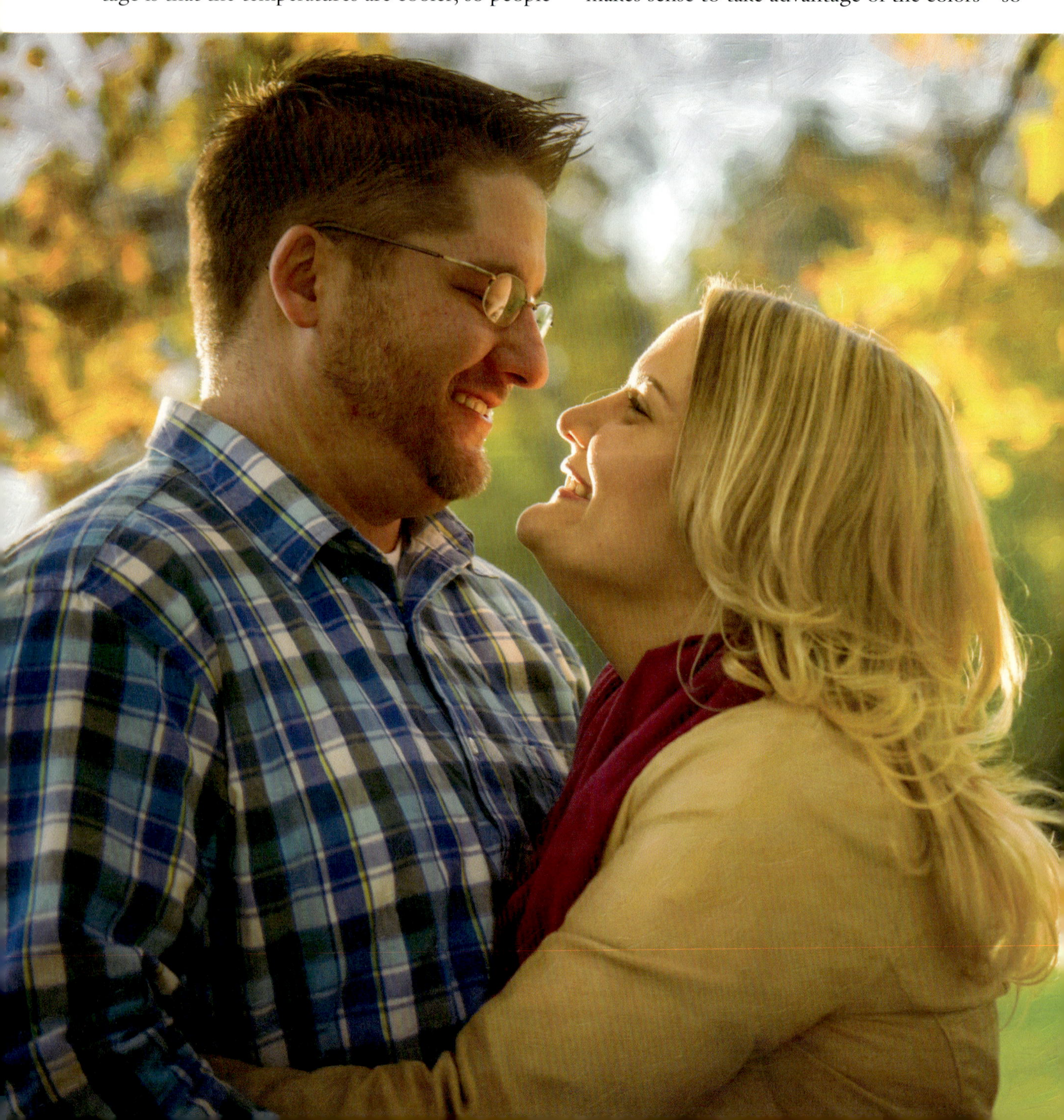

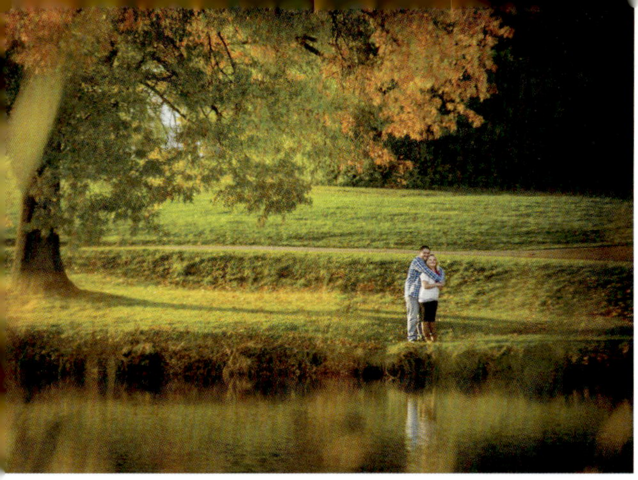

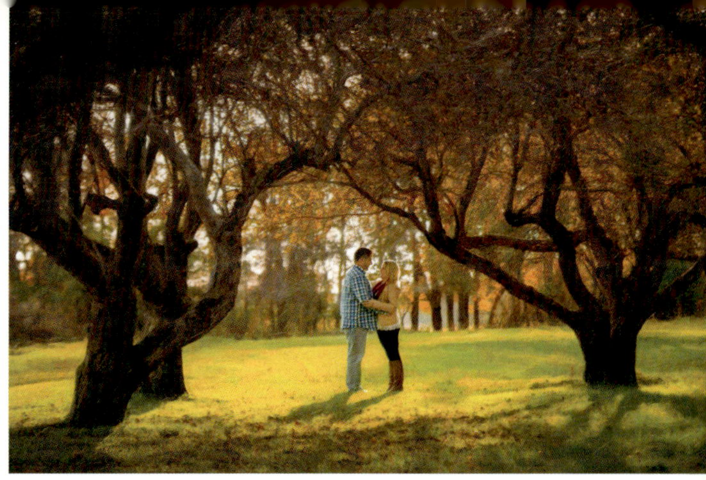

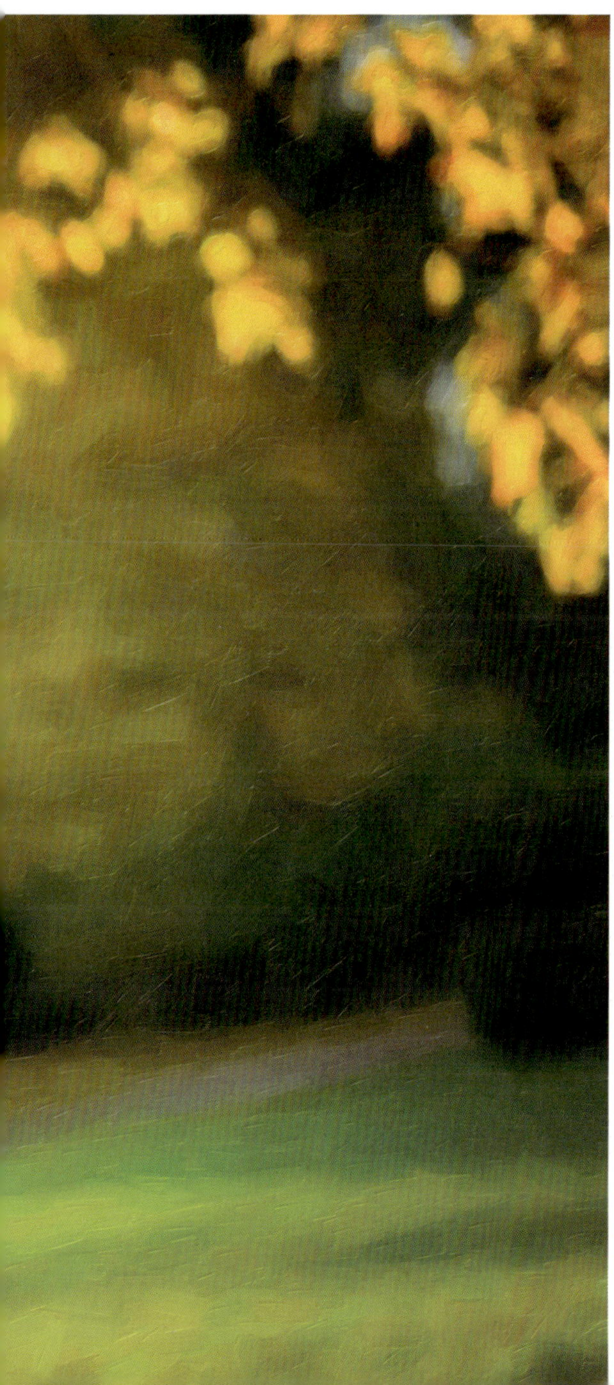

we steer couples away from indoor sites or locations like the waterfront (popular at other times of year) and toward locations with lots of trees.

Lighting

Backlighting makes fall colors glow. If needed (as in the large image to the left), add fill flash to balance the subjects with the scene.

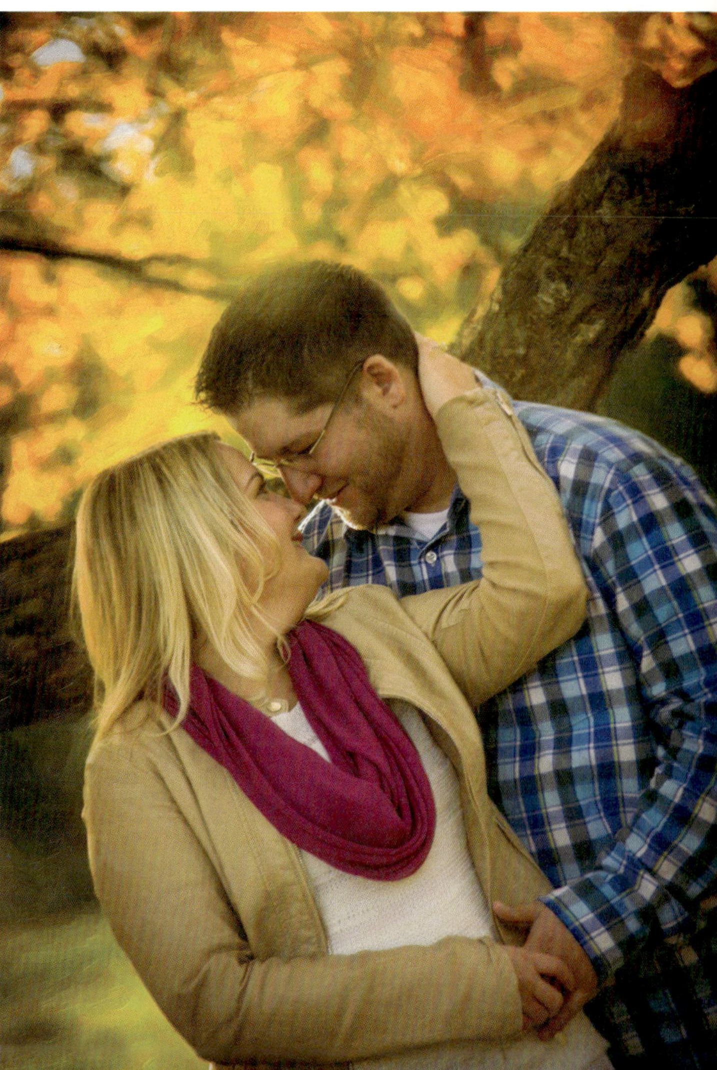

28 Winter Sessions

If you live anywhere above the equator, most likely you're going to see snow at some point. We live in Buffalo, NY, so we have no problem getting our fair share of it. Fortunately, snow doesn't stop us from shooting portraits outdoors. We actually look forward to photographing in it. Many of our couples love winter and winter

Cold Gear

You want to warm yourself up, but your lenses will fog up if you shift them from the cold outside to the warm car. I usually put my camera gear in the trunk, so it's safe but not exposed to those temperature changes.

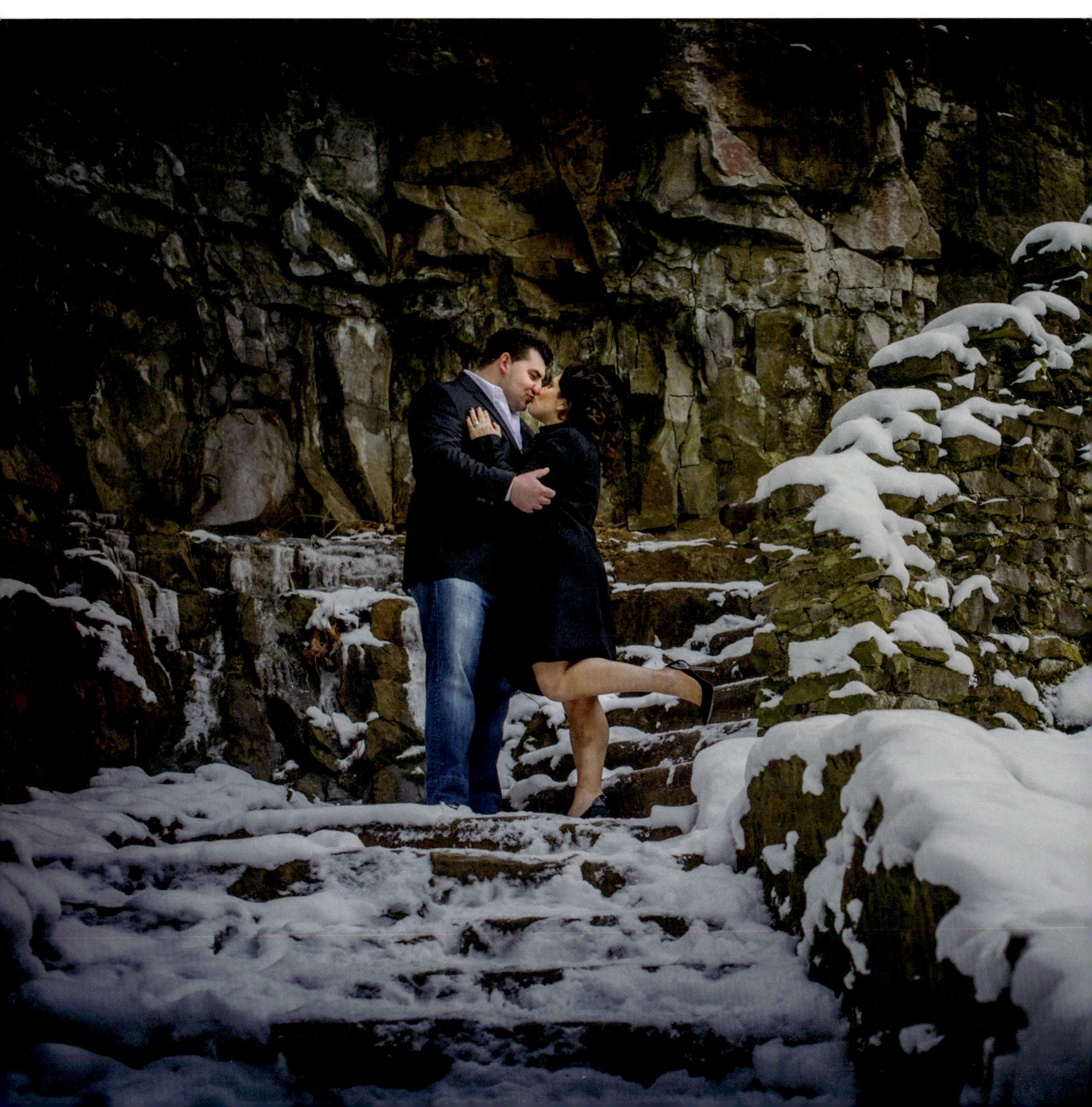

activities—and the monochromatic look of winter landscapes is very well suited to portraiture.

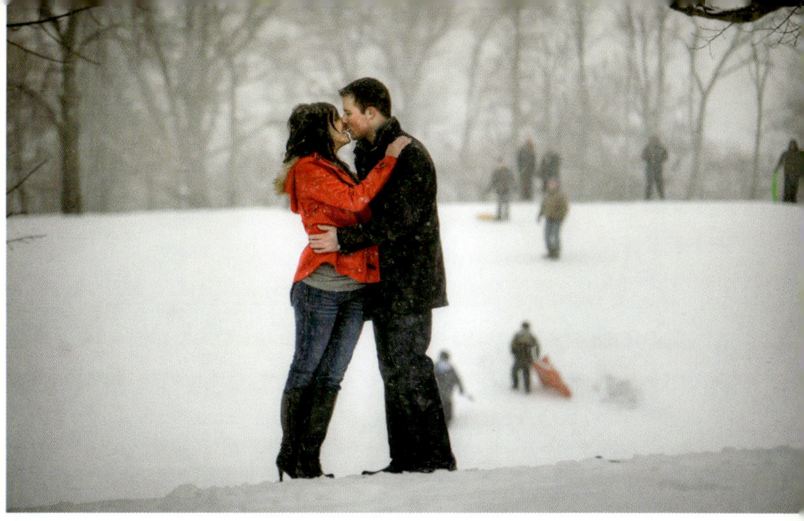

Playful and Romantic

When shooting in a winter scene, you can encourage the couple to get playful and silly by suggesting a little snow fight. Then, they can warm each other up by getting close and romantic. The posing options are limitless.

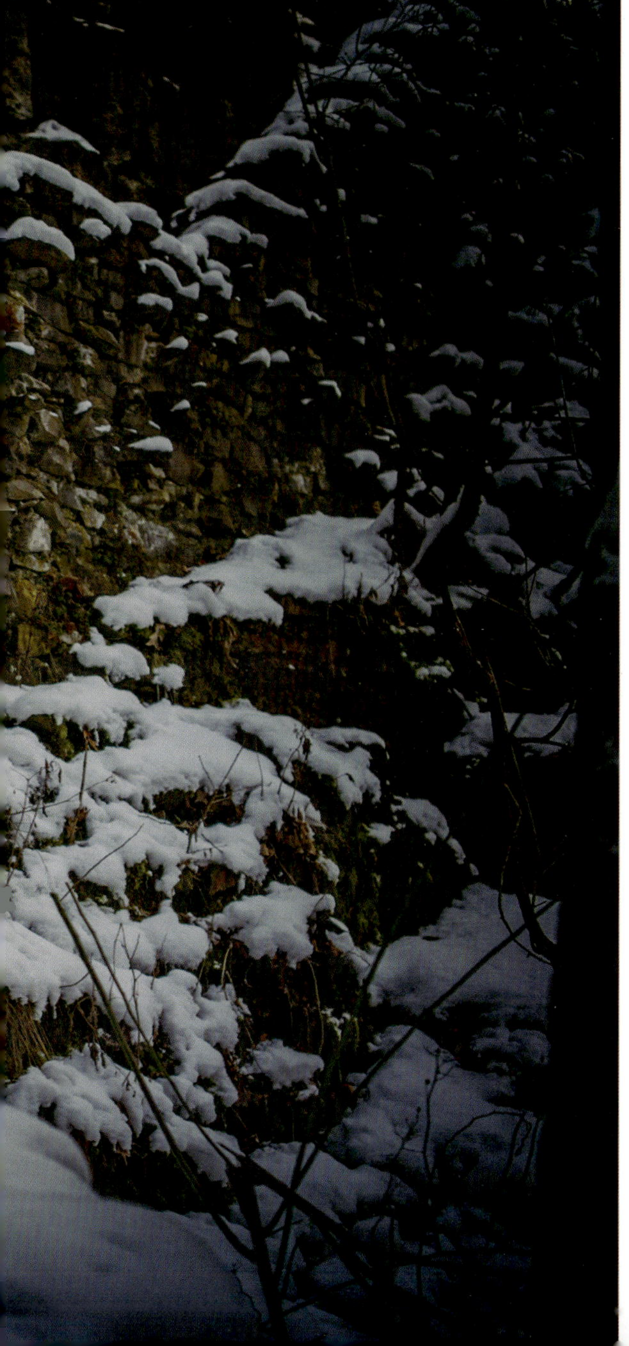

The monochromatic look of winter landscapes is very well suited to portraiture.

Take Time to Warm Up

No matter where you end up shooting, you should try to keep the cars nearby so the couple can warm up from time to time. When it's cold out, people's cheeks and noses will get very red. Their eyes and noses will also start to water if it's very cold. Allowing the couple (and yourself) some time for breaks will make the shoot more comfortable.

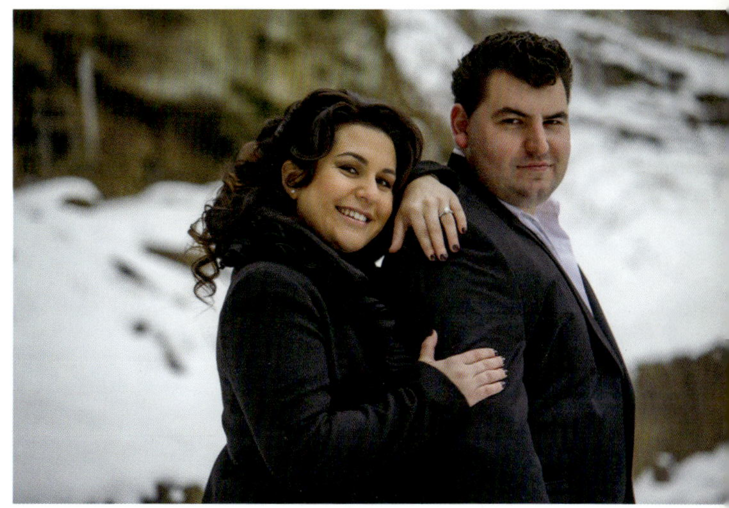

29 Contrasting Settings

As you can see from the images on the facing page, this couple's wedding was all about pink (I even turned the foliage pink in the top right photo). For their engagement shots, I wanted to create images that would contrast with the dreamy, fairy-tale look of their wedding. We decided to shoot at a stadium and then at their friends' nearby home, which sits on the shore of Lake Erie. The idea was to capture clean, natural images using the late afternoon light.

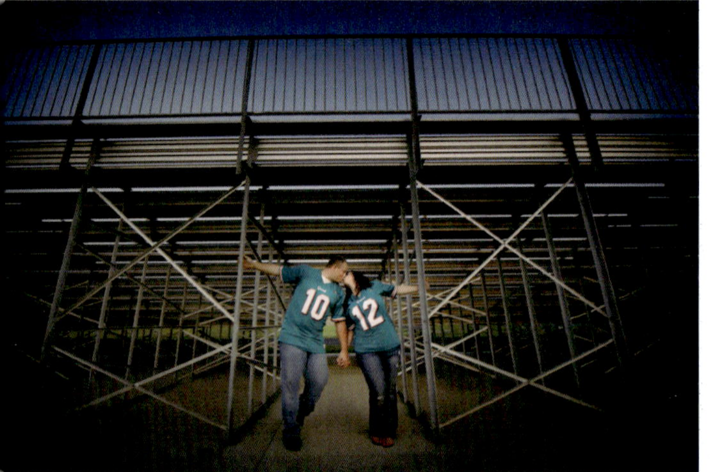

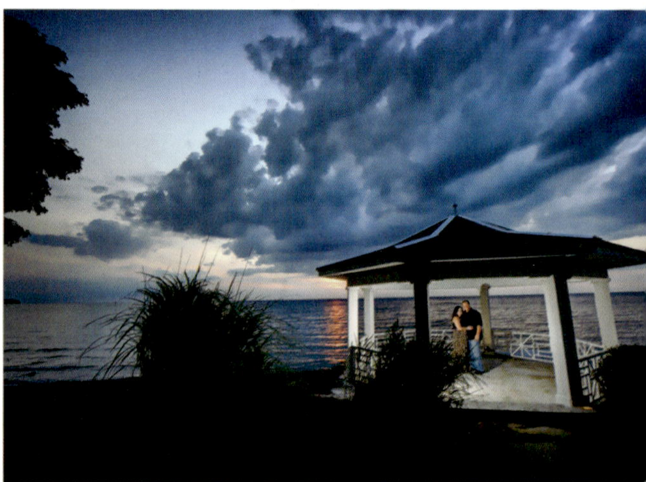

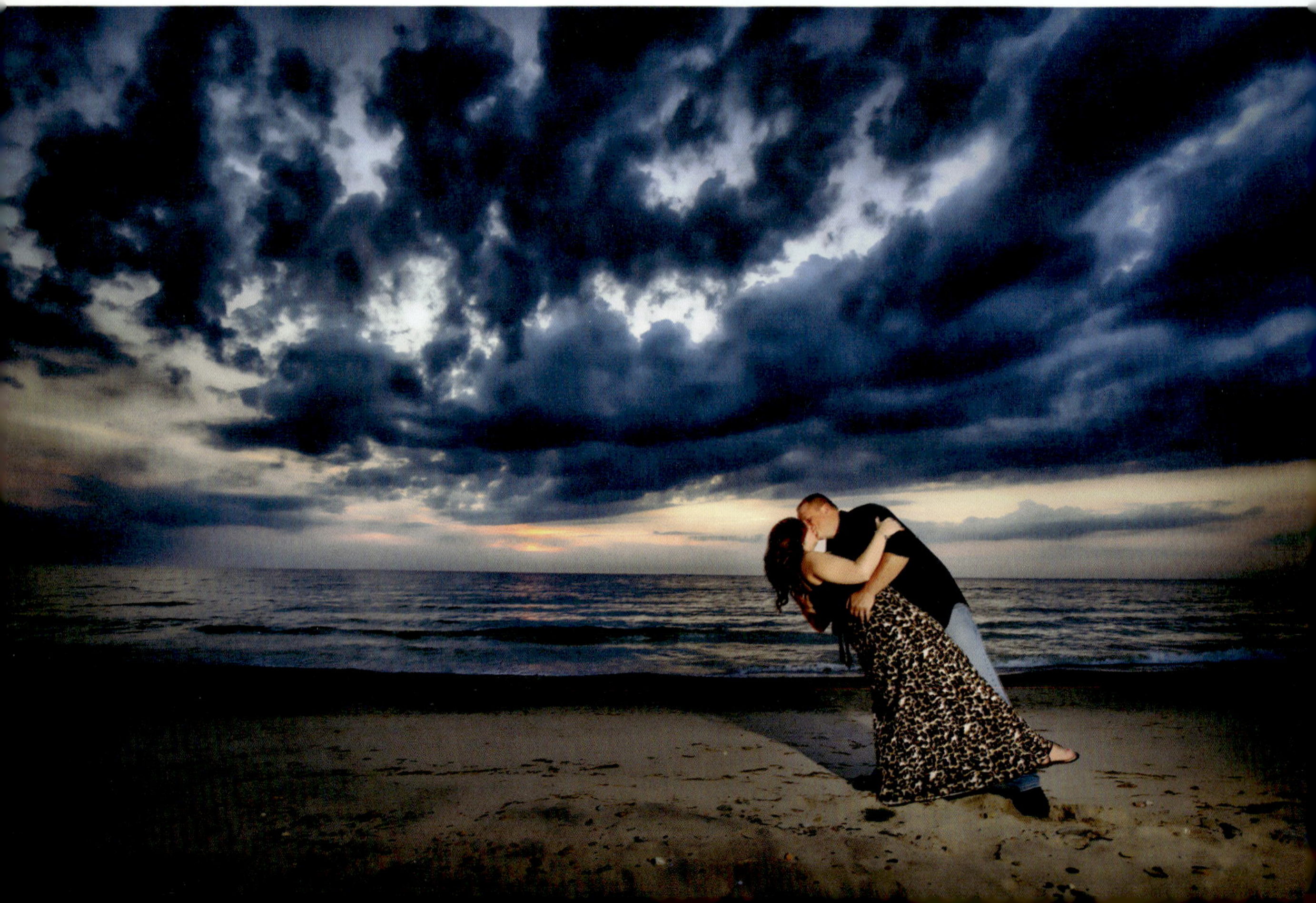

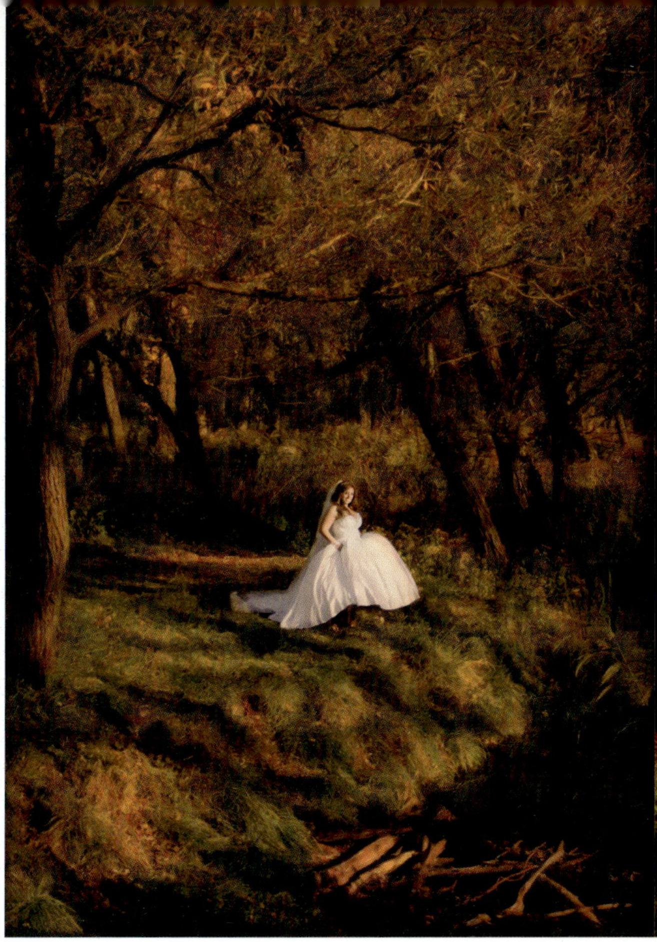

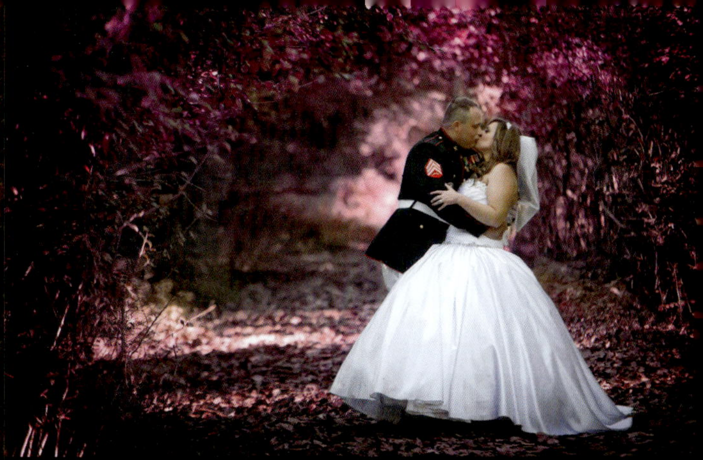

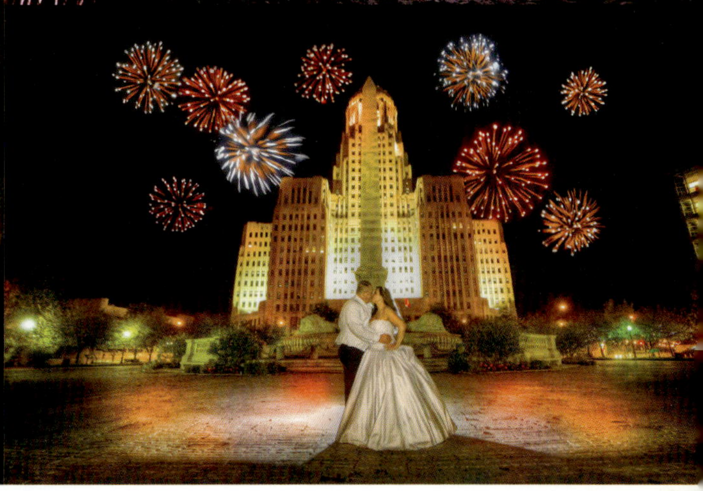

▲ These images from the couple's wedding show the style and color palette of the event. As you can see, the engagement images were designed to have a very different (but complementary) look and feel.

Locations and Lighting

As seen on the facing page, we started at a nearby school for shots of the couple in their "save the date" jerseys (*top left*). There's another shot from this part of the session in section 31. As the sun dropped, we moved to the friends' property and created images in a gazebo near the shore (*top right*). To balance the couple against the dramatic sky, I bounced an SB900 flash (positioned behind a bush) up into the roof of the gazebo. This lit up the whole area. Our next stop was the shore, where I added manual flash at half power from camera right (*bottom*). This popped the couple out of the dark background and gave them warm, natural skin tones against the cool sky.

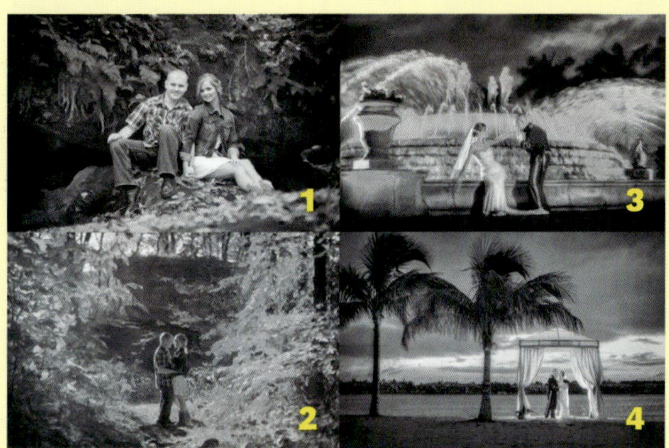

Two Locations, Two Very Different Looks

Next Two Pages ➤

This couple's engagement session was just a month before their wedding, so capturing contrasting seasons wasn't possible. Fortunately, we were able to shoot in two very different locations. **Images 1 and 2:** Their engagement session was shot at Rock City Park (near Olean, NY), where we worked deep into the forest about 45 minutes before sunset. **Images 3 and 4:** Their Florida wedding images have an entirely different look, giving us the contrast and variety we like to deliver to our clients.

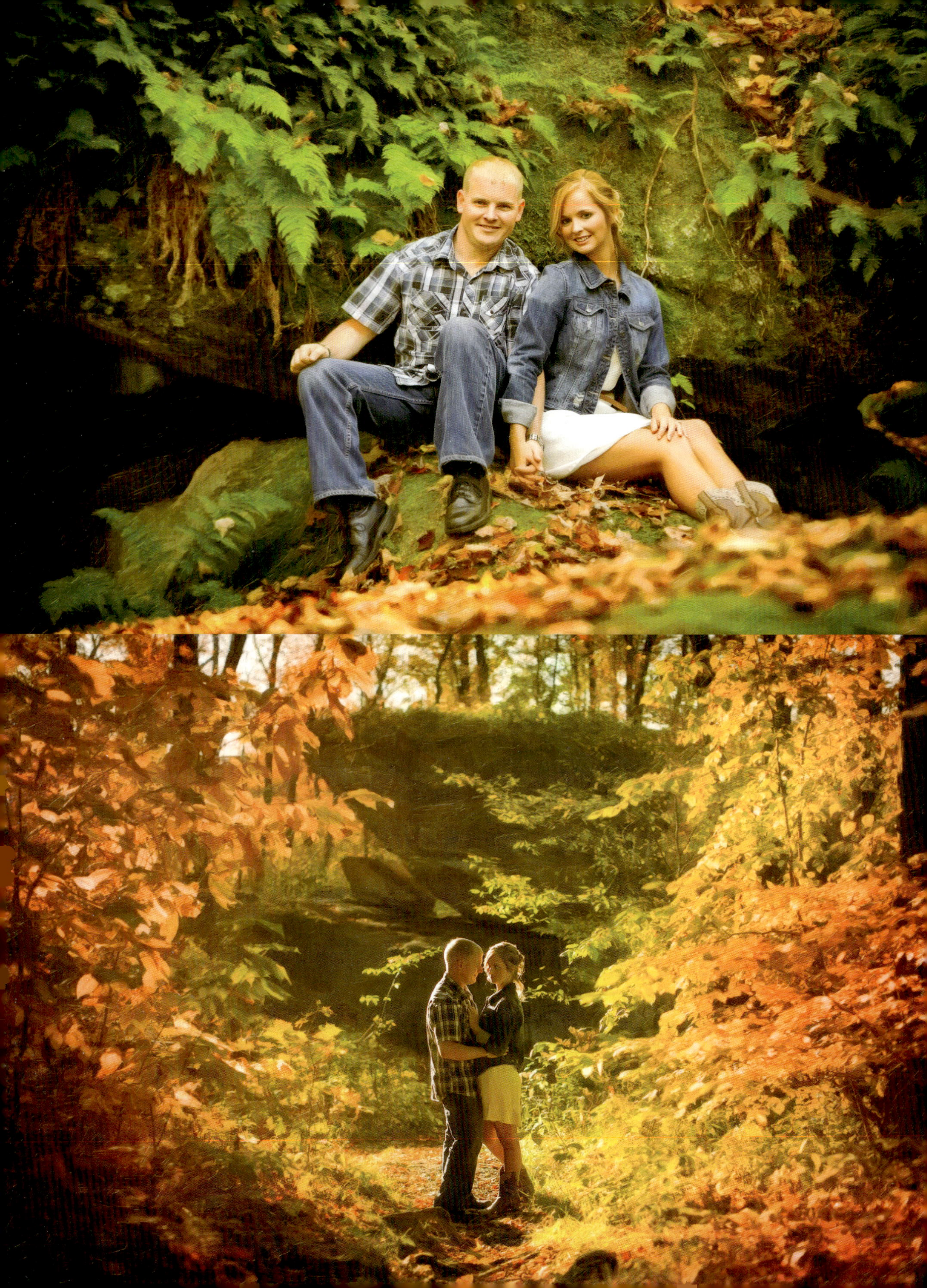

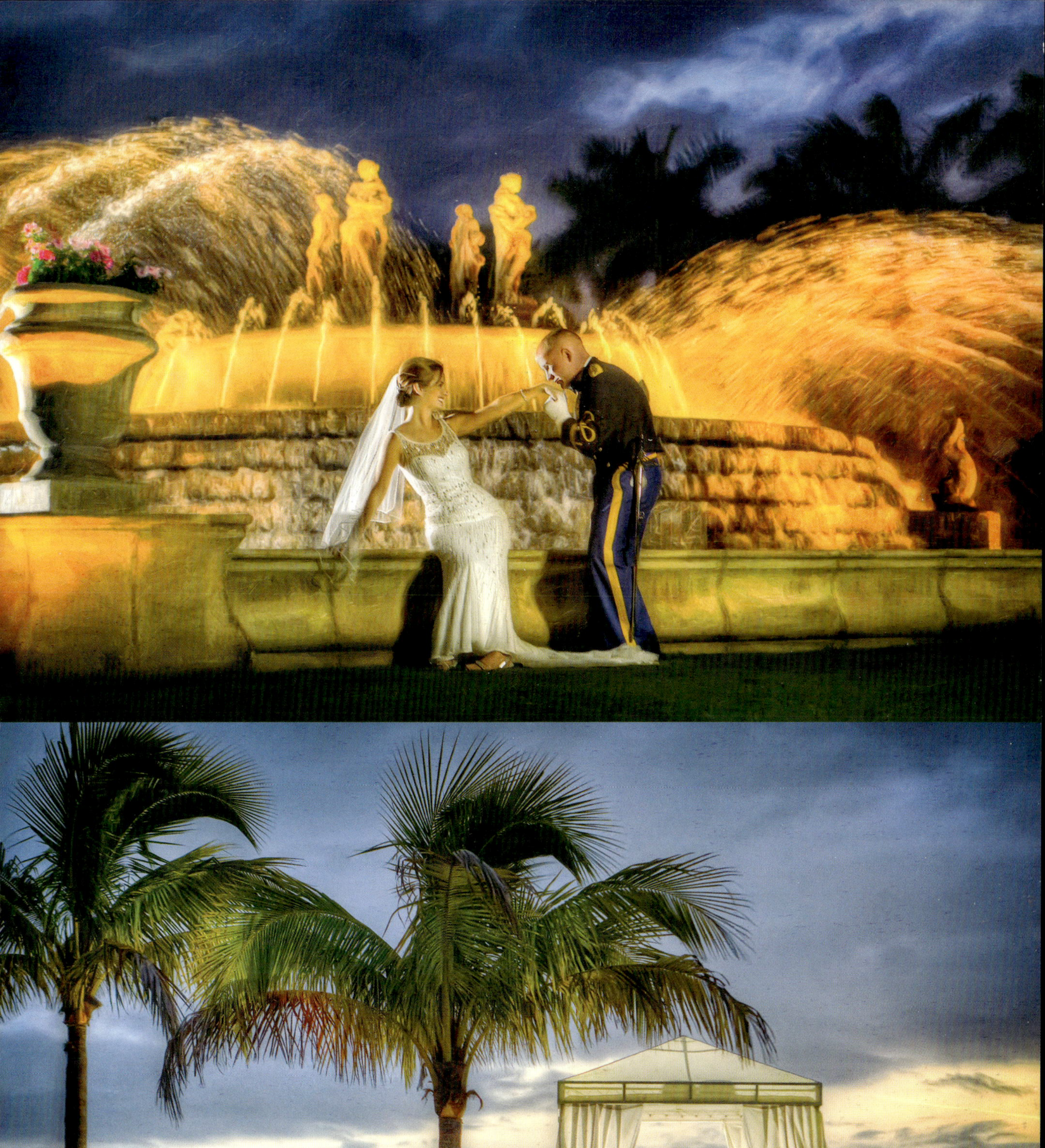

Cars

Whether it's the couple's own vehicle or one you come across during the course of your session, cars make great props and can add character to the images.

Farm Truck

Becker Farms in Gasport, NY, offers many scenic shooting areas—including the old farm truck in the image below. This is a flatbed truck, but I didn't like that look so I had them move around to the front of the vehicle. We were working late in the day with a clear blue sky; to add some color, I applied a film bleed effect. It looked like an orange cloud and filled the negative space.

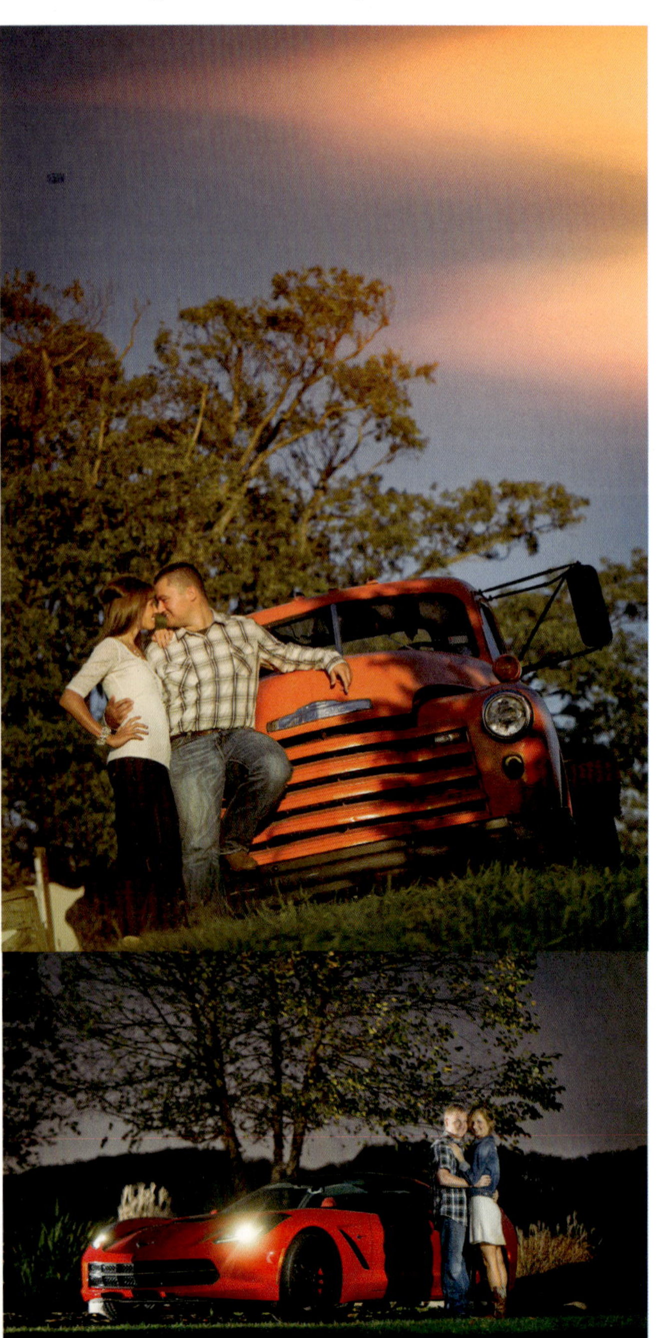

Corvette

After their session, we were invited back to the couple's house—where the dad of the bride-to-be showed up with a special edition 2014 Corvette from his dealership (*bottom left*). He was really proud of it, so we ended up photographing the couple with the car, then taking portraits of Dad with it, too. I placed SB900 flash units behind the car and to camera right (on the couple). The rest of the light is from the last glow of sun on the horizon and the car's headlights.

Car Collectors

The Salvatore family is known for their car collection (on display at the family's restaurant), so we decided to add a car to the couple's sunset shot at Spring Lake Winery in Lockport, NY.

For the first image (*facing page, top*), I added an Ice Light to camera right to illuminate the subjects. I placed an SB900 behind the tree to camera left, separating the hood of the car from the background. A Lowel light on the trees brought up their texture.

As the sun dropped (*facing page, bottom*), it made sense to turn on the headlights—but I wanted them to fall on something, so we set up a table with wine glasses and a bottle.

Comparing the two images, you can see how much the sky often changes in a short amount of time—especially at the end of the day.

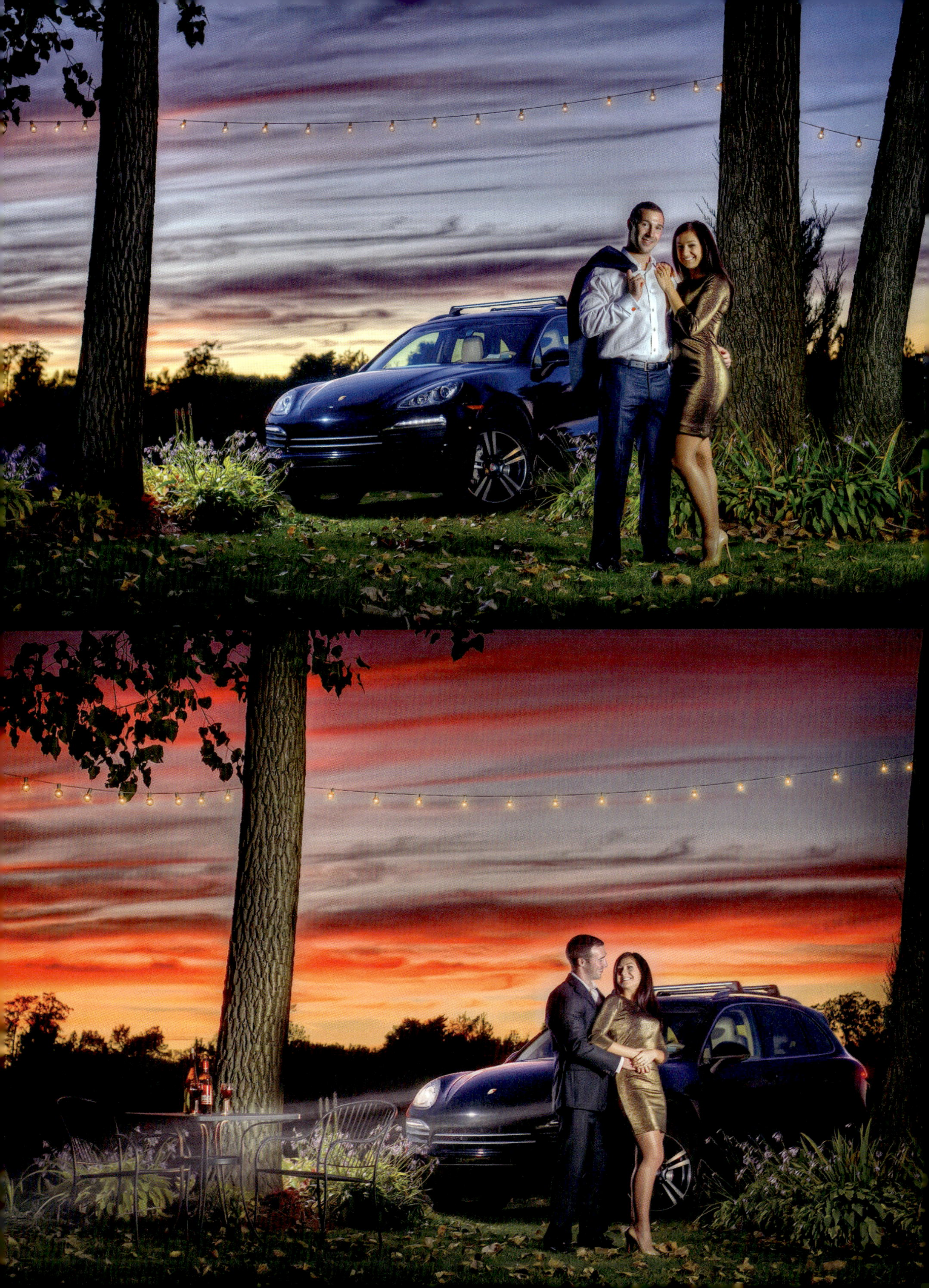

31 Pets

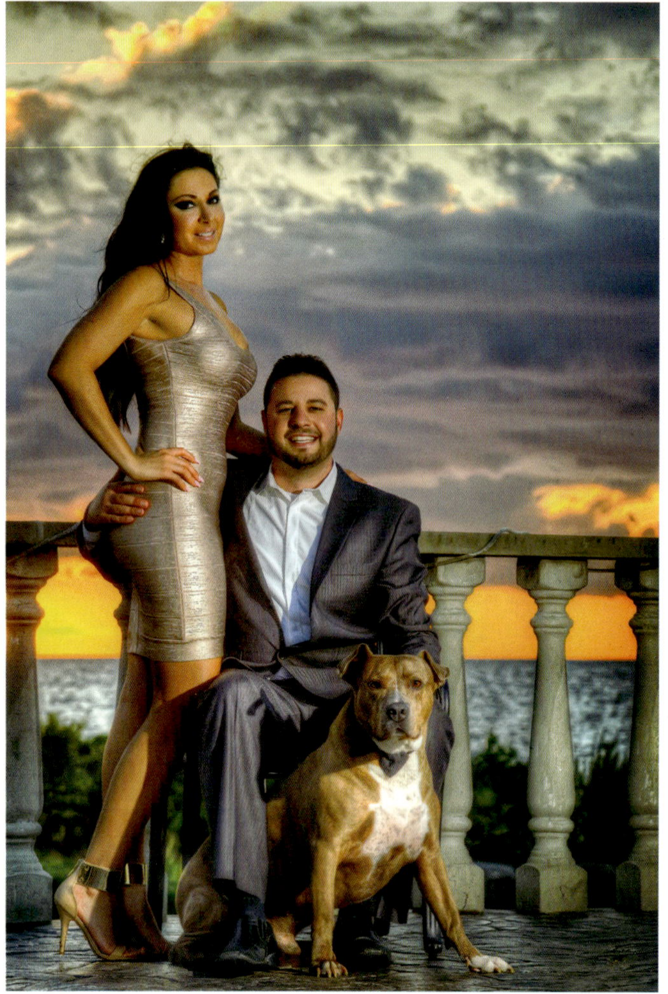

Couples love their pets—and many of our clients want these important members of the family to be included in their engagement sessions. For these shoots, we start off with the pet images and we add thirty minutes to the beginning of the session to let the animals get relaxed. Often, the couple will get stressed out during these images because they want the pets to be perfect. Remind them that their pets will feed off that stress, so it's better for them to relax.

We ask them to just interact and leave it to us to get the pet's attention. To do this, Danielle stands next to the camera and makes noises or motions to draw the pet's gaze. Sometimes the clicking of the camera alone is enough to keep a curious dog locked in on the lens.

Ask Them to Bring a Friend

Have a friend or family member accompany the couple to the shoot and plan to take off with the pet when you're done with them. This will let you concentrate on the people once the pet portion of the session is done. If this is someone the dog likes, they can also help get the dog's attention.

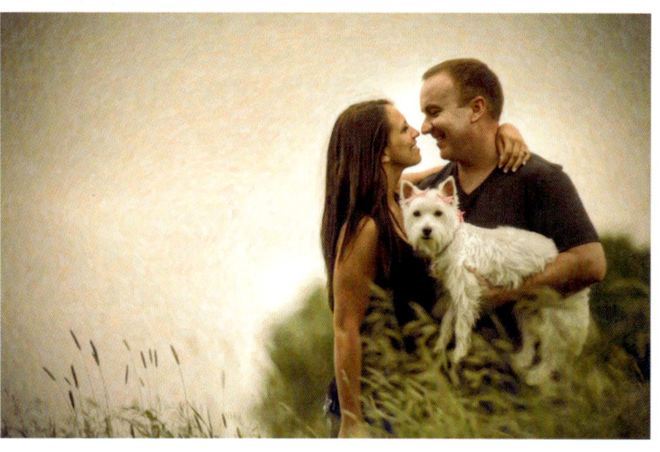

(top) This might look like a relatively simple portrait of a nice little family, but the dog was not interested in staying where we wanted him. We had to keep following to where he wanted to sit (at which point, he was ready to move on). Having the man hold him in place finally helped us get this image. We worked with the sunset behind them and added one SB900 to the right.

(bottom) We were shooting in the wet grass, so I had the man pick up the dog. This is a good way to get the pet's face up closer to the subjects' faces.

Football Fans

These Miami Dolphins fans (*top right*) had jerseys made with their wedding date (10/12). For a portrait with their dog at the football field, I had them get down to canine level. I shot the image using just the late date sunlight on their faces. Minimizing equipment is another way to help keep dogs calm and more cooperative.

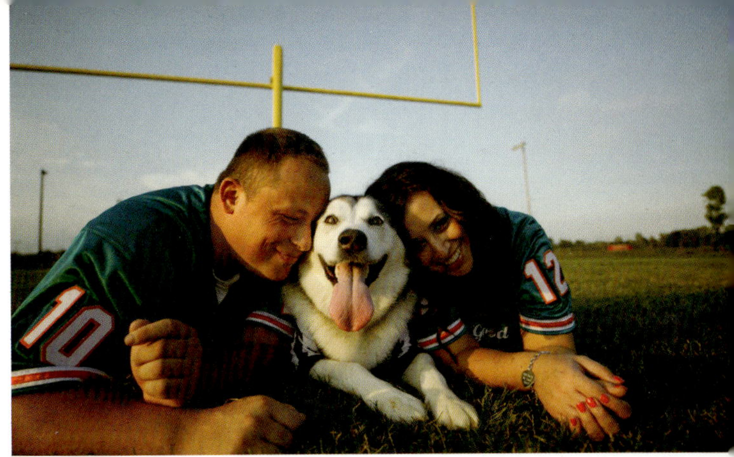

Energy Level

Some dogs are really energetic. Here (*right*), we got *one* shot that worked out perfectly. That was the result of being patient shooting in burst mode. Three people were behind me trying to get the dogs' attention—with their faces right around mine to keep the dogs looking at the lens.

Of course, some dogs are relaxed and having a good day—which makes them very easy to photograph. With the dogs in the image below, we were able to get lots of great looks.

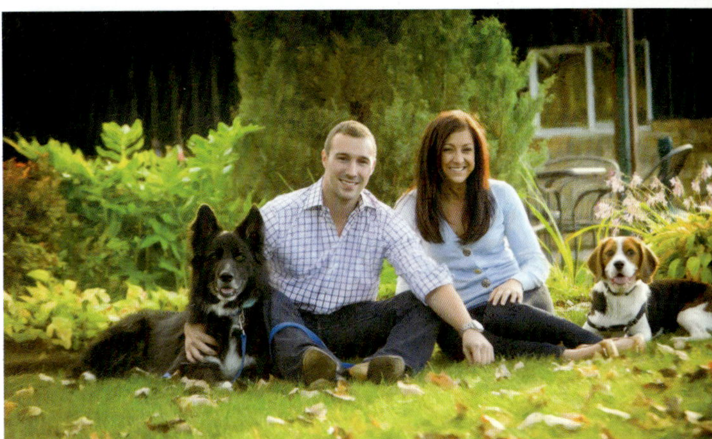

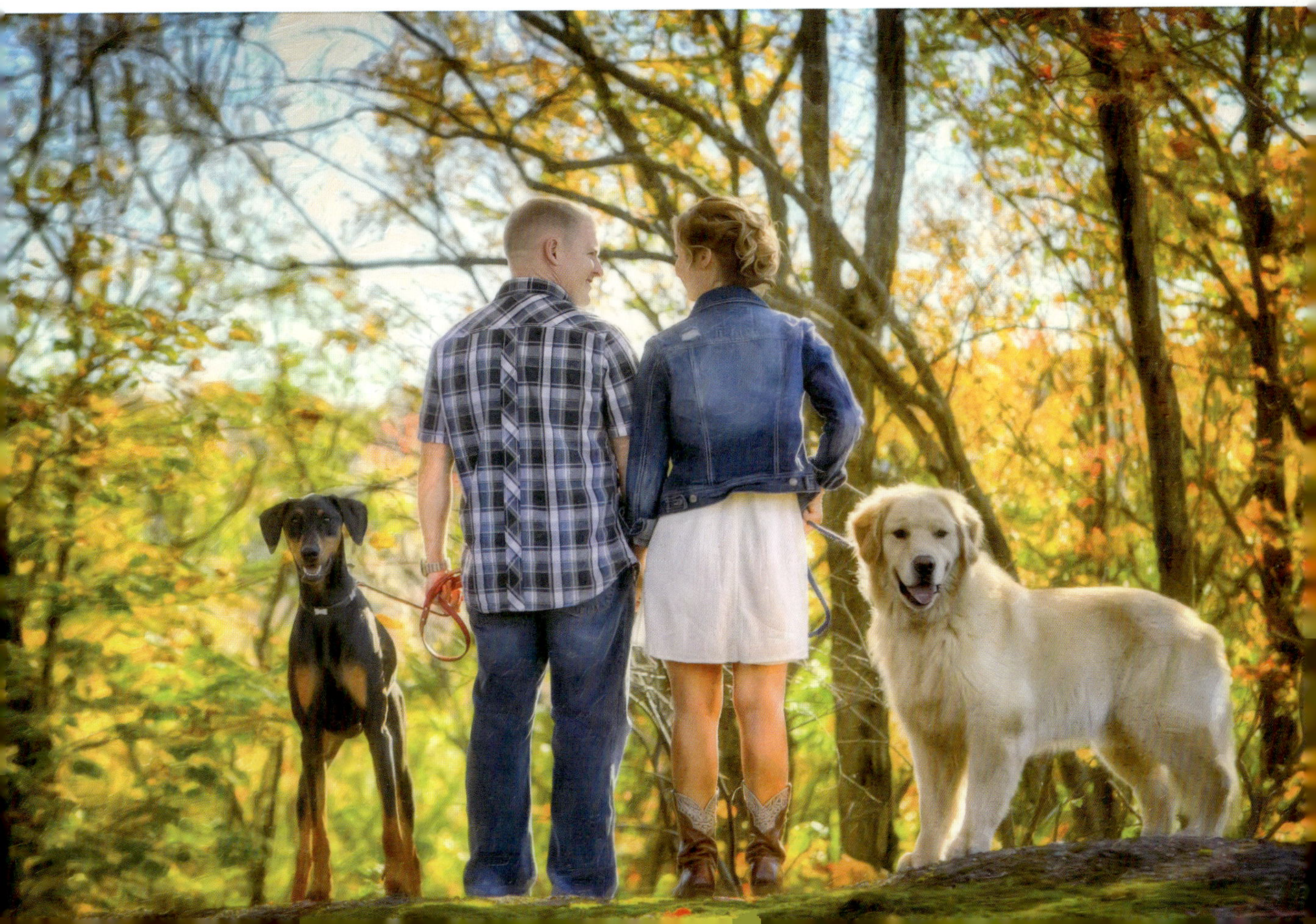

32 Unexpected Moments

When you're out shooting on location, things are going to happen—unexpected things. If you don't let them throw you for a loop, they can sometimes make for even more powerful images (and they definitely make the shoot even more memorable for your subjects). We've had kids appear out of nowhere (see section 18), a bench collapse (see next two pages), a cop appear on horseback and become part of the session, and much more. When it happens, we always try to go with it and approach the unexpected with a "Well, let's just try this!" perspective.

Here Comes the Horse

When shooting the image below, we saw the horse coming their way and everyone got sort of excited about what might happen. I really wanted them to stay focused on each other, so I asked the couple to ignore the horse—but I kept teasing them, telling them, "It's getting closer! It's getting closer!" Their uncertainty about where the horse really was—and how close it might be to them—produced some wonderful and very natural reactions.

How Much Is that Doggie in the Window?

The bride-to-be loves seeing this dog (*facing page, top*) in a shop window as she walks to work every morning, so when we were in the area, she wanted to stop by and see if the dog was there. From that point, creating the portrait was a simple process of lining up the dog, the couple, and their reflection.

Chicken Wrangling

For this session with a vintage look (*facing page, bottom*), we got the couple into position—but then a stray chicken or two started to appear at the edges of the frame. Danielle rose to the challenge of wrangling the chickens, running around and trying to get the birds to congregate in front of the posed couple. We kept them focused on each other, but their expressions reveal the fun and humor of the whole situtation.

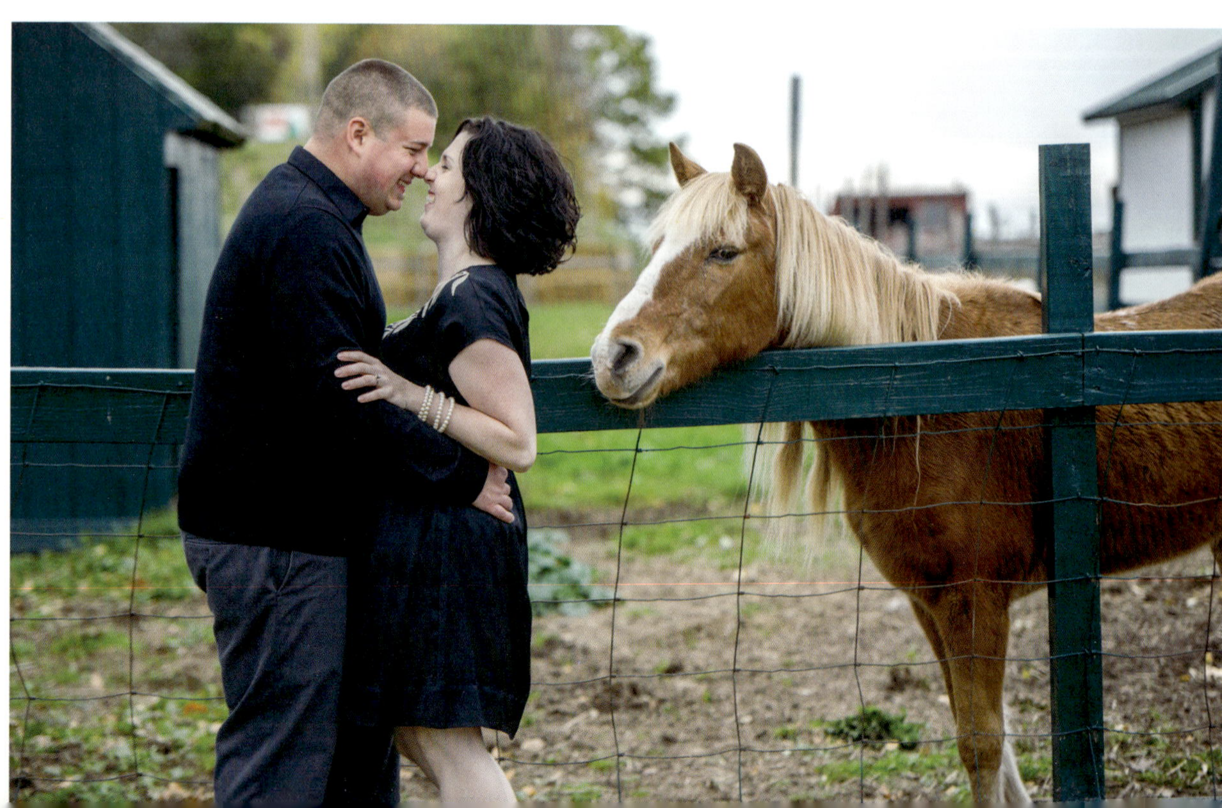

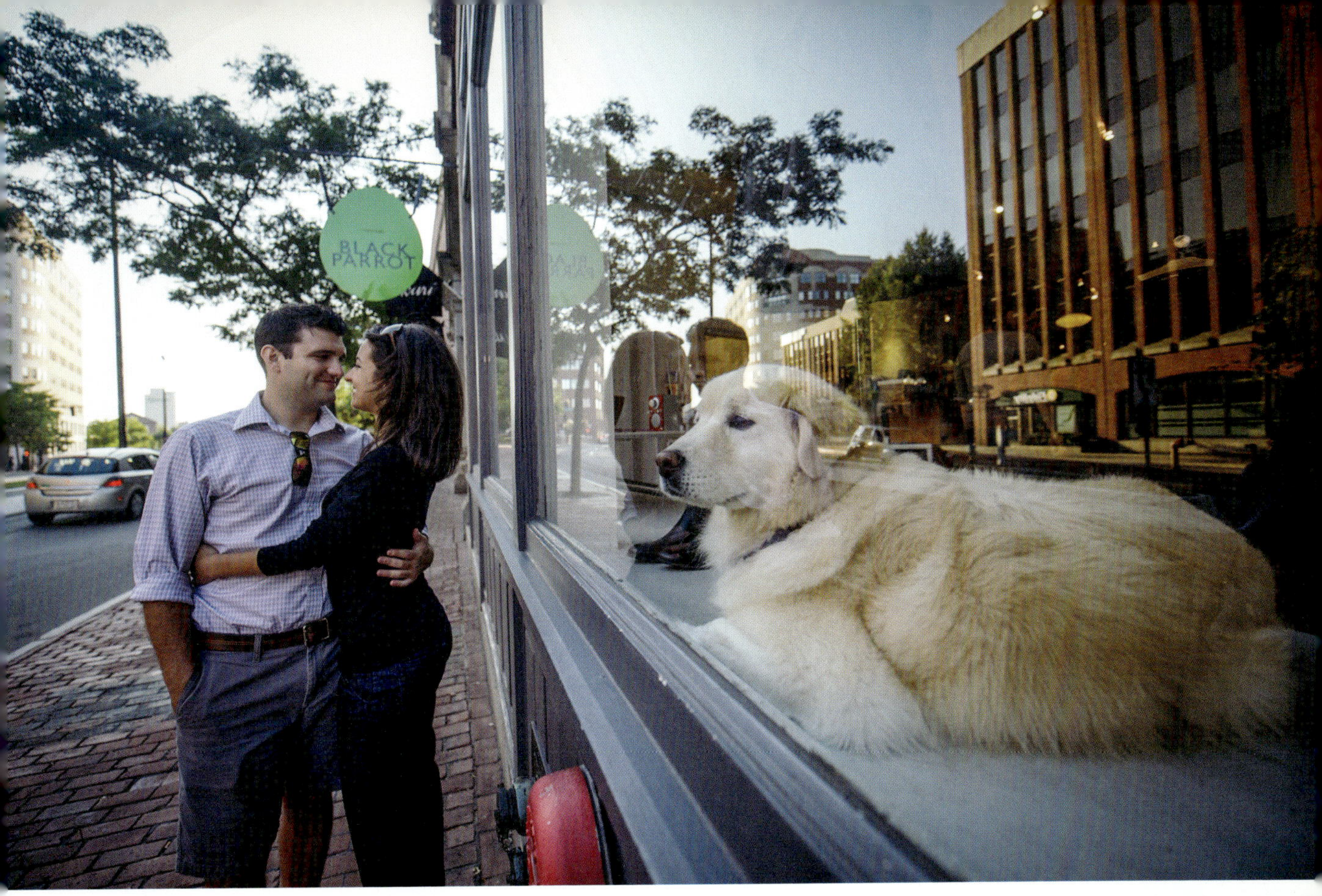

BLACK PARROT

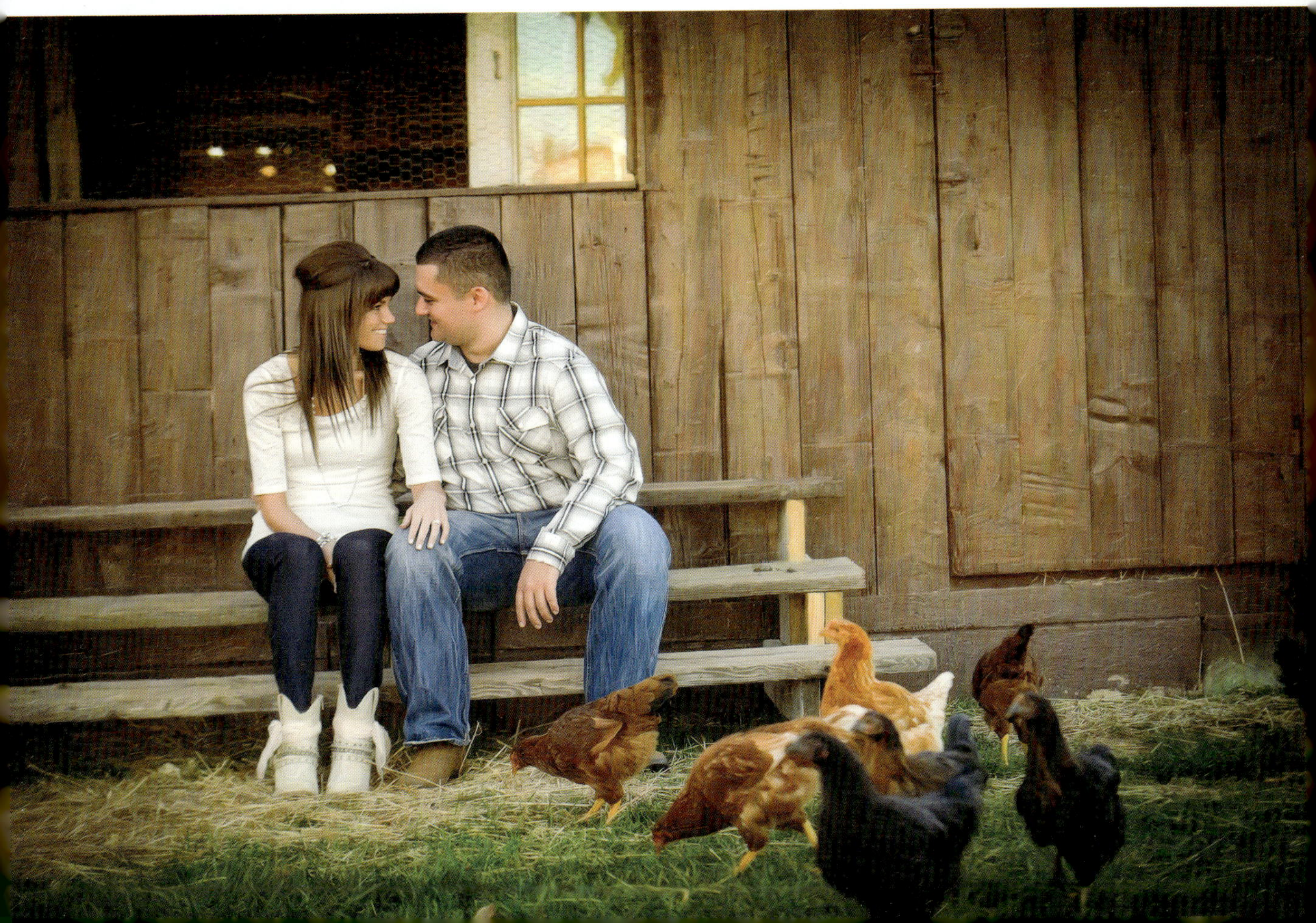

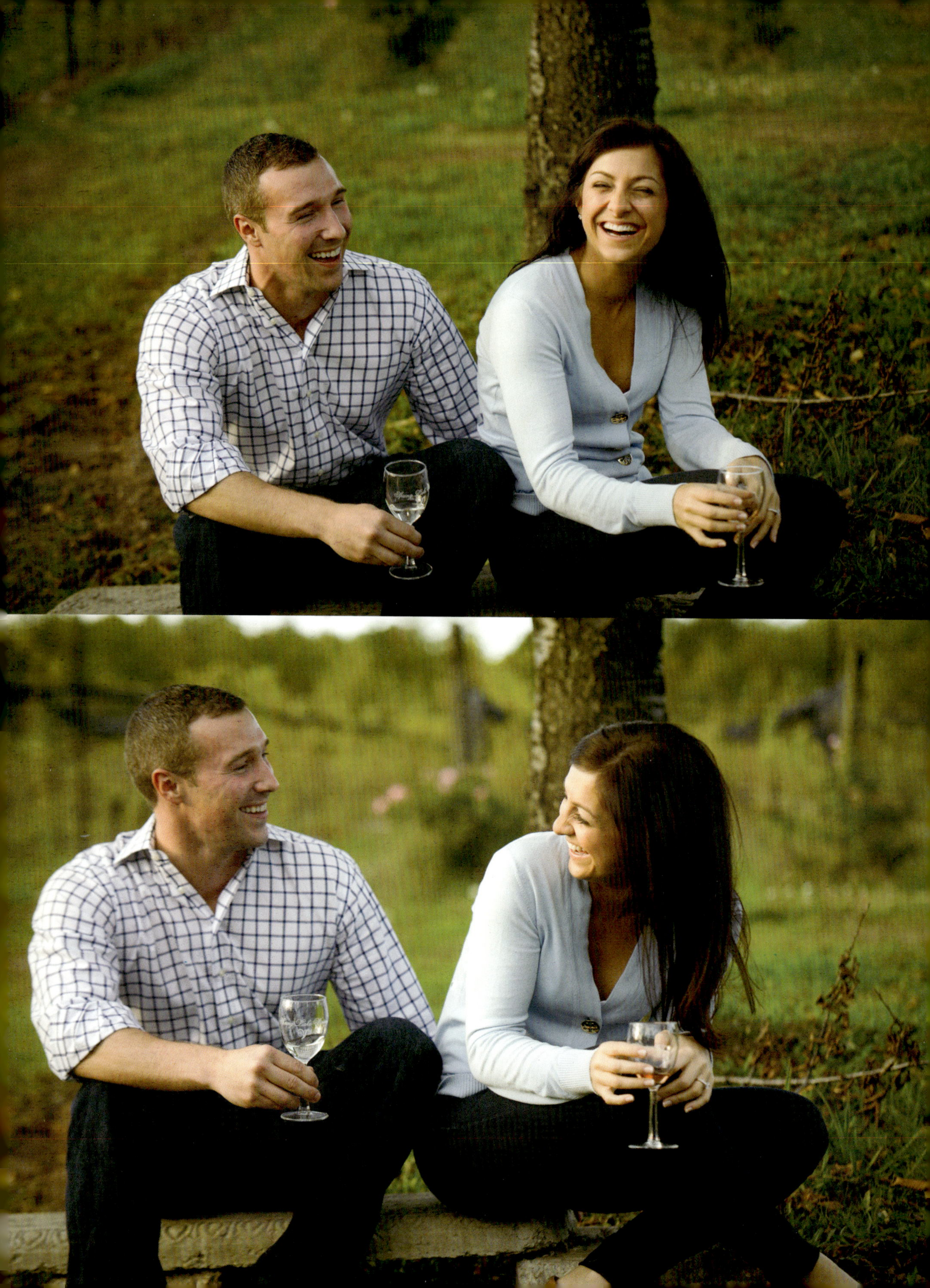

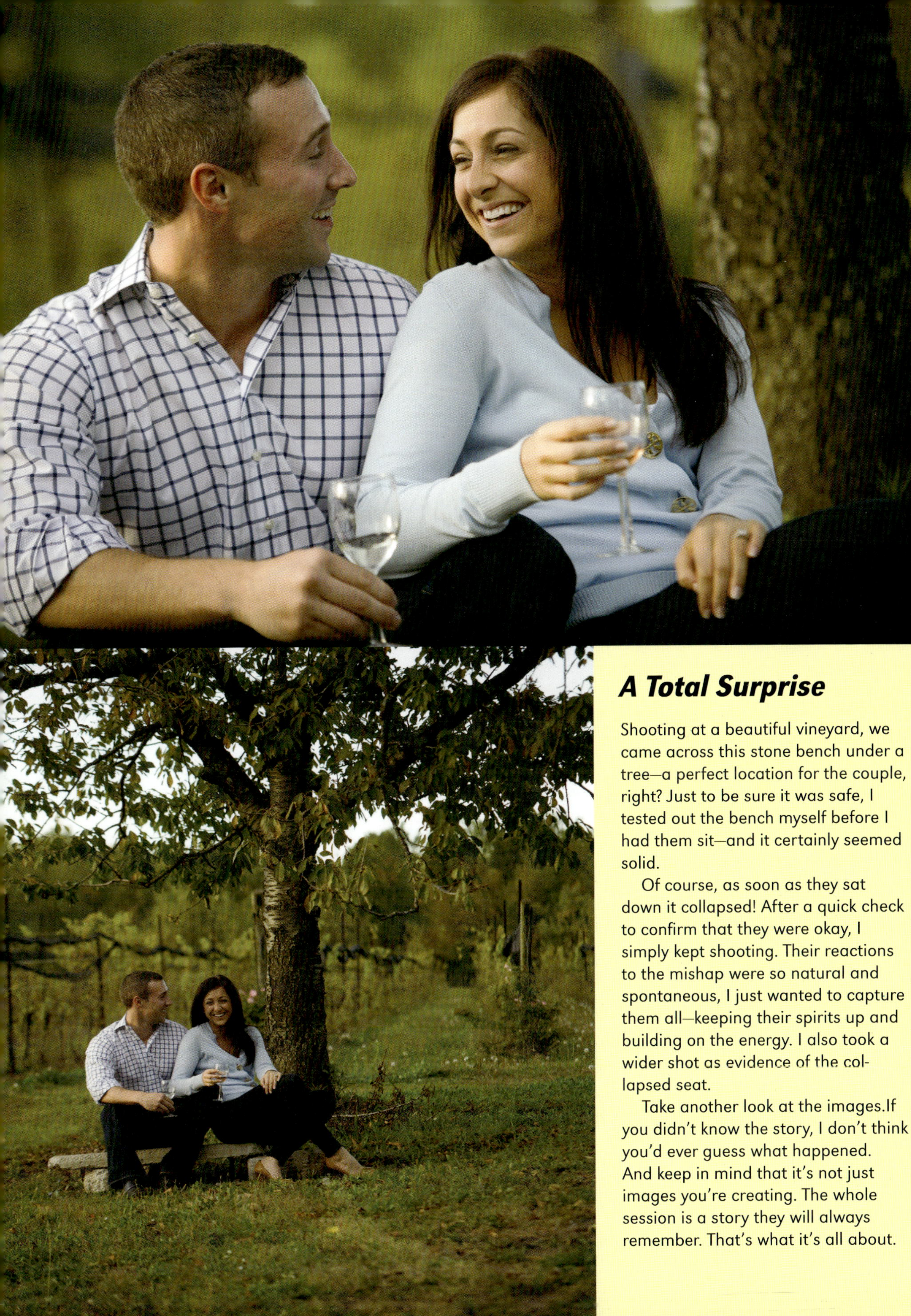

A Total Surprise

Shooting at a beautiful vineyard, we came across this stone bench under a tree—a perfect location for the couple, right? Just to be sure it was safe, I tested out the bench myself before I had them sit—and it certainly seemed solid.

Of course, as soon as they sat down it collapsed! After a quick check to confirm that they were okay, I simply kept shooting. Their reactions to the mishap were so natural and spontaneous, I just wanted to capture them all—keeping their spirits up and building on the energy. I also took a wider shot as evidence of the collapsed seat.

Take another look at the images.If you didn't know the story, I don't think you'd ever guess what happened. And keep in mind that it's not just images you're creating. The whole session is a story they will always remember. That's what it's all about.

33 Late Afternoon Into Golden Hour

In the previous sections of this book, you've probably already gotten the idea that lighting plays a key role in the success of engagement images (as it does in *all* photography, for that matter). While the location selection takes place based on the style we're trying to create, how we'll photograph the couple in that location is largely decided by the existing light—or the logistics of adding light when the existing light is insufficient or unflattering.

When to Shoot

Our favorite time to shoot is in the late afternoon and into Golden Hour. From there, we may continue to shoot into the evening, depending on the location and the couple's preferences.

When planning a Golden Hour shoot, centered on sunset, it's important to start *before* the sun drops. You want to have some shooting time for your subjects to get loosened up. Once the sky is great, all the nerves should be gone and you'll be ready to capture the perfect moment.

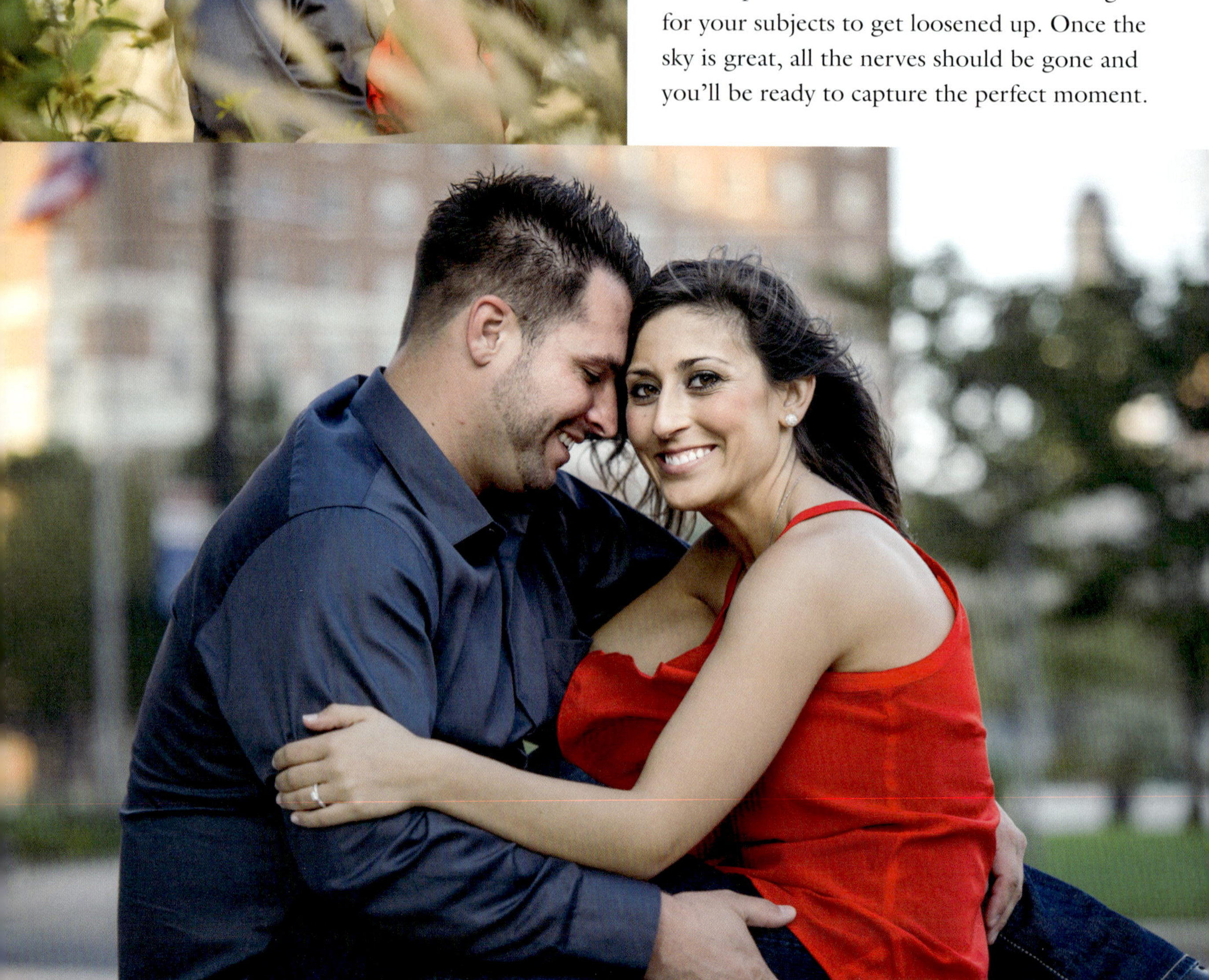

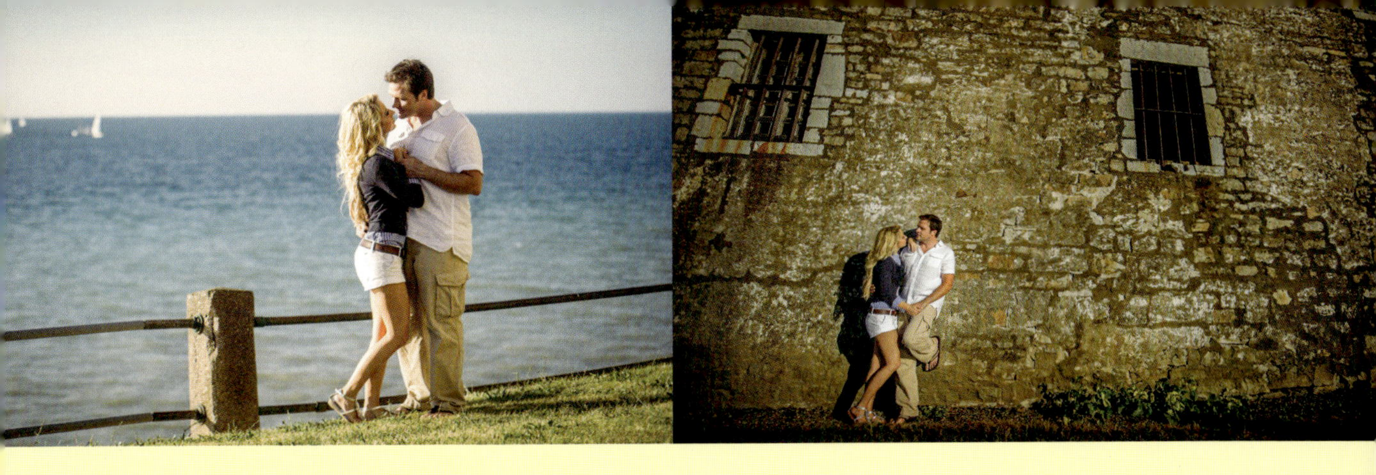

Work the Scene—and the Light

For these summer engagement portraits, we decided to shoot by the water—but of course I also took full advantage of the good lighting I found in other parts of the scene. These two images were taken about ten feet apart. For the first shot, I posed the couple at the fence and I stood near the wall. For the second shot, we simply reversed the camera/subject positions. This gave us two totally different looks—backlighting by the water and angled front lighting by the stone wall.

Downtown

This couple loved the downtown area, so that's where we decided to go for their session. We started with few late-afternoon shots (*facing page*). These let the couple loosen up and get used to being photographed. When sunset rolled around (*below*), we were ready to make the most of that beautiful, golden light.

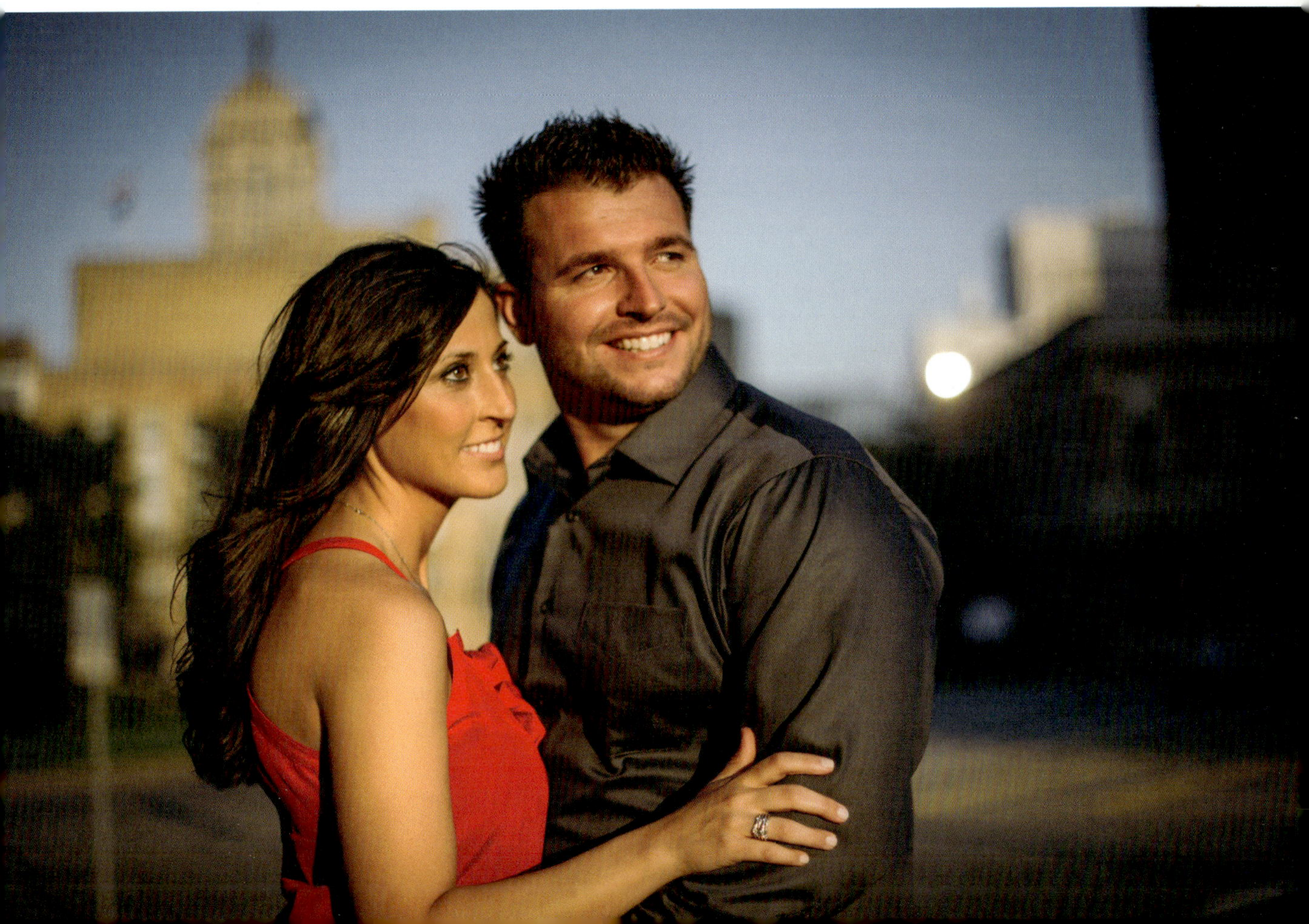

34 Sunset Lighting

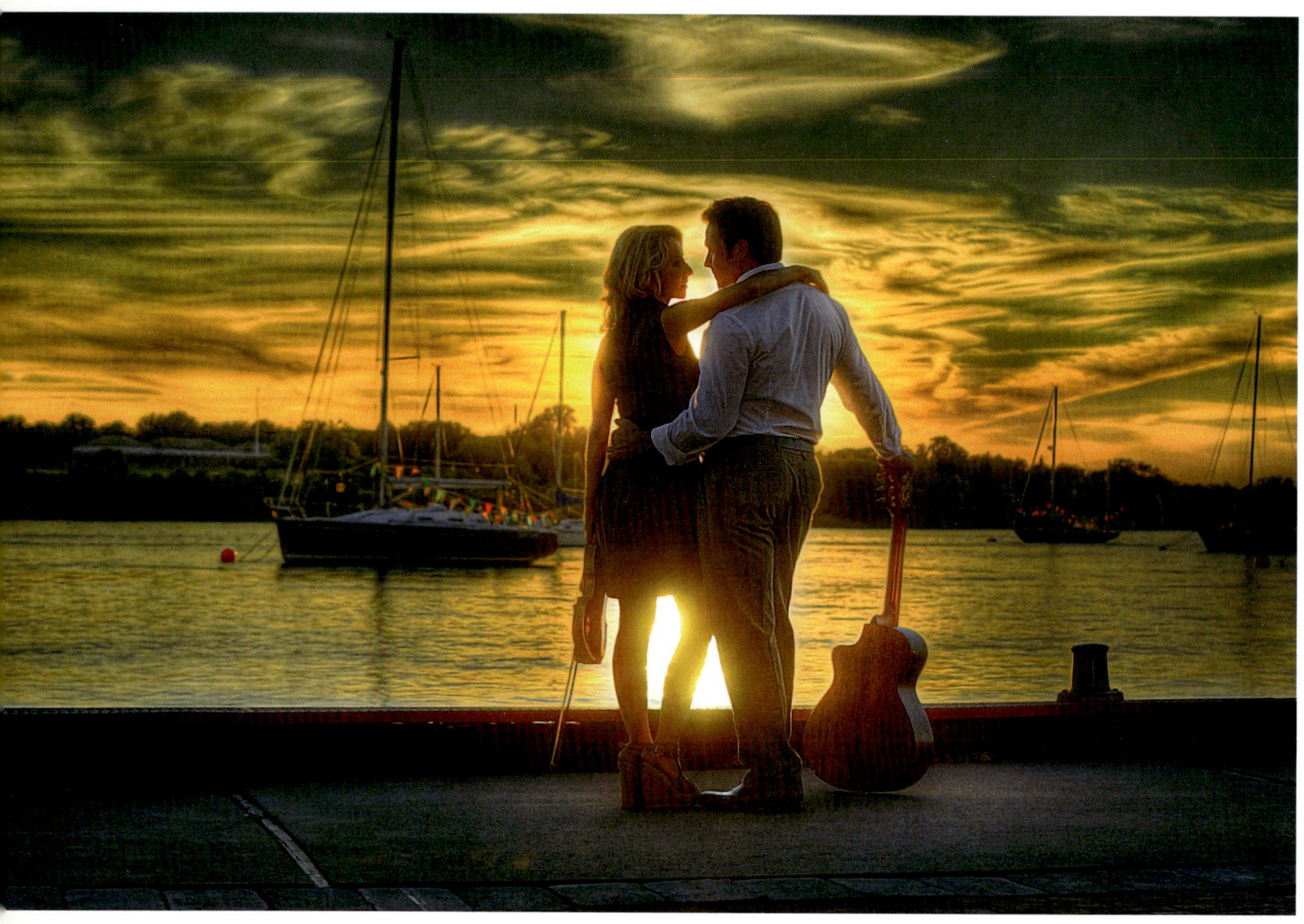

Personalize It

The subjects in the image above are both musicians, so they brought their instruments to the session to make the images more special. When photographing them, I metered for the sky then brought up the exposure on them just a bit to give me some detail. I also shot from a lower angle to put more of their bodies against the sky.

Sun Angle

A different light angle yields a different look (*facing page, top*). Here, the sun was not directly behind the couple but a little bit to their left. This added nice separation between his dark suit and the background. I shot from a lower angle and used Photomatix to bring out the clouds.

A Found Moment

I saw this opening in the trees (*facing page, bottom*) and had him pick her up while she kicked her legs. I also tried a pose where they looked at each other and kissed, but her hair fell forward and obscured his face. This pose provided much better definition between the two subjects.

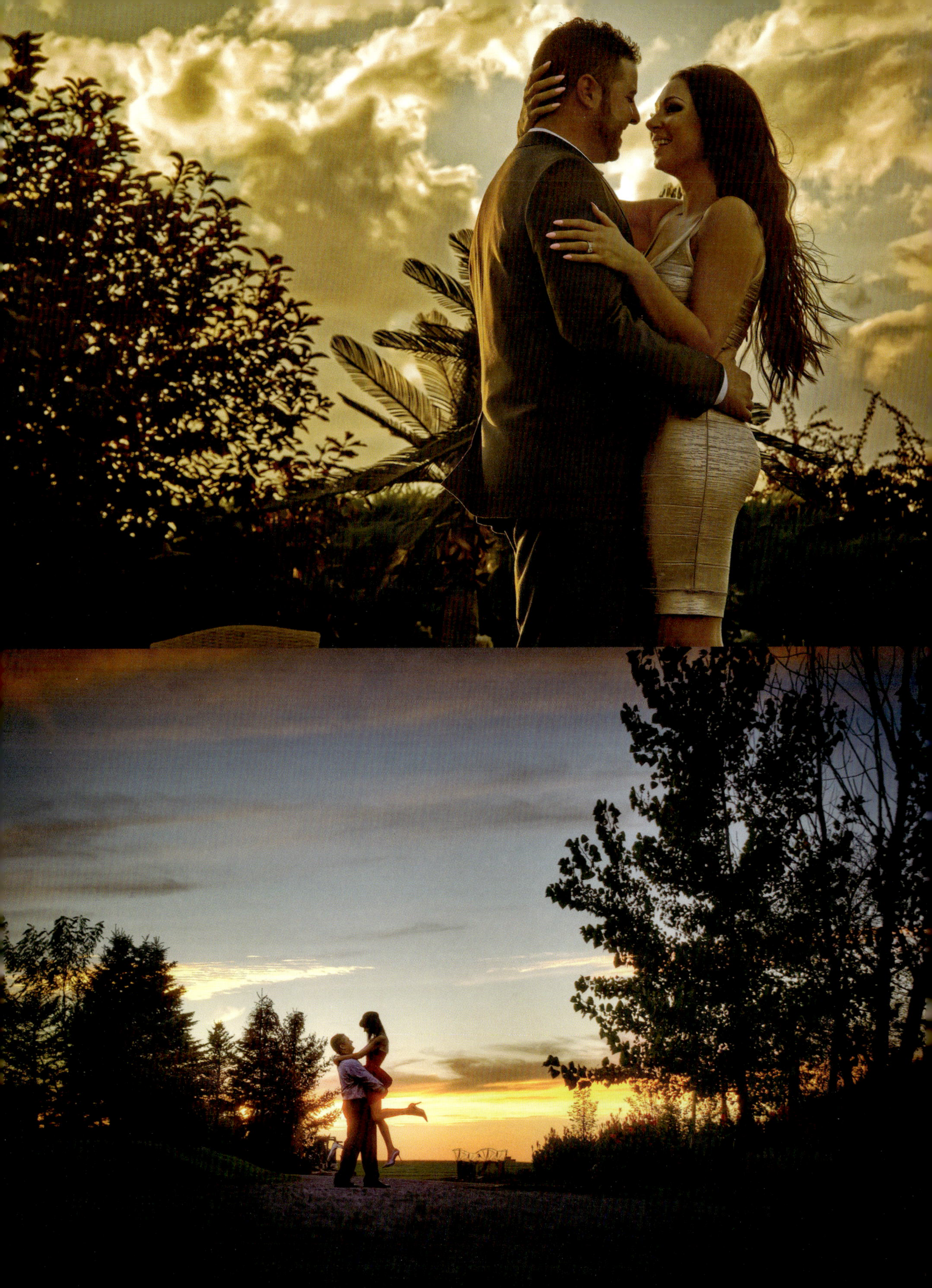

Portraits at Night

Clothes Selection

We ask couples to prepare two looks for their session. First, we want a dressier look—a date night look. Second, we want a dress-down outfit, something casual. We advise them to avoid wearing whites/blacks and to skip anything with a visible logo.

We usually like to have couples start in their dressier outfit, then change into their casual attire later in the session. That's especially true if a car is the only changing area we'll have access to.

We like to have couples start in their dressier outfit, then change into their casual attire later in the session.

When I have a specific look in mind, I try to gear their clothing selection to what I've envisioned—but I also want them to be honest to themselves and not feel like they're in costume.

Central Park at Night

The couple below was photographed using the ambient light only—the light from the street lamp seen to the right of the frame. With a longer exposure and a bit of dodging and burning, I was able to capture the tones I wanted. (A bigger obstacle to success was the rats running all over as we shot—definitely *not* adding to the romance!)

Twilight Grove

At the top of the facing page, we return to the couple and scene in section 30. Here, I rotated

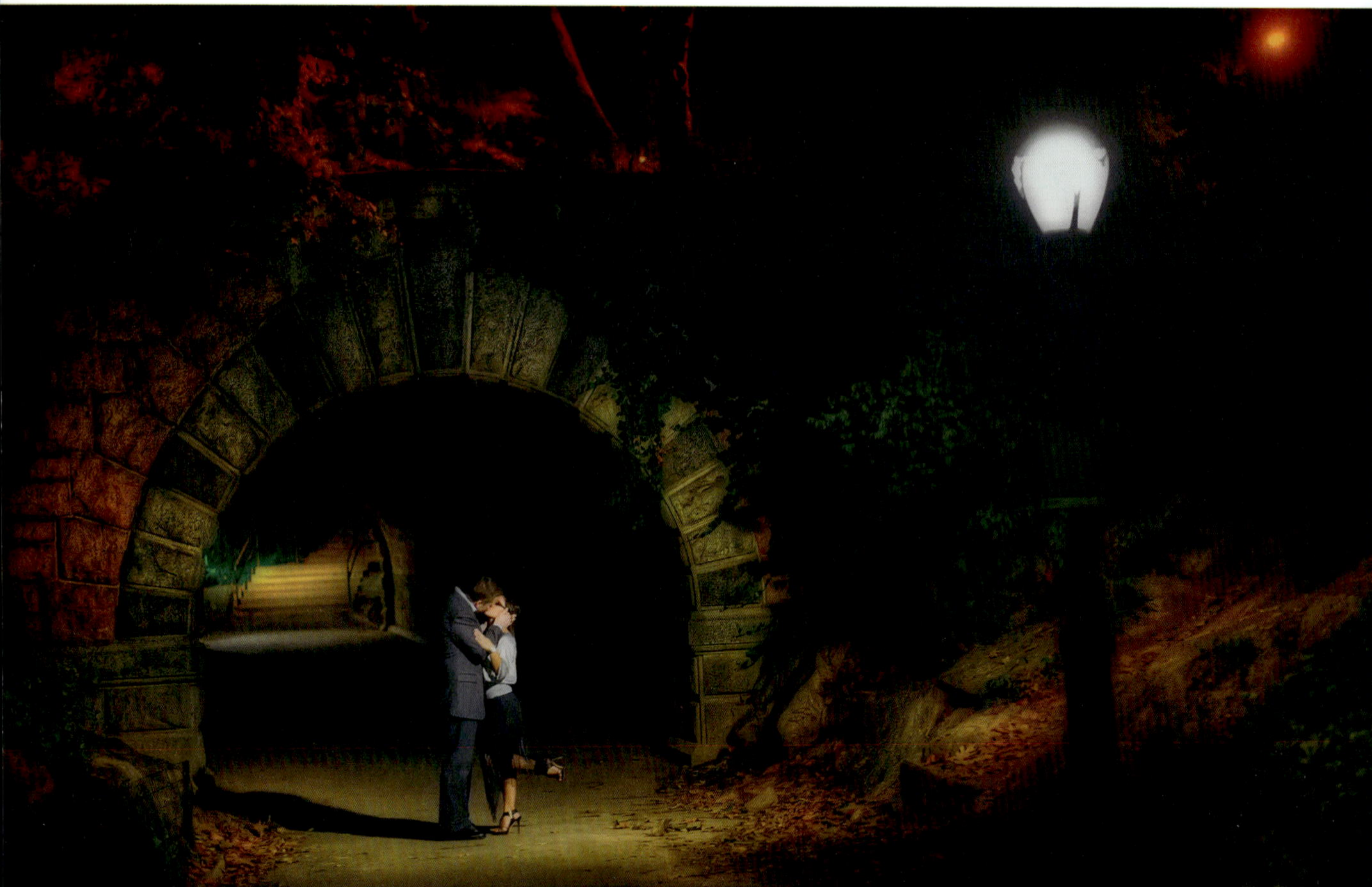

them to capture the blue twilight sky as a background for the orange glow from a string of tungsten lights overhead. The couple was lit with an Ice Light and an SB900 was placed about 50 feet behind them to light up the trees. In post-production, I dodged the string of lights.

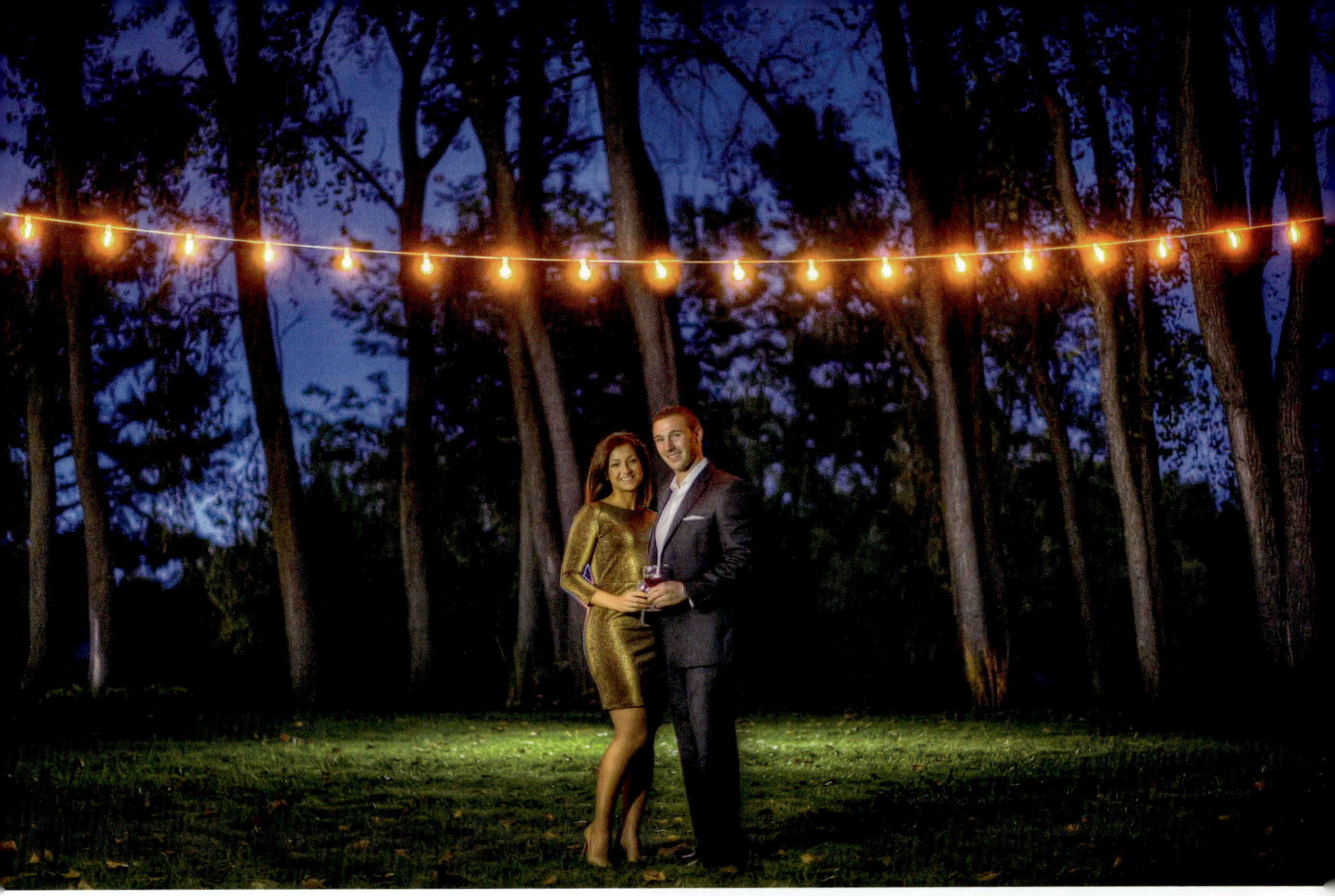

Theater Marquee

We'd already shot a lot of colorful shots inside the theater (see sections 9 and 37 for examples), so this black & white image (*right*) added nice contrast and helped capture the pure emotion of the moment. It also fits the period of the vintage sign in the background. Working on the street outsidc thc theater, I positioned the couple and camera to get the marquee in my frame—along with nice reflections of both the sign and the couple. A Lowel light to camera right illuminated the couple and brought up their reflection.

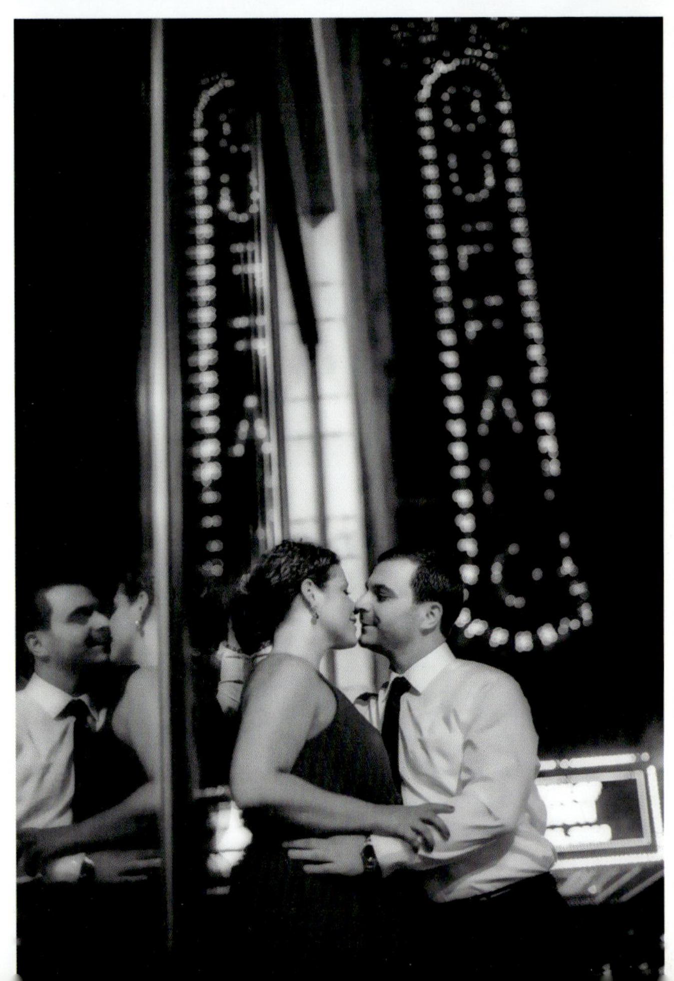

36 Using the Changing Light

For this engagement session, we traveled to a state park about ninety minutes away. This is the kind of shoot you simply can't do on a wedding day—but it was a location that was especially meaningful to the couple, a park where they liked to go on dates and where he proposed. In these three images, you can also see how we work with changing available light throughout the course of a single session.

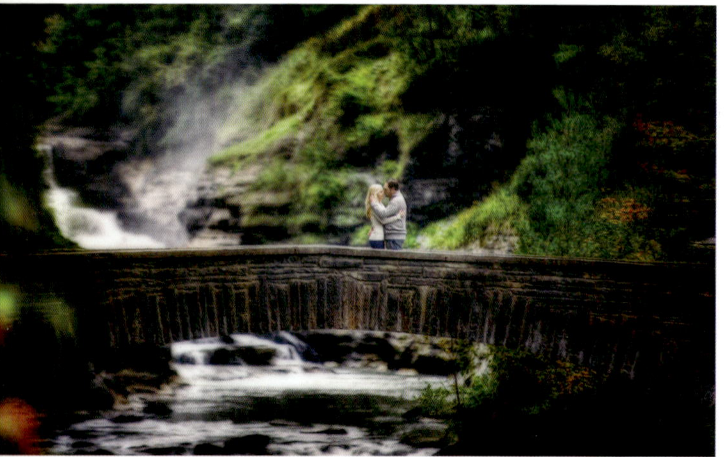

Just Before Sunset

The first image (*left*) was shot just before sunset. We trekked our gear to the bottom of the gorge and set up with a 200mm lens on a path alongside the river, shooting back toward the couple with a waterfall just visible behind them.

Starting before sunset gives us a little wiggle room if anyone is running late. It also lets us get clicking (and get the couple comfortable) before the light is perfect. The best sunset light may only last fifteen minutes, so we want to be ready to take full advantage of it.

In postproduction, I used a tilt-shift effect to soften the background, making it look even more magical. I masked out the couple to keep them sharp.

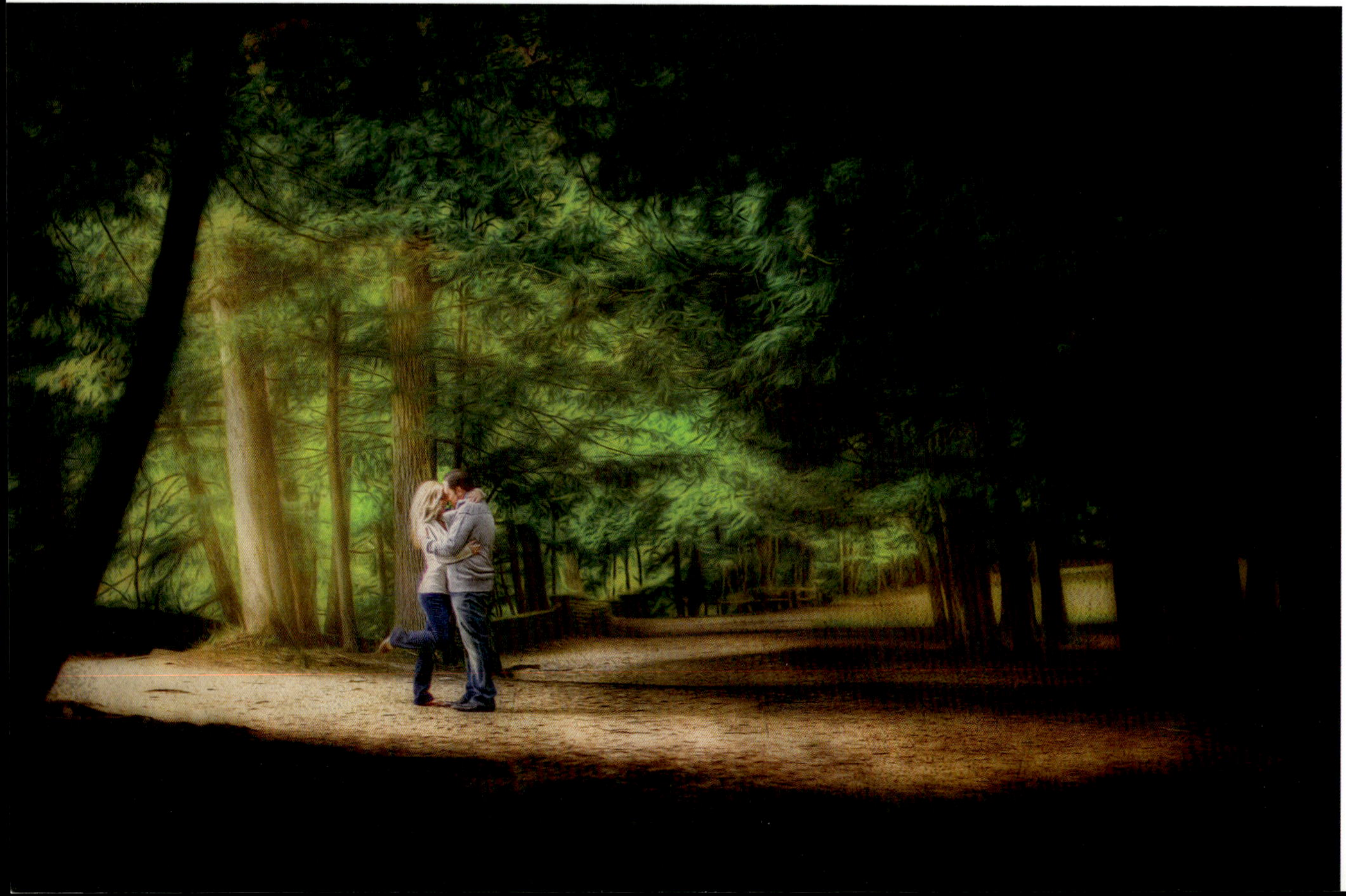

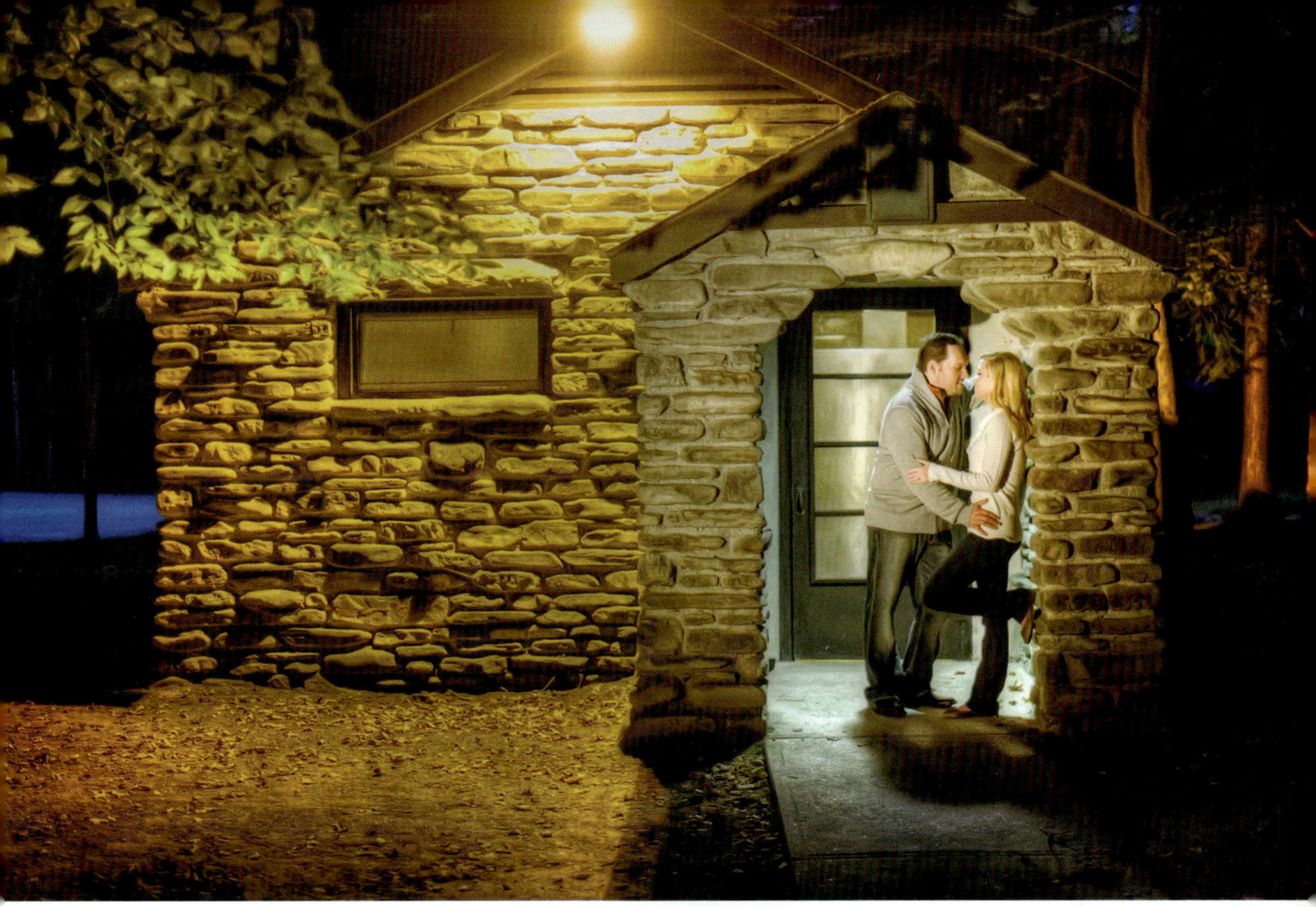

Sunset

As we continued exploring the park around sunset, we found a beam of light shining through the dense forest. This created nice directional light on the couple and a natural vignette around them (*bottom image, facing page*).

Evening

Walking back to our cars, we came across a beautiful stone building (*above*)—and a complex mixed lighting situation. Atop the building, illuminating it and the yard, was a tungsten light fixture. In the portico behind the couple, there was a fluorescent light. To the far left of the frame, the background was lit by the fading evening light. To ensure the right tonality on the subjects, my wife and assistant Danielle positioned a tungsten Lowel light to camera left.

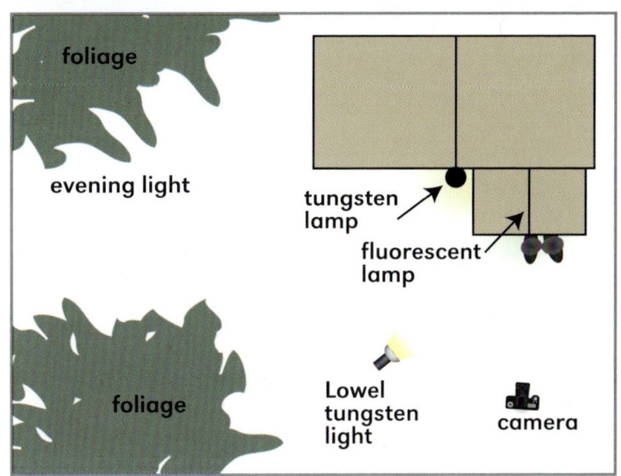

I shot with a tungsten white balance to keep the couple's skin tones neutral, but this setting had a secondary effect: it made the blue tones in the background really pop. I liked the look, so I enhanced it using Photomatix in postproduction. The result is a great mix of gold, blue, and green.

37 Ice Light Portraits

Shooting with the LED Ice Light is convenient and produces beautiful results. Just turn it on, dim it down a bit, and watch the effect on your subject as you move the light into the right position. That's it—you're ready to take your shot. With LED lighting, what you see is what you get. The Ice Light basically gives you a portable window in your lighting kit. What could be more simple or flattering?

A Private Moment

To give my couple (*below*) a bit of a private moment together, I had them step off the street. Danielle stood in the alley with the Ice Light. It was just about night, and the store lighting was starting to come on, so I wanted to balance them against it—and this was a spot where I could hide Danielle pretty well. I also liked that the solid color of the wall behind them helped visually separate the couple from the rest of the more complex street scene.

At the Theater and Onto the Street

The Ice Light also works beautifully indoors—as you can see in the images on the facing page, shot in an ornate old theater. For the top image, Danielle was at camera right with the Ice Light. She was quite close to the subjects, so the light has a softer look. It also gave us good falloff around them for an almost spotlighted look with a natural vignette. Notice, too, the contrast between the warm tungsten room lights and the natural skin tones from the daylight-balanced Ice Light.

For a second shot in the theater, we pulled a bench out into the hallway and designed a pose that suited the venue. Danielle held the Ice Light to camera right, but back a little bit. I posed the couple between two of the overhead lights—but they were so dim in comparison to the Ice Light that I didn't really have to worry about shadows or color problems from them.

After a quick clothing change, we moved outside the theater to an elevated train platform

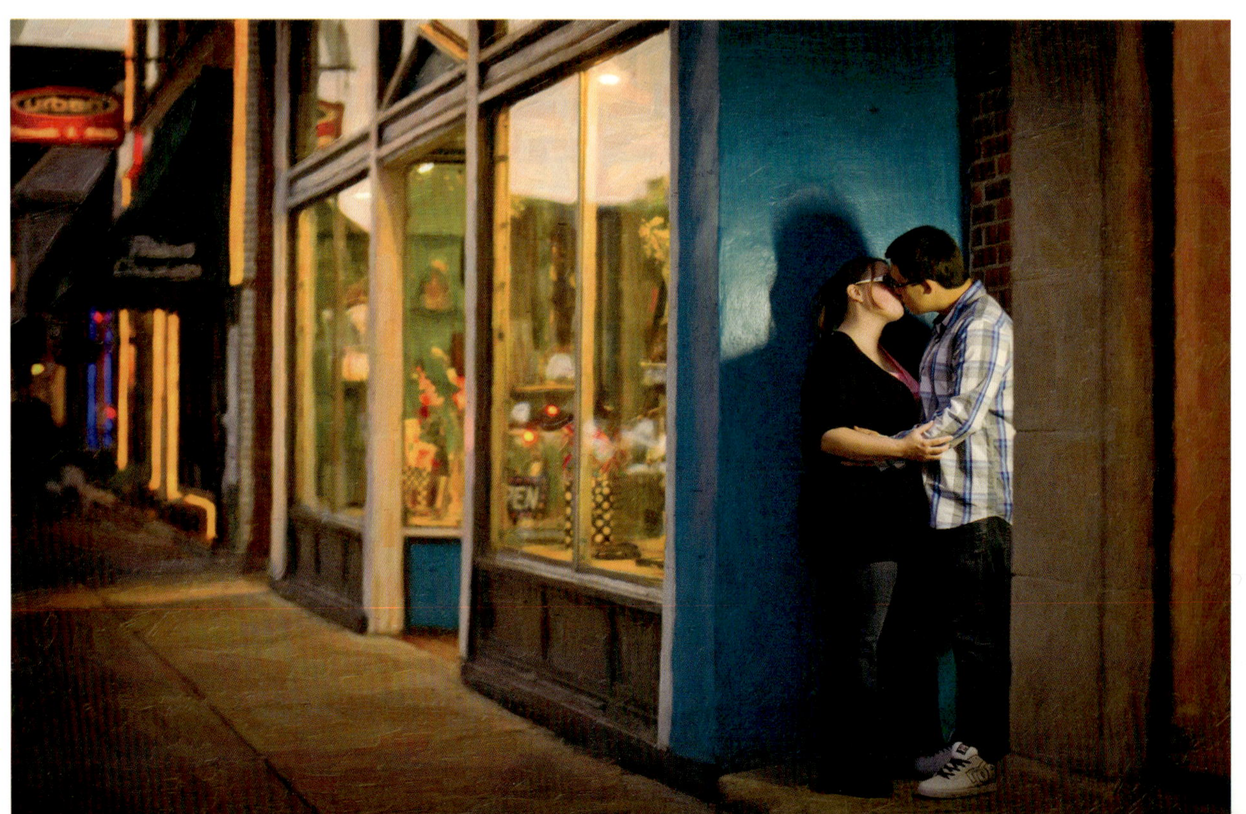

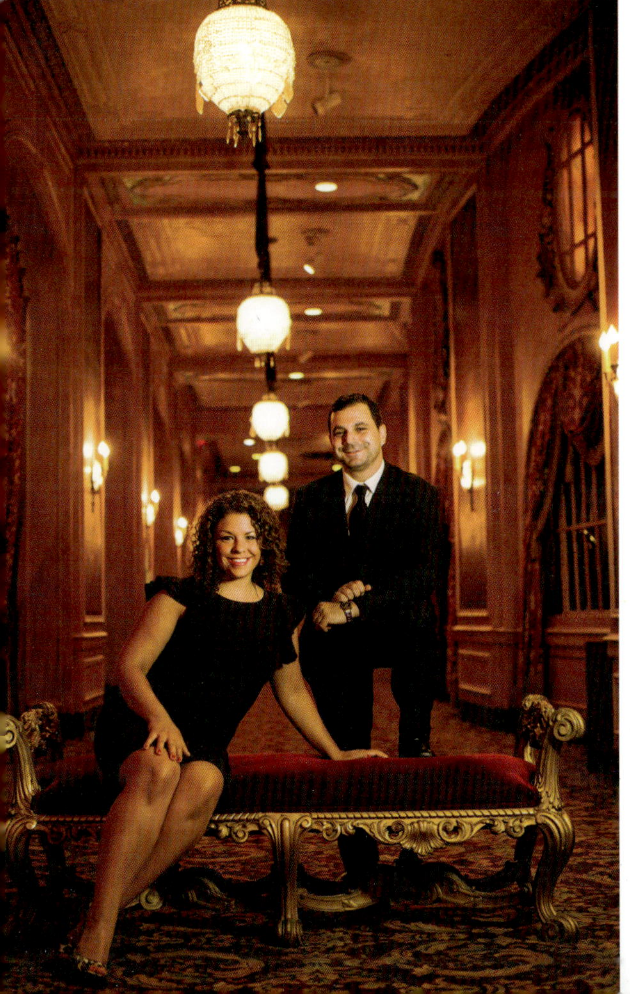

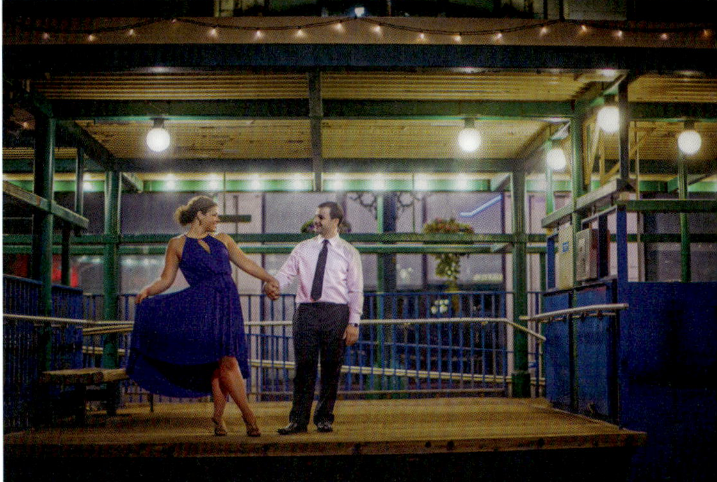

(*above*). Danielle backed up with Ice Light to let it illuminate the whole scene. I shot with a fluorescent white balance to match the lights on the platform. I positioned myself at a low angle (track level) and I asked her to pick up her dress in order to add some movement to the pose.

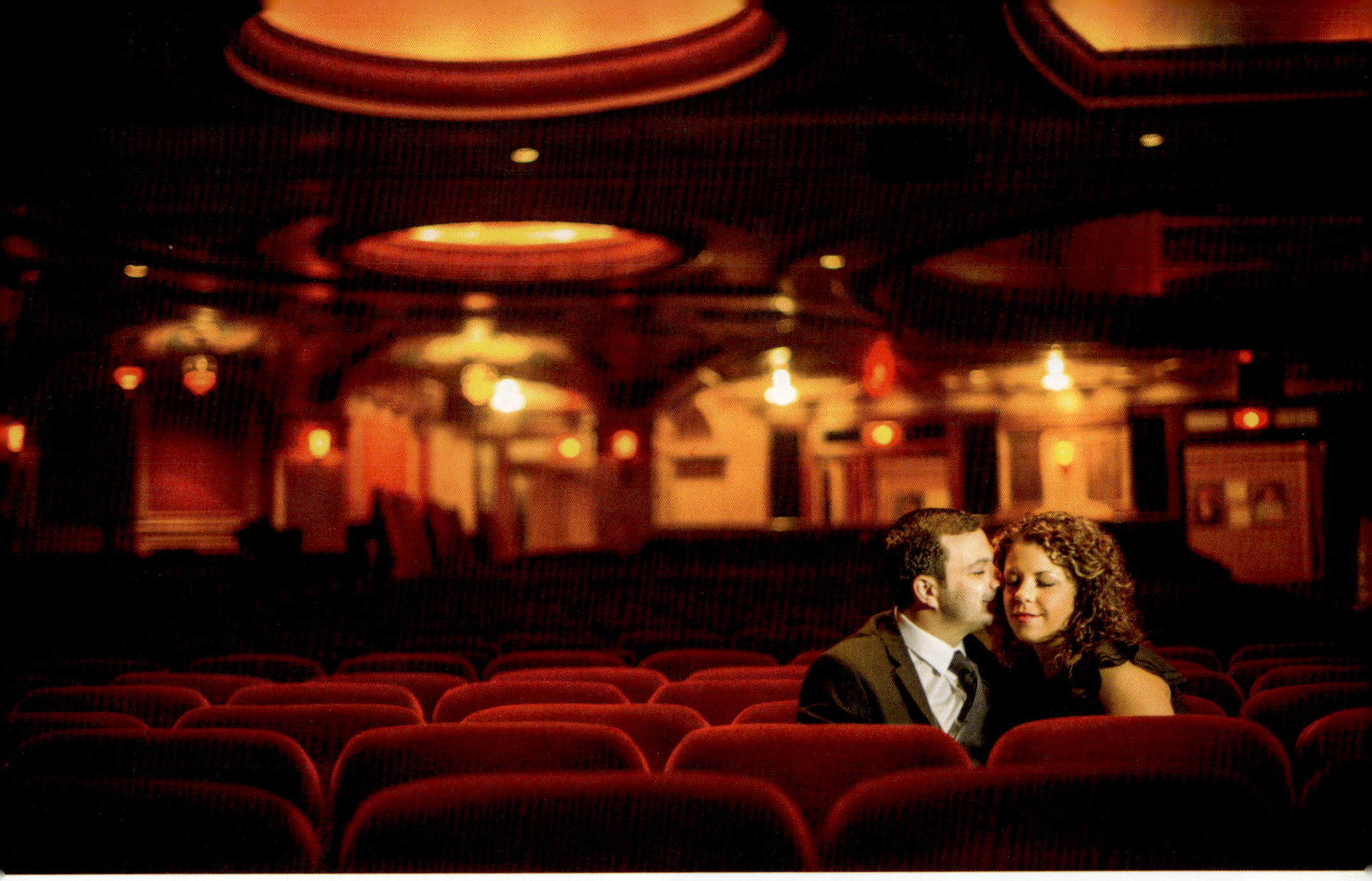

38 Lowel Light Portraits

One of the nice features of the Lowel light is its spotlight setting, which gives you a narrow, intense beam of light that stays constrained over significant distances.

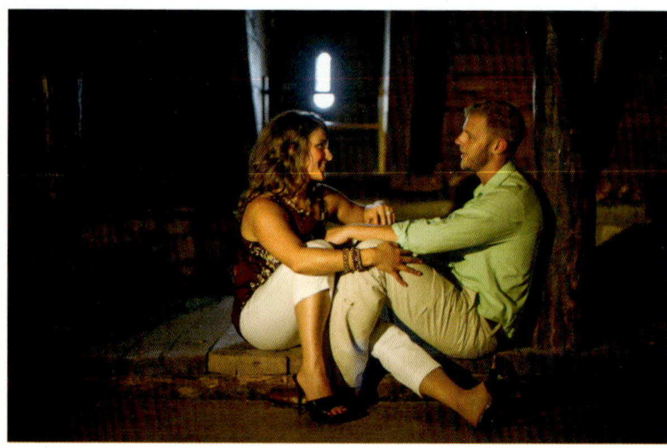

For a scene like the one below, this made it an optimal choice. The small image shows the couple silhouetted in the doorway. To bring them up, as seen in the larger image, we needed to add fill. With the Ice Light or with flash, Danielle would have had to be *in* the shot. Even with a snoot on a flash, it probably wouldn't have worked. The Lowel light was a perfect choice—and its tungsten white balance made it coordinate well with the minimal room lighting for a nice, warm glow against the daylight.

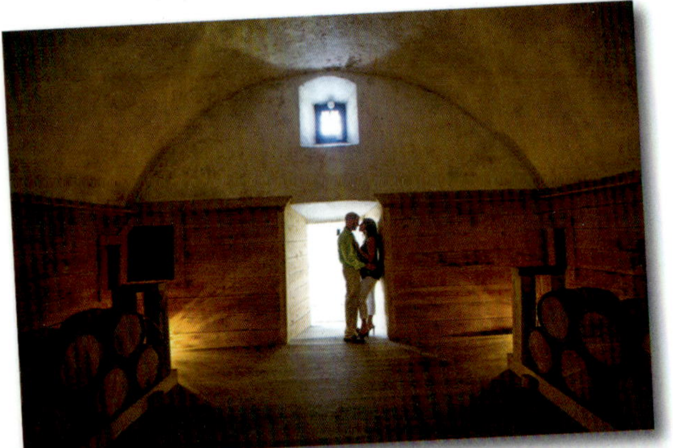

The images above and on the facing page show other applications of the Lowel light with the same couple at other parts of the same old fort.

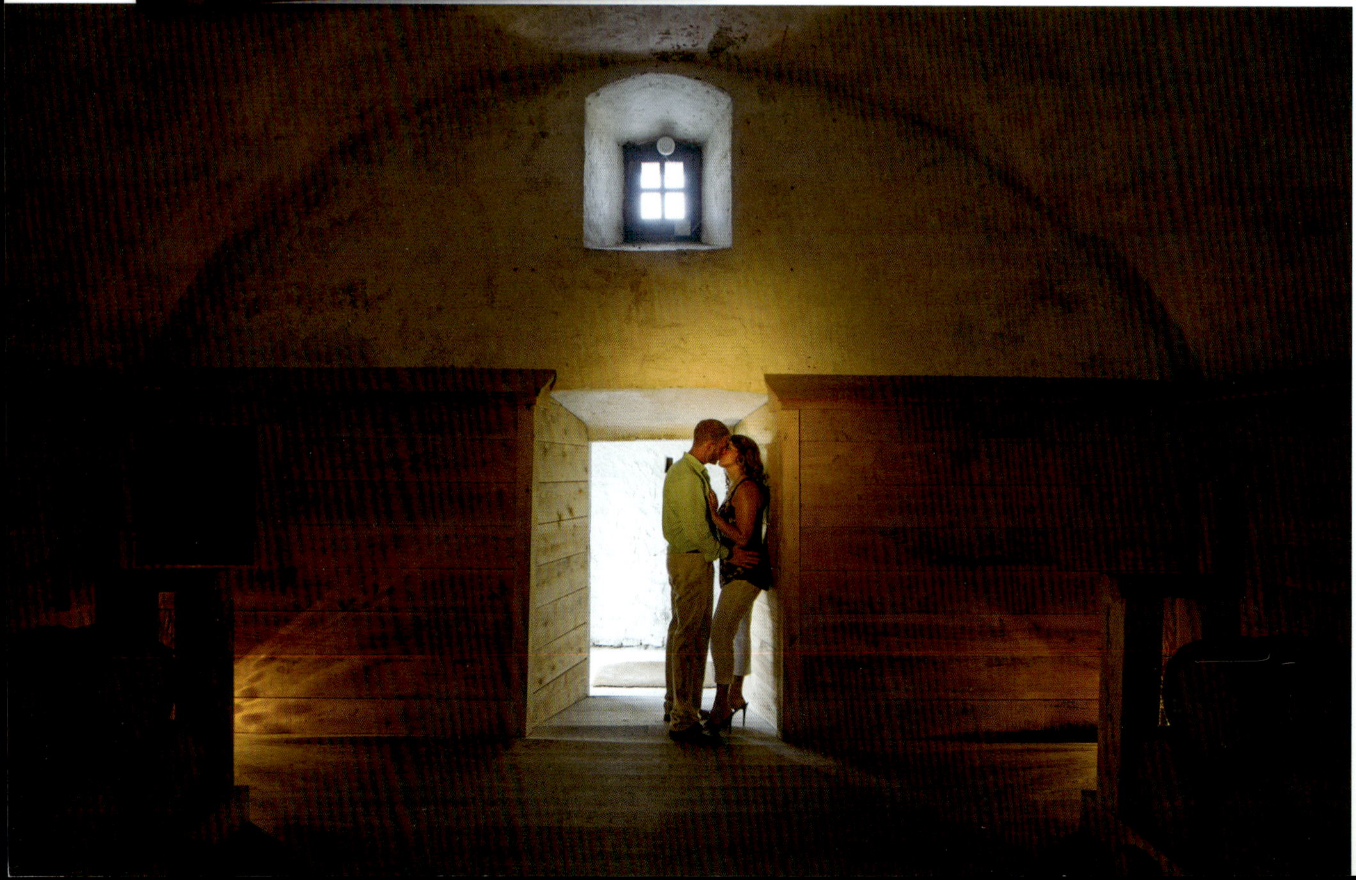

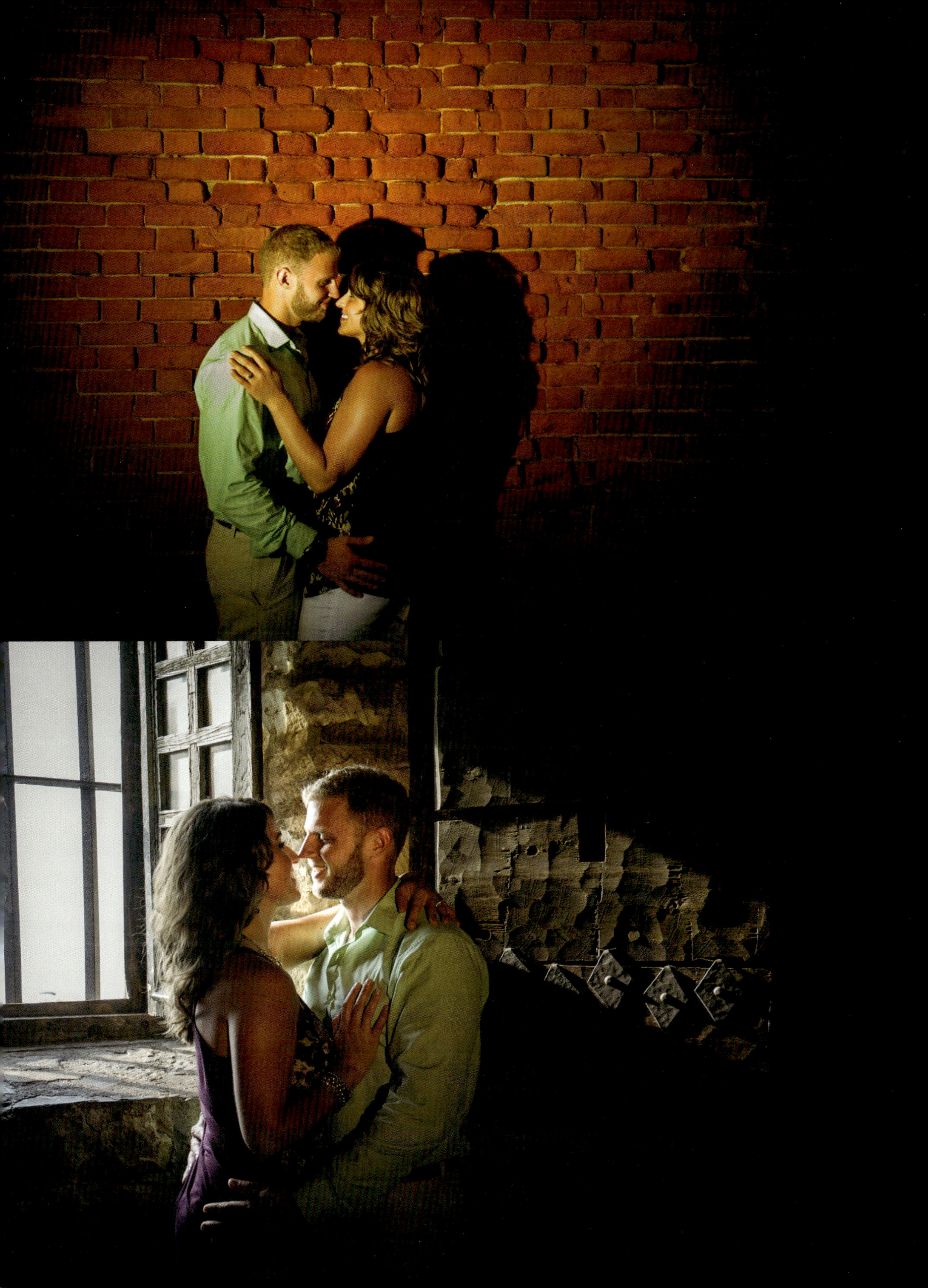

39 Adding One Flash

Keep It Simple

Adding flash to your images can make a huge difference—and it doesn't have to be overly complicated. For the image below, I was working with natural backlighting, so all I needed was some fill from the front to keep the couple in balance. Danielle stood to camera left with an SB900 and cupped her hands around it to create a spotlight effect (we didn't want to wipe out the detail on the grass around the couple). In postproduction, I brought up some of the shadow detail and added texture on the sky. Simple!

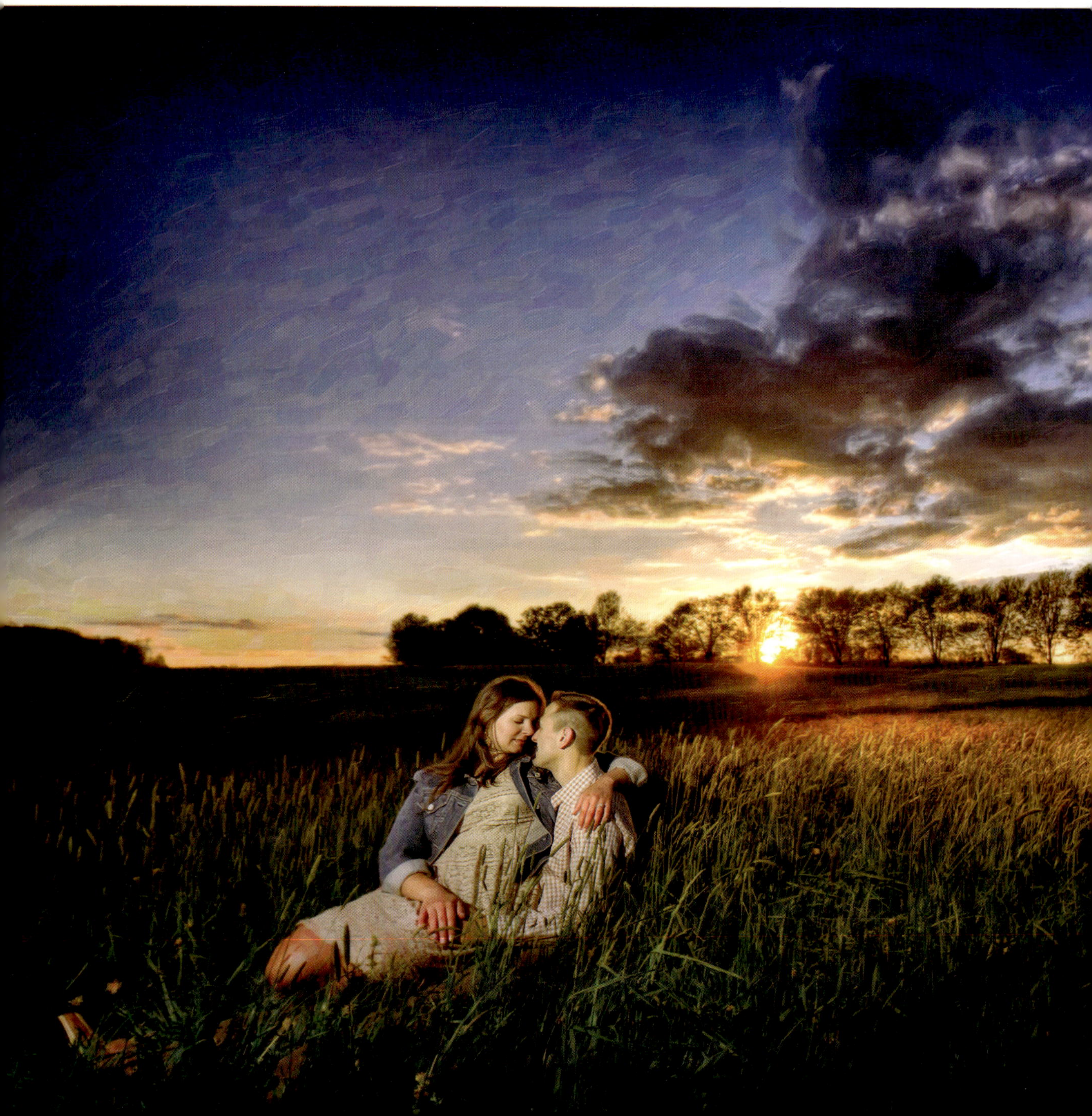

Backlighting—Plus More Backlighting

When photographing the couple against the last light of the setting sun (*right*), I could have opted to create a pure silhouette. Instead, I added a little more backlighting for separation and to create some detail on their faces. To do this, I placed an SB900 at a low power setting on the ground behind them (no light stand to retouch out!). It looks almost like they might be standing at the edge of a pool of light from a street lamp.

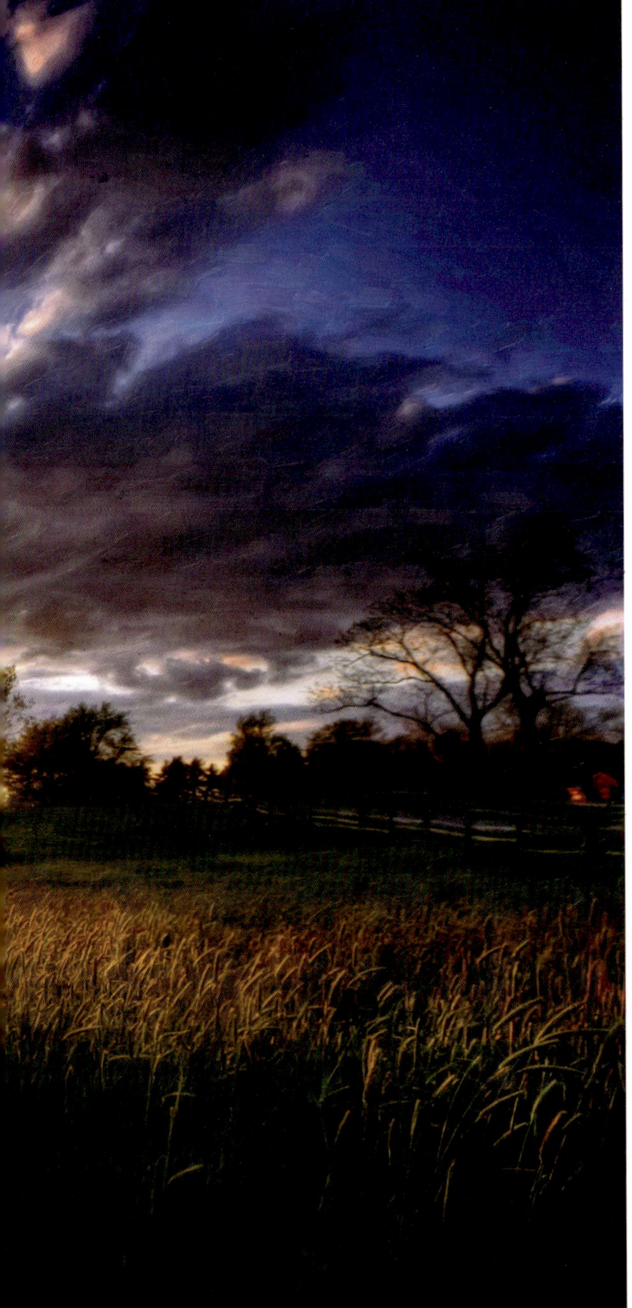

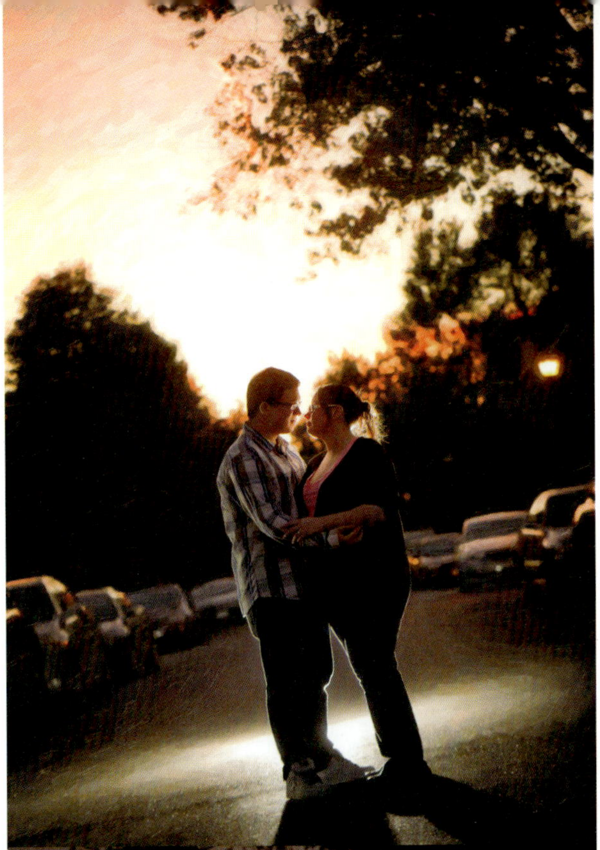

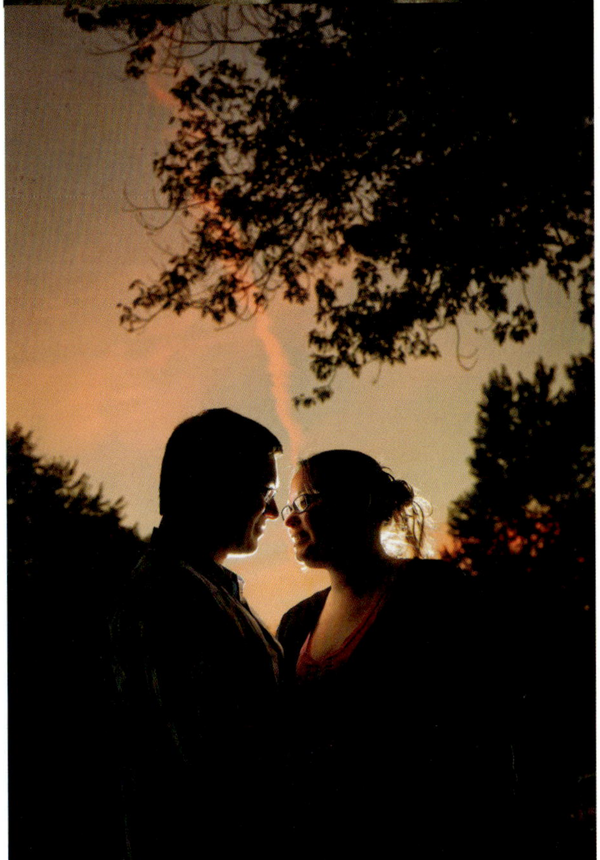

40 Multiple Light Sources

This couple's session took place on a gray, gloomy day. In fact, the weather was so ominous that the bride wondered if we should shoot at all. By adding lighting, we were able to give the couple images they loved—without rescheduling the session.

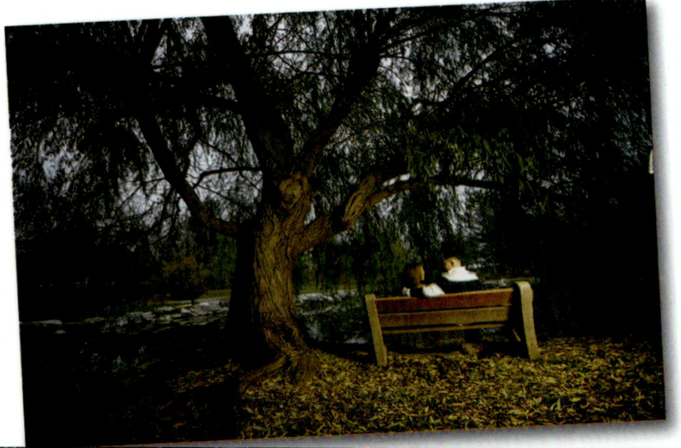

Evening Park Bench

As shown in the smaller photo (*below*), I initially photographed the seated couple with light from an SB900 flash to camera right. There was so little ambient light, though, that the background just didn't look as good as I knew it could. To bring it up, we first tried putting a second flash on the ground in front of them—but this didn't allow us to put the light at the right angle. The solution was to have Danielle get down low in front of them (she was actually lying on the bank of the river) and bounce an SB900 flash up into the tree. This light skimmed up across them and brought all of the beautiful foliage into view. We also left the first SB900 in place (high to camera right) to keep the couple from being rendered in silhouette.

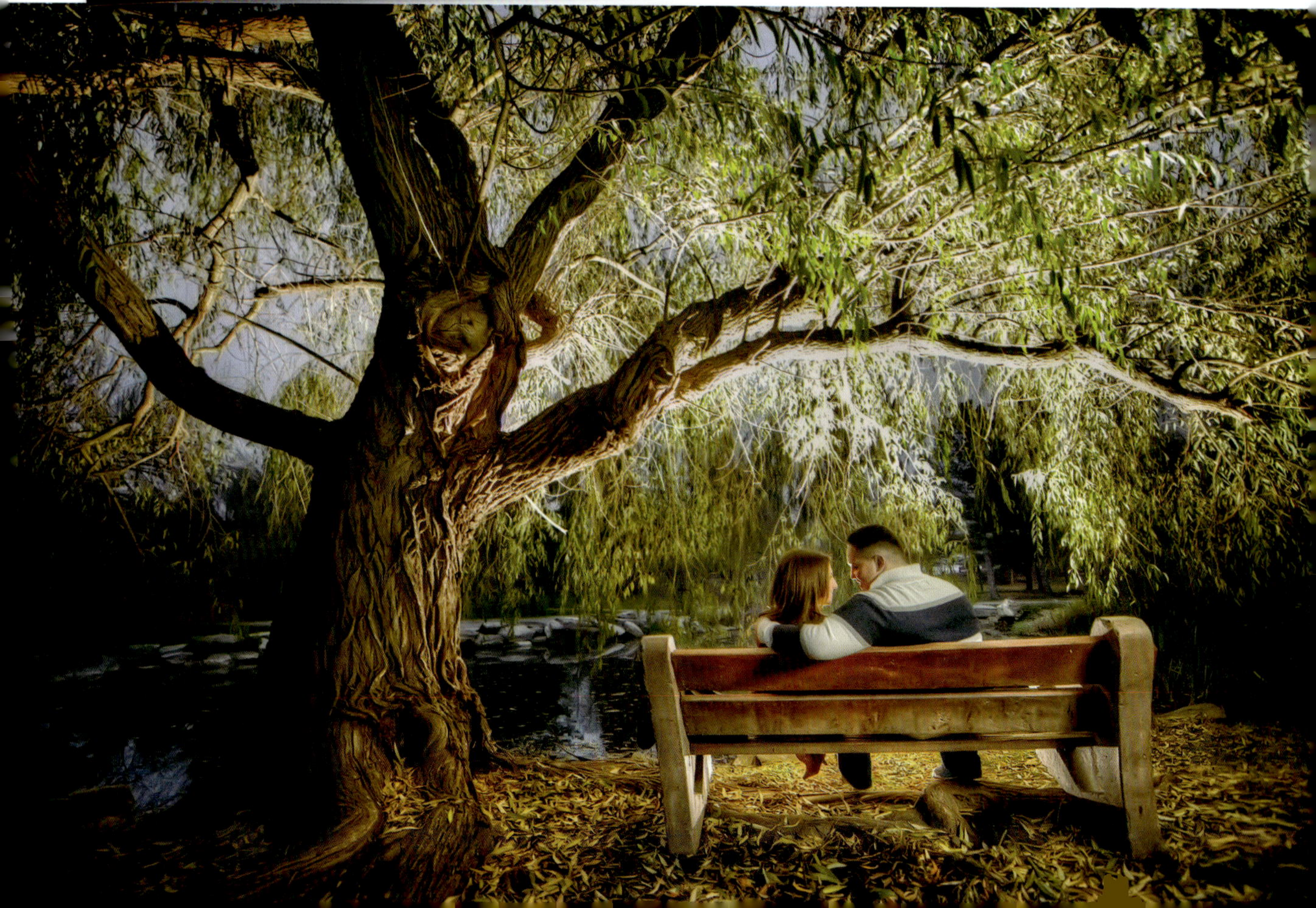

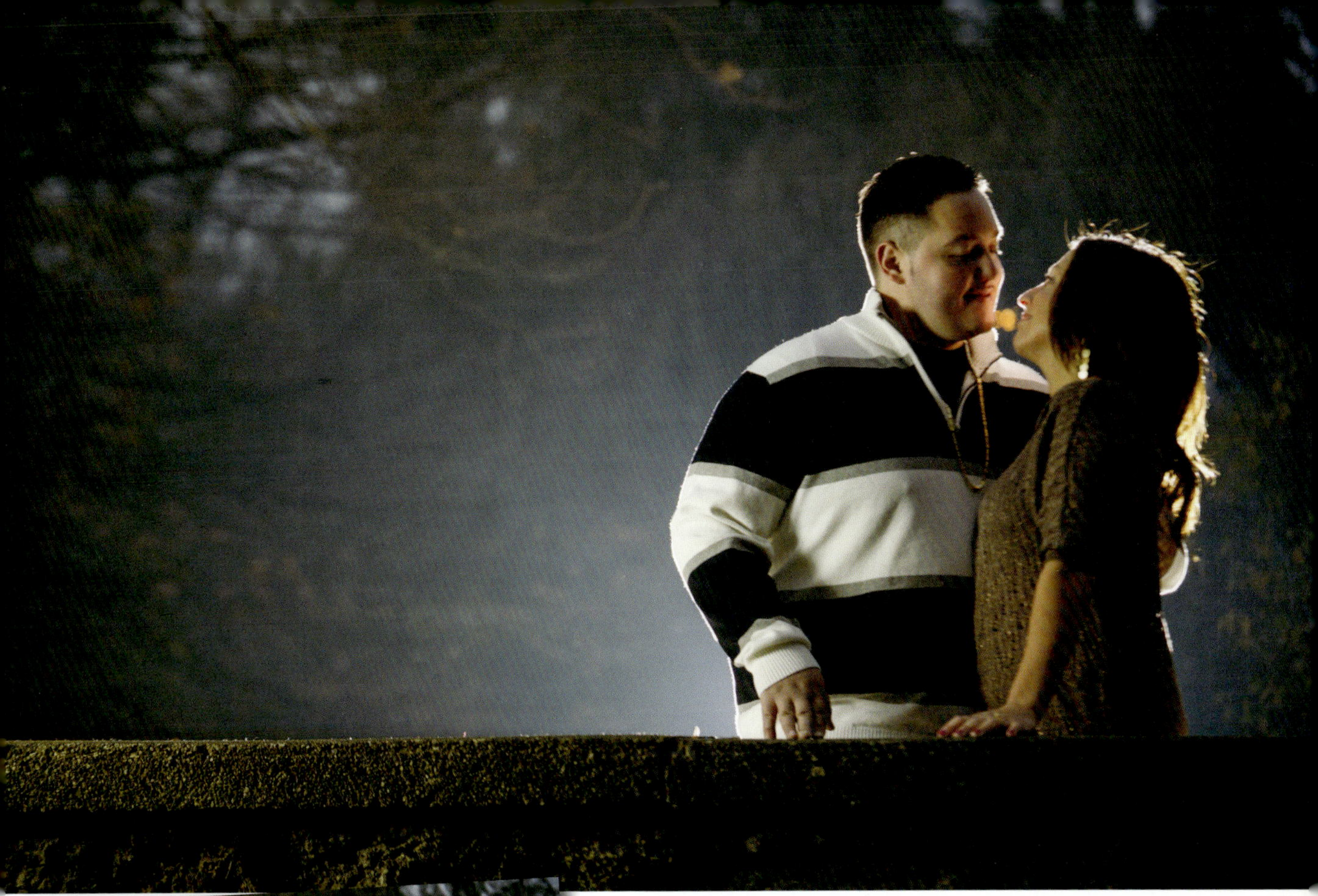

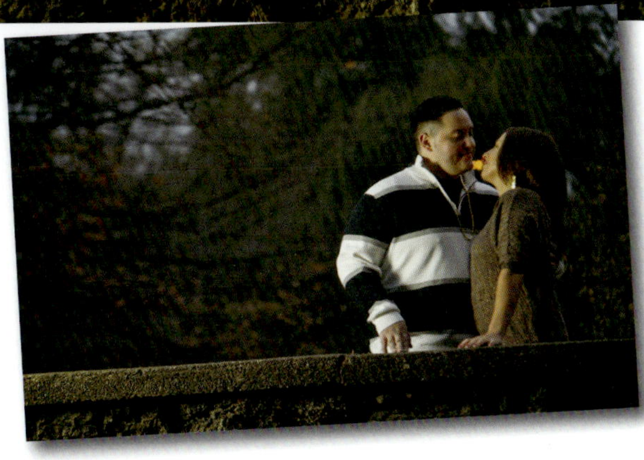

seem more private. An SB900 behind them was filtered through the hazy evening air for some nice backlighting. Danielle held the Ice Light to camera right for light on the front of the subjects.

The image above shows another similar scene where I used the SB900 for backlighting. Compare this to the inset image (*left*), where the backlight was not fired. It makes a huge difference.

Two More Locations

This location (Glen Falls Park in Williamsville, NY) offers a variety of nice backgrounds, so we continued our session there to take advantage of them. One of the spots I liked was a nice stone wall next to a pond (*right*). I photographed the couple from across the pond to put some tall grasses in the foreground and make the moment

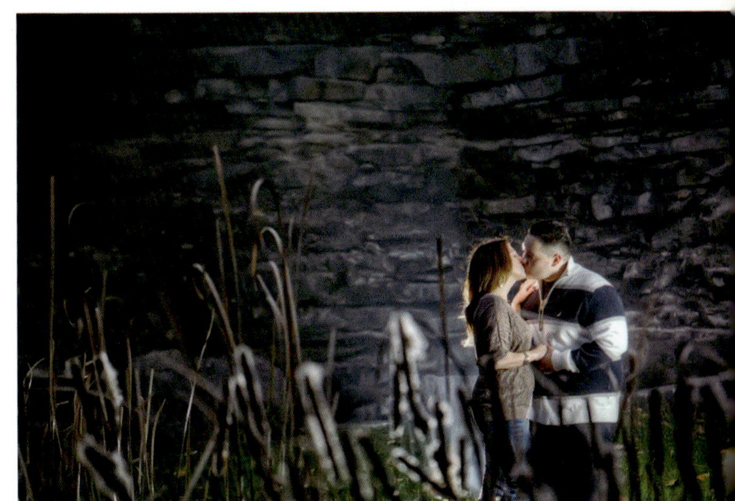

41 Lighting the Scene

Finding Light in the Scene

It's great when you come across a background that is already well lit—like New York City's iconic Radio City Music Hall (*below*). To make full use of this beautifully lit building, we shot from a few angles and took advantage of the reflections in a pool (*bottom right*) to catch even more of the light. We also changed up the lighting on the couple, working with an SB900 flash in front of them and then behind them for rim lighting.

Adding Light to the Scene

Often, you'll encounter scenes that can be brought to life with the addition of lighting. That was the case with the images on the facing page.

The Albright Knox Art Gallery (*top*) is a popular wedding photography location, so we tend to skip it for weddings and go for evening engagement shots instead, giving our couples a different look. All the light in this portico came from two SB900 flashes placed behind the pillars. I placed the couple facing the sunset, then shot up toward them from a lower angle with a wide-angle lens.

The couple under the stone arch (*bottom*) was lit from behind with an SB900 on the ground. This added rim lighting on the couple to separate them from the scene, but it also lit up the whole tunnel. We shot this image as the sun was going down; without the flash, the stone arch would have been quite dark with very little detail.

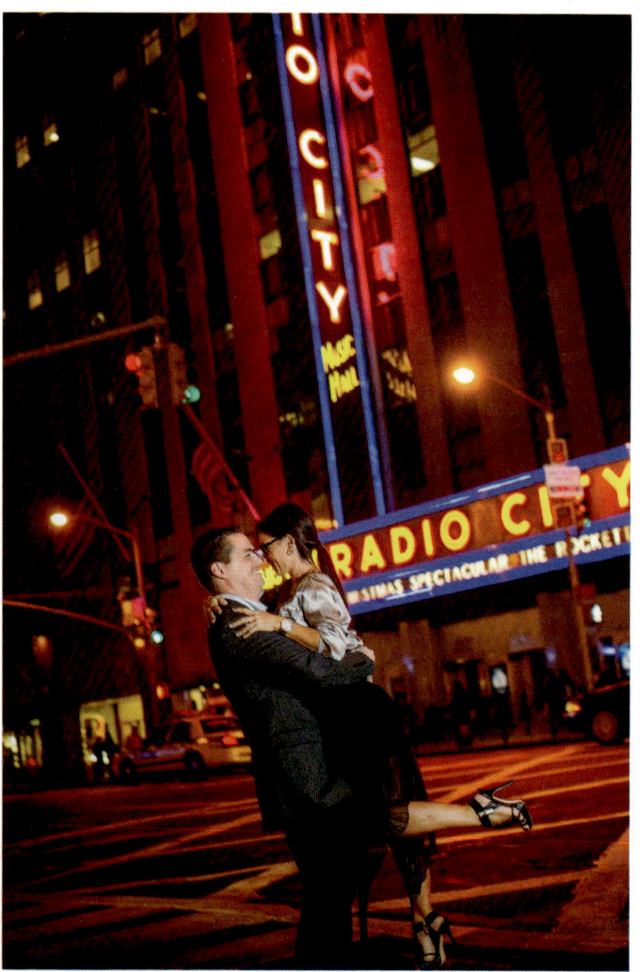

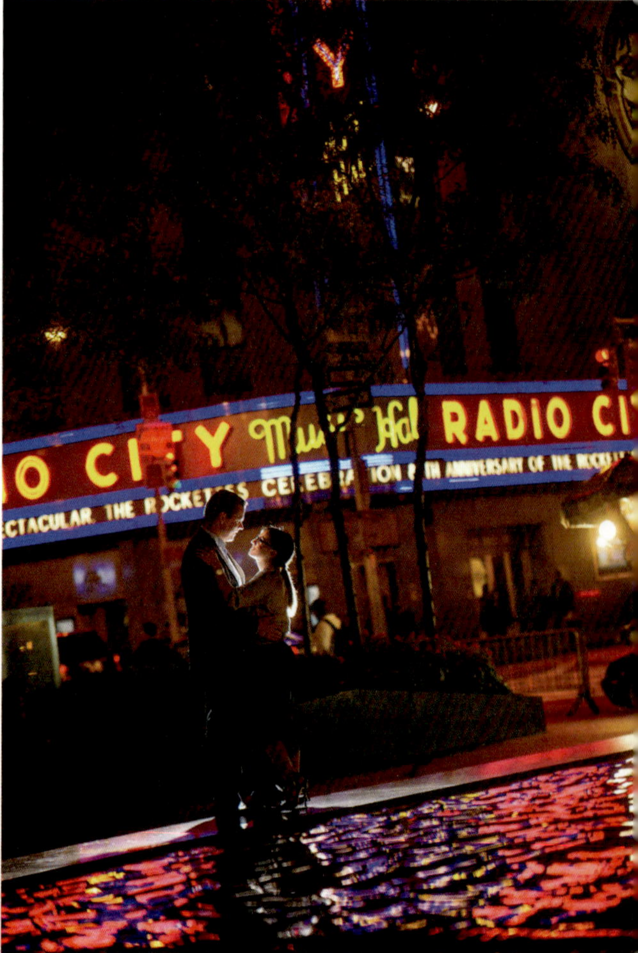

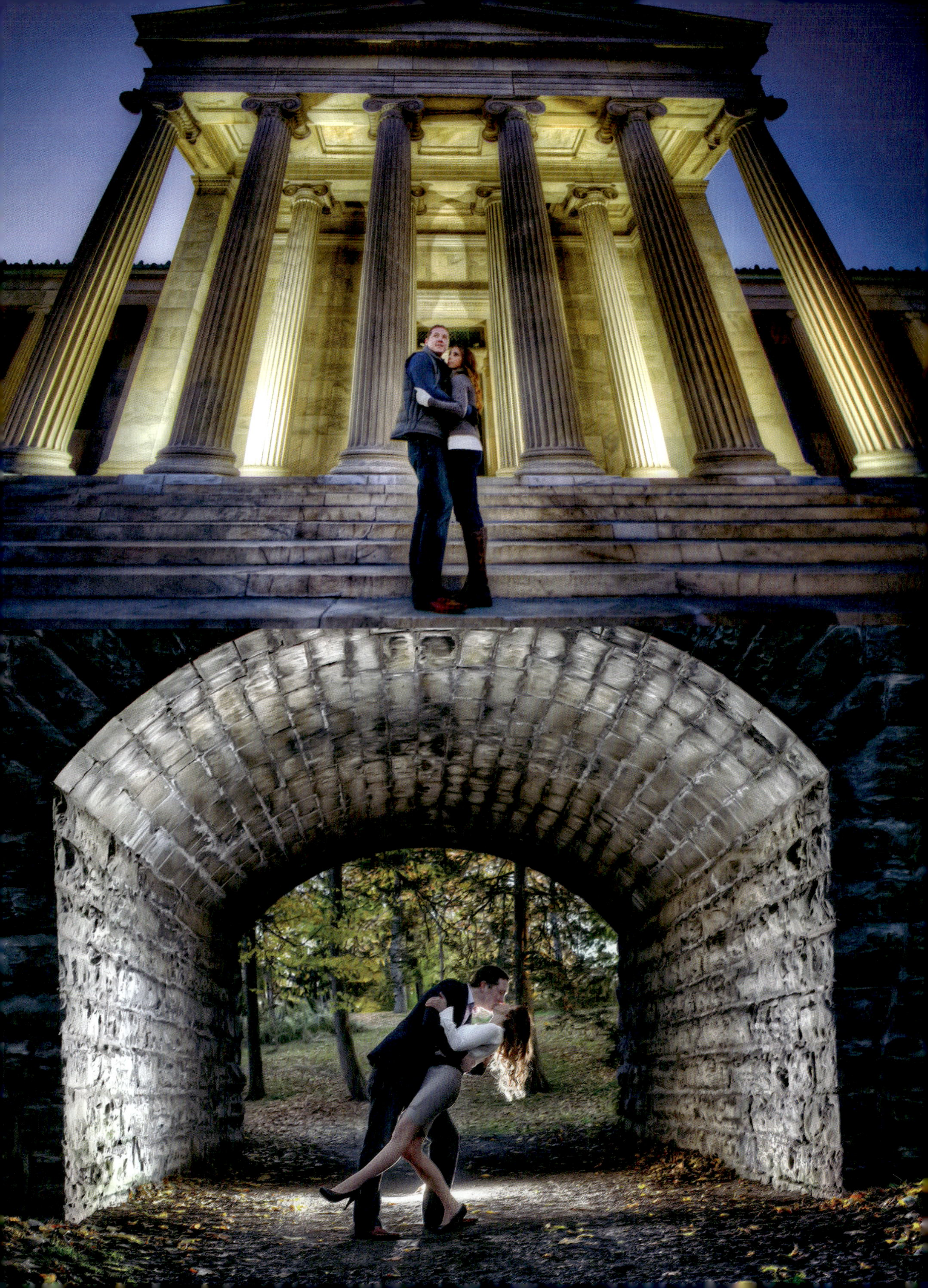

Bounce Light

Bouncing light can let you work without the addition of supplementary light sources—or make the light sources you do choose to add perform a double duty.

Bounce the Ambient Light

When shooting the images on the facing page, we were working in the late afternoon and I posed my couples with the sun behind them (and, for the top image, a bit to the side). Adding fill from a reflector was the simplest way to open up the shadows while keeping the nice rim lighting.

Reflectors come in many surface finishes and knowing which to choose will have a substantial impact on the look of your images. For the portrait next to the lake, Danielle held a gold reflector to camera right to fill the shadows with warm light that gave the couple a nice golden glow. For the portrait in the vineyard, however, the sunlight was already quite warm; adding a gold reflector would have made the couple look too orange. Instead, I had Danielle hold a gold/silver striped reflector high to camera left. This added a hint of warmth but kept their skin tones fairly neutral.

Bounce the Flash

For the image below, I chose a red wall as the background to complement the couple's Red Sox jerseys—but the location was *really* dark. Splashing the light from an SB900 flash up onto the wall made it record as vibrant red. Since the ceiling above them was all white, the same upward flash bounced back down and over them for just enough light on their front sides.

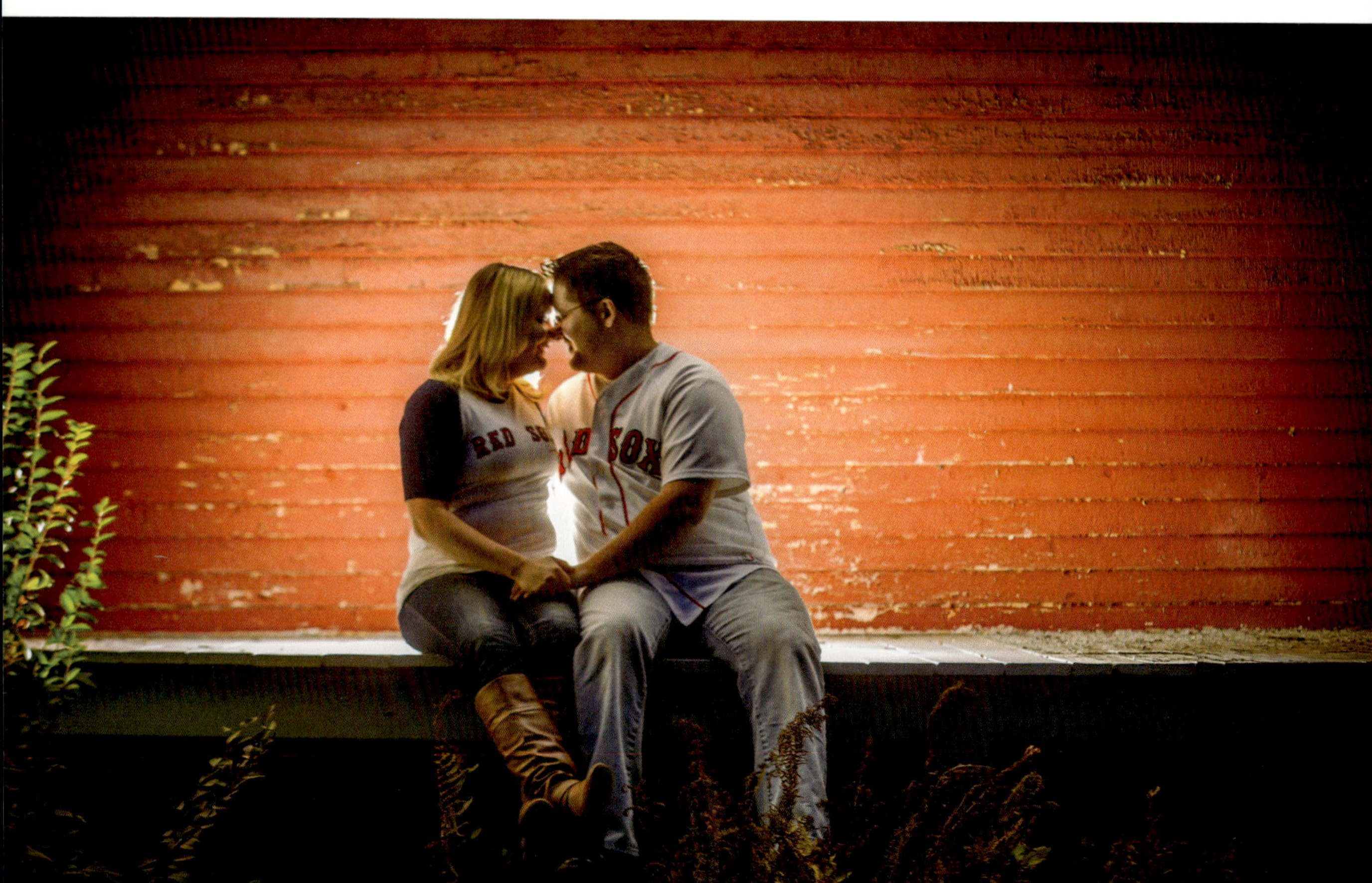

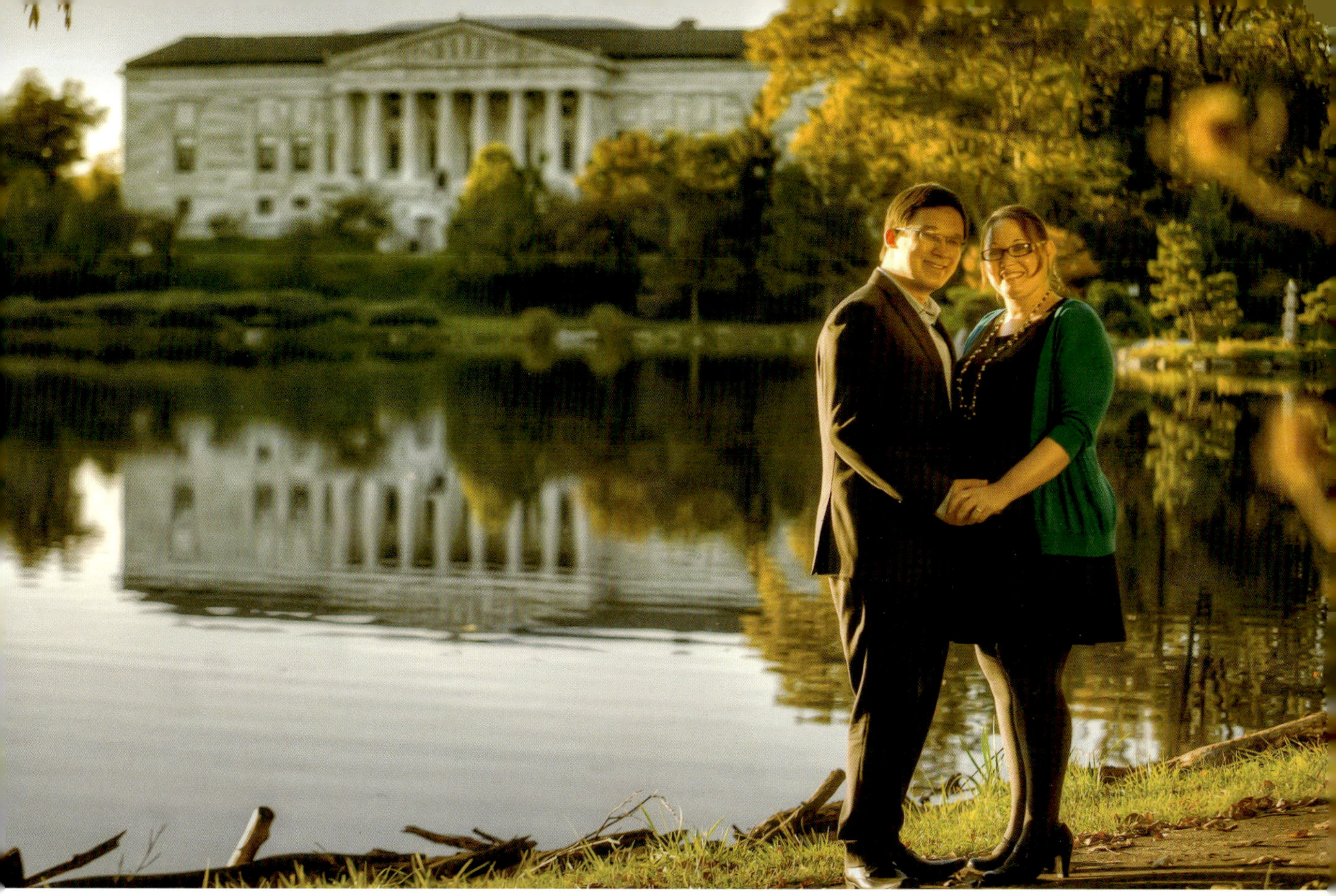

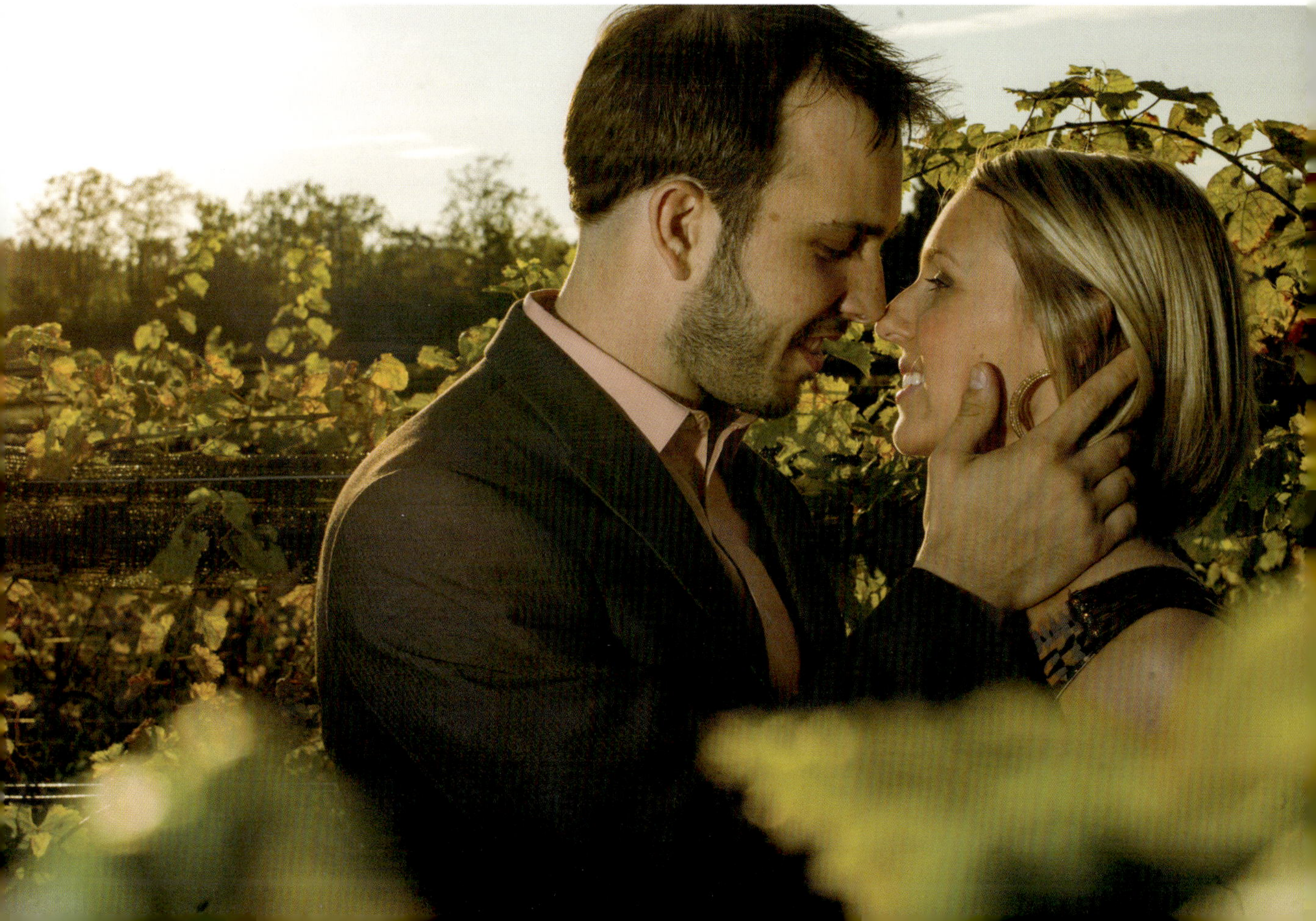

43 Mixed Light and Color Balance

Tungsten/Twilight

The bottom images on this page and the facing page were both made using a mix of late-day ambient light and tungsten lighting.

For the image below, the couple was seated at their kitchen table (we saw another shot from their cooking-themed session in section 14). Danielle was inside with the couple, holding a tungsten Lowel light to camera right for soft fill that balanced with the other interior lights (flash would have been too blue). I shot from outside with my white balance to tungsten. In the cool twilight, this rendered the white window trim as a rich blue that contrasted beautifully with the warm tones inside.

The same approach worked for the bottom image on the facing page, where a Lowel light was used to balance with the string of lights above the couple. Again, shooting with a tungsten white balance made the ambient-lit setting a rich blue. (Flip back to section 35 for a different mixed-light portrait of the same couple and setting.)

Fluorescent/Sunset

For the top image on the facing page we were shooting around sunset with the couple lit by a fluorescent street lamp that was above them and a bit to the left. Changing to a fluorescent white balance that matched the street light changed the color of the sunset, too. This color shift gave them a little more variety, since the other sunset shots from the session were much warmer. It still looks "normal," though, because sunsets come in so many different colors.

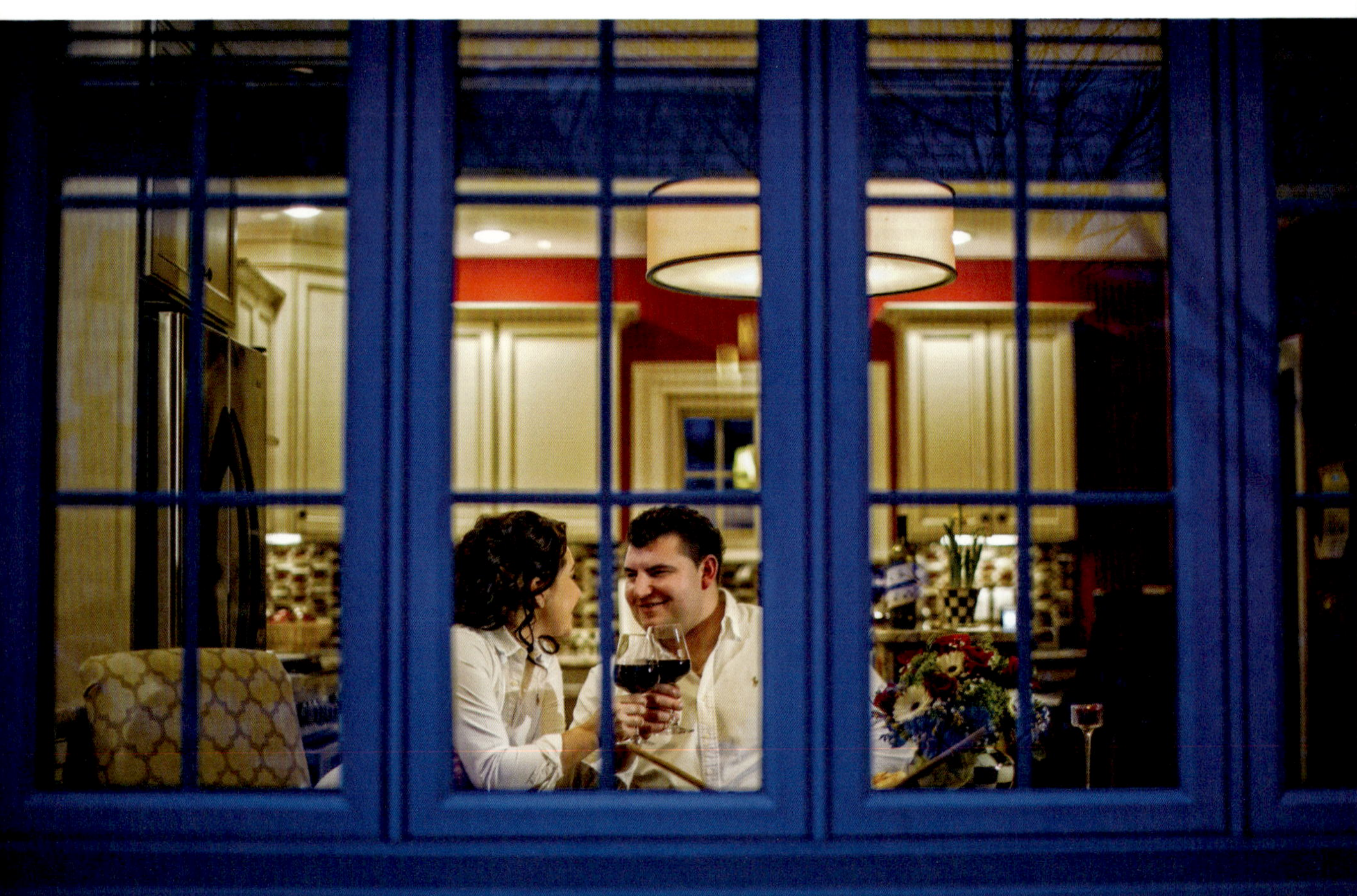

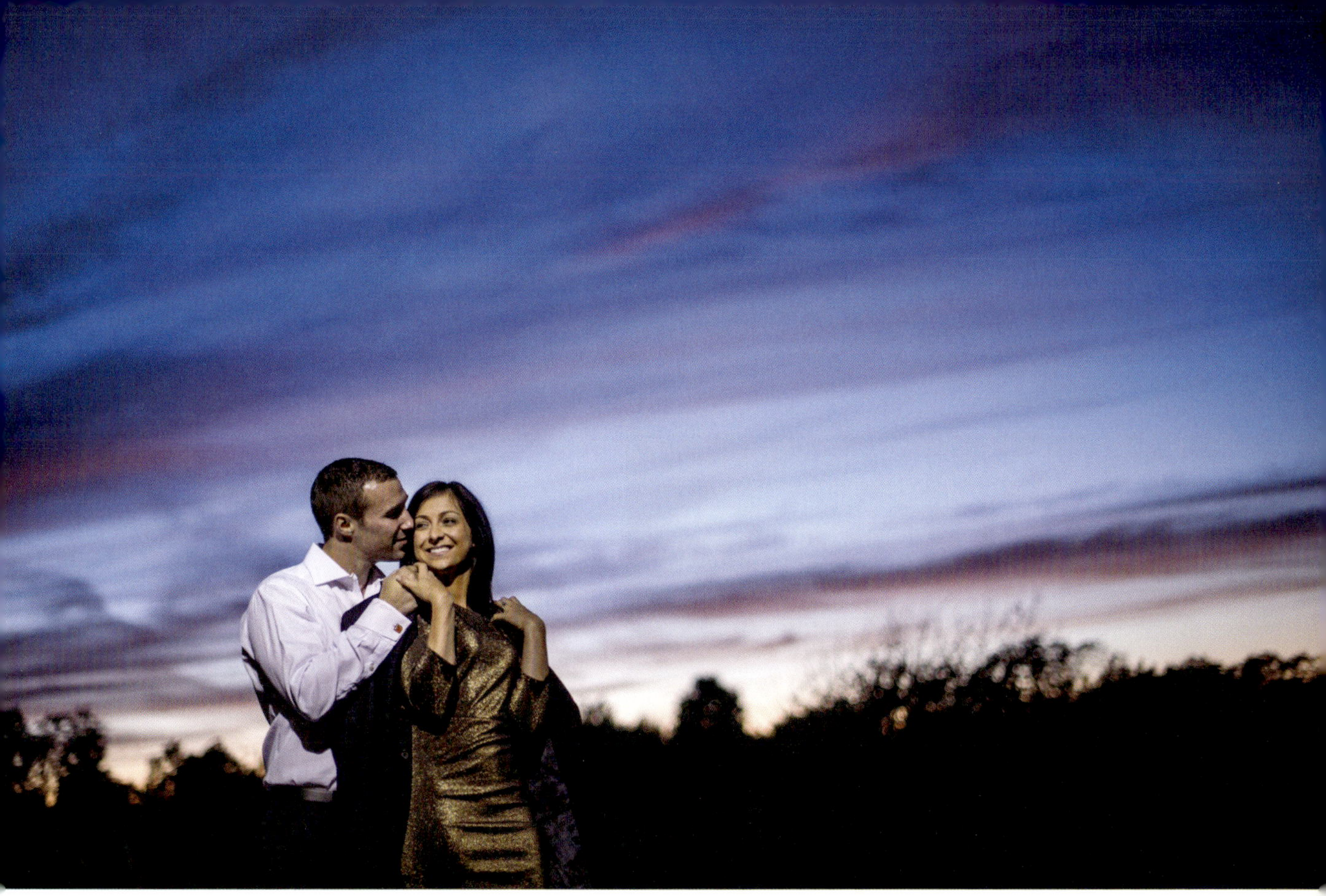

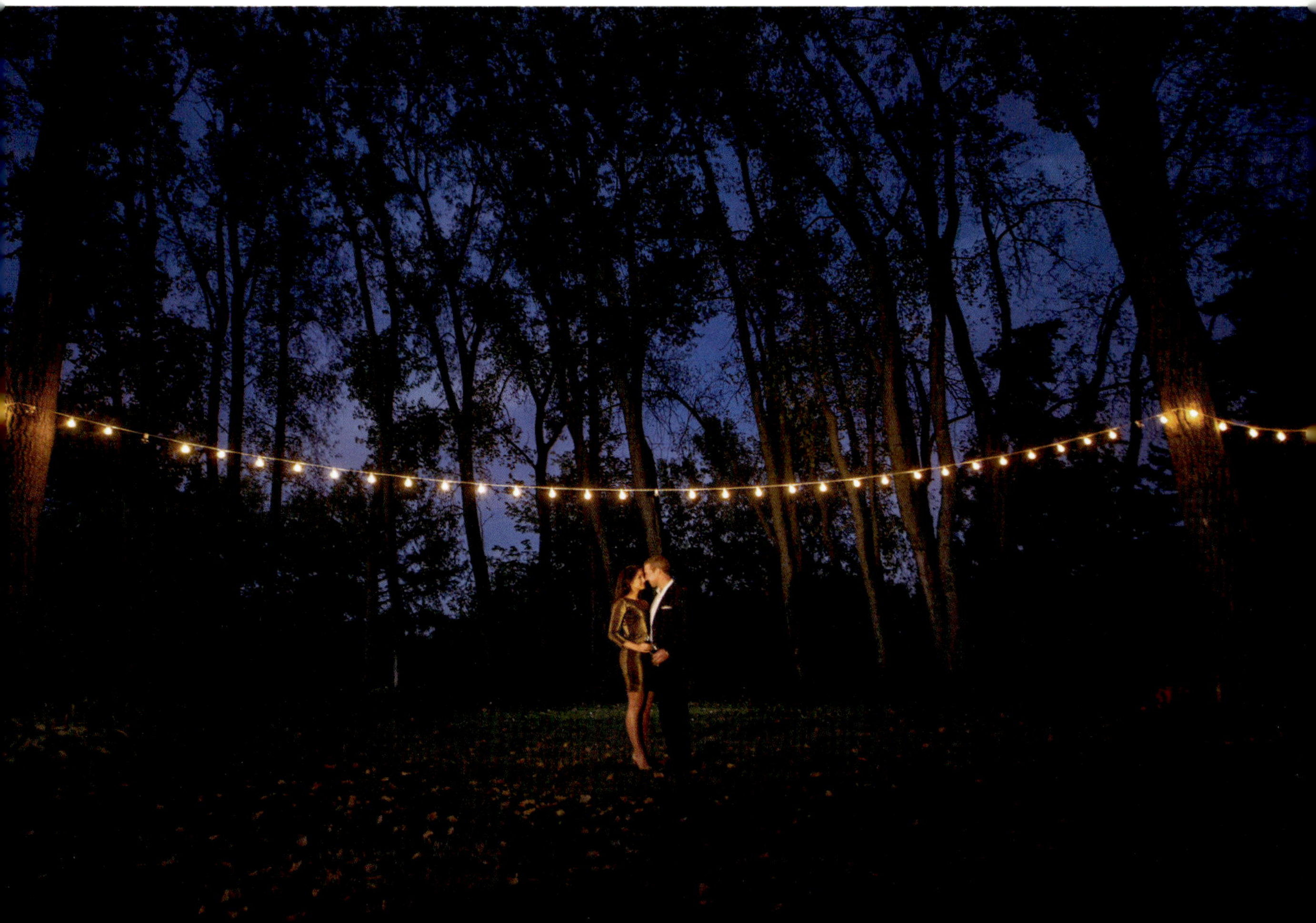

44 Subject Placement and Composition

Going hand-in-hand with finding (or creating) the right lighting on the subjects is choosing the right position for them in the scene. Guidelines like the Rule of Thirds can help—but sometimes you have to take it a step farther.

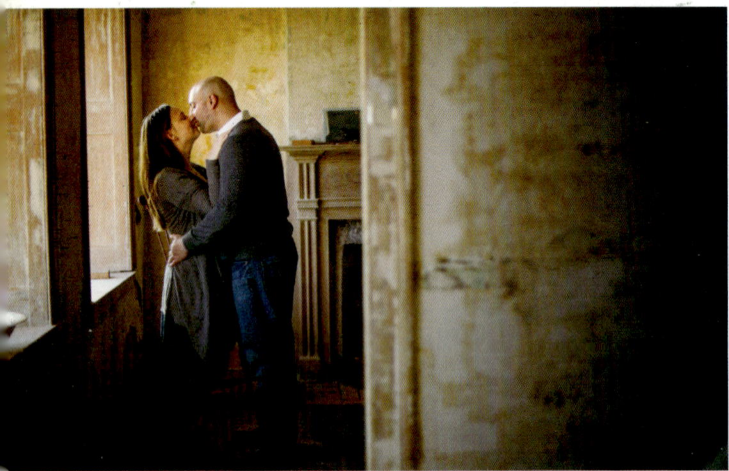

Think about framing and leading lines (see sections 9 and 10). Consider using elements in the foreground. Look for opportunities to create frames within frames. Your objective is to draw the viewer's eyes to the couple, but then give them some additional area of interest that will cause their gaze to linger on the image.

◄ This building was being restored and there wasn't much in the room to the couple's right, so I used the wall in the foreground to cut off what I didn't want to show.

▼ Here we see almost the same effect. The blurred red wall of the barn in the foreground helps keep the emphasis on the subjects—who are additionally framed within a door opening.

► Natural environments also provide attractive and effective framing options.

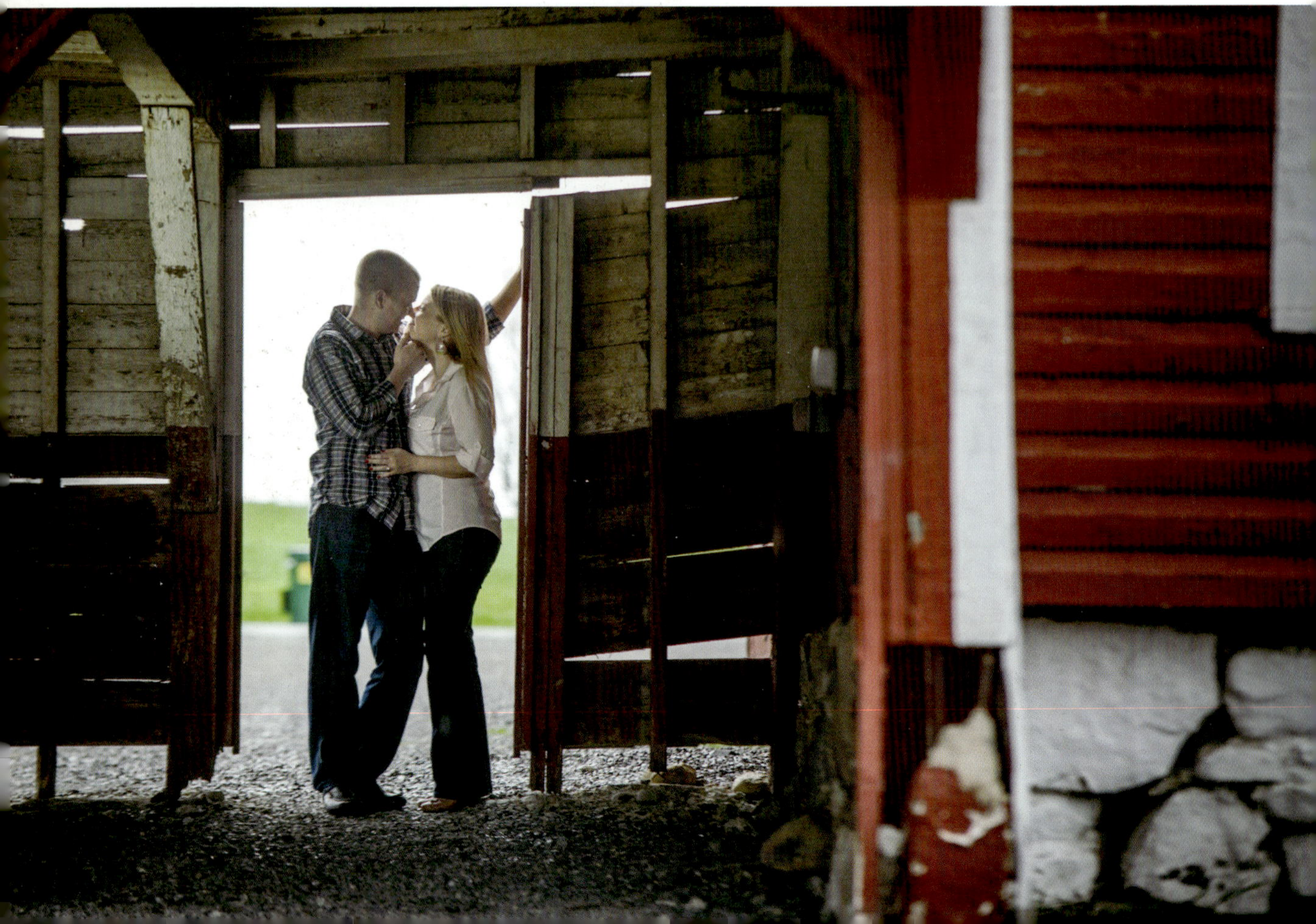

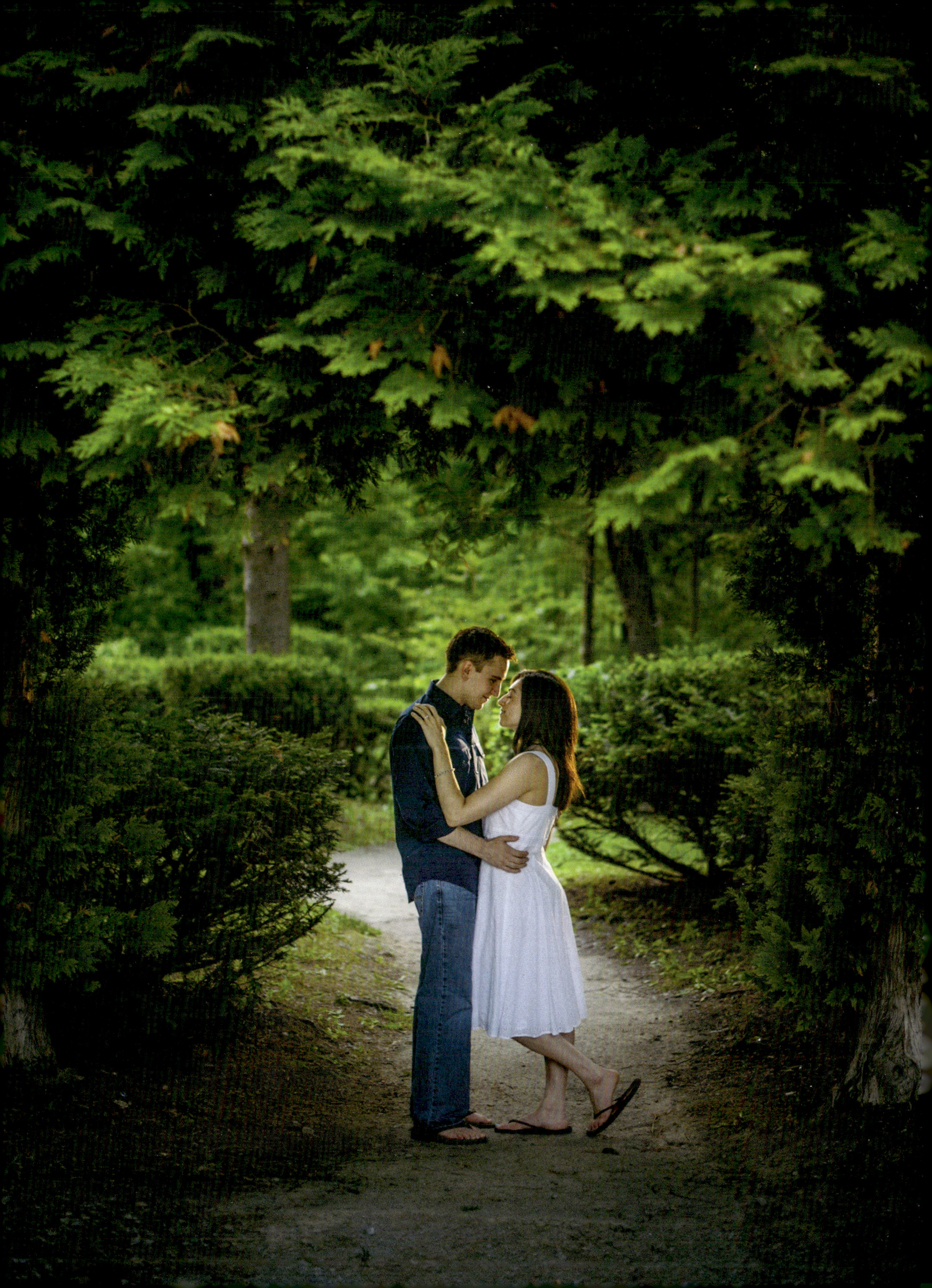

45 Directing the Poses

I keep the silly jokes and funny banter going throughout the session, helping me get real smiles from the couple. When I'm setting up the guy in a pose, I'll even pretend to be the girl and step in really close, putting my hands on him and then asking him slyly if he feels uncomfortable. It always makes the guys laugh—which is especially important since the men tend to need more encouragement to loosen up.

As the session progresses and they feel more comfortable, we can start to get more subtle expressions. I'll ask them just to be silent and look at each other without smiling. Sometimes I'll step back out of sight and shoot from a distance, just letting that connection unfold between them. I watch them interacting and get a nice variety of images with them looking at each other and looking at the camera.

People do pay attention. By the end of the session, most couples are doing a lot of posing on their own—being more themselves and more genuine, but within the guidelines.

This puts us in a good position for the wedding day, because I can just say, "Remember when we did X? Do that again."

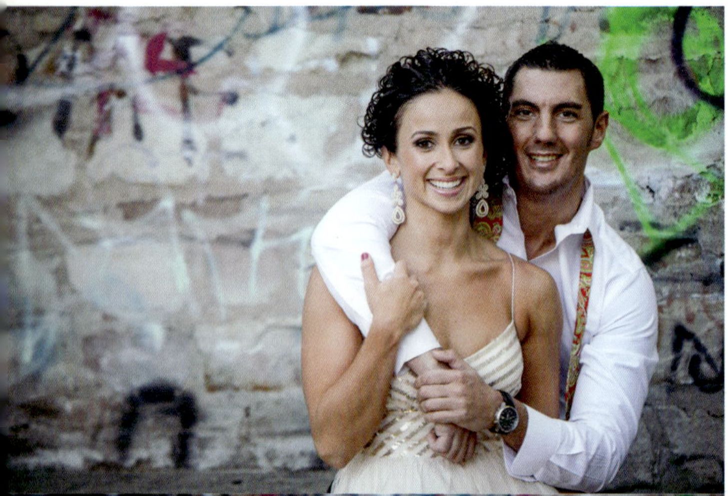

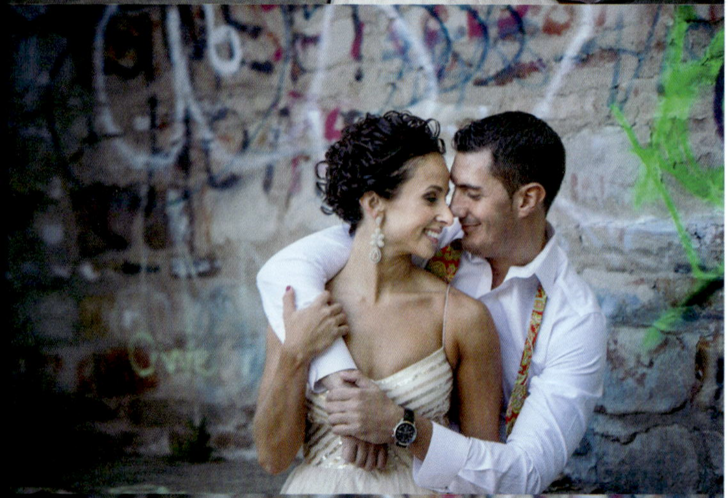

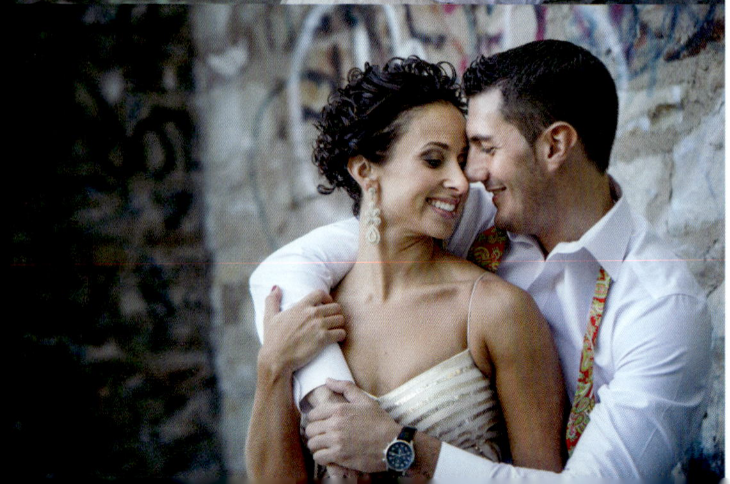

▼ Danielle took this image to show the overall scene where all the posing variations here were created.

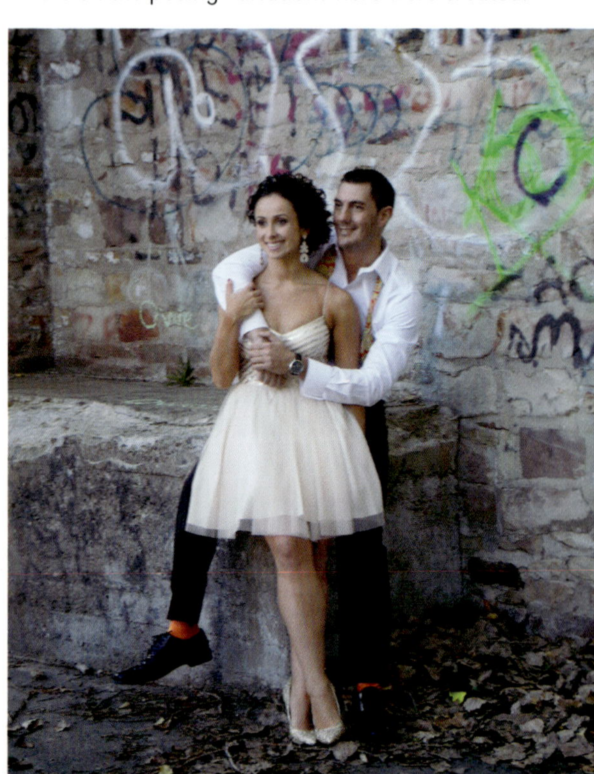

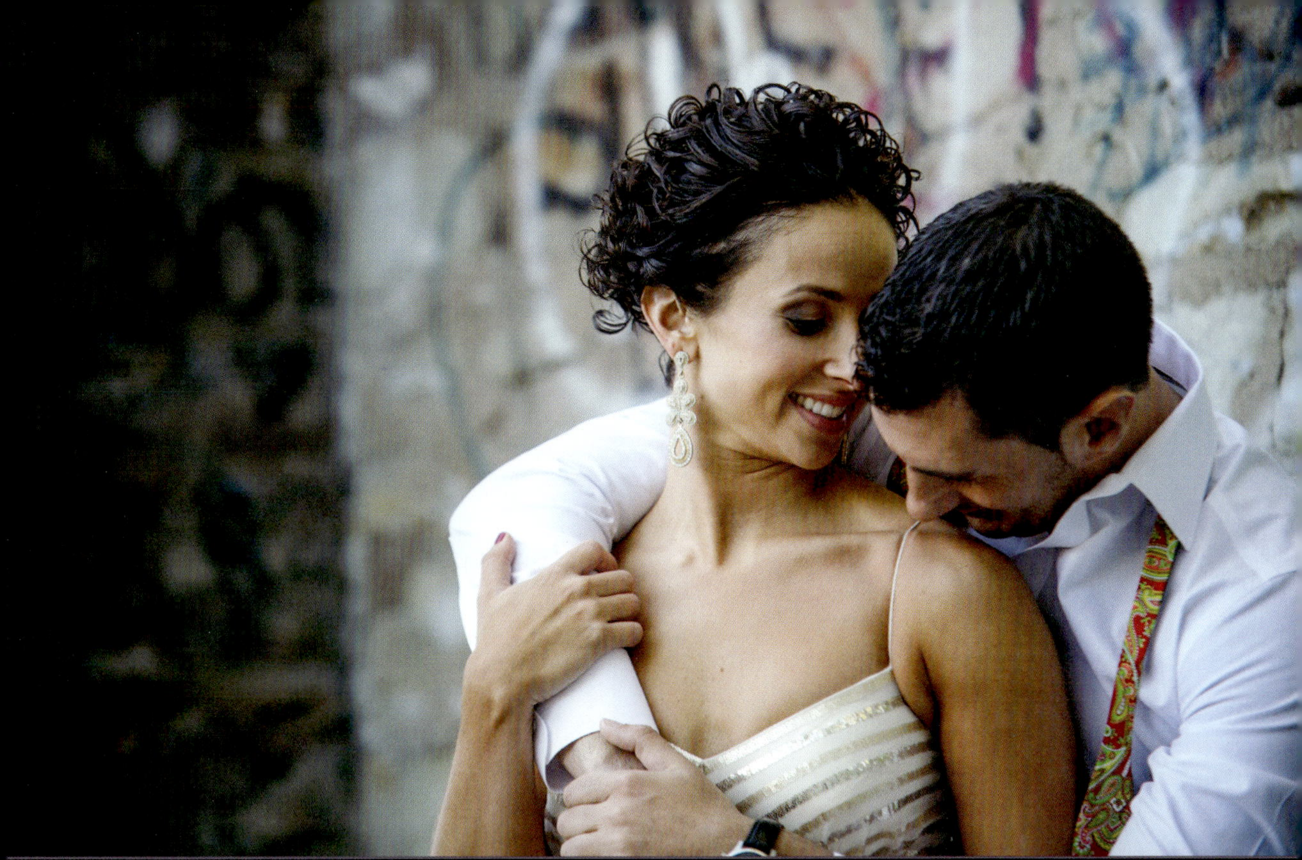

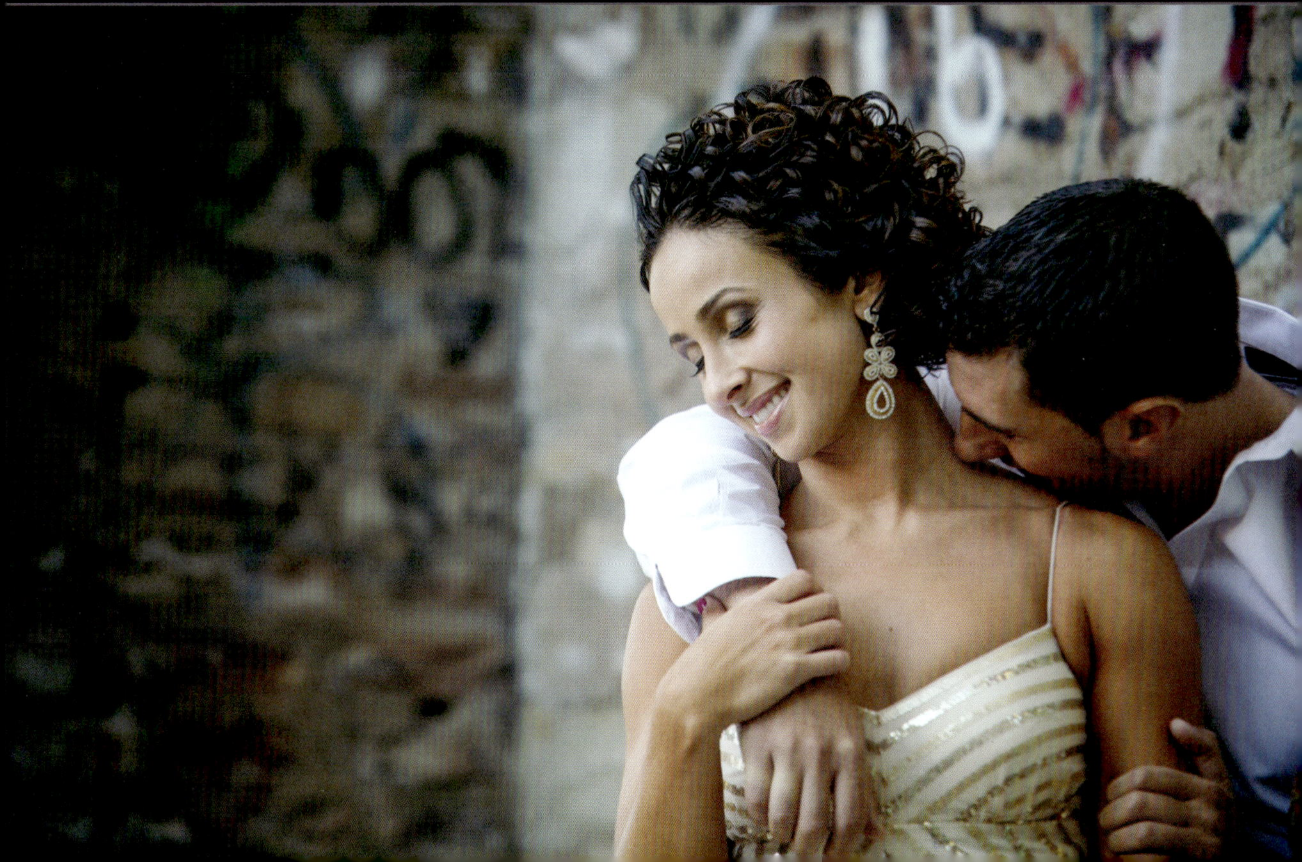

Standing Poses

Standing poses can be used with any outfit, but they offer a particularly good opportunity to show off the couple's fancier clothing.

Add Some Movement

People often feel a little more comfortable in front of the camera when they are moving—it doesn't make them feel (or look) like they are trying too hard to pose.

To add some movement to standing poses, I try having the couple walk toward me as I shoot. Then I have them walk away, stop, and look back at me. We repeat this process a few times. I get something a little different on each pass, so the couple ends up with a nice variety of poses to choose from.

If the couple has a choreographed dance for their wedding, I love having them "perform" for me. This gives us poses that are really elegant—and look a lot different from the standing shots most people are used to.

Not All Full-Length

Just because your couple is standing doesn't mean you have to shoot full length. If you see that they have a nice interaction going on, zoom in and shoot closer. Images like the ones on the facing page make perfect photos for their parents—especially with the engagement ring showing!

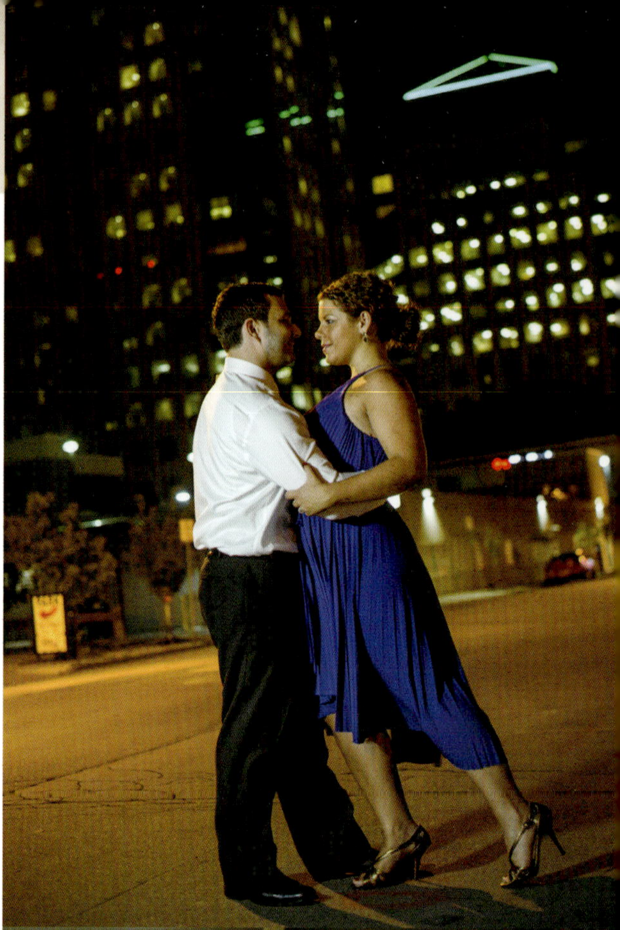

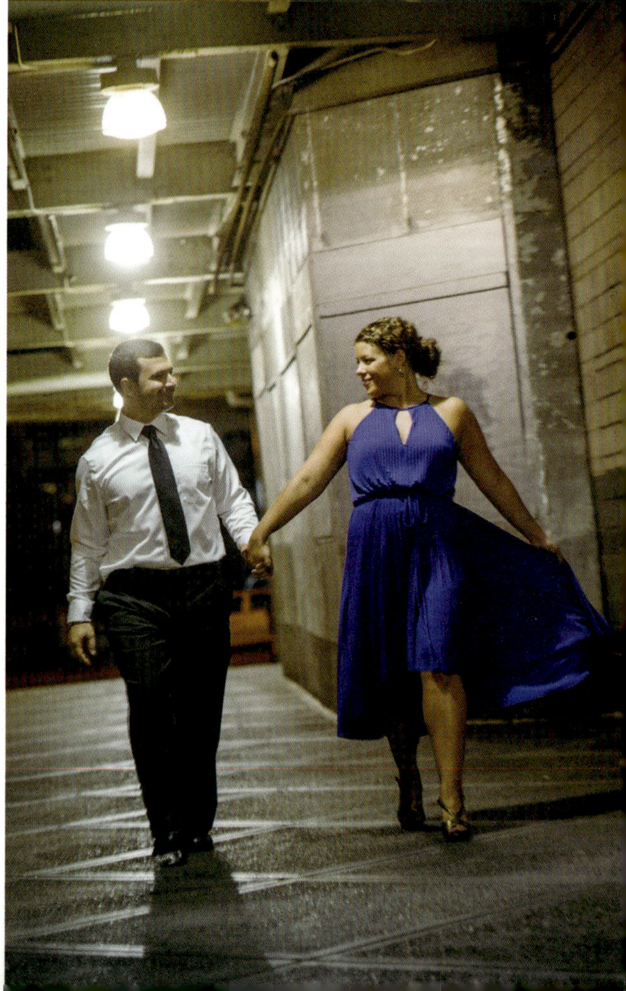

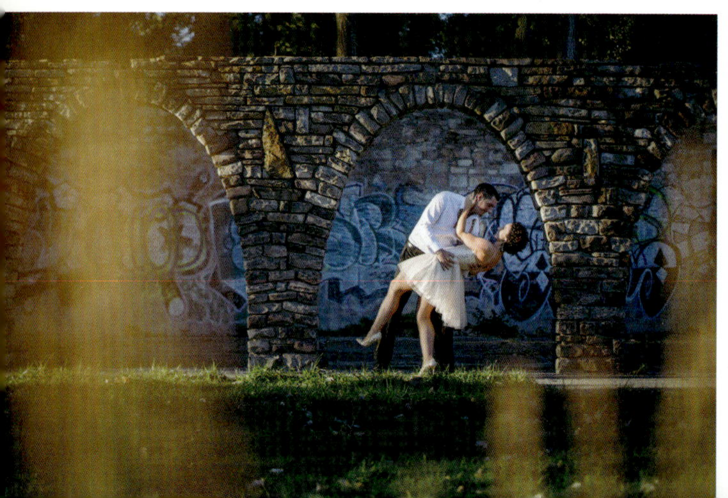

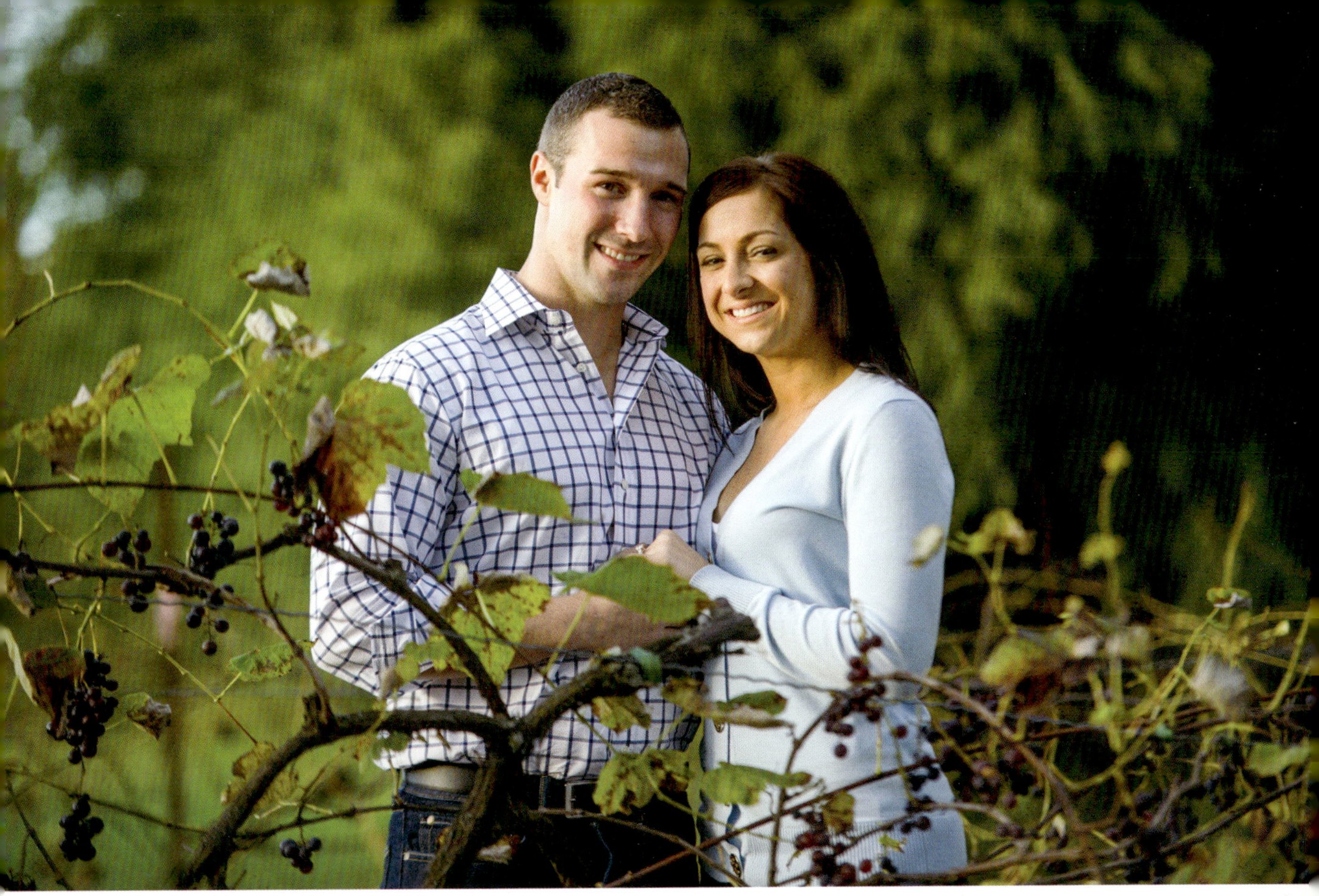

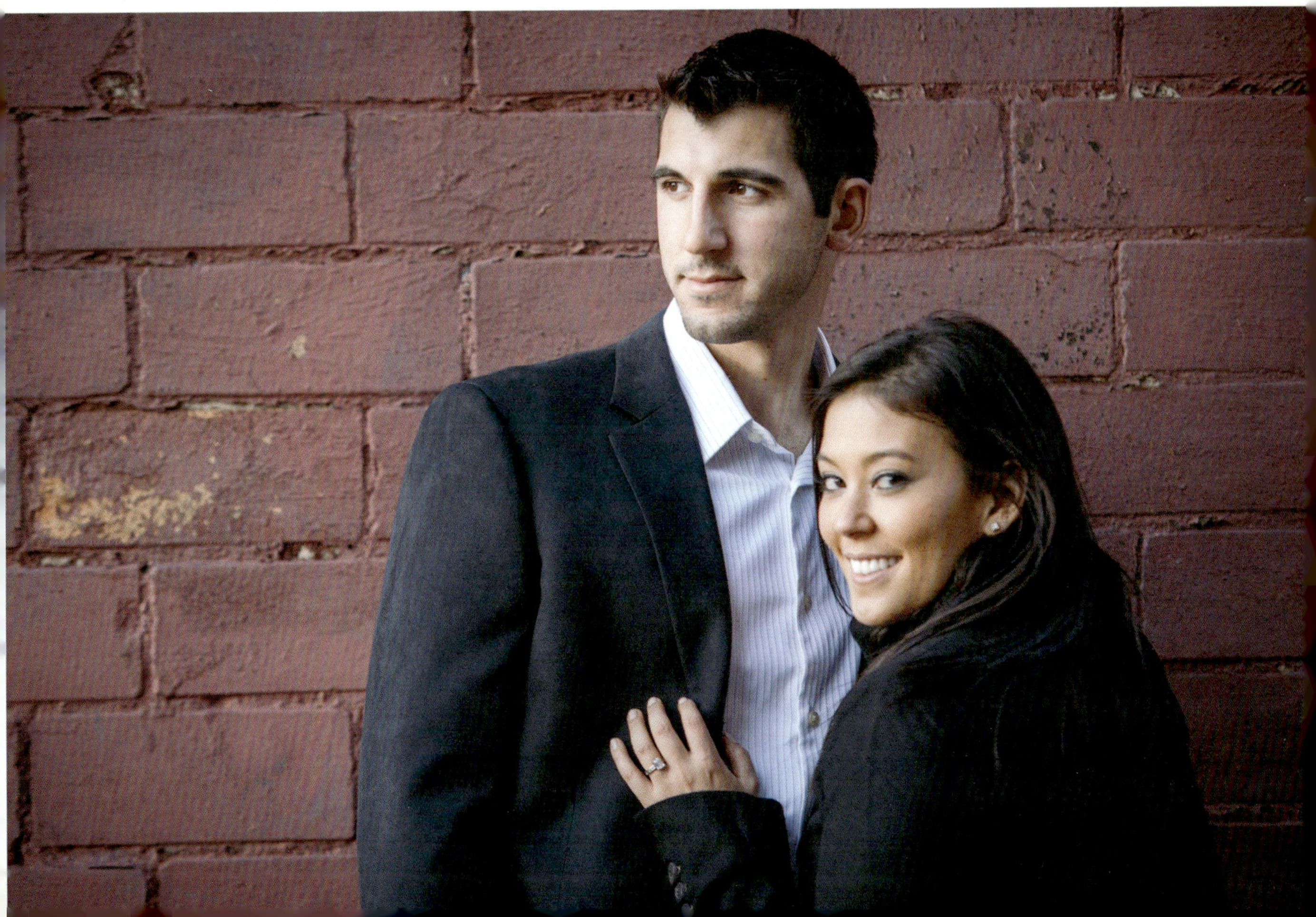

47 Seated Poses

The Scene

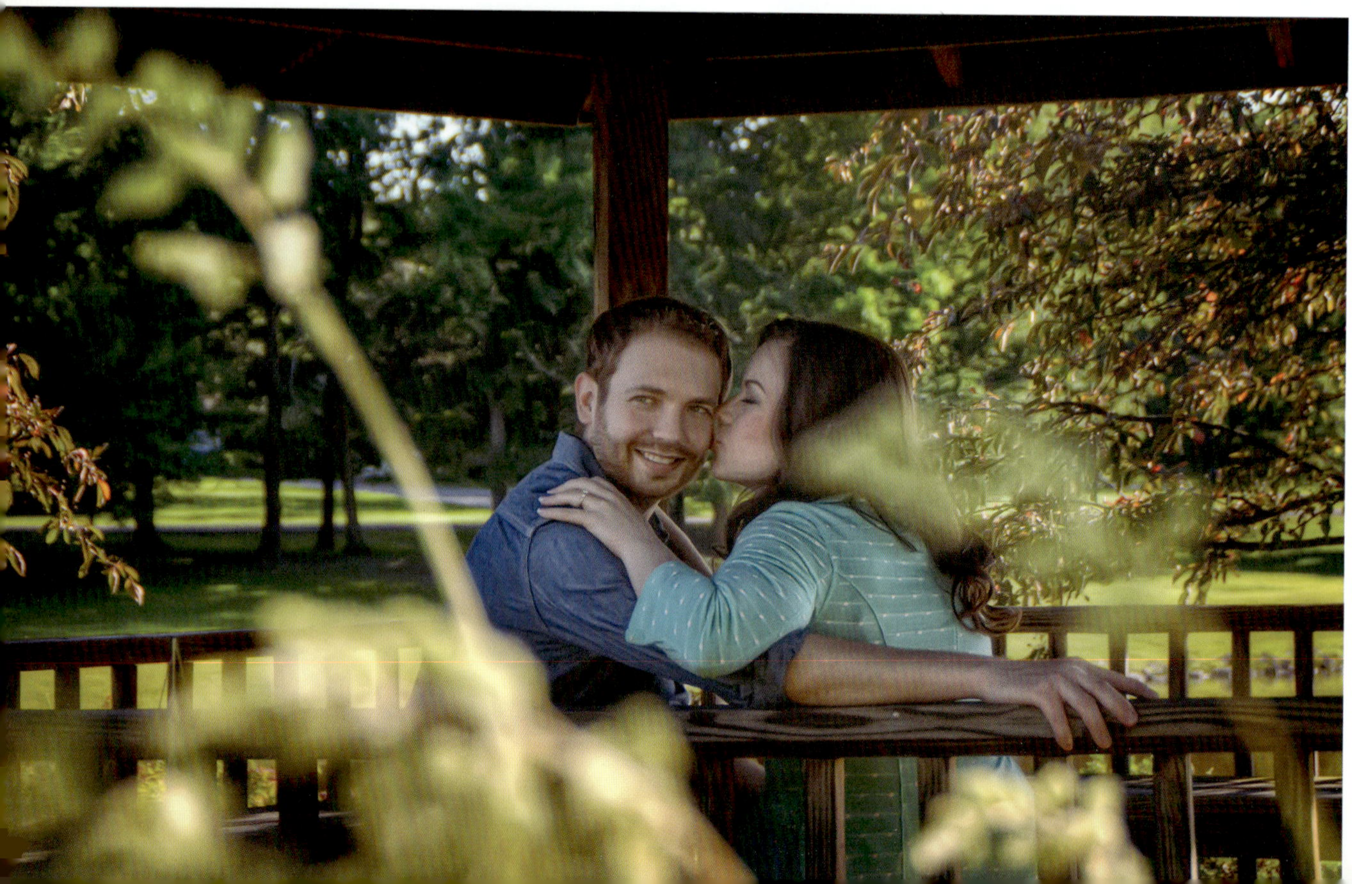

Sometimes, switching to a seated pose lets you take better advantage of a scene; getting lower gives you a totally different perspective. For the image below, I couldn't have shown the railing as a prominent background element if the couple

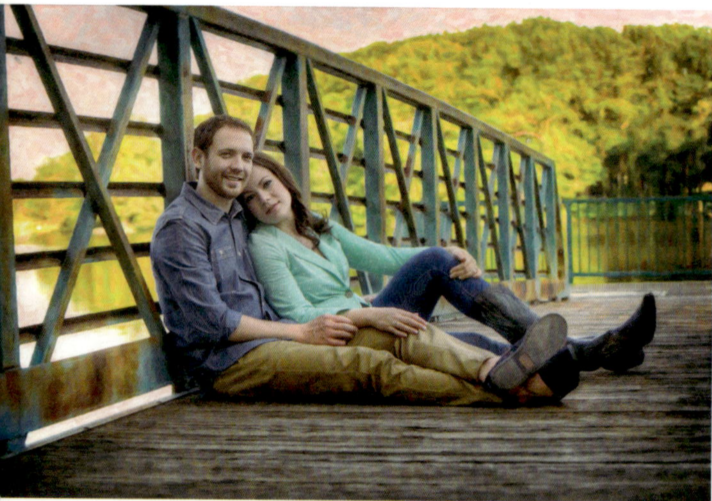

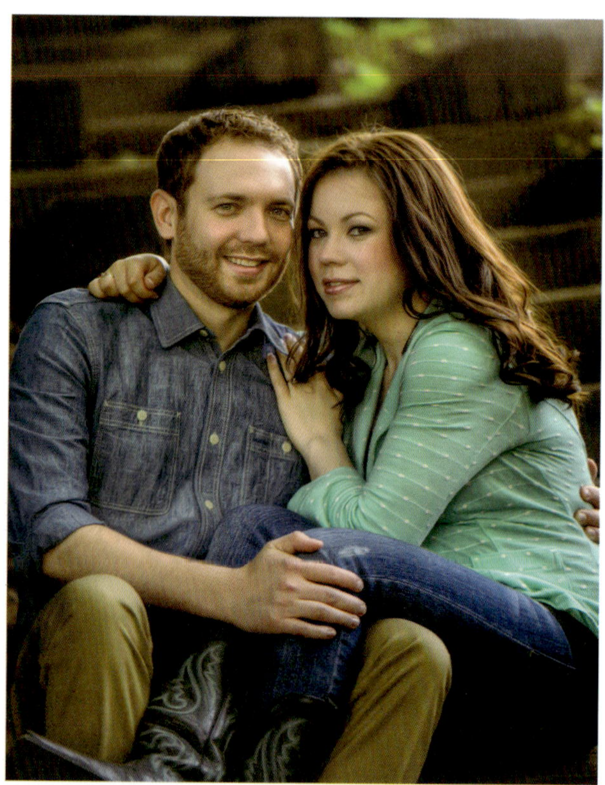

had been standing. The same is true for the image of the same couple posed on the stone steps.

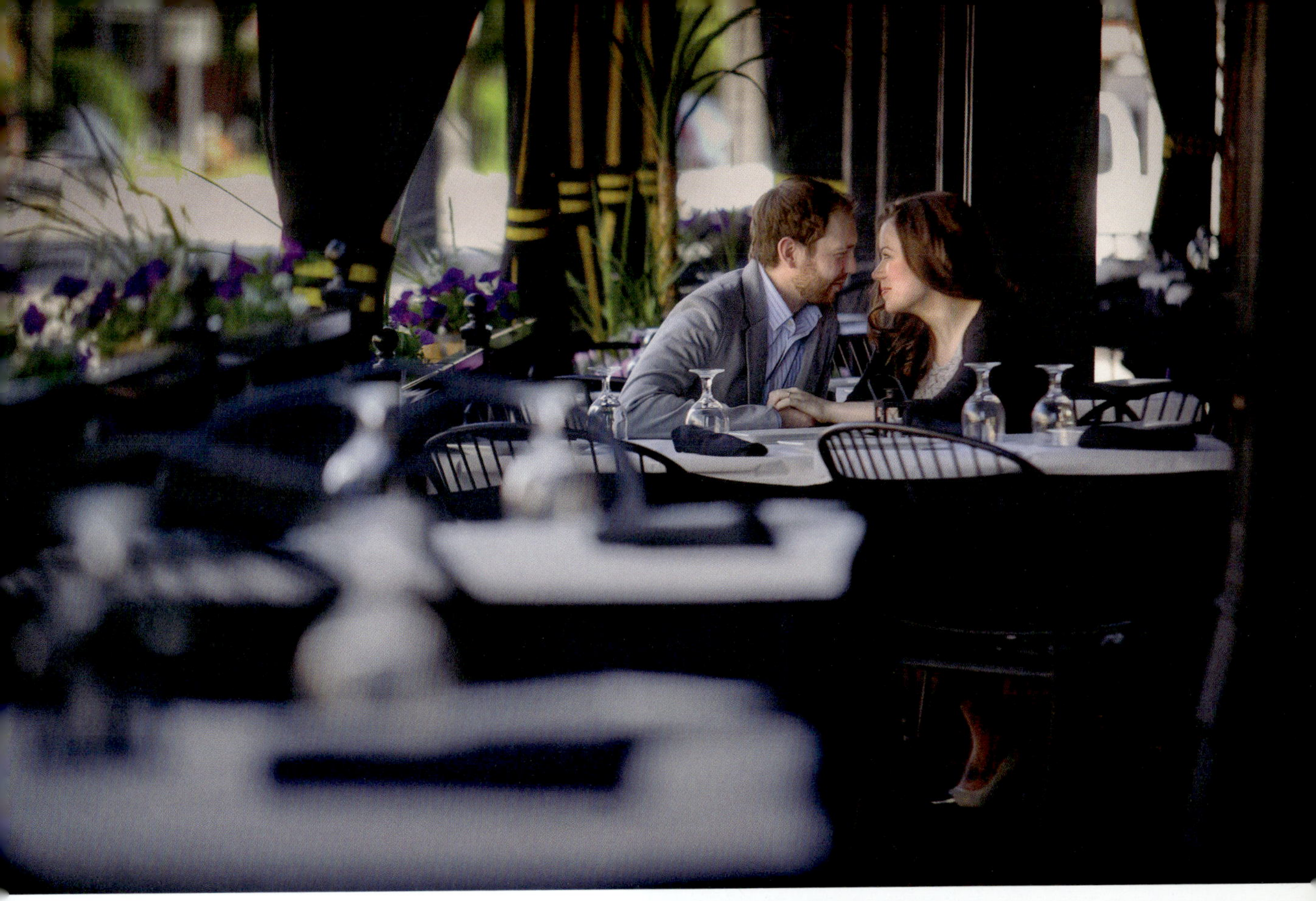

The Clothing

For the most part, we use seated poses when couples are in their more casual outfits. There are some exceptions, though. For instance, the image above of the couple in the restaurant shows them in dressier clothes. Sitting is just the natural pose for people in a restaurant.

A Break and a Better Connection

If we've been doing a lot of standing poses or walking around for a while, a seated pose also gives the subjects a little break. Sitting together also seems to make it easier for couples to connect and intermingle their bodies in the frame. That can lead to a better sense of their romantic connection in the portraits.

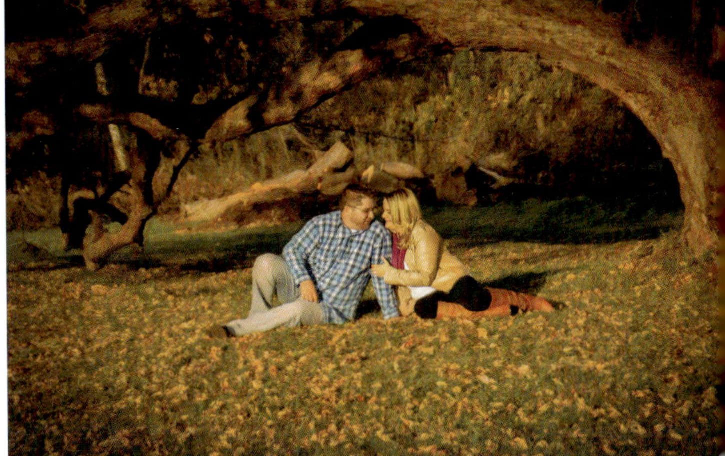

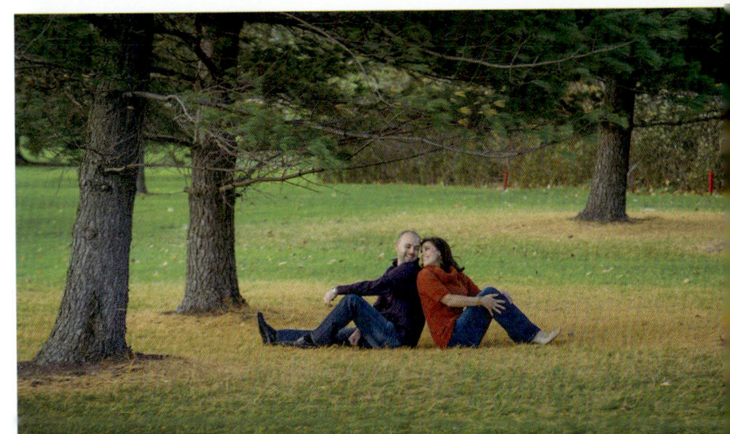

48 Reclining Poses

Transforming the Background

As we touched on in section 19 (and the images that follow it), reclining poses often make sense because they help you make use of a background that's not so great. By creating a frame with the foreground and background, this pose makes almost any area work. You don't need special lighting to make it work, either. Even if the sun is from right overhead, you'll get bounce from the ground (or you can add a reflector to further refine the look).

Putting Couples at Ease

The fun and close contact of these poses makes most couples smile and laugh, which is great for putting them at ease—especially earlier in the session. Best of all, the images always look great, so showing them a few shots in these poses is a quick way to boost their confidence if they're feeling awkward. It will also make them more likely to trust you when, down the road, you ask them to do something else they aren't expecting.

Precautions

Obviously, these poses are best suited to casual outfits. If you don't have a blanket, be sure to ask the couple if they're okay with the idea. While the girl usually comes away clean, the guy will likely get a little dirty on his back. For the same reason, it's smart to make this one of the last shots before the end of the shoot or before the couple changes into their more formal outfits.

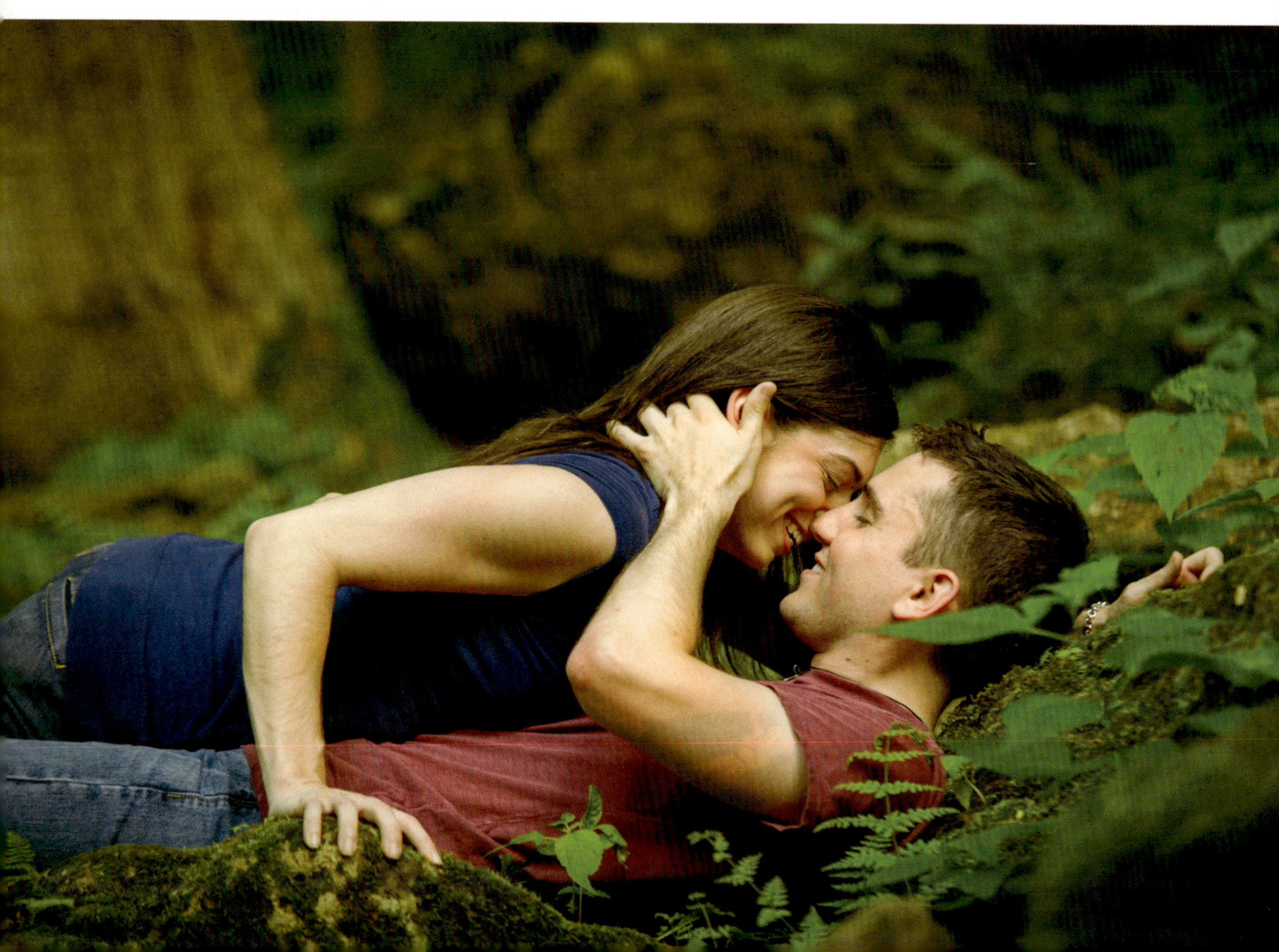

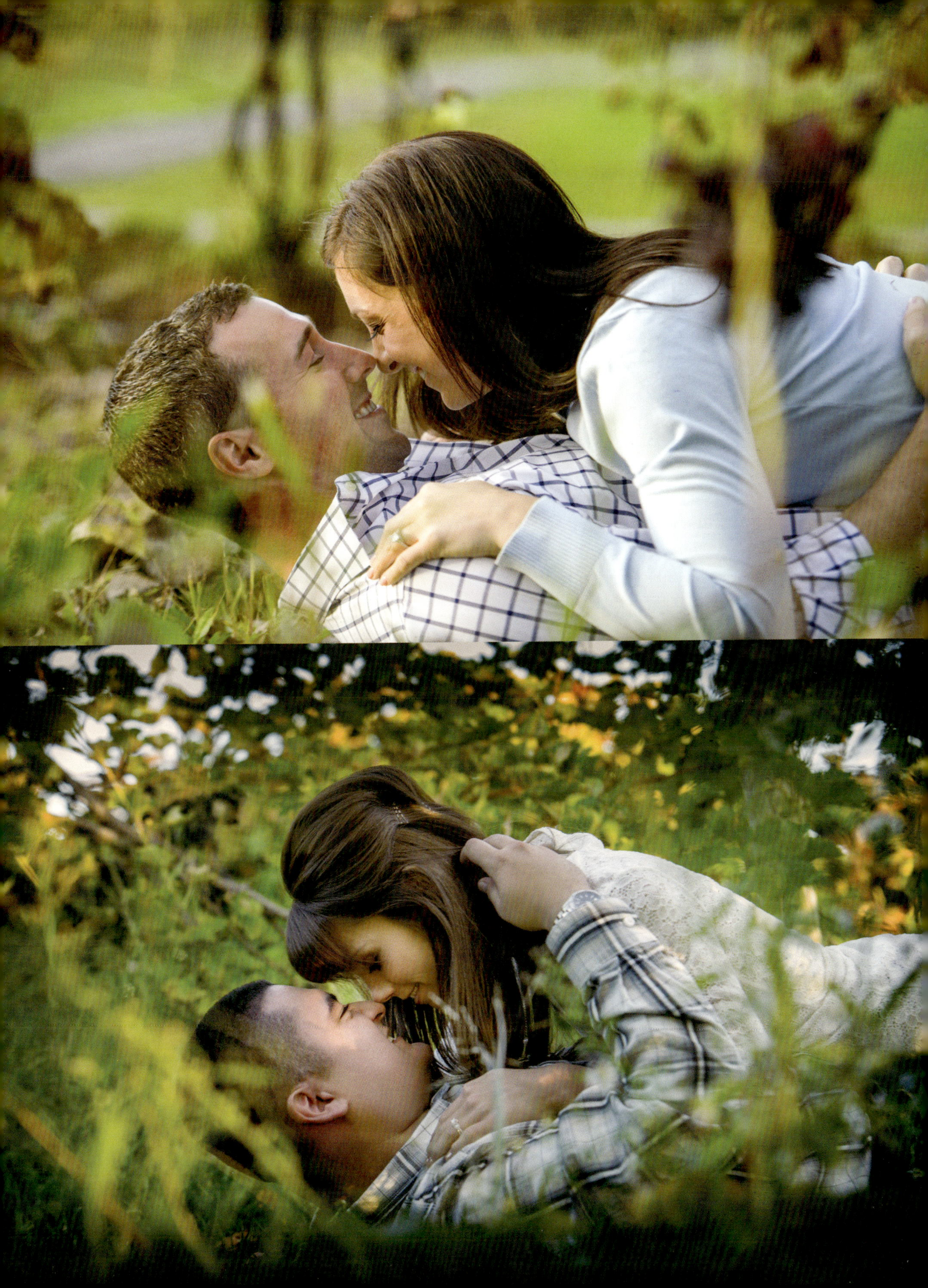

49 Have Fun with It

Posing certainly doesn't have to be static. A pose that brings some action to the scene can work really well—particularly for couples who tend to be a little less demonstrative or who are having a little trouble loosening up.

Piggyback Ride

One of my favorite things to do is to ask the guy to give his soon-to-be wife a piggyback ride. It's not something most grownups do—but everyone knows exactly how to do it, so no further instruction is needed. Everybody feels a little silly and off-balance when trying this, which is exactly why it works so well. It's so unexpected and unfamiliar that they immediately stop paying attention to the camera and start interacting genuinely.

That's part of the fun for me as the photographer, too—I don't know exactly what is going to happen, either. How long will he carry her around? How hard will she squeeze him? One thing is for sure: it always yields some great smiles and laughter.

Close Contact

In these examples, notice how the pose inherently puts them in close physical contact—something I'm always asking for when posing. They literally have to hold onto each other and their faces are positioned inches a part, so you see the expressive contact between them as well.

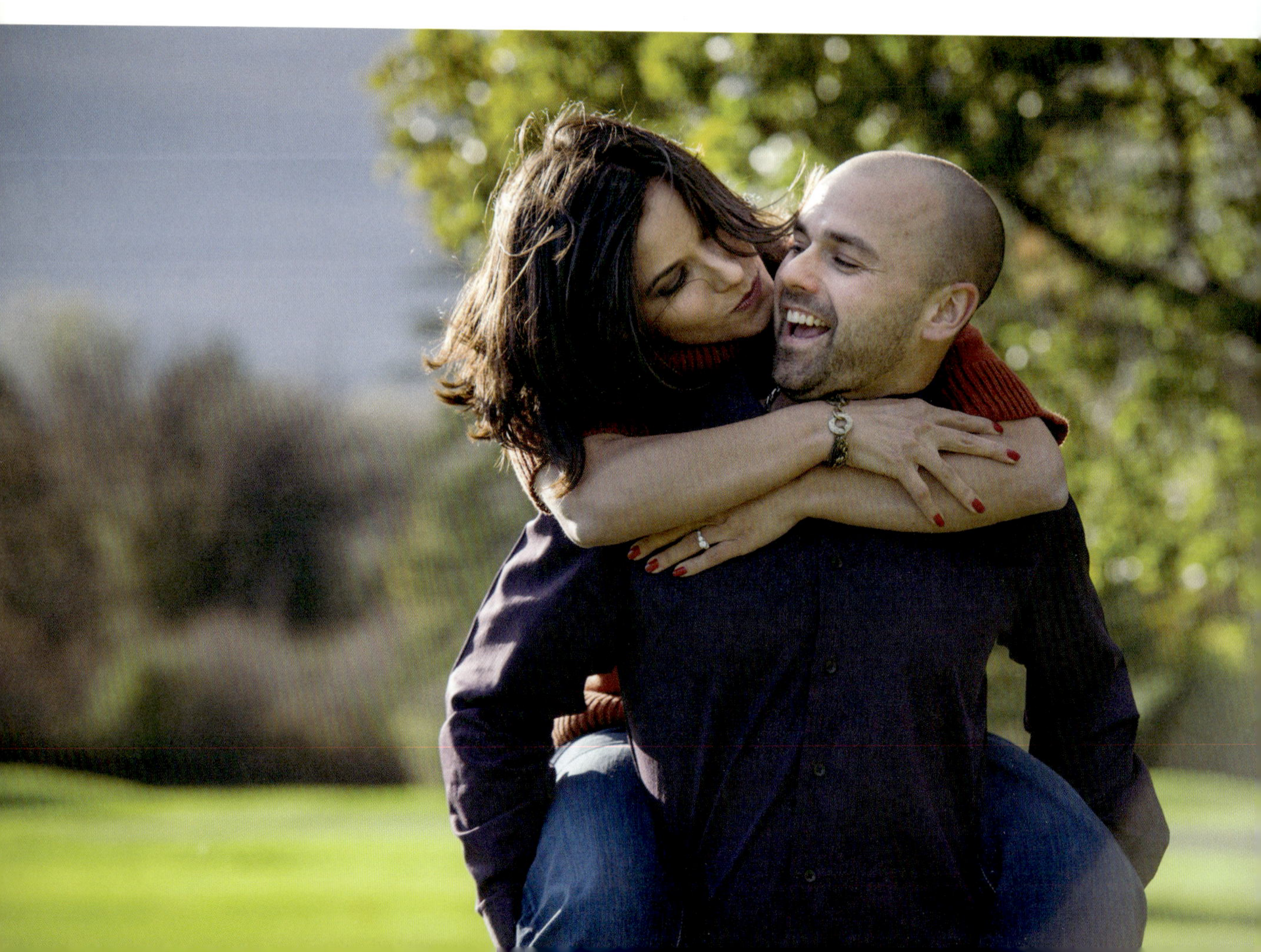

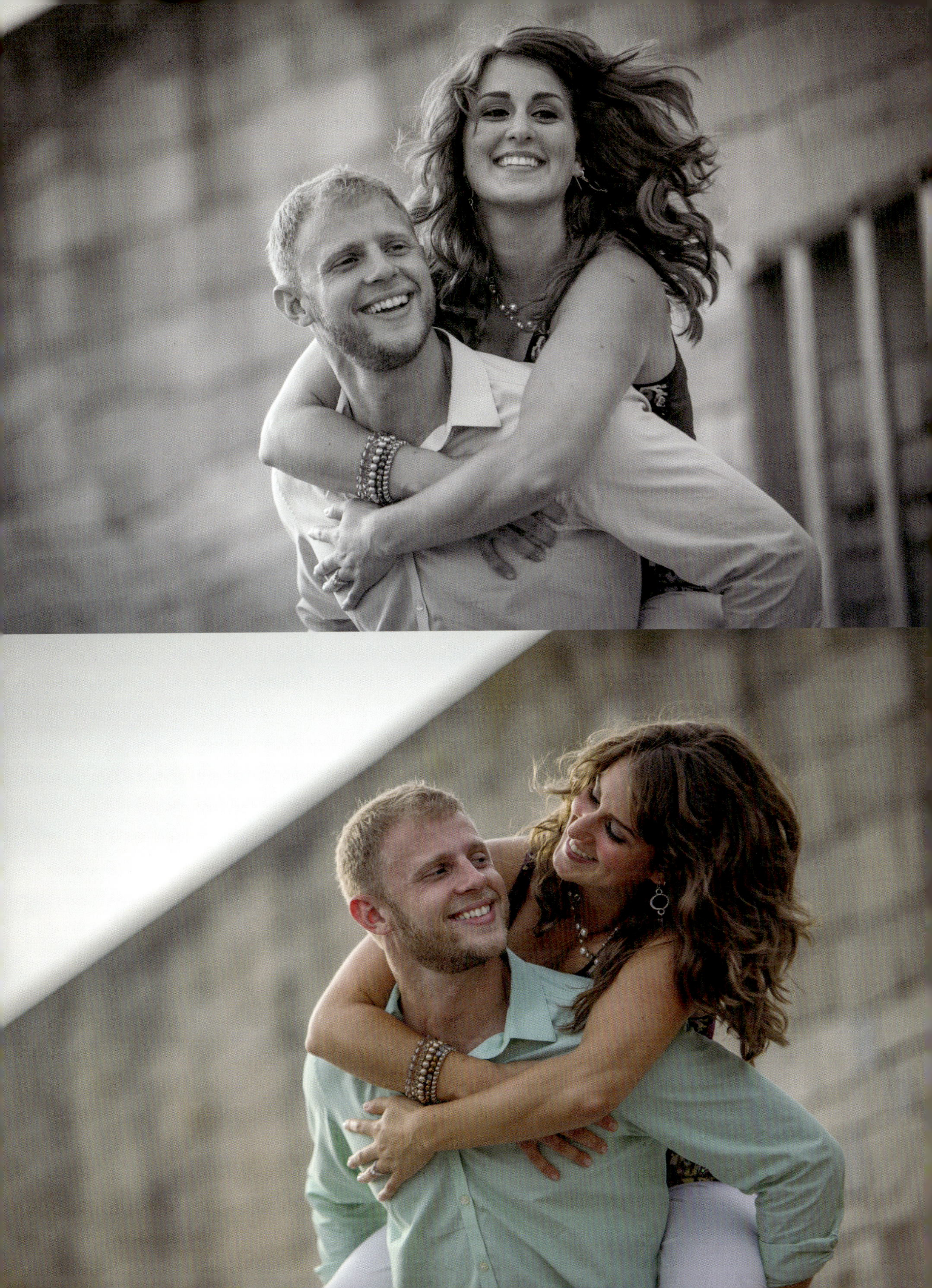

The Right Expressions

The right expression can make or break your portraits. I look for natural expressions ranging from smiles to more serious looks that show the intensity of their connection. Here's a tip: when you have the couple look at each other, make sure it doesn't come off like a staring contest; have them tilt their heads a little to soften it or ask them to look down a little.

Natural Kisses

I tell couples that when I ask for a kiss, I don't want them to give me the same exact kiss every

Let Nice Expressions Shine

A simple background lets nice expressions shine. Compare the final image (*top*) with the pull-back shot (*bottom*) to see how cropping and camera angle transformed this scene.

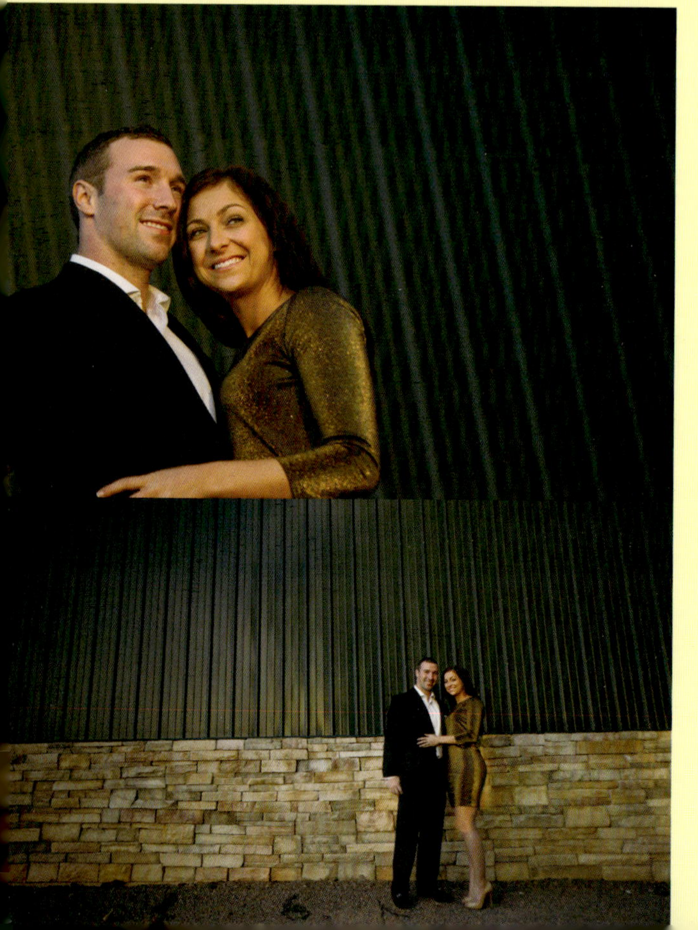

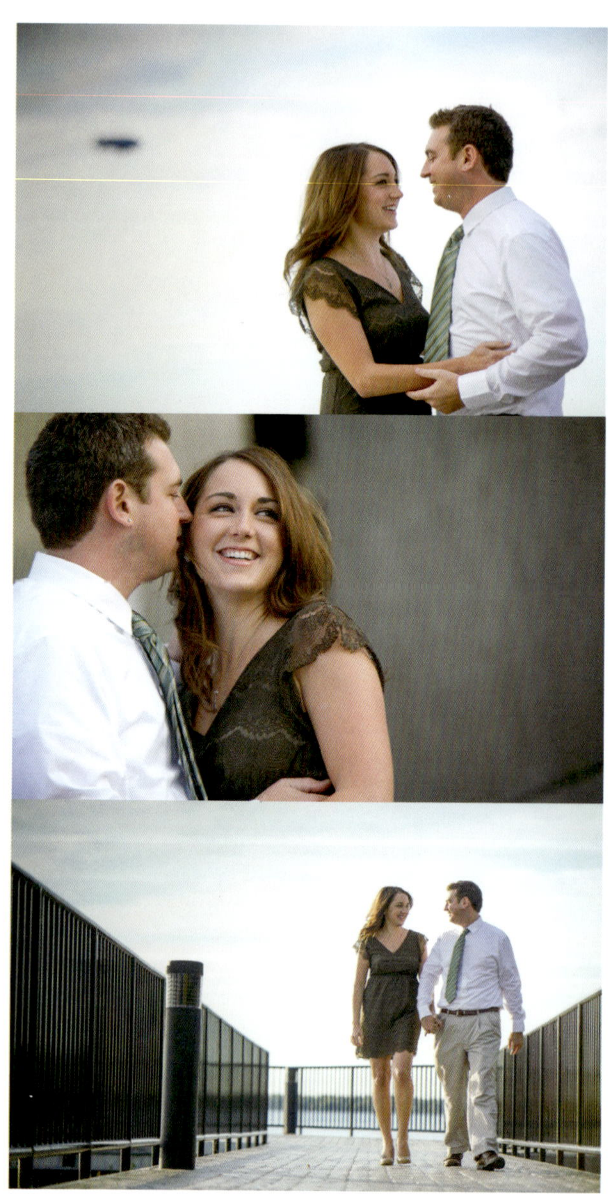

time. I want to them to tease each other. He might go in for a kiss on the cheek (or neck or ear) when she's expecting a kiss on the lips. She might grab him for a kiss.

We have had a few couples who didn't want to kiss at all (for personal or religious reasons). In this case the "tease each other" approach becomes even more important. I ask them to pose like they're *about* to kiss—like they really want to kiss but are holding back.

I ask them to pose like they're about to kiss—like they really want to kiss but are holding back.

Give Them Some Space

Like many couples, the pair seen here and on the facing page started off feeling a little nervous and unsure about the session and what was expected of them.

To loosen them up and help them feel more natural, I had them walk and interact. Giving them some space and some freedom helped build their confidence—and I sealed the deal by showing them some beautiful images. By the time we shot the image below, they were totally relaxed.

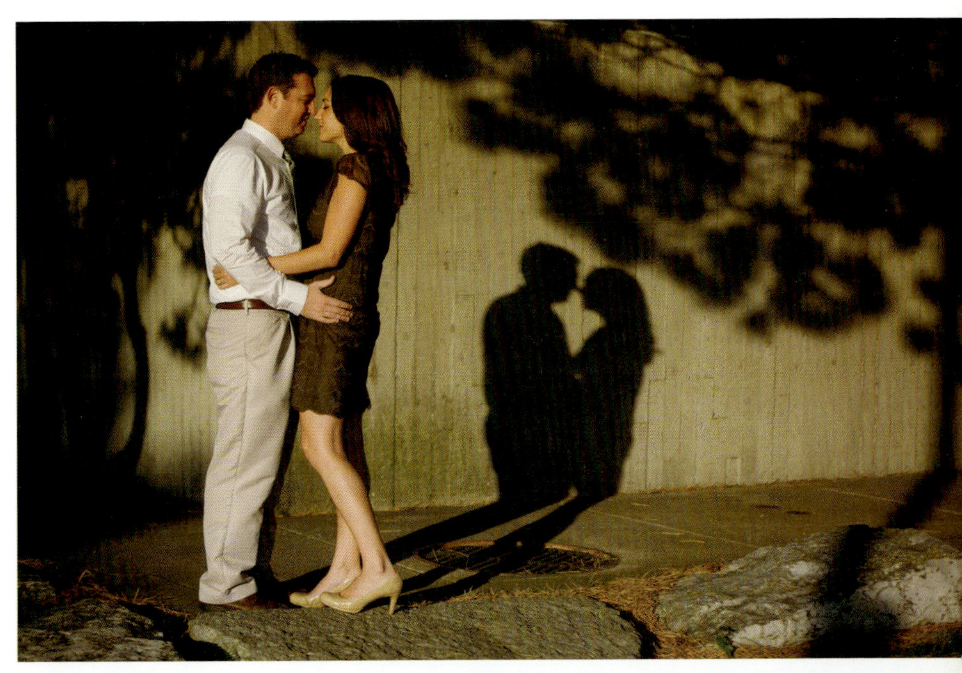

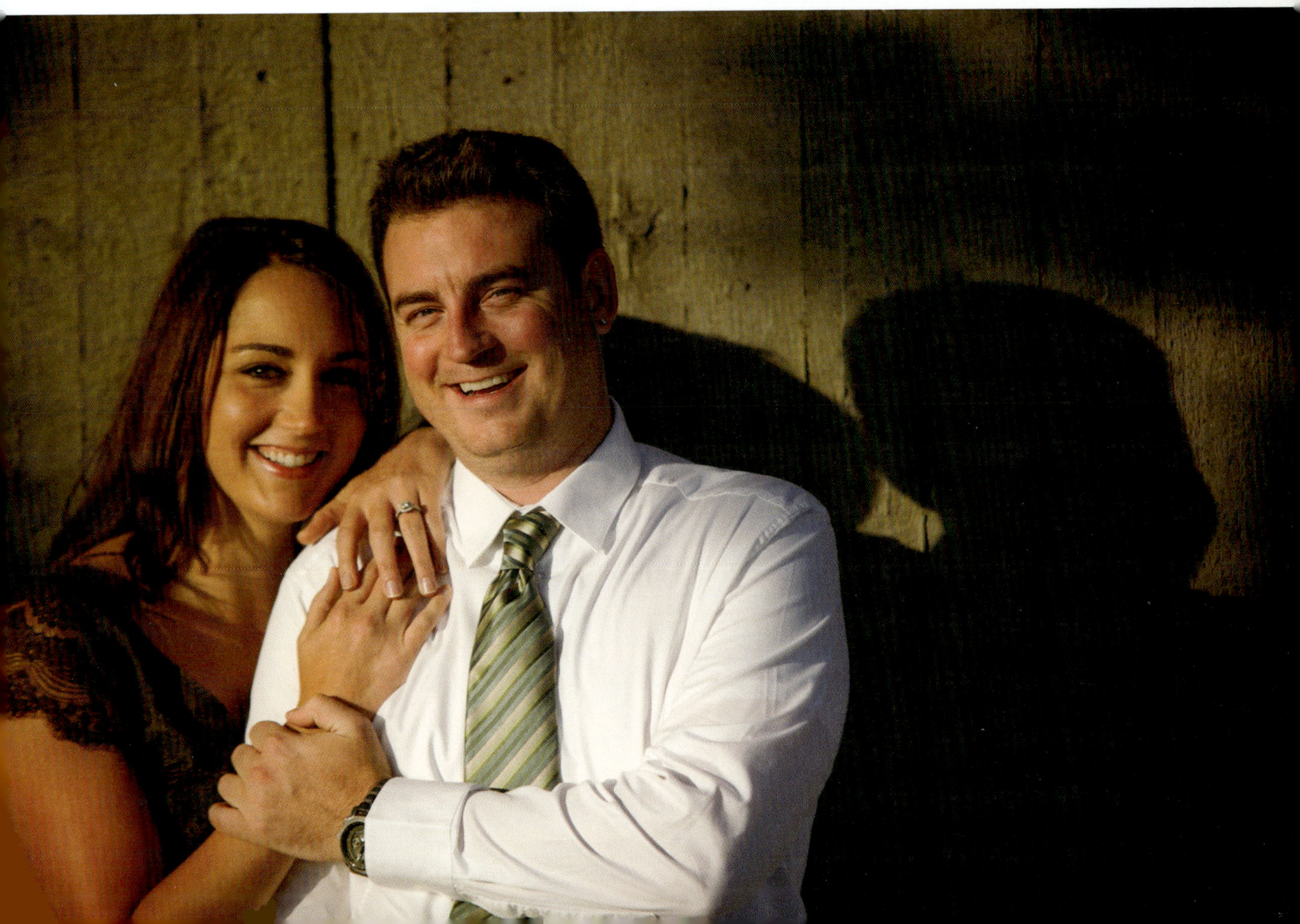

51 After the Shoot

After we've created a lot of great images together, it's time to wrap up the session. At this point, we take a few minutes to go over the next steps in the process with our couple. In particular, we want to give them a rough time frame so they know when to expect their images.

Depending on the season, we'll usually tell them they'll see their portraits in a couple weeks. We're very often able to deliver them sooner than that (often within a few days), but we think it's much better for our business to underpromise and overdeliver.

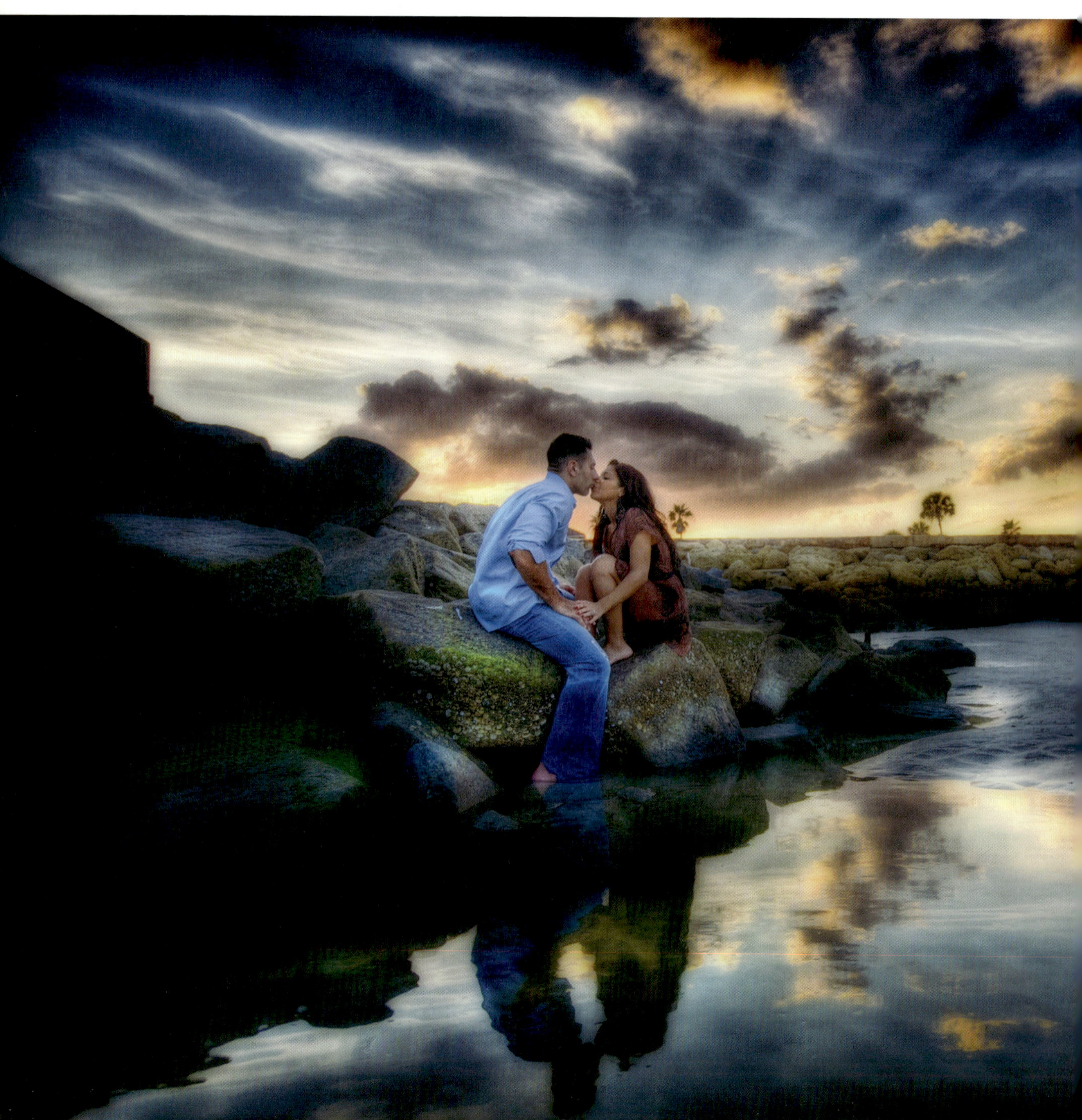

We also want to make sure that the couple knows how to access their images on our password-protected web site. Additionally, we let them know what products (like small prints to share) we suggest they order through our affiliated print provider and which products (like wall prints and albums) we'd like them to order through us so we can ensure the highest quality. (More on the subject of products and ordering appears in section 54.)

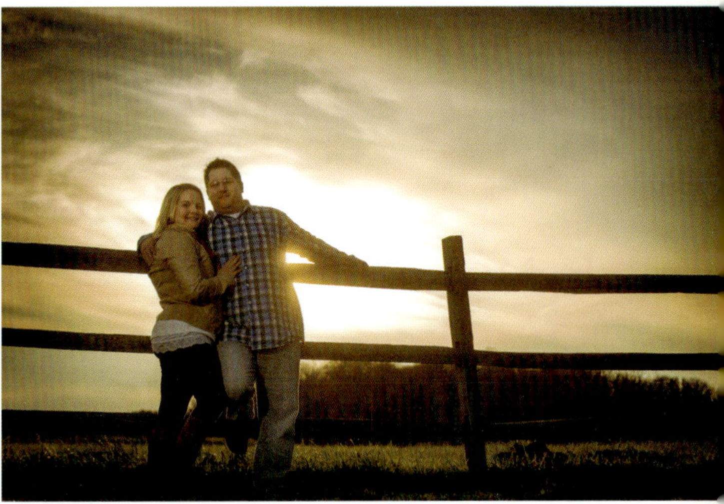

We think it's much better for our business to underpromise and overdeliver.

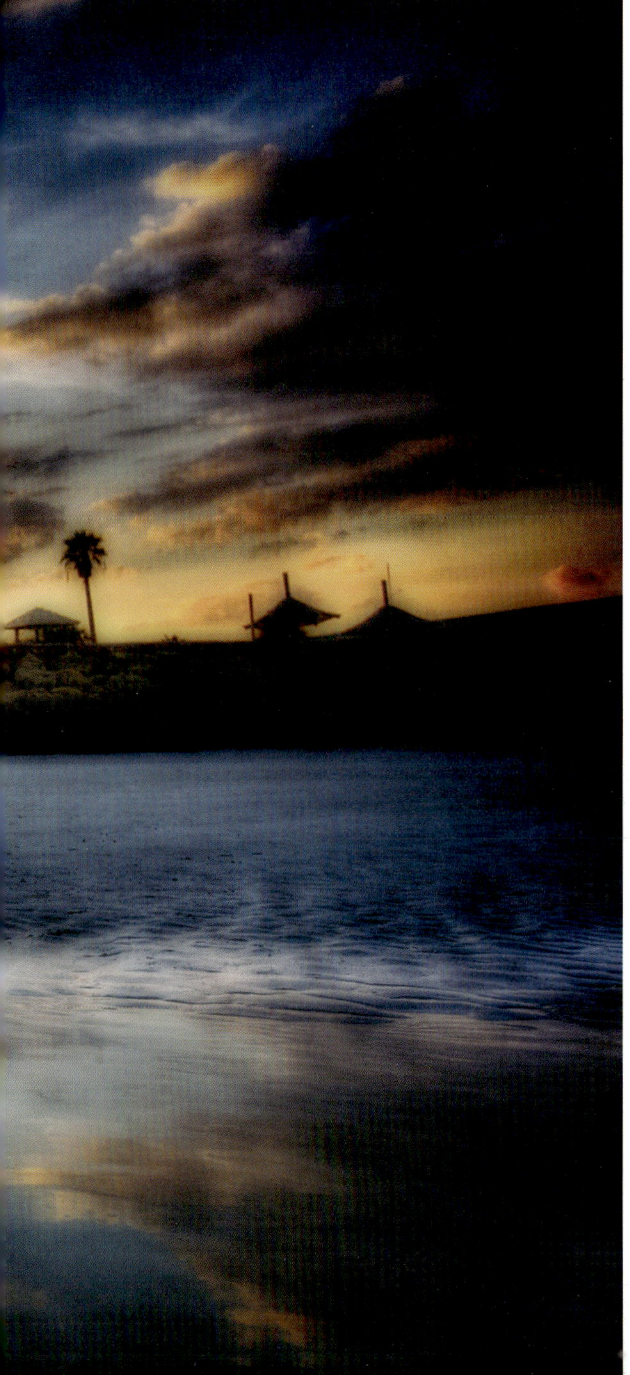

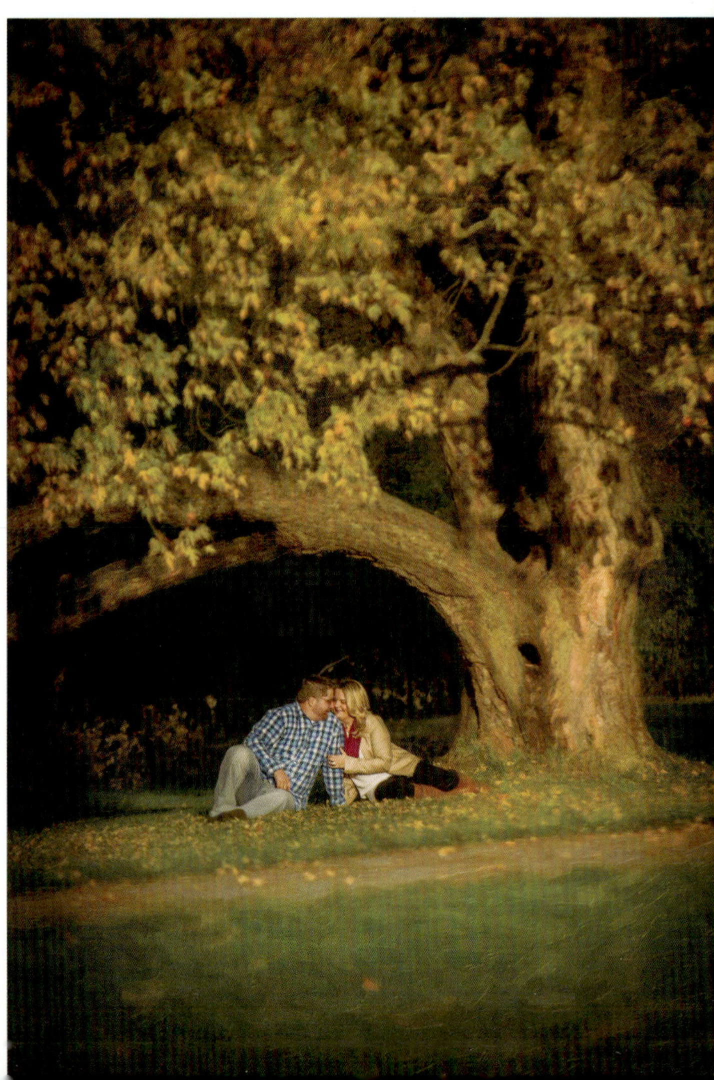

Archiving

At most engagement shoots, I create about five hundred images. When we return home from the session, all of those images are archived for long-term storage—even those ones we suspect we'll never use. Better safe than sorry!

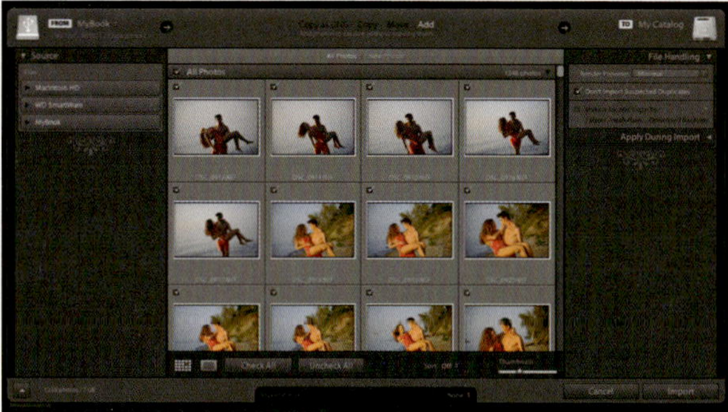

Step 1—All of the images are imported to Lightroom.

Preliminary Editing

Working from this set of five hundred, Danielle culls down the selection (removing images with any obvious problems like closed eyes or missed focus) to about three hundred.

She then proceeds to do some basic editing, including lighting adjustments, cropping, and correcting horizon tilts. If there are several similar images in the series, she'll also identify the best one. In Lightroom, the corrections she makes to this image can then be copied and pasted to the other images in the same series, which saves a lot of time.

The image on the facing page shows one of the final images from the same session featured in the screen shots below.

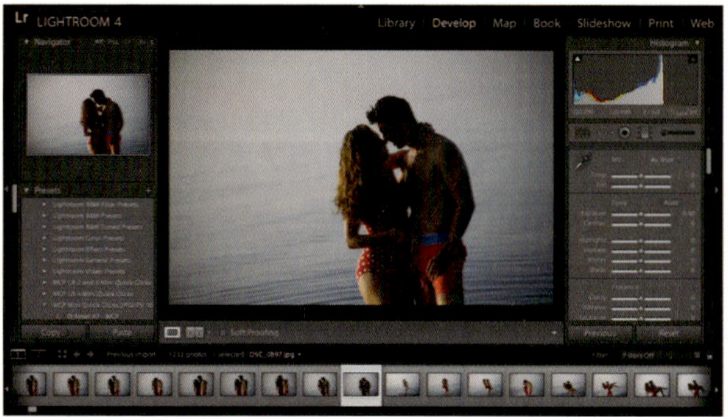

Step 2—From the Library, we go to Develop to bring up the sidebar of adjustments.

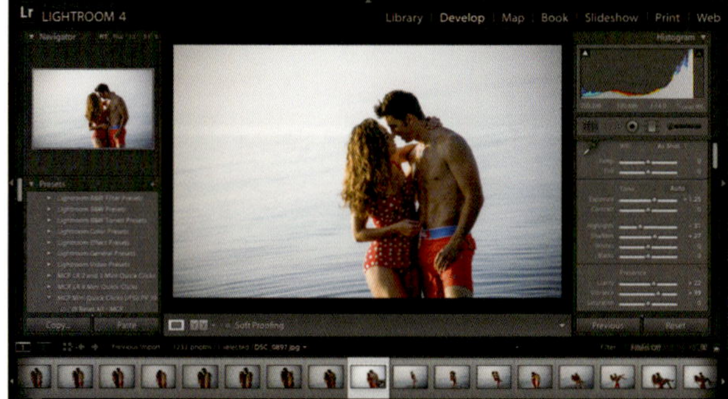

Step 3—For this image, we raised the exposure, toned down the highlights, and bumped up clarity/vibrance.

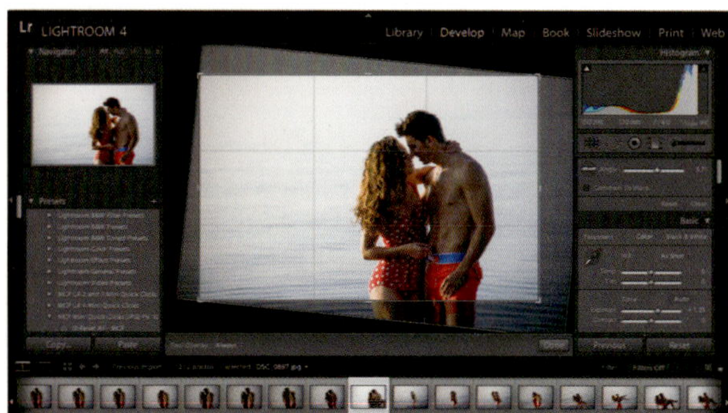

Step 4—With the crop tool, the angle slider was used to straighten the horizon and leave the couple on a one-third line (as per the Rule of Thirds).

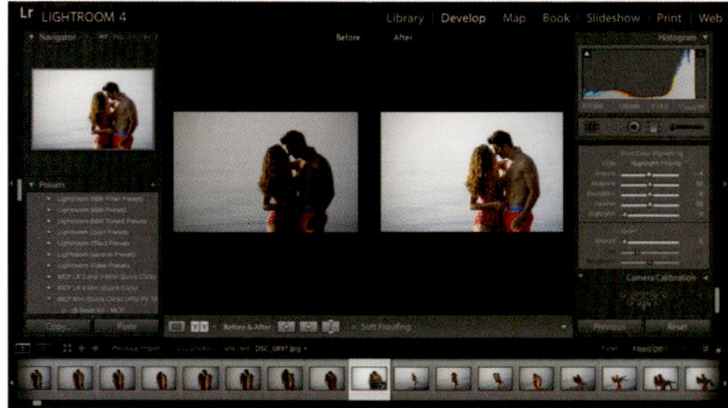

Step 5—The before and after, side by side.

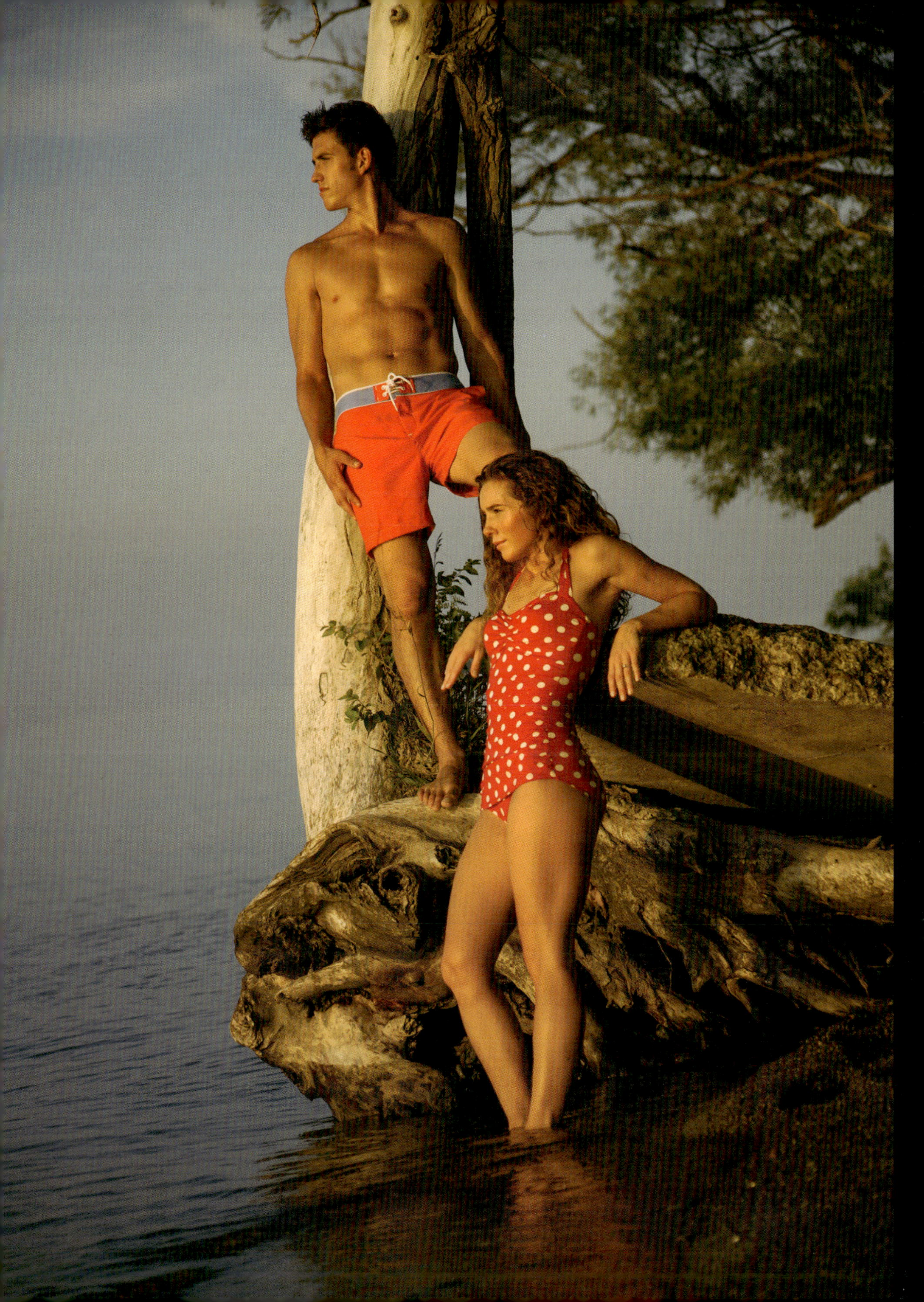

53 Advanced Artistic Postproduction

Photomatix

To go from the original capture to a final look, I brought this image into Photomatix. You can use the presets they give you on the right as a starting point, then play with the sliders to the left to refine the look. No two images are going to use the same presets or sliders, so I experiment and see what they do for each image. As you gain experience, it will become a more intuitive process.

Here, I wanted a grungy look to suit the location, but I didn't want it to take away from the couple. To make sure they stood out, we shot with an Ice Light above the couple (to the left) so it looked like there was a work light there.

The final result in Photomatix will sometimes look too grungy—but don't worry; I only use certain parts of the Photomatix image.

Camera Raw

Next, I opened up the Raw file in Camera Raw and played with the sliders in until I was happy with the results.

Photoshop

I brought the Photomatix file into Photoshop on a layer above the image imported from Camera Raw. I duplicated the bottom layer and dragged that *above* the Photomatix layer. In case I wanted to start over, this made it easy to backtrack to the original image. My next step was to create a layer mask and get ready to play.

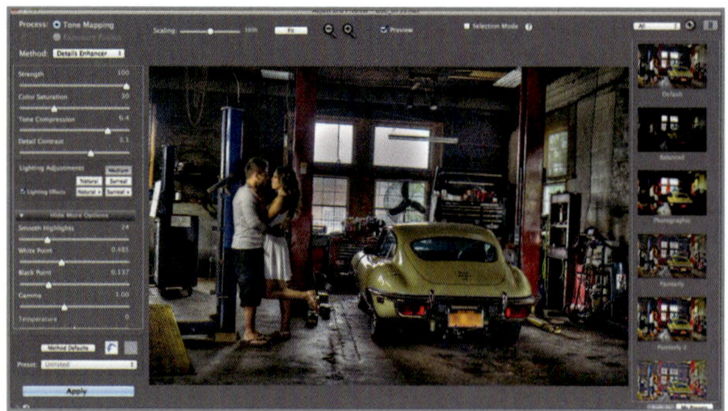

Step 1—The image is loaded into Photomatix.

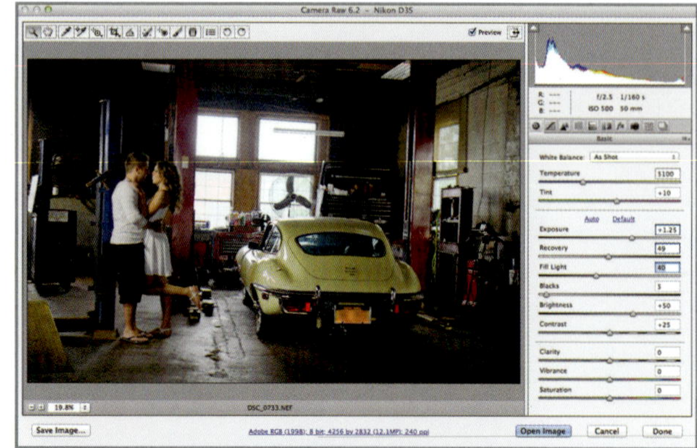

Step 2—The original image is refined in Camera Raw.

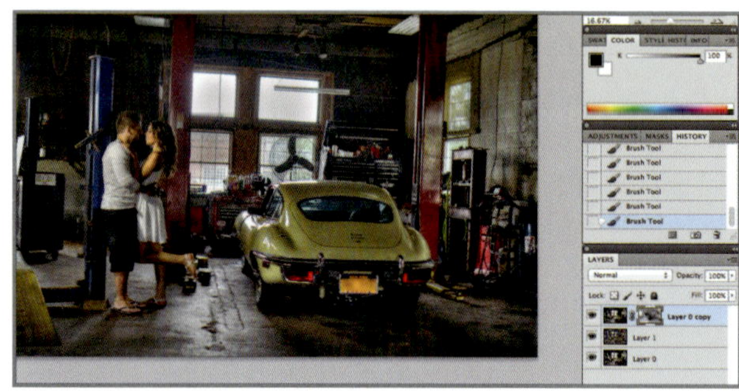

Step 3—The Photomatix and Camera Raw images are placed on different levels. A mask is added.

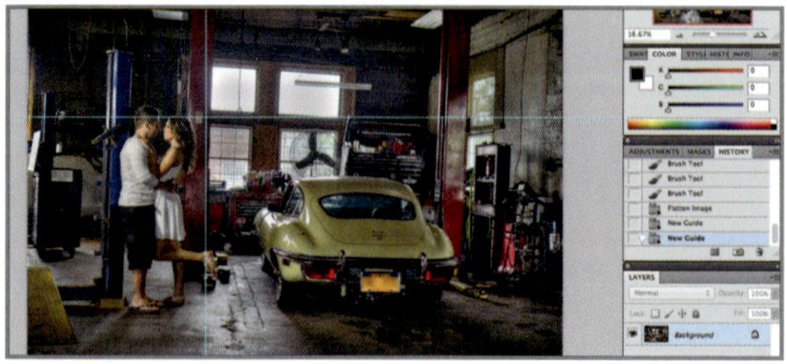

Step 4—I dropped in guides as a reference to straighten the image.

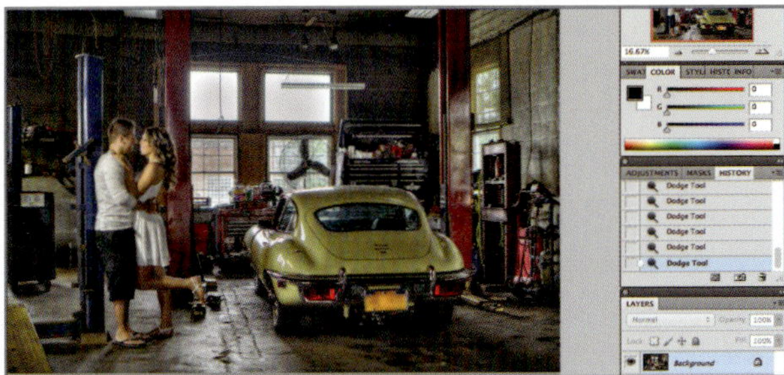

Step 5—A little selective tonal adjustment was done with the Burn and Dodge tools.

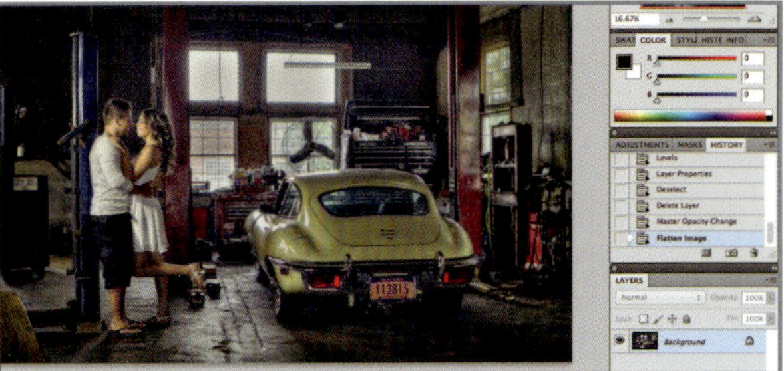

Step 6—I flattened the final image when I was done with my edits.

With a large, soft brush at about 30 percent opacity, I used black to paint in parts that I liked from the underlying Photomatix image. For this image, I focused on bringing in more detail from the car, windows, and tools. I do *not* use any of the skin from Photomatix because it tends to look dirty or bruised when processed this way.

Once I had the image looking good and had cloned out anything distracting, I put guides on the strongest horizontal and vertical lines of the image and rotated it until they were straight.

Final Details

From there, I can the use image as is—or finish it with filters or another technique. This is the part that will separate you from anyone else who uses techniques like these. Do whatever suits *your* style. But, whatever you do, make sure that it doesn't take away from the couple.

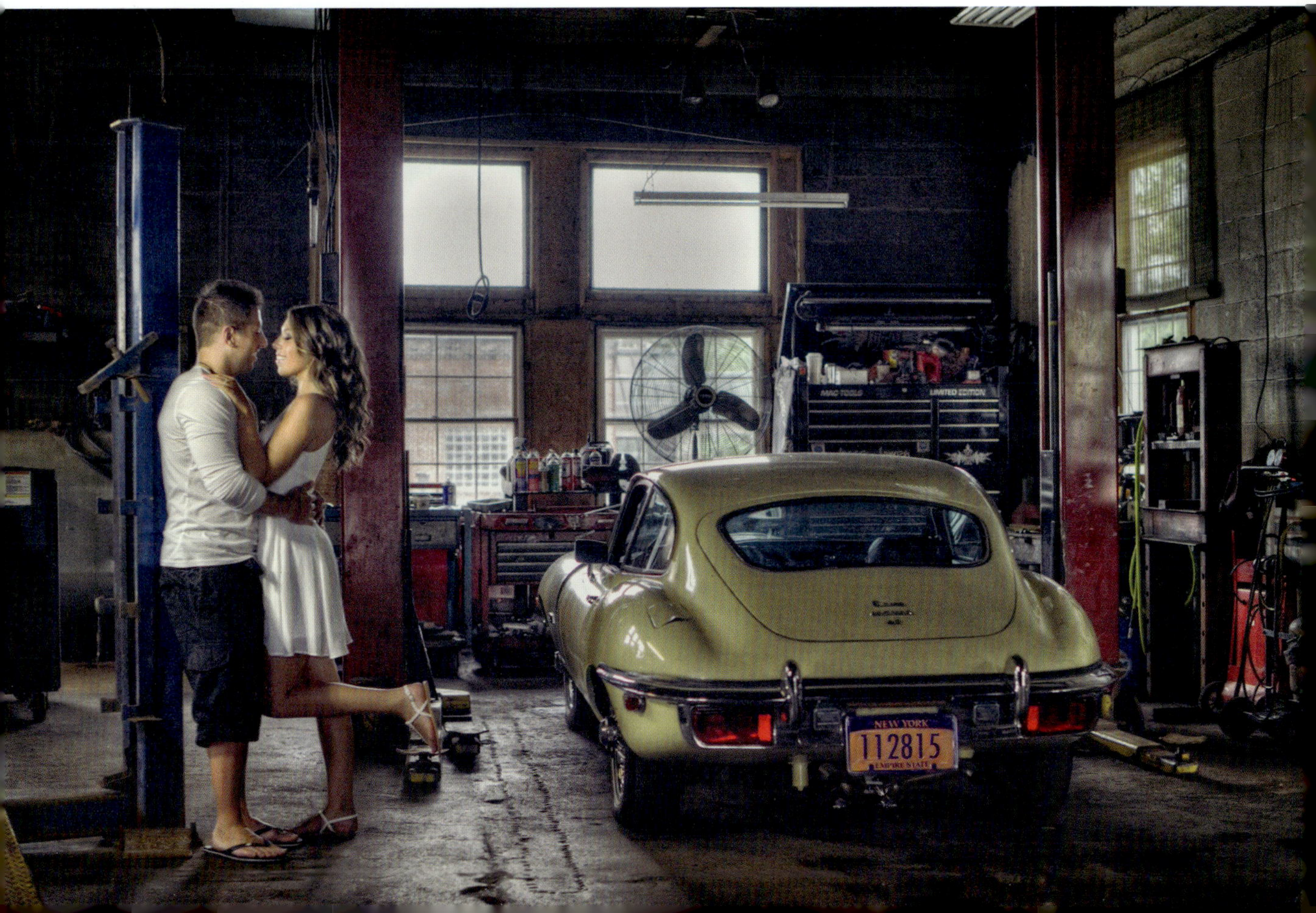

54 More on Postproduction

Usually, the last photo I do during an engagement shoot is a silhouette. We put the artificial lighting away and just shoot it naturally. This image shows off the amazing sunset or the location we shot at and has a hint of the couple.

Bringing in Some Detail and Color

When the couple chooses that silhouette as one of their favorite images, I like to bring out some detail. To do this, I open the image in Photomatix and play with the sliders until I'm happy. If you look back at section 53, you'll see that the sliders for this image are completely different from that one. I wanted this image to be a lot more colorful to show off that beautiful sunset.

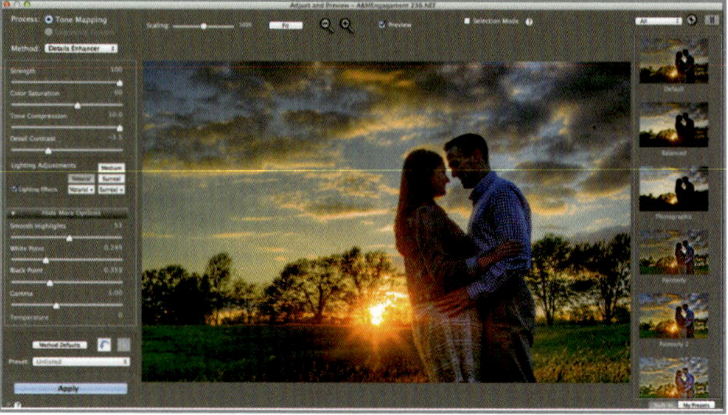

Step 1—Adjusting the image in Photomatix.

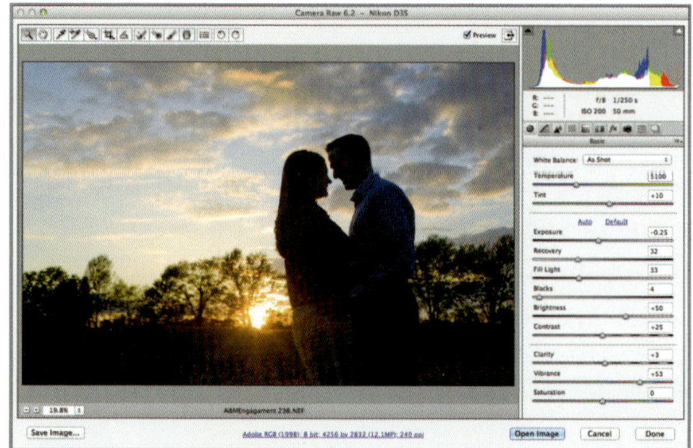

Step 2—Adjusting the image in Camera Raw.

In Camera Raw and Photoshop

As in the previous example, I opened the RAW file in Photoshop via Camera Raw. I placed the Photomatix file on top of the original image, then duplicated that layer and dragged it above the Photomatix layer. I created a mask and chose a large, soft brush at 30 percent opacity and painted onto the areas I liked the most from the HDR image. Remember not to overdo it; you don't want to create halos around the couple or the trees. If it was a beautiful sunny day, the clouds shouldn't be dark and stormy. Make sure they are lighter with some nice color. Don't oversaturate the couple; you just want a hint of what they look like. We already have photos of them with lots of detail, so we want this shot to be different.

HDR in Lightroom

There are people who are intimidated by Photoshop and Photomatix. For you, Lightroom is getting so good that you can have an HDR effect without using HDR software. Playing with the highlights, shadows, and brushes can give you the look you want without any specialized software.

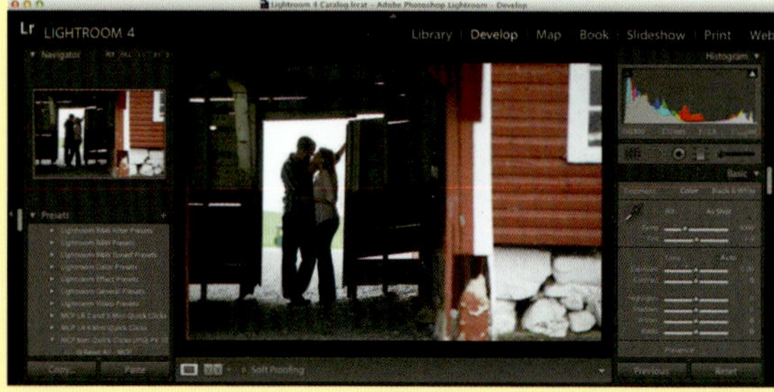

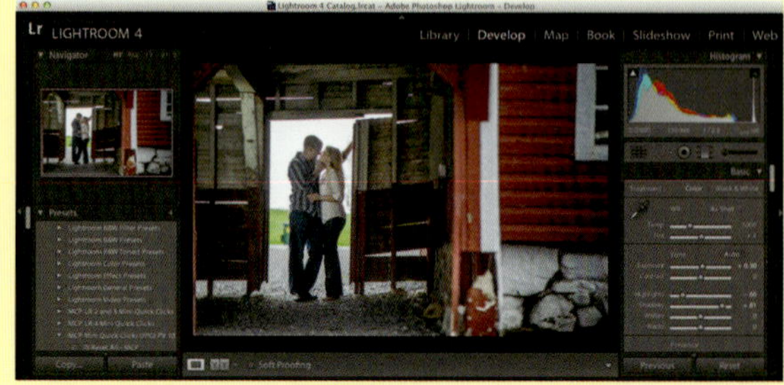

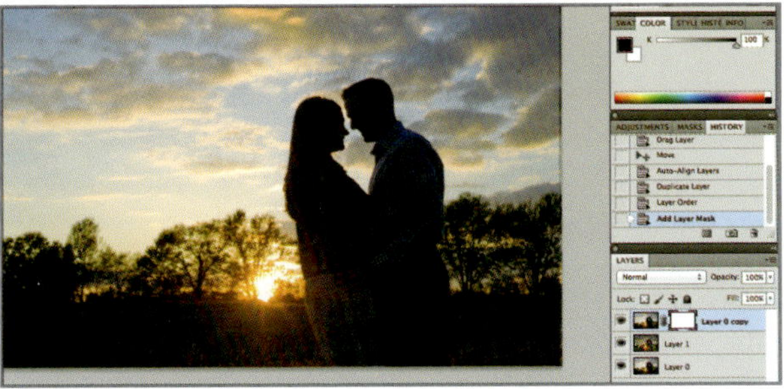

Step 3—The Photomatix and Camera Raw images are placed on different levels. A mask is added.

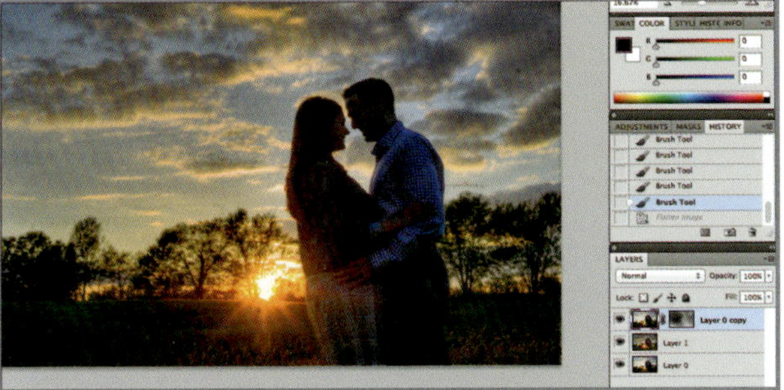

Step 4—Painting on the mask brought in HDR details.

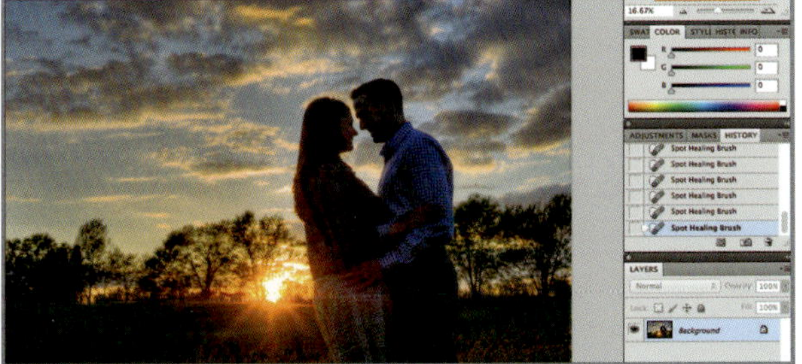

Step 6—Small distractions are cloned out.

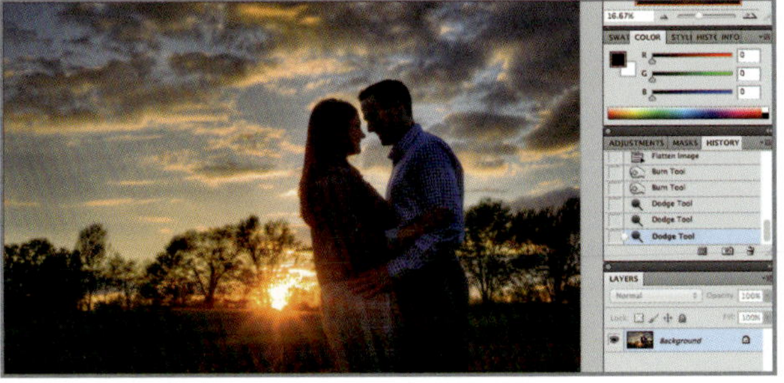

Step 7—Selective tonal adjustments are made with the Dodge and Burn tools.

Finishing Touches

Finally, I cleaned up the image, cloning out any dust spots from the sensor and anything distracting. At that point, it's time to finish the image with your own personal touch. For me and this image, I just warmed up the colors a little bit and added a dark vignette.

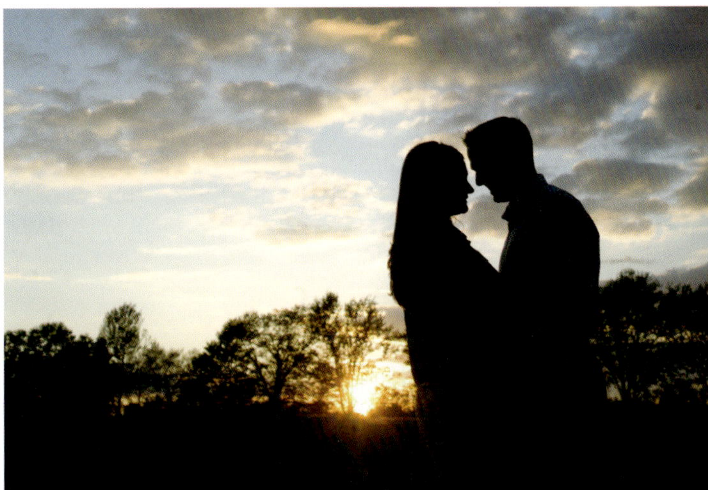

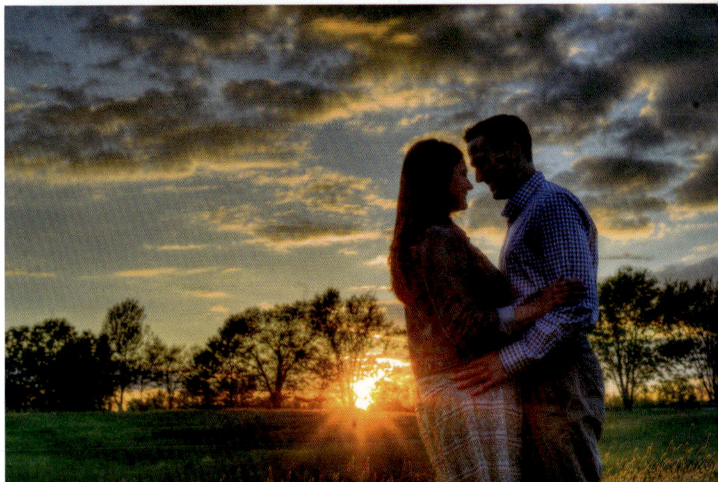

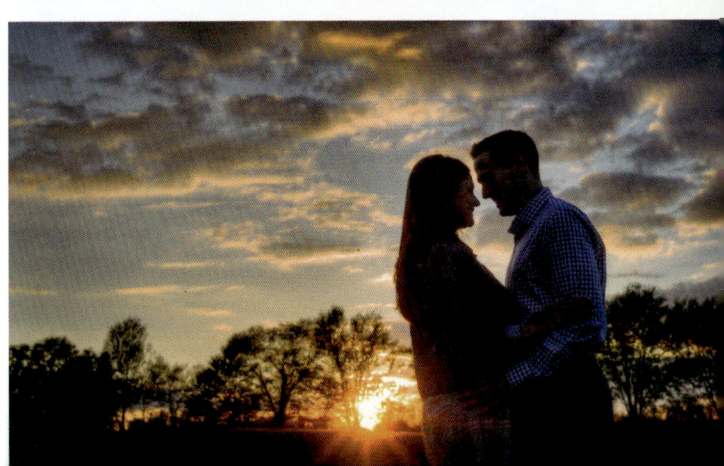

➤ The original image (top), the tone-mapped image (center), and the final image (bottom).

55 Why We Release the Files

Once I have created the fifteen or so artistic edits, Danielle and I review all of the images together and upload the files for the couple.

What We Give Them

We give our clients both the final edited images and the "proofs," so they always have both versions. Over the decades, tastes and styles change; this gives them the greatest flexibility in how they can use their images. We don't add watermarks to these files for the same reason. Clients have a year to download their files from the site.

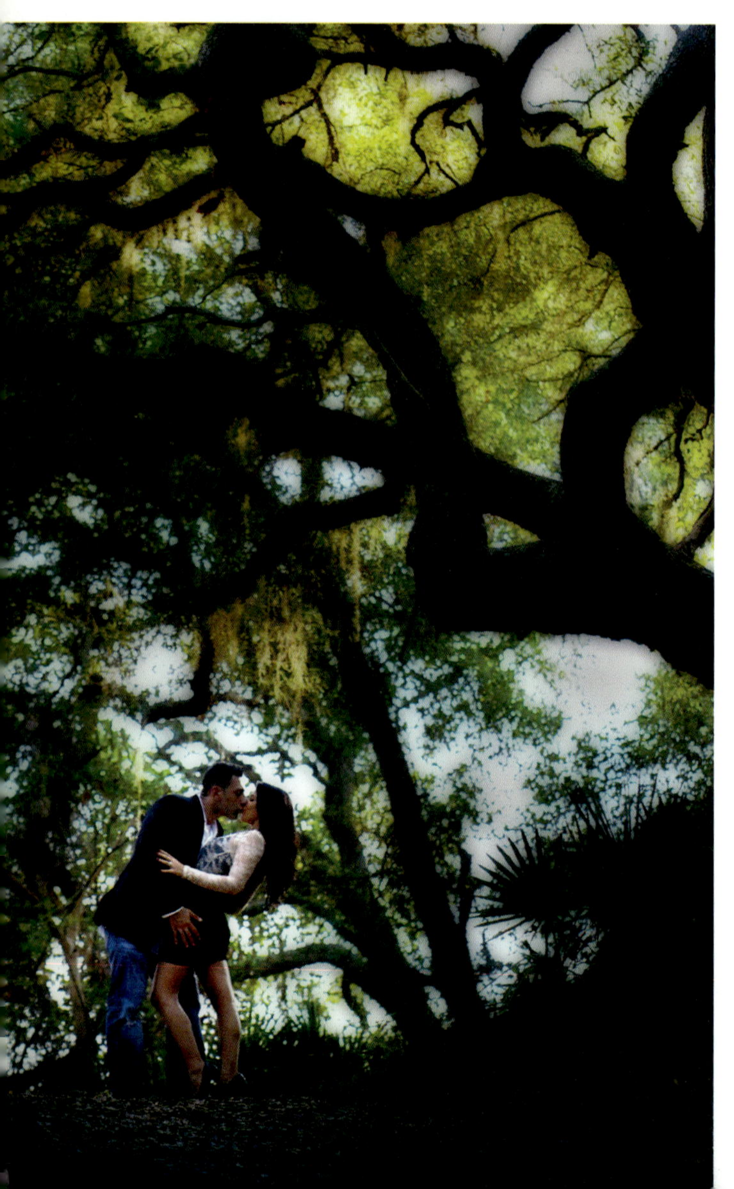

Why We Give Them the Files

Photographers used to regard the prints and albums in their packages as an integral part of their product. We feel that clients are primarily paying for *us*, and we charge fees that reflect that so we're not waiting on print orders to make our money from the event. We offer an à la carte selection of high-end products, but we also give our clients their image files so they can order small prints, use the images on their save-the-date cards, and much more (see section 55 for some designs clients have created with our images).

It just doesn't make sense for us to spend time managing a client's order of twenty 4x6-inch prints for friends and family when anyone with an Internet connection can order those prints for themselves. We also offer direct ordering via our web site through a reliable third-party lab that gives us a little kickback when clients choose use their services.

Creative Products by Our Clients

The most important benefit of giving clients their files is that their friends and family see a lot more of our images.

Products We Sell

The products we do prefer to produce for our clients are the high-end ones that particularly benefit from more expert control. These include larger prints, sign-in books, and albums (custom-designed by Danielle). From the beginning of our conversations with them, we educate our clients about the high-quality, customized products they can order from us.

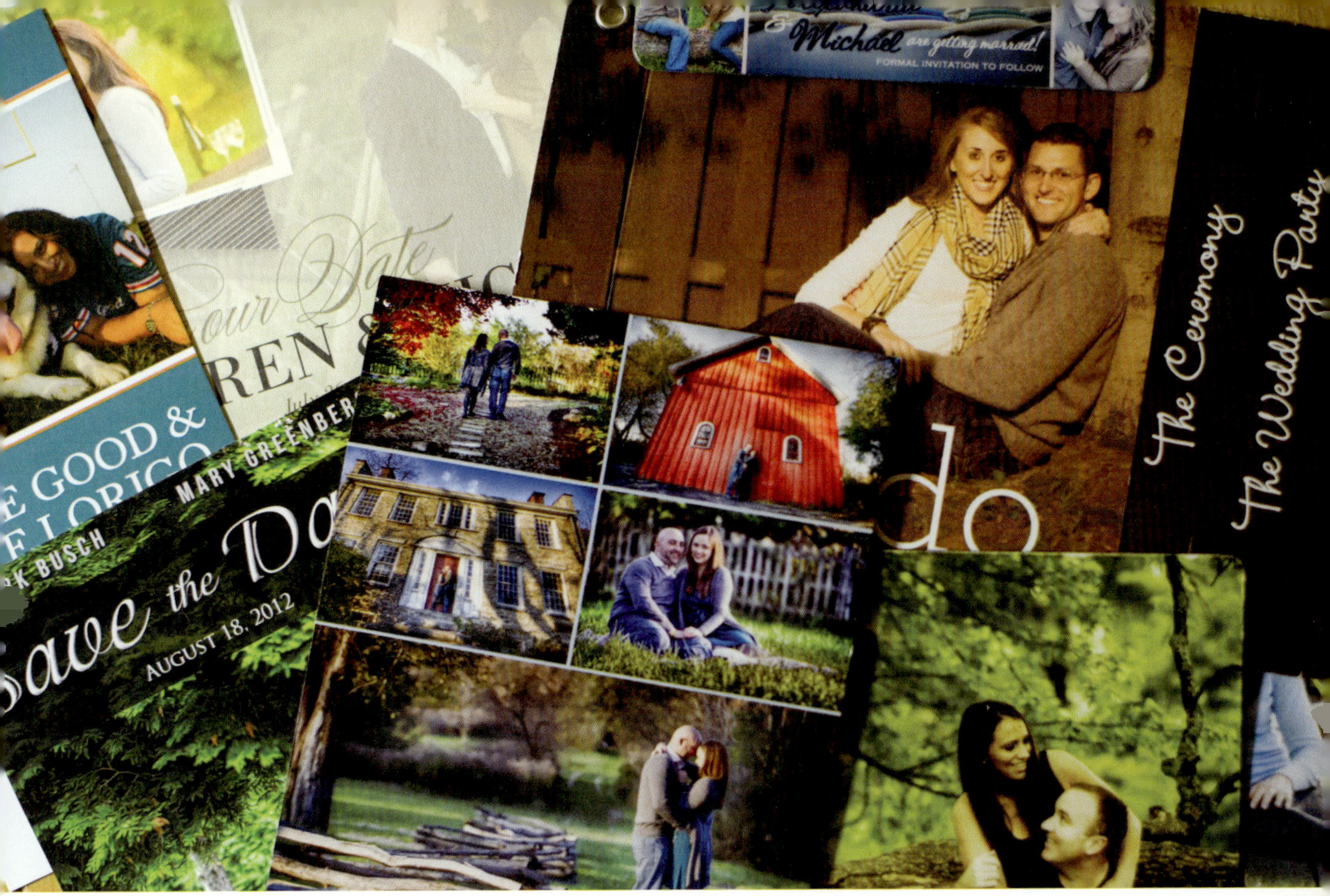

Our couples are always excited to share their images on social networking sites, they mail them out as invitations and thank-you cards, and create all sorts of other products. Above and to the right are just a few recent examples of how clients have put our images to work on their save-the-date cards and invitations. They also love to showcase our work on their sign-in boards and some people have even made calendars, magnets, and other products to share with their friends and families.

Our Clients Are Our Sales Force

All of this sharing and creating means that lots of people see the images and want to know who shot them—so we *never* have to advertise. Our happy clients are our most powerful sales force. Their referrals keep our phone ringing with new events from all over the country!

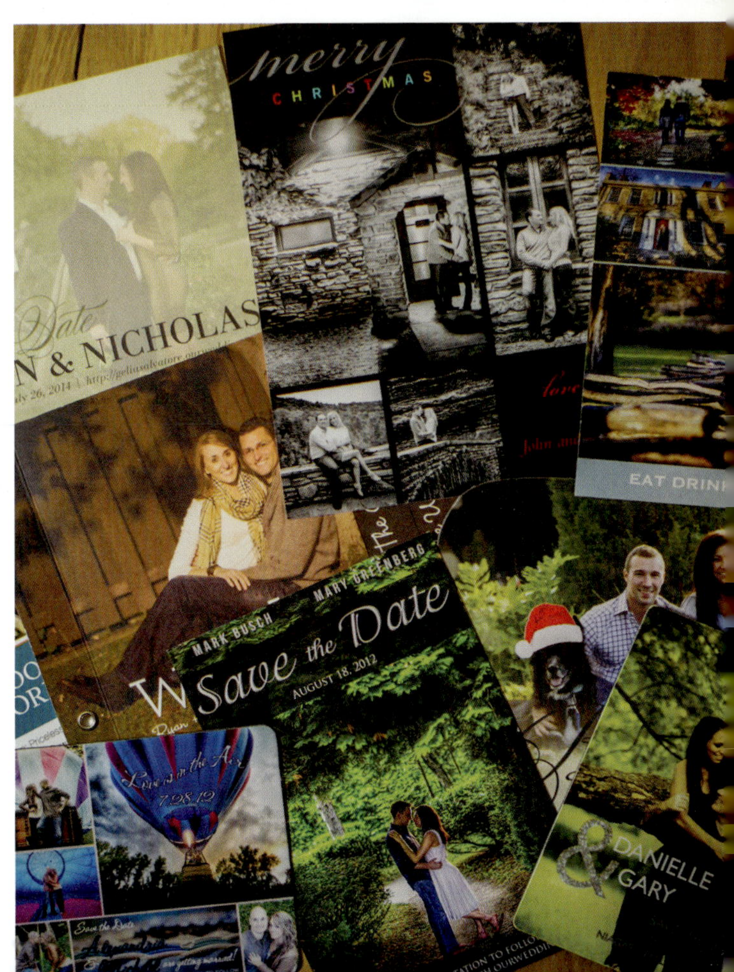

Conclusion: Great Impressions

An engagement session is most likely going to be the third impression you make on the couple—your portfolio or web site being the first and your consultation being the second. By the time you meet up for the photography, you should have established a relationship with the couple through the meetings, e-mails, and phone calls you've used to establish all the details of the session.

For many couples, this shoot is the point where the engagement becomes *real.* Sure, they've been planning a wedding—but it becomes more official when they get professional images done. Accordingly, they're going to be excited and a little nervous for the shoot. It's your job to help them relax, put them at ease, and win their trust.

You should give them great images, but you should also give them a great experience! They should be talking about this session for the rest of their lives—so make it count. Take advatage of the the fact that, for once, time is on your side! Get creative with outfits that match the locations, and schedule the shoot so you can take advantage of the day's best lighting.

And when the shoot is done, it's time to show off the images. This is when you're going to make your *first* impression on all of the most important people in your clients' lives. If you do a great job on the engagement session, just imagine how excited everyone will be to see the images from the wedding!

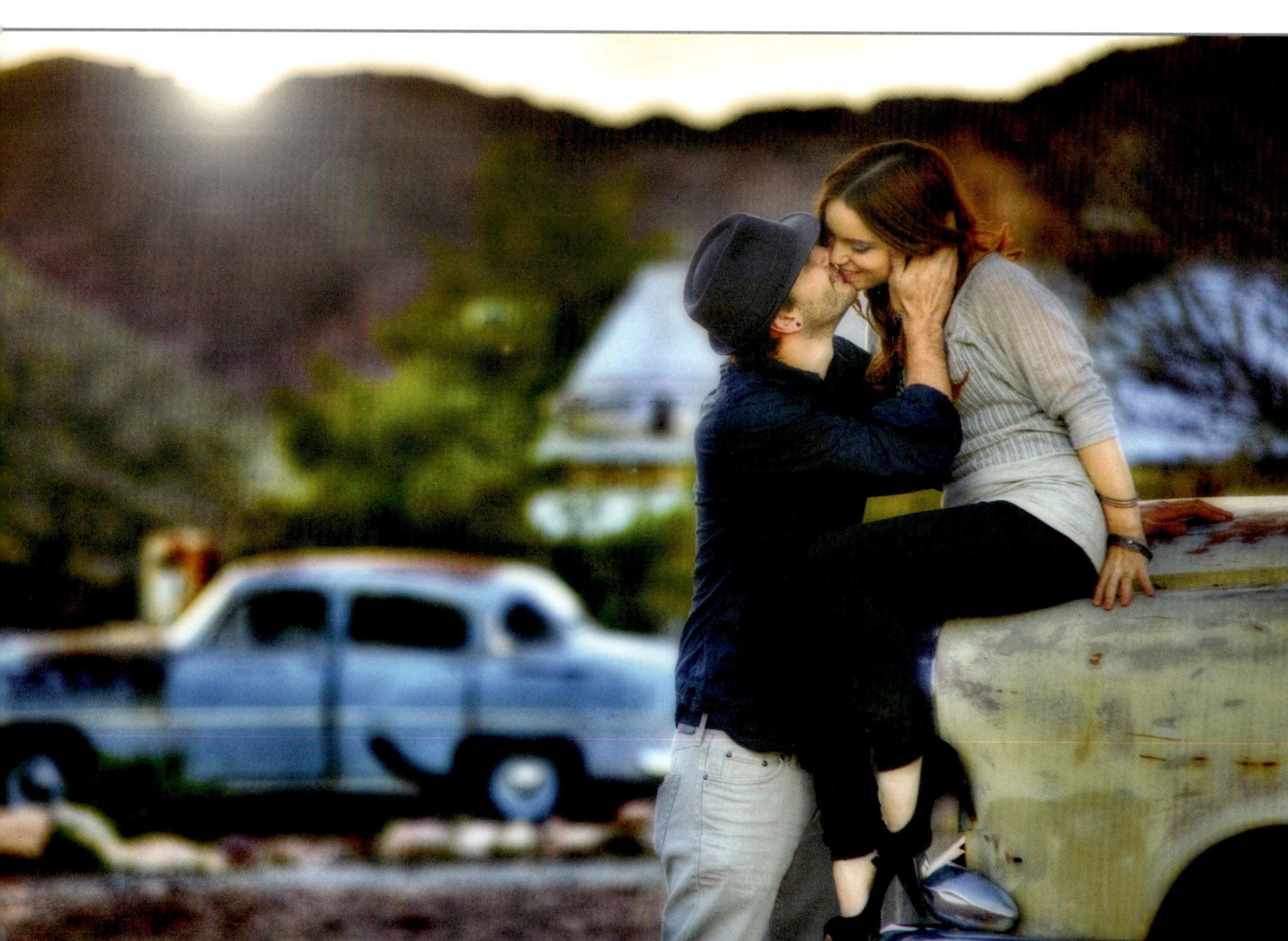

Index

OTHER BOOKS FROM

Amherst Media®

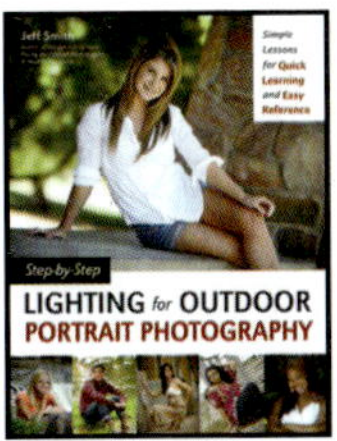

Step-by-Step Lighting for Outdoor Portrait Photography

Jeff Smith brings his no-nonsense approach to outdoor lighting, showing how to produce great portraits all day long. *$27.95 list, 7.5x10, 128p, 275 color images, order no. 2009.*

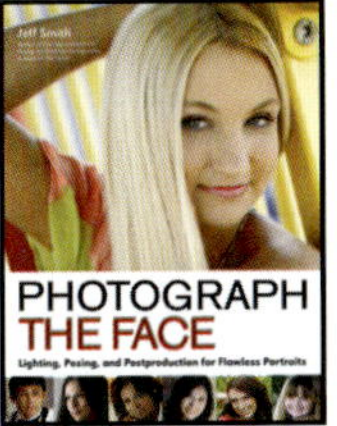

Photograph the Face

Acclaimed photographer and photo-educator Jeff Smith cuts to the core of great portraits: making the subject's face look its very best. *$27.95 list, 7.5x10, 128p, 275 color images, order no. 2019.*

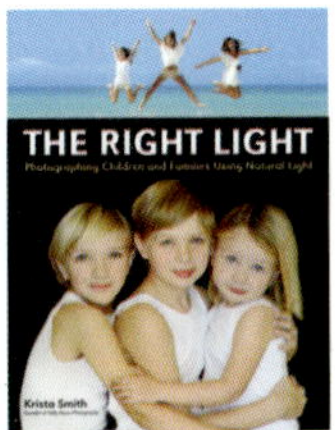

The Right Light

Working with couples, families, and kids, Krista Smith shows how natural light can bring out the best in every subject—and produce highly marketable images. *$27.95 list, 7.5x10, 128p, 250 color images, order no. 2018.*

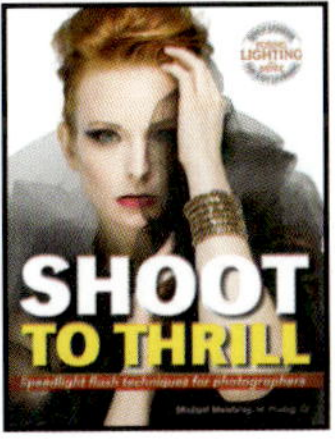

Shoot to Thrill

Acclaimed photographer Michael Mowbray shows how speedlights can rise to any photographic challenge—in the studio or on location. *$27.95 list, 7.5x10, 128p, 220 color images, order no. 2011.*

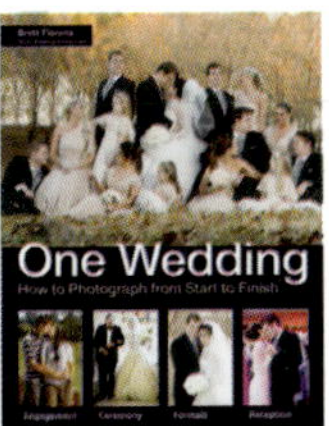

One Wedding

Brett Florens takes you, hour by hour, through the photography process for one entire wedding—from the engagement portraits, to the reception, and beyond! *$27.95 list, 7.5x10, 128p, 375 color images, order no. 2015.*

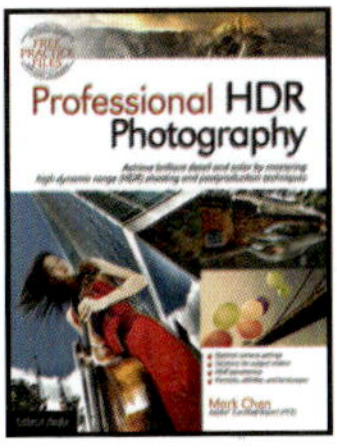

Professional HDR Photography

Mark Chen shows how to achieve brilliant detail and color with high dynamic range shooting and post-production. *$27.95 list, 7.5x10, 128p, 250 color images, order no. 1994.*

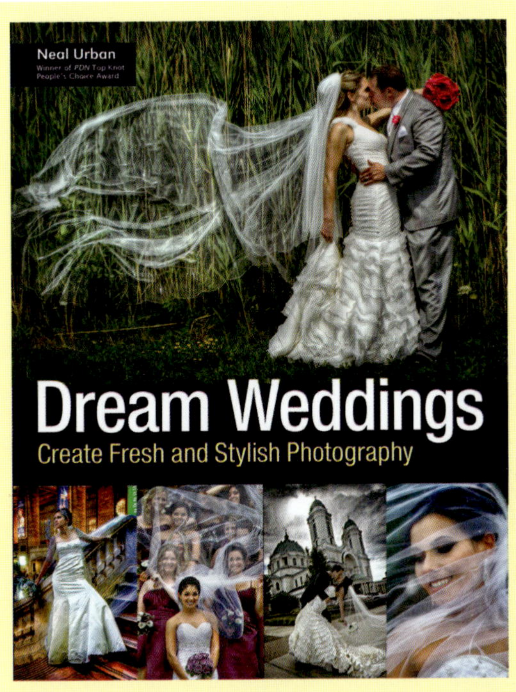

Dream Weddings

Create Fresh and Stylish Photography

Celebrated wedding photographer Neal Urban shows you how to capture more powerful and dramatic images at every phase of the wedding photography process. *$27.95 list, 7.5x10, 128p, 190 color images, order no. 1996.*

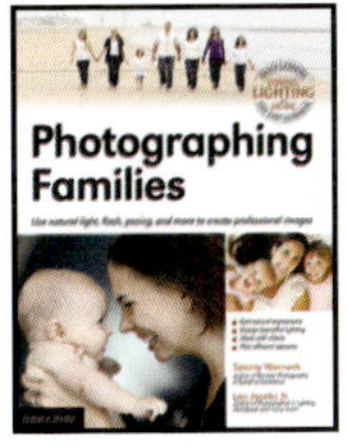

Photographing Families

Tammy Warnock and Lou Jacobs Jr. demonstrate the lighting and posing skills needed to create professional-quality portraits of families and children. *$27.95 list, 7.5x10, 128p, 180 color images, order no. 1997.*

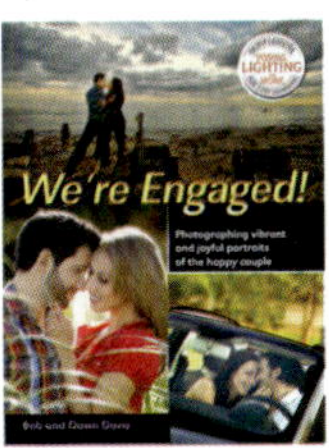

We're Engaged!

Acclaimed photographers and photo instructors Bob and Dawn Davis reveal their secrets for creating vibrant and joyful portraits of the happy couple. *$27.95 list, 7.5x10, 128p, 180 color images, order no. 2024.*

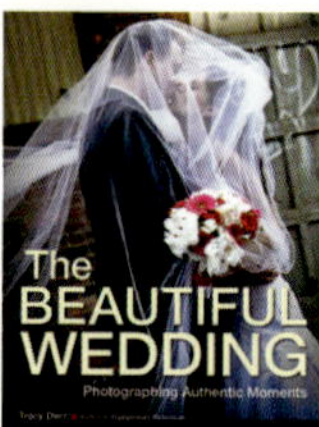

The Beautiful Wedding

Tracy Dorr guides you through the process of photographing the authentic moments and emotions that make every wedding beautiful. *$27.95 list, 7.5x10, 128p, 180 color images, order no. 2020.*

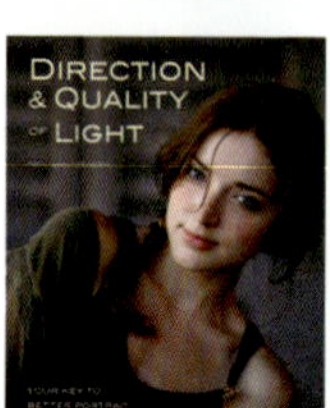

Direction & Quality of Light

Neil van Niekerk shows you how consciously controlling the direction and quality of light in your portraits can take your work to a whole new level. *$29.95 list, 7.5x10, 160p, 194 color images, order no. 1982.*

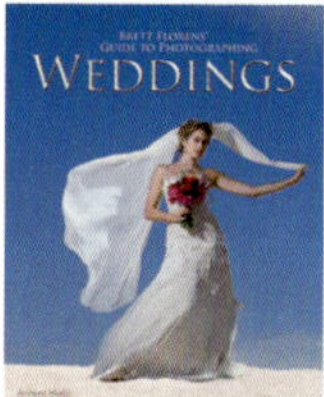

BRETT FLORENS' Guide to Photographing Weddings

Learn the artistic and business strategies Florens uses to remain at the top of his field. *$19.95 list, 8.5x11, 128p, 250 color images, index, order no. 1926.*

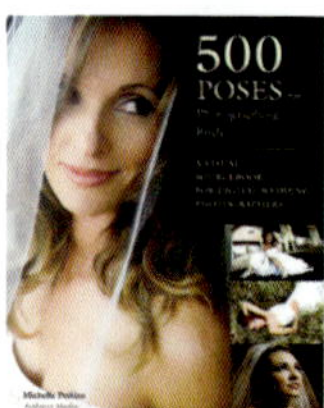

500 Poses for Photographing Brides

Michelle Perkins showcases an array of head-and-shoulders, three-quarter, full-length, and seated and standing poses. *$34.95 list, 8.5x11, 128p, 500 color images, index, order no. 1909.*

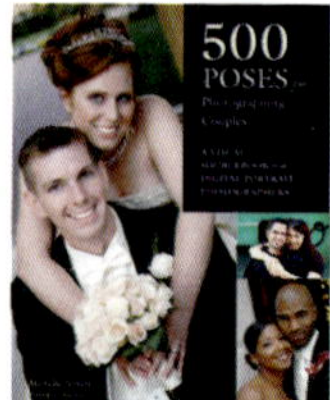

500 Poses for Photographing Couples

Michelle Perkins showcases an array of poses that will give you the creative boost you need to create an evocative, meaningful portrait. *$34.95 list, 8.5x11, 128p, 500 color images, order no. 1943.*

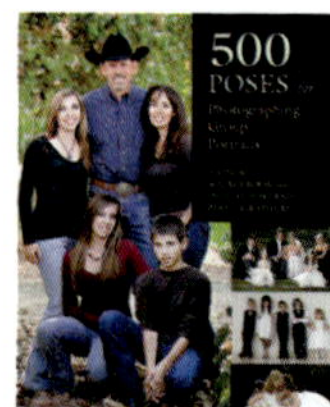

500 Poses for Photographing Groups

Michelle Perkins provides an impressive collection of images that will inspire you to design polished, professional portraits. *$34.95 list, 8.5x11, 128p, 500 color images, order no. 1980.*

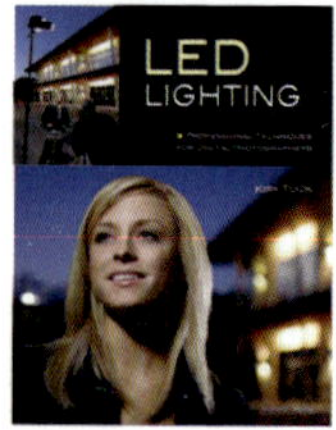

LED Lighting: PROFESSIONAL TECHNIQUES FOR DIGITAL PHOTOGRAPHERS

Kirk Tuck's comprehensive look at LED lighting reveals the ins-and-outs of the technology and shows how to put it to great use. *$34.95 list, 7.5x10, 160p, 380 color images, order no. 1958.*

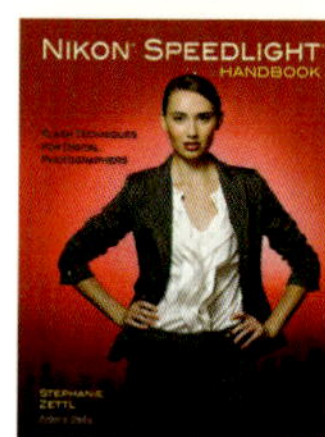

Nikon® Speedlight® Handbook

Stephanie Zettl gets down and dirty with this dynamic lighting system, showing you how to maximize your results in the studio or on location. *$34.95 list, 7.5x10, 160p, 300 color images, order no. 1959.*

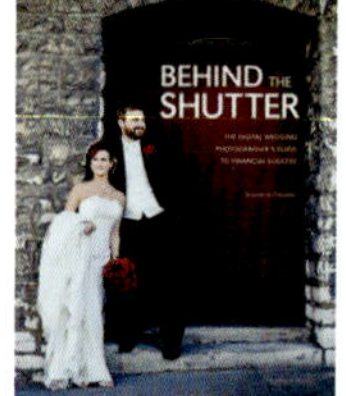

Behind the Shutter

Salvatore Cincotta shares the business and marketing information you need to build a thriving wedding photography business. *$34.95 list, 7.5x10, 160p, 230 color images, index, order no. 1953.*

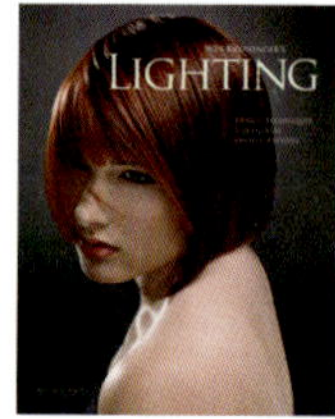

WES KRONINGER'S Lighting Design Techniques FOR DIGITAL PHOTOGRAPHERS

Create setups that blur the lines between fashion, editorial, and classic portraits. *$19.95 list, 8.5x11, 128p, 80 color images, 60 diagrams, index, order no. 1930.*

MORE PHOTO BOOKS AVAILABLE

Amherst Media®
PO BOX 586
BUFFALO, NY 14226 USA

Individuals: If possible, purchase books from an Amherst Media retailer. To order directly, visit our web site, or call the toll-free number listed below to place your order. All major credit cards are accepted. *Dealers, distributors & colleges:* Write, call, or fax to place orders. For price information, contact Amherst Media or an Amherst Media sales representative. Net 30 days.

(800) 622-3278 or (716) 874-4450
Fax: (716) 874-4508

All prices, publication dates, and specifications are subject to change without notice. Prices are in U.S. dollars. Payment in U.S. funds only.

WWW.AMHERSTMEDIA.COM

FOR A COMPLETE LIST OF BOOKS AND ADDITIONAL INFORMATION